RESPONSIBLE PARENTS AND PARENTAL RESPONSIBILITY

This book examines the area of 'parental responsibility' in English law and what is expected of a responsible parent. The scope of 'parental responsibility', a key concept in family law, is undefined and often ambiguous. Yet, to date, more attention has been paid to how individuals acquire parental responsibility than to the question of the rights, powers, duties and responsibilities they have once they obtain it. This book redresses the balance by providing the first sustained examination of the different elements of parental responsibility, bringing together leading scholars to comment on specific aspects of its operation.

The book begins by exploring the conceptual underpinnings of parental responsibility in the context of parents' and children's rights. The analysis highlights the inherent constraints and limitations of 'parental responsibility' and how its scope has deliberately been curtailed in certain contexts. The book then considers what parental responsibility allows and requires in specific areas, for example, naming a child, education, religious upbringing, medical treatment, corporal punishment, dealing with any contracts entered into or property owned by the child, representing the child in legal proceedings, consenting to a child's marriage or civil partnership and the law's response to the death of a child. In the final section, the idea of the 'responsible parent' is considered in the contexts of child support, contact, tort and criminal law.

Responsible Parents and Parental Responsibility

Edited by

REBECCA PROBERT

STEPHEN GILMORE

AND

JONATHAN HERRING

·HART·
PUBLISHING

OXFORD AND PORTLAND, OREGON
2009

Published in North America (US and Canada) by
Hart Publishing
c/o International Specialized Book Services
920 NE 58th Avenue, Suite 300
Portland, OR 97213–3786
USA
Tel: +1 503 287 3093 or toll-free: (1) 800 944 6190
Fax: +1 503 280 8832
E-mail: orders@isbs.com
Website: http://www.isbs.com

Hart Publishing Ltd, 16C Worcester Place, Oxford, OX1 2JW
Telephone: +44 (0)1865 517530 Fax: +44 (0)1865 510710
E-mail: mail@hartpub.co.uk
Website: http://www.hartpub.co.uk

British Library Cataloguing in Publication Data
Data Available

ISBN: 978-1-84113-880-0

Typeset by Columns Design Ltd, Reading
Printed and bound in Great Britain by
CPI Antony Rowe, Chippenham, Wiltshire

Foreword

As a construct of English law, parental responsibility is very strange. A major reason for creating it was to de-emphasise the idea of parents as right-holders with respect to their children, and to focus attention more directly on their duties to them. Yet the definition of parental responsibility is:

all the rights, duties, powers, responsibilities and authority which by law a parent of a child has in relation to the child and his property (Children Act 1989 s 3(1)).

So it includes responsibilities *and* rights, not to mention powers and authority. It would seem to be better described as the full complement of juristic relations a parent could have regarding a child: full legal parenthood in fact. Except that 'legal' parenthood seems to mean something less. Legal parenthood usually derives from a biological relationship and seems to be simply what is left if parental responsibility is taken away or never conferred. Yet legal parenthood is not an empty legal relationship (there are consequences). It is, however, a good deal weaker than having parental responsibility. Not that there are *no* responsibilities attached to legal parenthood, even without parental responsibility! There is, for example, the support obligation. No wonder students, courts and parents get thoroughly confused.

It might take a small book to sort out the confusion. It would be a useful, though ultimately rather arid task. For parental responsibility is not only a legal issue. It refers to the vastly important range of issues which goes to the heart of the relationship between the generations: issues dealing with how children should be brought up and, in particular, the interaction between the role of parents and the state and its institutions. Since most children find themselves in the care of (or under the control of) some adults in their childhood, usually their actual parents, society could just let them get on with it. Since most parents have an interest in their children doing well, it might not be a bad arrangement for children. But history tells us otherwise. And in any case, the risks to children might be increased in the modern world because social and technological change has meant that, while in the past children were an important means of creating wealth for parents, today children are more likely to be a net economic liability for parents. Anyway, for whatever reason, society is unwilling to leave things solely to parents. On the other hand, it does not want to nationalise child upbringing completely, for a multitude of good reasons. The bureaucracy would be horrendous. Those ill-disposed to totalitarianism would worry about the power the dominant political class would have to indoctrinate the population. The (possibly) primeval urges of parents to design the characters of those they create would have to be smashed. Some might feel the children, too, were losing out on something.

So we steer a path between these extremes. How we negotiate it throws up opportunities for endless debate. But it is not sterile debate. It is urgent and significant to people's lives. This book demonstrates just how urgent and significant it is. A glance through the contents shows this. Many subjects are topical and controversial: corporal punishment, religion, child support and juvenile offending, for example. Others are perhaps less in the public eye, but remain important. We must be grateful to the editors and contributors for giving these subjects such detailed attention.

John Eekelaar, FBA

Preface

Most of the chapters in this volume were originally presented to fellow contributors as a paper for discussion at a seminar at King's College London in January 2008. Dr Kathryn Hollingsworth also attended the seminar as a discussant and provided helpful comments on the papers, for which we are very grateful. We should also like to record our thanks to Lord Plant of Highfield, then Head of King's College School of Law, for kindly agreeing to fund the seminar. Our thanks also go to Ms Carolina Cordero, Secretary in the School of Law, for her assistance in organising the day.

Following the seminar discussion, the papers were reworked in the light of comments before being edited for this collection. At this stage Liam D'Arcy Brown provided invaluable assistance in proofreading the final contributions, for which we are most grateful.

Finally, for kindly agreeing to write the foreword, we are especially grateful to John Eekelaar.

The Editors
September 2008

Contents

Foreword   v
Preface   vii
List of Contributors   xi

1   Introduction: Parental Responsibility—Law, Issues and Themes   1
STEPHEN GILMORE, JONATHAN HERRING AND REBECCA
PROBERT

Part I   Parental Responsibility: General Issues   **21**

2   Is Anything Now Left of Parental Rights?   23
ANDREW BAINHAM

3   Establishing and Ending Parental Responsibility: A Comparative
View   43
JENS M SCHERPE

4   The Limits of Parental Responsibility   63
STEPHEN GILMORE

5   The Degradation of Parental Responsibility   85
HELEN REECE

Part II   The Content of Parental Responsibility   **103**

6   The Shaming of Naming: Parental Rights and Responsibilities in
the Naming of Children   105
JONATHAN HERRING

7   Parental Responsibility and Religion   123
RACHEL TAYLOR

8   Parental Responsibility and Education: Taking a Long View   143
DANIEL MONK

9   Parental Responsibility and Corporal Punishment   165
SHAZIA CHOUDHRY

10   Parental Responsibility and Children's Health Care Treatment   185
LYNN HAGGER

11   'Don't Spend It All at Once!': Parental Responsibility and
Parents' Responsibilities in Respect of Children's
Contracts and Property   201
ELIZABETH COOKE

12   **Children's Representation by Their Parents in Legal Proceedings**   215
CAROLINE SAWYER

13   **Parental Responsibility and Children's Partnership Choices**   237
REBECCA PROBERT

14   **Parental Responsibility, Relational Responsibility: Caring for and Protecting Children after their Death**   255
JO BRIDGEMAN

Part III Responsible Parenting   **271**

15   **Financial Support for Children after Parental Separation: Parental Responsibility and Responsible Parenting**   273
NICK WIKELEY

16   **Parental Responsibility and the Responsible Parent: Managing the 'Problem' of Contact**   295
JULIE WALLBANK

17   **Parental Responsibility for Juvenile Offending in English Law**   315
ROGER LENG

18   **Parental Liability for Harm Caused by Children: A Comparative Analysis**   333
PAULA GILIKER

Index   **353**

List of Contributors

Andrew Bainham is a Fellow of Christ's College Cambridge and Reader in Family Law and Policy at the University of Cambridge. He was a founder member and first chair of the Cambridge Socio-Legal Group. For over a decade he was editor of the *International Survey of Family Law*, published on behalf of the International Society of Family Law. He is the author of *Children: The Modern Law* (3rd edn, Jordans, 2005). He is currently consultant to the Centre for Social Justice in connection with its ongoing Family Law Review. He is the author of many articles in the field of family law, the most recent of which is 'Arguments about parentage' (2008) 67 *Cambridge Law Journal* 322. He is the editor of *Parents and Children* (Aldershot, Ashgate, 2008).

Jo Bridgeman is a Senior Lecturer in Law at the University of Sussex, where she is a founder member of the Child and Family Research Group and the Centre for Responsibilities, Rights and the Law. Her research and publications are in the field of healthcare law and the law regulating the care of children. Jo's recent monograph *Parental Responsibility, Young Children and Healthcare Law* (Cambridge, Cambridge University Press, 2007) offers a critical analysis of moral, social and legal responsibilities for the healthcare of babies, infants and young children, informed by and developing the feminist ethic of care. This perspective also informs her work on the legal regulation of care, which is developing a conceptual framework of relational responsibility.

Shazia Choudhry is a Lecturer in Law at Queen Mary, University of London, and has also taught at the University of Newcastle (2002 to 2005). Prior to her academic work, she was a practising solicitor. Her areas of expertise and research interests are in family law, the impact of the European Convention on Human Rights on various aspects of family law and the issue of 'rights' within family law in general. Shazia has published a number of articles on this subject which have been widely cited both nationally and internationally.

Elizabeth Cooke is a Professor of Law at the University of Reading; her main interests are in property law and family law. The sixth edition of *The Family, Law and Society*, written with Brenda Hale, David Pearl and Daniel Monk, was published in summer 2008. From July 2008, she is serving for five years as a Law Commissioner for England and Wales.

Paula Giliker is Professor of Comparative Law at the University of Bristol. She has previously taught at the University of Oxford and Queen Mary, University of London. Paula has published extensively in the field of comparative contract and tort law, is the co-author of *Tort* (3rd edn, Sweet & Maxwell, 2008) and recently edited *Re-examining Contract and Unjust Enrichment: Anglo-Canadian Perspectives* (Leiden, Brill, 2007).

Stephen Gilmore is Lecturer in Family Law at King's College London. He is particularly interested in the law on parental responsibility and the resolution of parental disputes. Recent publications include: 'Contact/Shared Residence and Child Well-being: Research Evidence and its Implications for Legal Decision-Making' (2006) 20 *International Journal of Law, Policy and the Family* 344; and 'Disputing Contact: Challenging Some Assumptions' [2008] 20 *Child and Family Law Quarterly* 285. He is currently co-authoring the third edition of *Hayes and Williams: Family Law, Principles, Policy and Practice* (Oxford, Oxford University Press) for publication in 2009.

Lynn Hagger is a Lecturer in Law at the University of Sheffield. Her research interests are in medical law in general and children's issues in particular. Her publications focus on the empowerment of children through the use of human rights instruments. She is currently writing a book on this theme which is due to be published in June 2009: *The Child as Vulnerable Patient: Protection and Empowerment*. Her research interests have been greatly assisted by her parallel career in the NHS as a non-executive director for 20 years. She was Chairperson of the Sheffield Children's Hospital NHS Foundation Trust for nine years until January 2008. Here she established a Clinical Ethics Forum and Patients' Advisory Group to help to ensure that ethical standards of care were offered to patients and their families.

Jonathan Herring is a Fellow in Law at Exeter College, University of Oxford. He is author of several books, including *Criminal Law: Text, Cases and Materials* (Oxford, Oxford University Press, 2008); *Family Law* (Harlow, Pearson, 2007); *Medical Law and Ethics* (Oxford, Oxford University Press, 2008); and *Criminal Law* (Basingstoke, Palgrave, 2006). He has also written widely on issues relating to criminal law, family law and medical law. In 2007 he was the George P Smith Distinguished Visiting Professor-Chair at the University of Indiana. He is currently working on a book on family law and human rights (with Shazia Choudhry) and a book on law and older people.

Roger Leng is Reader in Law at the University of Warwick. His work spans the fields of criminal law, evidence and procedure. He is a former editor of the *International Journal of Evidence and Proof* and has held consultancies with the Law Reform Commission of Canada and the Royal Commission on Criminal Justice. His most recent book (with R Taylor and M Wasik) is *Blackstone's Guide to the Criminal Justice Act 2003* (Oxford, Oxford University Press, 2004).

Daniel Monk is a Senior Lecturer in Law at Birkbeck College, University of London. He has published articles on various issues relating to children's rights, education law and the sociology of childhood, and is co-author (with B Hale, D Pearl and E Cooke) of *The Family, Law and Society* (6th edn, Oxford, Oxford University Press, 2008). He is the co-editor (with J Bridgeman) of *Feminist Perspectives on Child Law* (London, Cavendish, 2000) and (with L Moran and S

Beresford) of *Legal Queeries* (London, Cassells, 1998). He is Assistant Editor of *Child and Family Law Quarterly*.

Rebecca Probert is a Senior Lecturer at the University of Warwick, teaching family law and child law. She has just completed a book on the Clandestine Marriages Act of 1753—*Marriage Law and Practice in the Long Eighteenth Century: A Reassessment*—which is due to be published by Cambridge University Press in 2009. She is also co-author (with J Masson and R Bailey-Harris) of *Cretney: Principles of Family Law* (London, Sweet & Maxwell, 2008), editor of *Family Life and the Law: Under One Roof* (Aldershot, Ashgate, 2007) and co-editor (with Jo Miles) of *Sharing Lives, Dividing Assets: An inter-disciplinary study* (Oxford, Hart, 2009).

Helen Reece is a Reader in Law at Birkbeck College, University of London. Her current research interests include conceptions of responsibility in the context of the family. She is the author of *Divorcing Responsibly* (Oxford, Hart, 2003). Other recent publications include 'From Parental Responsibility to Parenting Responsibly' in Michael Freeman (ed), *Law and Sociology: Current Legal Issues* (Oxford, Oxford University Press, 2006) and 'The Autonomy Myth: A Theory of Dependency' (Review article) [2008] 20 *Child and Family Law Quarterly* 109.

Caroline Sawyer is Reader in Law at Oxford Brookes University. Her research interests include issues of legal competence and legal personality, especially of children and non-nationals. She is currently working on statelessness and British citizenship as well as the legal status of children.

Jens M Scherpe is a Fellow of Gonville and Caius College Cambridge, and a University Lecturer in Law at the University of Cambridge, where he teaches comparative law and family law. Previously he was Research Fellow and Head of the Department for the Law of the Nordic Countries at the Max Planck Institute for Comparative and Private International Law in Hamburg. He is a member of the International Advisory Board of the *Zeitschrift für das gesamte Familienrecht* (FamRZ) and member of the Wissenschaftliche Vereinigung für Familienrecht eV.

Rachel Taylor is Penningtons Tutor in Law at Christ Church, University of Oxford. Her research interests are in Family Law and Human Rights Law. Recent publications include: 'Reversing the Retreat from Gillick? *R (Axon) v Secretary of State for Health*' [2007] 19 *Child and Family Law Quarterly* 81 and (with Jonathan Herring) 'Relocating Relocation' [2006] 18 *Child and Family Law Quarterly* 517.

Julie Wallbank is a Senior Lecturer in Law at the School of Law, University of Leeds. Her areas of expertise and research interests are family law, feminist legal theory and gender and the law. She has written widely on gendered aspects of family law, including the regulation of reproductive technologies, child support and contact.

Nick Wikeley has been a Judge of the Administrative Appeals Chamber of the Upper Tribunal since November 2008 and is an Emeritus Professor at the University of Southampton. His books include *Child Support in Action* (Oxford, Hart, 1998), with Gwynn Davis and Richard Young) and *Child Support Law and Policy* (Oxford, Hart, 2006). He was one of the authors of the report on the 'Relationship breakdown and child support study' (DWP Research Report No 503, 2008).

1

Introduction: Parental Responsibility—Law, Issues and Themes

STEPHEN GILMORE, JONATHAN HERRING AND REBECCA PROBERT

INTRODUCTION

THERE IS MUCH discussion in the media about what makes a good parent and the ills that fall on society because of inadequacies of parents. Often it is said that parents nowadays are not taking the burdens of parenthood seriously. Such discussions of parental irresponsibility by definition proceed on the basis that a responsible parent would act in a different way. Yet any parent knows all too well the difficulty of finding any consensus as to what constitutes responsible parenting. From the advice given by baby manuals to the opinions on the extent of supervision necessary for children or the latitude to be accorded to teenagers, parents are bombarded with—often conflicting—advice as to what they should be doing.[1]

Of course, newspapers and books on parenting exist for commercial reasons rather than to reassure the anxious parent or find a consensus. We might hope that the law would offer a better source of information as to what is expected of the responsible parent. Surely this is central to the legal concept of parental responsibility, loosely defined in section 3(1) of the Children Act 1989 as:

all the rights, duties, powers, responsibilities and authority which by law a parent of a child has in relation to the child and his property.

However, while much has been written on the theoretical nature of parental responsibility, relatively little is known (or has been written) about the content of the specific rights and duties that it comprises. They are nowhere spelt out in any legislation, and discussions of the nature and scope of parental responsibility must therefore draw on a combination of case law and learned treatises. Yet unless we know what powers and duties parental responsibility confers or imposes, important debates as to who has it—or should have it—occur in a

[1] See, eg 'A smack can keep children from crime, says police leader' *Sunday Telegraph* (4 March 2007); contrast 'Smacking can turn children into criminals' *Observer* (10 February 2008).

vacuum. The purpose of this book, therefore, is to provide what we believe may be the first attempt at a sustained, detailed discussion of the various rights, duties and powers that constitute parental responsibility in English law.

The book is divided into three sections. The first deals with some difficult, but important, generic issues relating to the establishment, nature, scope and limits of parental responsibility. The second, and most substantial section, looks at a broad range of practical matters, seeking to illuminate how the law interacts with some of the issues which regularly trouble parents, whether day-to-day issues (such as education, religion and punishment) or those in more exceptional situations (such as disputes over names, medical treatment, acting on behalf of children in legal proceedings and legal transactions, consenting to the marriage of a minor or dealing with the aftermath of a child's death). Overall, in each context the aim is to expose what parental responsibility allows a parent to do, and what is expected of the responsible parent. The third section of the book develops the idea of 'responsible parenting' by examining how the law in various contexts (tort, criminal law, child-support liability and child contact with a non-resident parent) characterises the 'responsible parent'.

Our purpose in this preliminary chapter is to set the scene for the discussions in the chapters which follow. In doing so, we have two principal aims. First, we supply some introductory background to the concept of parental responsibility, together with a basic account of the law relating to parental responsibility in order to avoid unnecessary repetition within individual chapters. Secondly, we provide an overview of the contributions, highlighting the various tensions and themes within the concept of parental responsibility which emerge.

PARENTS' RESPONSIBILITIES: MEANINGS AND ORIGINS

The focus in this book is upon individuals' responsibilities to particular children. This reflects one of several different senses in which the term 'parental responsibility' may be used: in this case, emphasising the word *parental* to denote that an individual, rather than the state, has been accorded the primary responsibility for a child's upbringing.[2] This has important implications for many of the issues discussed in the chapters which follow: if the responsibility for a child's upbringing is left to the parent, there is considerable scope for parental discretion.

Linked to this is a second sense, that such individuals (usually parents) may be held *responsible to other individuals or the state* for children's actions. In this understanding of parental responsibility, parents are held accountable and are expected to act responsibly. These aspects of parental responsibility surface in

---

[2]   J Eekelaar, 'Parental Responsibility: State of Nature or Nature of the State' [1991] 13 *JSWL* 37. There is debate as to the source of duties to care for children. On one view, these may be said to arise from the social allocation of a general duty to promote human flourishing: see J Eekelaar, 'Are Parents Morally Obliged to Care for Their Children?' (1991) 11 *OJLS* 340. Compare the discussion in C Barton and G Douglas, *Law and Parenthood* (London, Butterworths, 1995) ch 2.

various sections of the book, but are particularly prominent in the third. For example, within the criminal justice system (examined by Roger Leng), there is now 'a matrix of powers that can be used by the courts to instil "Parental Responsibility"';[3] and Paula Giliker, in her chapter, discusses how the law of tort may impose liability upon a 'parent' for damage arising from a child's act.

A third, and perhaps the most common, understanding of 'parental responsibility' among family lawyers is as a sphere of liberty or Hohfeldian privilege,[4] constituting the scope of parental decision-making with respect to a child. Here, parental responsibility connotes the idea of a bundle of parent/child 'jural relations' instrumental in promoting (or at least safeguarding) the child's interests.[5] The responsibility is to, or for, *the child*, rather than to others. As Lord Fraser put it in *Gillick v West Norfolk and Wisbech AHA and Department of Health and Social Security*[6] (hereinafter *Gillick*):

> parental rights to control a child do not exist for the benefit of the parent. They exist for the benefit of the child and they are justified only in so far as they enable the parent to perform his duties towards the child, and towards other children in the family.[7]

These three understandings of parental responsibility all predate the use of the term in an Act of Parliament, some by a considerable margin. It was not until the Children Act 1989 that the term was enshrined in legislation, following the recommendation of the Law Commission. The emphasis in *Gillick* on parental rights as derived from duties reinforced the Commission's view, expressed in its 1982 report, that:

> to talk of parental rights is not only inaccurate as a matter of juristic analysis but also a misleading use of ordinary language.[8]

It is important to note, however, that this assessment did not relate to parental rights generally, but rather to the issue of what light the common law threw on such rights. As the Commission pointed out, there were no recent cases that provided a comprehensive analysis of parental rights, nor, indeed, were there likely to be, given that the focus of the courts would generally be on the welfare of the child rather than the rights of the parent. Furthermore, it is clear from the discussion that followed that the Commission was aware of the power that parents enjoyed on a day-to-day basis, explaining that:

---

[3] K Hollingsworth, 'Responsibility and Rights: Children and Their Parents in the Youth Justice System' (2007) 21 *IJLPF* 190, 194.

[4] See WN Hohfeld, *Fundamental Legal Conceptions As Applied in Judicial Reasoning* (Newhaven, 1919); and see *Re KD (A Minor) Access: Principles* [1988] 2 FLR 139 at 153 (Lord Oliver of Aylmerton).

[5] BM Dickens, 'The Modern Function and Limits of Parental Rights' (1981) 97 *LQR* 462. See further A Bainham, *Children, Parents and the State* (London, Sweet & Maxwell, 1988) 48, and generally ch 3.

[6] [1986] 1 AC 112.

[7] *Ibid*, at 170D-E.

[8] Law Commission, 'Family Law: Illegitimacy' (Law Com No 118, 1982) [4.18].

under our law, unless and until a court order is obtained, a person with parental rights is legally empowered to take action in respect of a child in exercise of those rights.[9]

Was the terminological shift from rights to responsibilities accompanied by a substantive change in what was expected of a parent? The Law Commission did not envisage that it would be:

[s]uch a change would make little difference in substance but it would reflect the everyday reality of being a parent and emphasise the responsibilities of all who are in that position.[10]

Even the phrasing of section 3 of the 1989 Act echoed that of earlier legislation: previously, 'parental rights' had been defined as including both rights and duties;[11] under the 1989 Act 'parental responsibility' was likewise defined as encompassing both rights and duties. It is also important to note that the apparently more child-centred term, 'responsibilities', included in section 3 was flanked by the more parent-centred terms, 'powers' and 'authority'. Indeed, it could be argued that the latter terms qualify the meaning of 'responsibilities', since they appeared to be synonymous in the Commission's 1982 Report.[12]

Yet the fact that the new term was not intended to change the law does not mean that the law has not changed since then. The evolving nature of parental responsibility was one of the factors that dissuaded the Law Commission from attempting any list of the rights and duties that it comprised.[13] Back in 1990 Alexander McCall Smith posed the question: 'is anything left of parental rights?'; the changes of the past two decades make it appropriate for the question to be posed again, as Andrew Bainham does in his chapter, and possible for a different answer to be reached. Indeed, the incorporation of the European Convention for the Protection of Human Rights and Fundamental Freedoms (ECHR) into English law by means of the Human Rights Act 1998 has reinvigorated the debate as to the rights that parents enjoy. Conversely, the idea of children's autonomy rights—which by definition act as a constraint on parental responsibility—has not been significantly developed. This should not come as a surprise: as Stephen Gilmore points out in his chapter, the academic view that *Gillick* marked a great leap forward for children's rights is difficult to sustain upon a close reading of the case. The reasoning of Lords Fraser and Scarman was built upon a consideration of the best interests of the sexually active minor, not upon the right of the minor to be sexually active.

In addition, shifts in judicial opinion as to whether parental responsibility is a status that should be accorded to an interested father or a practical concept

---

[9] *Ibid*, [4.19].
[10] Law Commission, 'Family Law: Review of Child Law: Guardianship and Custody' (Law Com No 172 1988) [2.4].
[11] Children Act 1975 s 85(1).
[12] 'Illegitimacy', [4.19].
[13] 'Guardianship and Custody', [2.6].

reflecting the realities of being a parent have altered the meaning of having parental responsibility. As Helen Reece shows, it is possible for the court to award parental responsibility with one hand and constrain its exercise with the other: her chapter on 'the degradation of parental responsibility' might have been titled 'is anything now left of parental responsibility?'

If the answer to this were 'no', there would be no need for this book. But notwithstanding criticisms of, and challenges to, the concept, it does still form the central organising concept in the regulation of parent–child relationships. But to begin to understand this we need to consider the rights and duties that derive from the status of parenthood, and those that depend upon the possession of parental responsibility.

PARENTHOOD AND PARENTAL RESPONSIBILITY

A useful starting point, therefore, for understanding the nature and scope of parental responsibility in English law is to unpack the law's notion(s) of 'being a parent'. Bainham (in an earlier work) usefully observes that this requires engagement with three 'subtle, elusive, yet important distinctions' in terminology: 'parentage', 'parenthood' and 'parental responsibility'.[14] The term 'parentage' (particularly important to the child's interest in knowing his or her origins) focuses on a biological, principally genetic, connection between the providers of gametes and the resulting child. It is thus a matter of fact. By contrast, the term 'legal parenthood' represents the idea of who, as a matter of law, is recognised as a parent. In most cases, however, parentage and legal parenthood coincide because the general rule in English law is that legal parenthood is attributed according to biological connection[15] (the genetic father and gestational mother). This is not the place for a detailed examination of how English law attributes legal parenthood;[16] it will suffice to note that generally legal parenthood follows genetic parentage, but there are special rules in cases of assisted conception which can confer parenthood on men (and, under the Human Fertilisation and Embryology Act 2008, women[17]) who are not genetically related to a child,[18] and that legal parenthood can also be conferred by court order (for example, an adoption order).[19]

---

[14] A Bainham, 'Parentage, Parenthood and Parental Responsibility: Subtle, Elusive Yet Important Distinctions' in A Bainham, S Day Sclater and M Richards (eds), *What is a Parent? A Socio-Legal Analysis* (Oxford, Hart, 1999).

[15] Whether actual or presumed. For criticism of automatic deference to biology, see JG Dwyer, *The Relationship Rights of Children* (New York, Cambridge University Press, 2006).

[16] For an account of the law, see, eg N Lowe and G Douglas, *Bromley's Family Law* (10th edn, Oxford, Oxford University Press, 2007) ch 7.

[17] See Human Fertilisation and Embrology Act 2008, ss 42–46.

[18] See Human Fertilisation and Embryology Act 1990 s 28.

[19] Adoption and Children Act 2002 ss 46–51 and 67. It can also be conferred by a parental order under s 30 of the Human Fertilisation and Embryology Act 1990.

The important point for present purposes is that, once attributed, certain legal incidents attach directly to 'legal parenthood'.[20] The child and parent become members of the same family with all the attendant legal relationships with kin (such as the rights of intestate succession under the Administration of Estates Act 1925). Several other statutes confer rights or impose duties upon the status of parenthood. For example, the duty to maintain a child attaches to legal parenthood, including liability for child support payments under the Child Support Act 1991. Section 1 of the Children and Young Persons Act 1933 provides for an offence of wilful neglect of a person under 16 years of age; and a parent who is liable to maintain such a child is deemed to have neglected the child in a manner likely to cause injury if the parent has failed to provide adequate food, clothing, medical aid or lodging for him or her, or if unable to provide the same, he or she has failed to take steps to procure it. In addition, the parent of every child of compulsory school age has a duty to cause his or her child to receive efficient full-time education.[21] Further examples of rights attaching to parenthood can be found in the Children Act 1989. For instance, a parent has a right to apply automatically (without leave of a court) for any order under section 8 of that Act[22] (for example, a contact order or a residence order) and to apply to discharge an emergency protection order.[23] There is also a presumption of contact between a parent and a child who is the subject of a care order.[24]

In some cases, however, the exercise of parental rights (for example, the right to appoint a guardian or to object to a child's adoption) requires that the parent has parental responsibility for the child within the meaning of the Children Act 1989.[25] As with legal parenthood, the precise content of 'parental responsibility' is to be found in the common law and in other statutory provisions, and the chapters in the second section of the book seek to provide an in-depth account of the meaning of parental responsibility through detailed examinations of particular parental responsibilities. Whether a person has 'parental responsibility' within section 3, however, is itself a matter of law. The Children Act 1989 sets out who is allocated parental responsibility and the means by which parental responsibility can be acquired. A child's mother, and a child's father who is married to the mother, each have parental responsibility by operation of law.[26] A father who is not so married, however, must acquire parental responsibility in accordance with the provisions of the Children Act 1989.[27] He may do so if: (i) on or after 1

---

[20] See Bainham, above n 14, 33–34 for a useful summary.
[21] Suitable to his age, ability and aptitude, and to any special educational needs he may have, either by regular attendance at school or otherwise: see Education Act 1996 s 7.
[22] Children Act 1989 s 10(4).
[23] Children Act 1989 s 45(8)(a).
[24] Children Act 1989 s 34.
[25] Children Act 1989 s 5(3) and Adoption and Children Act 2002 ss 47 and 52(6).
[26] Children Act 1989 s 2(1).
[27] Children Act 1989 s 2(2).

December 2003, he and the mother jointly register the child's birth;[28] (ii) the mother agrees to his sharing parental responsibility by way of a parental responsibility agreement;[29] (iii) he obtains a parental responsibility order (PRO);[30] or (iv) he obtains a residence order, in which case the court must also grant him a PRO, which is not lost if the residence order is revoked.[31]

It is of course possible for persons who are neither biological nor legal parents to acquire parental responsibility. A step-parent (which includes a civil partner of the child's parent)[32] may also, with the consent of all holders of parental responsibility, agree to share parental responsibility, or may acquire it by court order.[33] Parental responsibility may also be conferred by way of a residence order, settling the arrangements as to the person with whom the child shall live.[34] It may be conferred in such a way on more than one person by a joint or shared residence order.[35] Defined applicants,[36] who have attained the age of 18 and who are not the parent of a child, may acquire parental responsibility through the making of a special guardianship order, which confers parental responsibility to the exclusion of other holders of parental responsibility.[37] Parental responsibility is also acquired when an adoption order is made.[38] It may also be conferred in public law proceedings by way of a care order[39] or an emergency protection order.[40] Finally, a person may acquire parental responsibility when appointed (by a court or by an individual) to act as a child's guardian in the event of the death of a person or persons who had parental responsibility.[41] Although the focus of this collection is on the content of parental responsibility, rather than the question of who should be entitled to have parental responsibility, the two questions cannot be divorced from each other entirely. As Jens Scherpe's chapter demonstrates, there is a wide variety of ways in which parental responsibility could be allocated. At a very basic level, the current rules on the allocation of

---

[28] Children Act 1989 s 4(1)(a). Current proposals to make joint birth registration almost universal have the potential to reduce the proportion of fathers without parental responsibility still further: see Department for Work and Pensions, 'Joint birth registration: recording responsibility' (Cm 7293, 2008). For discussion see A Bainham, 'What is the point of birth registration?' [2008] 20 *CFLQ* 449.

[29] Children Act 1989 s 4(1)(b).

[30] Children Act 1989 s 4, and see generally, S Gilmore, 'Parental responsibility and the unmarried father—a new dimension to the debate' [2003] 15 *CFLQ* 21.

[31] Children Act 1989 ss 8, 10 and 12(1).

[32] Amendment to s 4A introduced by Civil Partnership Act 2004 s 75(2).

[33] Children Act 1989 s 4A.

[34] Children Act 1989 ss 8 and 12(2).

[35] Children Act 1989 s 11(4). See S Gilmore, 'Court decision-making in shared residence order cases: a critical examination' [2006] 18 *CFLQ* 478, 491–2.

[36] See Children Act 1989 s 14A(5). This includes a local authority foster parent with whom the child has lived for a period of at least one year immediately preceding the application.

[37] Children Act 1989 ss 14A–14F. However, a special guardian needs the leave of the court to change a child's surname.

[38] Adoption and Children Act 2002 s 46.

[39] Children Act 1989 s 33(3)(a).

[40] Children Act 1989 s 44(4)(c).

[41] Children Act 1989 ss 5 and 6.

parental responsibility reflect what the Law Commission termed the 'parental claim'[42]—the idea that a parent in general has a better right to determine the child's future than a third party does. The extension of parental responsibility to persons other than a parent raises the question of whether the concept is parent-centred or child-centred: is the justification for the extension the status of the parent or the needs of the child?

Similar questions need to be considered where issues of shared parental responsibility arise. As can be seen, more than one person (whether or not a parent) may have parental responsibility at the same time.[43] Indeed, section 2(7) of the Children Act 1989 provides that each holder of parental responsibility may act alone in meeting his or her parental responsibility,[44] although the courts have seemingly undermined this provision by suggesting that parental responsibility introduces a 'right to be consulted on schooling, serious medical problems and other important occurrences in the child's life'.[45] Thus, the content of specific rights may affect who may exercise parental responsibility and how. The extension of parental responsibility to third parties also raises further questions about its content: does the fact that parental responsibility is accorded to a wider group of persons require us to narrow its content?

It is apparent from the preceding discussion that an important feature of the concept of 'parental responsibility' is the flexibility it brings, allowing its bundle of legal relations to be conferred on a person who is not a child's parent. But it does not follow that acquisition of parental responsibility under the Children Act 1989 confers all of the duties of parenthood, even though this would at first sight appear to be the effect of section 3 of the Children Act 1989. The content of parental responsibility can depend upon how it has been acquired. For example, if parental responsibility is conferred by a care order, or upon a non-parent by a residence order, it does not include the power to appoint a guardian, or to consent or refuse consent to the child's adoption.[46] The latter (but not the former) restriction also applies to a special guardian.[47] In addition, a local authority with parental responsibility cannot cause a child to be brought up in any religious persuasion other than that in which he or she would have been

---

[42]   'Guardianship and Custody', [2.4].

[43]   Children Act 1989 s 2(5).

[44]   Subject to any enactment requiring the consent of more than one person with parental responsibility and in so far as compatible with an existing court order: Children Act 1989 s 2(8).

[45]   *Re H (Parental Responsibility)* [1998] 1 FLR 855 at 859A (Butler-Sloss LJ). See also Morritt LJ in *Re D (Minors)*, (unreported) 20 March 1995: 'the effect of the PRO is one in which the father, for the benefit of the children, should be consulted and kept informed'. For specific examples of exceptions to s 2(7), see *Re G (Parental Responsibility: Education)* [1994] 2 FLR 964; *Re PC (Change of Surname)* [1997] 2 FLR 730; and *Re J (Specific Issue Orders: Child's Religious Upbringing and Circumcision)* [2000] 1 FLR 571. For criticism, see J Eekelaar, 'Do Parents have a Duty to Consult?' (1998) 114 *LQR* 337; J Eekelaar, 'Rethinking Parental Responsibility' [2001] *Fam Law* 426; and S Maidment, 'Parental Responsibility—Is there a Duty to Consult?' [2001] *Fam Law* 518.

[46]   Children Act 1989 s 33(6)(a) and (b); and s 12(3).

[47]   Children Act 1989 s 14C(2)(b).

brought up had a care order not been made.[48] In addition to these specific restrictions that appear in the legislation, the exercise of parental responsibility conferred by a PRO may be restricted by undertakings given by the applicant not to interfere in particular aspects of the child's upbringing[49] (an issue discussed in more detail by Helen Reece in her chapter).

This leads on to a further issue, namely the uncertainty surrounding who is responsible for different matters. It is difficult to find a coherent basis for determining for which issues a parent is responsible and which fall on the shoulders of those who have parental responsibility. Perhaps in some cases practical considerations, rather than thought-through principles, explain the law's operation. For example, although the duty to provide for a child is traditionally listed as an aspect of parental responsibility, the duty to make child support payments pursuant to the Child Support Act 1991 in relation to a child under the age of 18 is not an aspect of parental responsibility that is imposed on non-parents.[50] Instead, it falls on all parents, rather than just those with parental responsibility, reflecting, no doubt, the desire to ensure that more people are liable to pay than would be the case if parental responsibility was the sole basis of liability, as well as the realisation that it may be more difficult to find non-parents to assume the burden of parental responsibility if this brings onerous financial implications. By contrast, the defence of 'reasonable punishment' to an assault on a child is available not only to parents, but also to those acting in *loco parentis*, regardless of whether they have parental responsibility. In each area, therefore, there are distinctions between parents who have parental responsibility and those who do not, and between parents (with or without parental responsibility) and non-parents who have parental responsibility.

Nor is the concept of parental responsibility as set out in the Children Act 1989 inclusive of all the duties that parents owe to their children. The definition in section 3 of the Act refers to parental responsibility in relation to a child, who for the purpose of the Act is a person who has not attained 18 years of age.[51] However, there are several duties which a parent may owe to a child who has attained the age of 18. Such duties cannot, by definition, comprise 'parental responsibility' under the Children Act 1989 and are not therefore conferred when such parental responsibility is acquired. For example, orders for financial support for adult children may be made under the Matrimonial Causes Act 1973 or Schedule 1 to the Children Act 1989 and there would appear in principle to be no

---

[48]   Children Act 1989 s 33(6)(c).

[49]   *Re D (contact and parental responsibility: lesbian mothers and known father)* [2006] EWHC 2 (Fam).

[50]   The duty to maintain in the Child Support Act 1991 s 1 is owed in respect of a 'qualifying child', which definition requires the existence of a non-resident *parent*. While the courts see conferring parental responsibility as a matter with respect to the child's upbringing, to which Children Act 1989 s 1(1) applies, s 105(1) defines a child's upbringing as excluding his or her maintenance. See further Wikeley, ch 15.

[51]   Children Act 1989 s 105(1).

age limit on such orders;[52] and the duty to maintain a child within the Child Support Act 1991 extends to adult children under 19 years of age who are receiving full-time education which is not advanced.[53] Therefore, parents may have duties to their children that fall outside the scope of parental responsibility.

In addition, parents may have duties without having parental responsibility. Section 3(4) of the Children Act 1989 clarifies that the fact that a person has or does not have parental responsibility:

> does not affect any duty which he may have in relation to the child (such as a statutory duty to maintain the child).

As we have seen, however, the law provides that some parents shall not have 'parental responsibility', which suggests that there is some difference between simply being a parent and being a parent with parental responsibility. Sections 2 and 3(4) of the Children Act 1989 appear to indicate that while the former retains (some) duties attaching to legal parenthood, the latter (but not the former) in addition has all of the rights, powers and authority which a parent has in relation to the child and his or her property. Thus, *a parent's responsibilities*, and *parental responsibility* as defined by section 3 of the Children Act 1989, are not necessarily the same.[54]

It has been suggested by John Eekelaar, however, that the distinction between being a parent and being a parent with parental responsibility may be of rather limited significance. His argument is that important duties relating to a child's upbringing attach to parenthood,[55] and because *ought* implies *can*, a parent must have the rights, privileges or powers attending those duties in order to carry them through. In support of this view, Eekelaar points to the duty in section 7 of the Education Act 1996, that:

> [the] parent of every child of compulsory school age shall cause him to receive efficient full-time education ... either by regular attendance at school or otherwise.

He argues that 'the same must be true regarding medical treatment', for:

> if the [parent] has a duty to see his child is educated, he is also under a duty to tend to his health.[56]

---

[52]   Matrimonial Causes Act 1973 s 29. See M Letts, 'Children: The Continuing Duty to Maintain' [2001] *Fam Law* 839; and B Smyth, 'Child support for young adult children in Australia' (2002) 16 *IJLPF* 22. For a review of arguments and the position in the United States, see SL Bhai, 'Parental Support of Adult Children with Disabilities' (2007) 91 *Minnesota Law Review* 710.

[53]   Child Support Act 1991 s 55(1)(b). See also s 55(7) and (8) and SI 2001/157 ch 1, para 5(1) in relation to short-term provision to persons under the age of 19 who have just left full-time education.

[54]   See J Herring, *Family Law* (Harlow, Pearson Education Ltd, 2007) 385–6 for a list of the differences between rights given to a parent and those given to a parent with parental responsibility.

[55]   J Eekelaar, 'Rethinking Parental Responsibility' [2001] *Fam Law* 426.

[56]   *Ibid*, 427.

He further supports this view by reference to *Re O (A Minor) (Custody: Adoption)*,[57] a case in which the Court of Appeal upheld an unmarried father's claim to bring up his child in preference to prospective adopters. Eekelaar suggests that the court decided that the father had the better right to bring up the child, and argues that it must follow that he had the power to carry out that right whether or not he applied for parental responsibility.

At first blush, these appear to be powerful points; but on closer inspection there are several reasons for treating these arguments with caution. First, *Re O* is a case in which the parental right was conferred by the court's decision, so any attendant parental powers may arguably be said to flow from the same. It is not easy to see this case as authority for the proposition that fathers without parental responsibility and without court orders have such powers. Secondly, *Re O* was decided before the implementation of the Children Act 1989, so caution must be exercised in viewing this as an authority on the nature of parental responsibility under the Children Act 1989. Indeed, had that case been decided under the Children Act 1989, the relevant order would have been a residence order to the father, which would confer parental responsibility.[58] It is difficult to see why such an order would additionally need to confer parental responsibility if an unmarried father already has most, if not all, of the powers which flow simply from having the child living with him.

It might also be thought that it is asking too much of a specific provision such as section 7 of the Education Act 1996 to found more general duties to children. But in any event, the duty in section 7 applies only to children of compulsory school age, so it is a large jump to rely on this to found by analogy medical decision-making powers in general (ie for children under or over that age). In addition, a duty to tend to the child's medical needs, in the sense of causing to receive medical attention (cf causing to receive an education), does not necessarily imply decision-making powers as to treatment offered. A child minder without parental responsibility might be under a duty to obtain medical treatment at a local hospital for the child who is in pain and distress, but it does not follow that, upon the doctor's diagnosis of a medical condition requiring a serious operation at some point in the future, that the child minder would have a corresponding power to decide whether or not the operation is to be carried out. Indeed, it is difficult to derive parental powers to decide whether or *not* a child has medical treatment from the parental duty in section 7, since a parent cannot refuse to cause the child to receive an education.

Finally, it might certainly be thought to be counter-intuitive, in the light of the distinction made in section 2(1) and (2) of the Children Act 1989, that the acquisition of parental responsibility by a parent should make such little difference. The better view, therefore, may be that there are significant differences

---

[57] [1992] 1 FLR 77.
[58] Children Act 1989 s 12(1) and (4).

between a parent and a parent with parental responsibility, in terms of their *legal* responsibilities. Whether or not this *should* be the case is a matter that goes beyond the scope of this book. It is hoped, however, that this book will inform that debate, given that one reason why the debate has proved so complex is the uncertainty over the nature and meaning of parental responsibility. The content of parental responsibility will have an important impact on the question as to who should have it. If Reece is correct and the 'degraded' understanding of parental responsibility is now dominant, this makes the case against granting parental responsibility to all unmarried fathers more difficult to make. It may simultaneously make the case in favour weaker too, because if parental responsibility means so little there can be only a very limited disadvantage to an unmarried father in not having it. Others, however, may wish to argue that the case law is not consistent in downplaying the significance of parental responsibility.[59] Furthermore, it is clear that the possession of parental responsibility does still make a difference to the possessor's rights and duties to the child.

In summary, then, the responsibilities which an individual has in relation to a child depend upon whether the individual is a parent and whether (and if so how) the individual has parental responsibility for the child. The law is complicated further by the fact that there are rules relating to when parenthood and parental responsibility respectively are a necessary and/or sufficient condition of acting in matters relating to the child. As John Eekelaar has observed,[60] sometimes legal parenthood is necessary and sufficient; and likewise with parental responsibility.[61] On occasions, however, it is necessary to be both a parent *and* to have parental responsibility.[62] In yet other cases, either being a parent *or* having parental responsibility will suffice.[63]

As the foregoing discussion and the statutory definition of parental responsibility indicate, the concept of parental responsibility is far from straightforward. Indeed, the single phrase in section 3 of the Children Act 1989 appears to be overloaded with concepts and roles. It is perhaps inevitable that, as the courts have had to struggle with working out the role and definition of parental responsibility, cracks have begun to appear. Many of the tensions and themes within the concept are brought out in the chapters of this book.

---

[59]   See, eg Herring, above n 54, 384–5.
[60]   Eekelaar, 'Rethinking Parental Responsibility' [2001] *Fam Law* 426.
[61]   See, eg Children Act 1989 s 13(1); and the right to consent to marriage (on which see Probert, this volume).
[62]   See, eg consent to adoption.
[63]   See, eg Children Act 1989 s 10(4).

PARENTAL RESPONSIBILITY: TENSIONS AND THEMES

The Ideal Parent, the Acceptable Parent and the Unacceptable Parent

The media, the government and even the courts often make general statements about what parents ought to do. But the phrase 'ought to do' is ambiguous and it is not always clear whether it identifies a legal obligation from which clearly defined legal consequences will flow if it is not met, or is simply a statement of good practice, which is not enforceable. Hence, when the government encourages parents to feed children five portions of fruit or vegetables each day,[64] no one believes that if it is discovered that parents are failing to do this the police will be around to arrest the parents forthwith; or that an application for an interim care order will be successful simply on the ground that the parents have failed, again, to read a child a bedtime story. Such statements may be of what responsible parents should do, but are not enforceable aspects of parental responsibility.

This distinction is normally without difficulty in relation to statements from the government, but statements from the courts as to what parents ought to do can be problematic. The passage from Lord Fraser's opinion in *Gillick* (quoted above) immediately raises the question: what are the consequences if parents do not exercise their right of control for the benefit of the child?

In fact, family law does allow parents to raise their children in ways which may be harmful, subject to three limitations, as described below.

The Requirements of the Criminal Law

Clearly, a parent can be convicted of offences specifically designed to protect children and any general offence against the child, including offences against the person. This raises the issue, discussed by Shazia Choudhry in her chapter, of the extent to which a parent can use corporal punishment on a child. It is clear that a parent has no defence to a charge of assault occasioning actual bodily harm or more serious injury, but, as Choudhry explains, in relation to common assault the law exempts parents from what would otherwise be criminal acts, raising difficult questions regarding the human rights of children and their parents.

The Role of Public Law

Although a parent may raise a child in a way which harms the child, there comes a point when the type of harm will justify state intervention to protect and care for the child by way of a care or supervision order. This will be possible—

---

[64] <http://www.5aday.nhs.uk>.

although not necessary[65]—if the threshold criteria in section 31 of the Children Act 1989 are fulfilled. A court must be satisfied that the child is suffering or is likely to suffer *significant harm* attributable to the care the child is receiving not being what it would be reasonable to expect a parent to give. If the risk of significant harm is posed by a stranger rather than the parent or a carer, then the threshold criteria are not satisfied.[66] This reveals the extent to which care proceedings can be seen as indicating a failure of parenting, as much as a protection of children from harm. It is at this point that public law intervenes.

Private Applications

It is possible for an individual to challenge a parent's decision by an application under section 8 of the Children Act 1989, for example, an application for a specific issue order.[67] The court can then make an order applying the child's welfare as its paramount consideration.[68] This might be viewed, therefore, as an occasion on which a court could enforce the obligation of a parent to use his or her parental responsibility to promote the welfare of the child. Again, however, matters are not that straightforward, for three reasons. First, it has been determined that the parent with whom the child lives should be allowed to decide day-to-day issues.[69] So if the resident parent is engaging in conduct which is causing the child only minor harm, it is unlikely that a court will intervene.[70] For example, if a resident parent is feeding the child a diet which is less than ideal, another parent is unlikely to be able to challenge that aspect of parenting unless, despite the above principle about day-to-day care of the child, the court feels compelled to intervene in the child's interests. Secondly, there are many aspects of parenting on which the court may feel that there is no community consensus and hence a decision about welfare cannot be made. Thus, in *Re W (Residence order)*,[71] the Court of Appeal, in deciding a dispute between parents about children's residence, was willing to recognise that nudity in the home is an issue over which reasonable people disagree, and consequently the court was unwilling to suggest that a resident mother and her partner should not be naked in front of their children. This kind of argument is likely to apply to many issues about

---

[65] Even if a parent is causing a child significant harm, a court cannot make a care order or supervision order except upon application by a Local Authority or authorised person (the NSPCC): Children Act 1989 s 31.

[66] Unless the existence of the 'stranger danger' and consequent harm to the child can be said to be attributable to lack of reasonable parental care: see generally *Lancashire CC v B* [2000] 1 FCR 583.

[67] See generally S Gilmore, 'The nature, scope and use of the specific issue order' [2004] 16 *CFLQ* 367.

[68] Children Act 1989 s 1.

[69] *Re P (A Minor) (Parental Responsibility Order)* [1994] 1 FLR 578.

[70] Similarly, the courts have been reluctant to hear cases where children have sought to challenge their parents' decision over what are regarded as trivial issues (see *Re C (A Minor) (Leave to Seek Section 8 Order)* [1994] 1 FLR 26).

[71] [1999] 1 FLR 869.

which a third party may wish to complain. Thirdly, there is the issue of enforcement. A court will be reluctant to make an order which cannot be enforced. This will be true of many of the minutiae of day-to-day parenting.

The willingness of the courts to allow parents to raise children free from state intervention, unless absolutely necessary, should not be surprising. In a recent judgment, Hedley J made this point:

> Society must be willing to tolerate very diverse standards of parenting, including the eccentric, the barely adequate and the inconsistent. It follows too that children will inevitably have both very different experiences of parenting and very unequal consequences flowing from it. It means that some children will experience disadvantage and harm, while others flourish in atmospheres of loving security and emotional stability. These are the consequences of our fallible humanity and it is not the provenance of the state to spare children all the consequences of defective parenting. In any event, it simply could not be done.[72]

But recognising variable parenting need not be seen in such a negative light. It is not just about grinning and bearing the fact that some parents make a pretty bad job of parenting. Rather, not regulating parenthood to any great extent produces benefits. One of the joys of life is that everyone is different—a person's character, beliefs and appearance reflecting, to some extent, the way in which he or she was raised. What a dreary world it would be if all children had identikit parents, raising them according to a fiercely enforced manual. Indeed, Elizabeth Cooke in her chapter on parental responsibilities in the law of contract and property draws attention to the difference between what a responsible parent might do and what the law requires, and suggests that in that context responsible parenting works well without too much regulation. This leaves parents the freedom to raise children in ways that work best for the particular family. Interestingly, there are echoes of this in the recent government paper, *Every Parent Matters*:

> Families bring up children. The role of government is to ensure that all parents, not just those for whom it comes naturally, are able to ... make confident, informed choices which they feel are right for their family.[73]

Parental Discretions

As the foregoing discussion reveals (and as emphasised in Andrew Bainham's chapter), parents are, in effect, given a discretion as to how to raise their children However, as this and many other chapters of the book disclose, the discretion is more complex than might at first appear. For example, there is the issue of whether there are some areas where parents' discretion is protected to a greater extent than others. Rachel Taylor, in her chapter, argues that choices over

---

[72] *Re L (Care: Threshold Criteria)* [2007] 1 FLR 20 at [50]. See also *A Local Authority v N* [2005] EWHC 2956 (Fam).
[73] Department for Education and Skills, *Every Parent Matters* (2007) [2.6].

religious upbringing should be regarded as an aspect of a parent's rights to religious freedom. Court interference in a religious decision might, therefore, require even stronger justification than in other areas. That may be a controversial example, but there are others. In *Re E (Residence: Imposition of Conditions)*,[74] the Court of Appeal stated that only in exceptional cases would a court make an order restricting where a parent could live.

Further, there are some issues over which parental discretion is protected simply because it involves issues about which we do not know what is best for children. But there are others where the parental discretion is protected in order to protect parents' own rights. As this shows, in most decisions affecting children, the role of parents is not simply to stand in for the child (as illustrated by Caroline Sawyer in her discussion of the role of a parent in civil litigation); the parent has interests of his or her own. Parents' rights can, in some respects, trump issues relating to child welfare.[75] However, this can never be to the extent of leading to the child suffering significant harm. Such a formulation is very familiar to family lawyers nowadays, because it reflects the position under Article 8 of the ECHR. This recognises that a parent has a right to respect for his or her family life, which can be interfered with only if necessary in the interests of another individual (notably a child).

It would be wrong to suggest that all areas of the law recognise parental discretion to the same extent. Lynn Hagger's chapter, on the exercise of parental responsibility over health care issues, shows the willingness of the courts to overrule parental decisions in the medical context, even where the parent's decision is not obviously mistaken. However, as Hagger argues, this may overlook the expertise of the parents that comes from day-to-day interaction with and caring for the child. We might contrast, for example, the attitude of the courts to the nudity issues in *Re W* (discussed above) with the issue of whether children should have the MMR vaccine, addressed, for example, in *A and D v B and E*.[76] Both might be thought to be issues over which reasonable parents disagree, but it was only in the latter that the courts made a clear finding as to whether the parent was acting in the interests of the child. One explanation for this may be that in the medical cases there exists a ready expert who can speak authoritatively about one aspect of the child's best interests: namely the medical witness. By contrast, in many areas of child raising, there is no authoritative voice to declare what is best for children. Even among the 'super nannies', there is disagreement.[77] Indeed, it is a testament to the power of the medical profession that their expert opinion plays such a significant role in medical cases involving children.

---

[74]   [1997] 2 FLR 638, recently confirmed in *Re B (a child)* [2007] All ER (D) 371 (Jul).

[75]   See further J Herring, 'The welfare principle and the rights of parents' in Bainham *et al*, above n 14.

[76]   [2003] EWHC 1376 (Fam); and *B (Child)* [2003] EWCA Civ 1148.

[77]   J Brown, 'Tyranny of the child gurus: You don't have to be a paranoid parent' *The Independent* (22 May 2007).

Disputes between Holders of Parental Responsibility

From the discussion so far, it should be apparent that a parent who is the sole holder of parental responsibility has his or her discretion protected to a greater extent than a person who shares parental responsibilities with others. A sole holder of parental responsibility is unlikely to face challenges to any parenting decisions, unless the case involves public law issues. Where parental responsibility is shared, there are the added obligations of consultation in respect of important decisions (for example, changing a child's surname) and, of course, a greater likelihood that there will be challenges to a parent's decision.

However, this raises the question of whether all holders of parental responsibility should be equal. In the case of a dispute over an issue relating to the upbringing of a child, should the views of the resident parent count for more than the non-resident parent? As Julie Wallbank demonstrates in her chapter, much of the current discourse surrounding separated parents and parental responsibility emphasises that the responsible parent should seek cooperation between the parents. The resident parent is expected to facilitate contact, while there is no corresponding duty on the non-resident parent even to attend a contact session.[78] Similarly, as Nick Wikeley explains in his chapter, the Child Support Act 1991 presents the 'parental responsibility' of the non-resident parent as being restricted to the provision of financial support alone.

Parental Rights and Children's Rights

The exact role, if any, that children's rights and/or children's welfare should play in determining the scope of parental responsibility is an issue which has been troubling the courts and commentators for several years. Stephen Gilmore's chapter traces the development of the law, starting from the seminal *Gillick* case. He argues that early claims that the *Gillick* decision was one which heralded a recognition that children have rights to make medical decisions for themselves were exaggerated. In fact, the case was one in which the courts were endeavouring to ensure that children's welfare was protected, by ensuring access to contraceptive treatment, if the doctor thought that such prescription was in the child's best interests. Indeed, he is sceptical of claims that the current law has recognised that parental authority is usurped simply by children's capacity. Many commentators want the legal system to recognise children's rights, but as Gilmore argues it is not clear that the law actually matches their hopes.

Unsurprisingly, the discussion of the intersection of parental responsibility and children's rights naturally focuses on the complex and controversial issues surrounding children's medical treatment. However, other rights that children

---

[78] See the judgment of Thorpe LJ in *Re L, V, M and H (Contact: Domestic Violence)* [2000] 2 FLR 334.

possess should not be overlooked. Shazia Choudhry's discussion of the law regulating corporal punishment highlights how discussion of the rights of children and parents have come to dominate the legal discussions, rather than the question being seen as one simply of children's welfare. One explanation for this is that this is an issue over which parents disagree and therefore could easily be seen as a matter for discretion. By framing the issue as one of rights, it becomes less straightforward. Similarly, Rachel Taylor's discussion of religious issues highlights that, if the matter of religious upbringing is regarded as a question of the child's religious rights, rather than the parent's, the question becomes more complex. Yet the reluctance of the law to give weight to children's rights is amply illustrated by Jonathan Herring's chapter on names. Herring argues that the issue of a child's surname would be exactly the kind of area in which one could safely give children rights to make decisions, and yet in this context they appear to have none.

Parental Responsibility and the Public/Private Divide

Perhaps the appropriate exercise of parental responsibility requires a balance to be struck between the interests of children and parents. To focus entirely on maintaining that balance, however, might risk overlooking the broader interests of society which may be raised. Jonathan Herring, in his chapter, suggests that naming practices for children help to reinforce patriarchal attitudes about the family. While not everyone will agree with that, the example does indicate how apparently private decisions can be seen to have a wider impact on society. A further example is the issue of education, as explored in Daniel Monk's chapter. He demonstrates that the interaction of the exercise of parental responsibility over education and the wider public interest in education matters involves an uneasy balancing of interests.

The broader interests of society are also to the fore in the context of the criminal law, and Roger Leng reveals the complexity surrounding the criminal liability that parents can face for the conduct of their children. Interestingly, this jurisdiction has not adopted the same approach to tortious liability, and the chapter by Paula Giliker shows how other jurisdictions have imposed such liability on parents. Such liability rests on the assumption that parents are, or should be, able to control their children: the desirability of parental control is also considered in Rebecca Probert's chapter on the circumstances in which parental consent is needed for a child's marriage. Shifting policy concerns are very evident here: as she points out, at one time parents had the role of protecting their children from undesirable marriages, but nowadays the concern is rather that some parents are too much involved in such choices, for example, in cases of forced marriages.

Perhaps the most topical example of this issue is the area of financial support for children. In intact families, this is regarded as a most private matter.[79] However, as Nick Wikeley in his chapter on child support discusses, once the family separates the issue of child support becomes very much one of public concern, raising important political and social issues.

Real Life and Parental Responsibility

There is, perhaps, an air of unreality about some of the discourse surrounding parental responsibility. To the parent woken yet again in the early hours of the morning by the screaming baby; to the parent left shocked as the teenager slams the front door vowing never to return again; or to the parent holding the child they love more than their own life, the discussion of parental rights and obligations may appear sterile and out of touch with reality.

It is interesting to find cases where reality breaks though. Paula Giliker's study of the tort law cases refers to Lord Reid's comment that:

> Even a housewife who has young children cannot be in two places at once and no one would suggest that she must neglect her other duties, or that a young child must always be kept cooped up.[80]

Further, Browne-Wilkinson VC once remarked that:

> The studied calm of the Royal Courts of Justice, concentrating on one point at a time, is light years away from the circumstances prevailing in the average home.[81]

These judicial acknowledgements of the realities of family life are revealing. Although there are dicta indicating that high standards are expected, the judiciary here acknowledges that in the real world the parents cannot always promote their children's welfare nor protect them from harm.

Another aspect of this is explored by Jo Bridgeman in her chapter. As she emphasises, parents' responsibilities flow from their relationship with their children. This means that parental responsibilities cannot be stated in a list, but depend upon the characteristics and situation of the parents and the child.[82] It

---

[79] In such cases, claims cannot be made under the Child Support Act 1991: see the definition of qualifying child in s 3. Note too the provisions in Sch 1 to the Children Act 1989 providing that orders will come to an end if the parents begin to cohabit again.

[80] *Carmarthenshire CC v Lewis* [1955] AC 549 at 566. The 'even' here is revealing, presumably a 'working father' would be even less able to do these things. Also, clearly the fear that a 'housewife' in caring for her children may neglect her 'other duties' is of judicial concern.

[81] *Surtees v Kingston upon Thames RBC* [1992] PIQR P101 at 124.

[82] See also J Bridgeman, 'Parental Responsibility, Responsible Parenting and Legal Regulation', in J Bridgeman, H Keating and C Lind (eds), *Responsibility, Law and the Family* (Aldershot, Ashgate, 2008). For recent academic discussion of the concept of 'responsibility' in a family law context, see J Bridgeman and H Keating, 'Introduction: Conceptualising Family Responsibility' in Bridgeman, Keating and Lind *ibid*; and J Eekelaar, *Family Law and Personal Life* (Oxford, Oxford University Press, 2006), ch 5.

also means that they are not static; rather, they change over time as the relationship with the child develops. As Bridgeman also emphasises, the role played by other people in supporting the parents in their role needs to be acknowledged not only as significant in itself, but as affecting the content of parental responsibility.

CONCLUSION

We live in an age when many parents desperately want to 'succeed' at being a parent and be regarded as 'responsible parents'. The government also seeks to emphasise the importance of the role parents must play in raising their children. In this preliminary chapter, we have provided an outline of the law on parental responsibility. The analysis has revealed the intricacy of the concept of parental responsibility in English law—its different senses, its complicated relationship with the concept of legal parenthood, and the various aspects of its definition in section 3 of the Children Act 1989. We have suggested that, as the law has had to contend with this complexity and address questions surrounding the nature and appropriate scope of parental responsibility, inevitably tensions have arisen. Striking the right balance between the respective interests of children, parents and the state has long been a controversial issue within family policy debates. The balance is notoriously difficult to strike. Yet it is very important that we get it right.

It is our belief that these issues are likely to be informed by a clearer under-standing of the nature and content of parental responsibility and the law's expecta-tions of the responsible parent. It is to this end that the contributions in this book are aimed.

Part I

Parental Responsibility: General Issues

2

Is Anything Now Left of Parental Rights?

ANDREW BAINHAM

INTRODUCTION

A
LMOST 20 YEARS AGO, Alexander McCall Smith posed the question: 'Is anything left of parental rights?'[1] It was a good question then and it is a good question now. In the period after McCall Smith was writing, it had become distinctly fashionable, at least in the context of English law, to deny that a parent's position could properly be characterised in terms of rights. The Children Act 1989 set the tone for at least the next decade by abolishing the former notion of 'parental rights and duties'[2] and proclaiming instead 'parental responsibility'[3] as the central organising concept in the law of parent and child. Indeed, the title of this book reflects this very conceptual shift.

If viewed as a change of emphasis from the former proprietorial notions of ownership or possession of children to ideas of stewardship or trusteeship, the transition which the Children Act brought about is hardly controversial. Few people, including the great majority of parents themselves, would be at all comfortable with the notion that parents use children *primarily* for their own benefit. Even so, it might be wise to concede at the outset that the act of procreation, in so far as it is intentional (and many such acts of course are not), is an unquestionably adult-centred act. It is *those adults* who want the child. To say that a child is being planned and created for its own benefit is a distortion to which not many would subscribe. Neither, it must be said, does the claim that adoption is child-centred and exists solely for the child's benefit ring very true either.[4] There is, however, widespread agreement that the *primary* function of

---

[1] A McCall Smith, 'Is anything left of parental rights?' in E Sutherland and A McCall Smith (eds), *Family Rights: Family Law and Medical Advance* (Edinburgh, Edinburgh University Press, 1990).

[2] The Children Act 1975 s 85(1) defined 'parental rights and duties' as 'all the rights and duties which by law the mother and father have in relation to a legitimate child and his property'.

[3] Despite the clear intention to play down the existence of parental rights, the new concept of parental responsibility in the Children Act 1989 s 3(1) was so defined to include within it any such rights as parents might have.

[4] For a recent and, it is suggested, strikingly 'mother-centred' decision by the Court of Appeal on adoption, see *Re C (A Child) v XYZ CC* [2007] EWCA Civ 1206, which effectively upholds a mother's

parenthood is the responsibility to raise children and promote their best interests. The diminution in the significance attached to parental rights is accordingly in perfect harmony with the much greater importance attached first to the welfare of children and then to children's rights.[5]

But does this change of emphasis necessarily involve the abandonment of rights for parents? There have been plenty of those who have thought so. The House of Lords adopted an interpretation of the welfare principle which equated 'paramount' with 'sole' consideration, effectively meaning that any claims that parents might have could only be referable to their child's interests and not to their own and would be subsumed within the court's general investigation of the child's welfare.[6] The Law Commission felt able to state unequivocally that it was 'not only inaccurate as a matter of juristic analysis but also a misleading use of ordinary language' to talk of parental rights.[7] Furthermore, one leading commentator could speak about the 'emergence of children's rights' alongside the 'eclipse of parental rights'.[8] Such views rest on the apparent assumption that there is something inherently inconsistent in being in favour of children's welfare or rights and defending the existence of rights for parents.

In more recent years, substantial doubt has been cast on this position. There is now a growing feeling that parental rights, if not exactly thriving, may at least have been given a premature burial. The single event which has been most instrumental in this change of heart has been the implementation of the Human Rights Act 1998 and the rather quick realisation that the European Convention on Human Rights is, unsurprisingly, about rights. In so far as parents, or for that matter children, are asserting claims under the Convention, they are asserting rights. There is no question that parents, under Article 8, have rights to respect for their family life, which include rights in relation to their children. Admittedly, such rights are qualified by the 'rights and freedoms of others' and, in the balancing act which must be conducted under Article 8(2), there is a respectable view that the welfare of children must necessarily still predominate.[9] Accordingly,

---

decision to opt for a secret or confidential adoption without informing either the father or the wider birth family on either side. Judith Masson has also recently remarked that 'adoption is presented as a service for children who cannot be cared for by their birth families. However, much of adoption practice in the UK and elsewhere has focused on helping people to become parents': J Masson, 'International families: making new relationships at home and away' in R Probert (ed), *Family Life and the Law: Under One Roof* (Aldershot, Ashgate, 2007) 190.

    [5]   Children's rights as a concept was given a huge boost by the adoption in 1989 and subsequent almost universal ratification of the United Nations Convention on the Rights of the Child (UNCRC).
    [6]   *J v C* [1970] AC 668; and see generally NV Lowe, 'The House of Lords and the welfare principle' in C Bridge (ed), *Family Law Towards the Millennium: Essays for PM Bromley* (London, Butterworths, 1997).
    [7]   Law Commission, 'Custody' (Law Com WP No 96, 1986) [7.16]; and 'Illegitimacy' (Law Com No 118, HC 98, 1982) [4.18].
    [8]   J Eekelaar, 'The emergence of children's rights' (1986) 6 *OJLS* 161; and 'The eclipse of parental rights' (1986) 102 *LQR* 4.
    [9]   Importance has been attached to the decision of the European Court of Human Rights in *Yousef v The Netherlands* [2003] 1 FLR 210, holding that, where under the European Convention on Human

some conclude that there is not a great deal of difference between this exercise and the process of applying the welfare principle without recourse to the Convention. This seems to be a widely held view among the family judges.[10] It is not one which has found as much favour with academic commentators, who are inclined to feel that the welfare principle itself is in need of a revamp.[11] It is not my intention here to add to this debate.

We should also note that the idea that parents lack rights, so difficult now to defend in the European context, would be even more difficult to defend in the United States. There, the Supreme Court has resolutely and repeatedly asserted the existence of parental rights,[12] latterly alongside children's rights.[13] There is no doubt whatsoever that in the United States parents' rights have strong constitutional dimensions. Indeed, it has been said that parental rights 'have come to be regarded in American constitutional law as among the most protected and cherished of all constitutional rights'.[14] Therefore, there is a real risk that if we in England were to persist in our denial of parents' rights, we would find ourselves rather isolated in the developed world in doing so and not at all in tune with either Europe or the United States.

However, could it be that this is all just a semantic argument? Twenty years ago, I offered the view that:

> the label which the law attaches to parental authority is not nearly as important as the substantive question of its extent and duration.[15]

I still believe this to be the case. The truth is that there can be endless jurisprudential and philosophical arguments about the nature of rights, duties and discretions. Rather than add to this literature, I want to try here to focus on

---

Rights (hereafter 'ECHR') the rights of parents and children conflict, the child's rights will be the paramount consideration. It may be doubted, however, whether the Court had a complete understanding of the English interpretation of 'paramount' as meaning 'sole' consideration. It seems very unlikely given that the jurisprudence under Art 8 is habitually concerned with balancing rights and not ignoring them.

[10] Many examples could be given of the English judiciary's unwavering commitment to the welfare principle in the face of arguments about human rights. However, for a comparatively recent one, see the Court of Appeal decision in *Re S (Adoption Order or Special Guardianship Order)* [2007] EWCA Civ 54, in which the Court said that it was unlikely that in most cases Art 8 would add anything to the court's central task of applying the welfare principle.

[11] See, eg S Choudhry and H Fenwick, 'Taking the rights of parents and children seriously: confronting the welfare principle under the Human Rights Act' (2005) 25 *OJLS* 453; J Herring, 'The Human Rights Act and the welfare principle in family law—conflicting or complementary?' [1999] 11 *CFLQ* 223; and, for the author's view on this question, A Bainham, *Children: The Modern Law* (3rd edn, Bristol, Jordans, 2005) 38–40.

[12] The leading cases being *Meyer v Nebraska* 262 US 390 (1923); *Pierce v Society of Sisters* 268 US 510 (1925); and *Wisconsin v Yoder* 406 US 205 (1972).

[13] For detailed analysis of the leading decisions on children's rights in the United States, see RH Mnookin and D Kelly Weisberg, *Child, Family and State* (5th edn, New York,, Aspen, 2005) ch 1, especially 75 *ff*.

[14] M Guggenheim, *What's Wrong with Children's Rights* (Cambridge, Mass., Harvard University Press, 2005) 23.

[15] A Bainham, *Children, Parents and the State* (London, Sweet & Maxwell, 1988) 60.

the *essence* of the independent interests which parents may have in relation to their children, reflected in the special legal status conferred upon them, and the extent to which the legal system should recognise them. I will argue that parents *do* have independent interests which are not referable exclusively to promoting their children's welfare and that the legal system should explicitly and unapologetically endorse them. Whether or not these independent interests should be recognised is at the heart of the parental rights debate. I will accordingly refer to parental rights and interests quite interchangeably throughout this chapter. I will go on to argue that the most important interest parents have lies in the defence of their superior status—superior, that is, to all other adults. This arises automatically on the birth of the child and it sets parents apart from all of those others who may have an interest in the child. It will be my case that the term 'social parent' is something of a misnomer, an invention by academics for the benefit of academic analysis, and that the greatest threat to parents' interests lies in the prevalent tendency to confuse *parentage* with *parenting,* as it has recently been put by Thérèse Callus.[16]

DO PARENTS HAVE INDEPENDENT INTERESTS?

One widely held position is that parents have no independent rights or interests because everything they do is derived from the responsibility they have for their children. Commentators agree that parents must discharge certain minimum duties to their children, including feeding, clothing, arranging necessary medical attention and providing an education.[17] Macleod has called this the 'Minimum Provision Thesis'.[18] Beyond this, it is generally acknowledged that parents enjoy a wide discretion in the manner in which they raise their children. It is clear, for example, that although parents must educate their children,[19] the *kind* of education provided is up to them. It is therefore their choice whether or not the child is privately educated or educated within the state school system. Similarly, once we move beyond essential medical care, more routine medical decisions are a matter for individual parents.[20]

A key question is how this parental discretion should be characterised and whether, in exercising it, a parent is entitled to have regard not simply to what is best for the child, but also to his or her own benefit. One view, described by

---

[16]   T Callus, 'First "Designer Babies", Now À La Carte Parents' (2008) 38 *Family Law* 143.

[17]   Criminal liability may arise from wilful neglect to attend to these basic needs of the child, principally under the Children and Young Persons Act 1933 s 1.

[18]   CM Macleod, 'Conceptions of parental autonomy' (1997) 25 *Politics and Society* 117, 120.

[19]   Education Act 1996 s 7: see further Monk, this volume.

[20]   Even in the case of serious medical decisions, it has been accepted by the Nuffield Council on Bioethics that 'parents have interests and that it is reasonable for these interests to be given some weight in any relevant deliberations about critical decisions for a child who is, or who will become, severely ill'. See *Report on Critical Care Decisions in Fetal and Neonatal Medicine* (2006) [2.29], and see further Hagger, this volume.

Archard as the 'priority thesis', is that 'any rights that parents do have are constrained by, and derive from, a prior duty to care for their children'.[21] This derivative notion has been applied by Montague to parental discretion. According to Montague, while it cannot be denied that parents enjoy a large amount of discretion, we can account for:

> any latitude that parents have in making decisions affecting their children's lives in terms of permissions people have to select the specific ways in which they fulfill their obligations.[22]

According to this view, the parent who, say, forces his or her children to attend church twice on a Sunday, despite the fact that the children detest church and protest loudly on every occasion, is not acting in his or her own interests at all, but is merely selecting the way in which he or she fulfils his or her parental obligations. Bernard Dickens, in a seminal article, also highlighted the discretion enjoyed by parents and again saw the modern function of parental rights as enabling parents to discharge their duties, albeit that those duties in his view were best characterised as avoiding harm to the child rather than promoting the child's best interests.[23]

Others have doubted that all parental actions can be seen as taken entirely for the child's benefit and see in some of them an element of parental interest. Alexander McCall Smith himself tried to identify a category of 'parent-centred rights'.[24] For him, the key factor was to try to identify the *beneficiary* of the right in question. A 'child-centred parental right' was justified by its furtherance of the child's best interests or welfare. In contrast, a 'parent-centred parental right' touches upon 'the parental response to the basic moral issue of *what sort of child they wish to raise*'.[25] The significance of this latter type of right, into which category McCall Smith placed the above issue of religious direction, appeared to him to be that:

> [T]he parent has a wide range of discretion to pursue goals which society as whole might find undesirable, but which it will tolerate.[26]

Part of the reason for the existence of such rights is that 'they reflect something to which the parent is entitled by virtue of being a parent'.[27] Furthermore, to continue with the example of religion, the infringement of the right to instil religious values in the child 'involves distress to the parent, not necessarily to the child'. In cases like this, it was McCall Smith's view that it was not the exclusive

---

[21] D Archard, *Children, Family and the State* (Aldershot, Ashgate, 2003) 94.
[22] P Montague, 'The myth of parental rights' (2000) 26 *Social Theory and Practice* 47, 63.
[23] B Dickens, 'The modern function and limits of parental rights' (1981) 97 *LQR* 462.
[24] Above n 1, 9–10.
[25] *Ibid*, 9.
[26] *Ibid*.
[27] *Ibid*, 10.

purpose of parental rights to serve the interests of children. It was also to take into account 'self-serving parental wishes'.[28]

Archard is also fundamentally unhappy with the tendency to speak only in terms of parental duties or to view the parent as 'merely an agent of the child's welfare'. For Archard, the parent also has interests which are bound up with the activity of parenting:

> Being a parent is extremely important to a person. Even if a child is not to be thought of as the property or even as an extension of the parent, the shared life of a parent and child involves an adult's purposes and aims at the deepest level … parents have an interest *in parenting*—that is, in sharing a life with, and directing the development of, their child. It is not enough to discount the interests of a parent in a moral theory of parenthood. What must also merit full and proper consideration is the interest of someone in being a parent.[29]

In a similar vein, Macleod also recognises the independent interests of parents:

> [T]hose who accept the responsibility of raising children frequently do so because the project of creating and raising a family is an important, indeed often fundamental, element of their own life plans. Viewed from this perspective, parents cannot be seen as mere guardians of their children's interests. They are also people for whom creating a family is a project from which they derive substantial value. They have an interest in the family as a vehicle through which some of their own distinctive commitments and convictions can be realized and perpetuated.[30]

I will call this view, shared by McCall Smith, Archard and Macleod amongst others, 'the independence thesis'. It may be contrasted with the 'priority thesis' because it recognises in one form or another that parents have independent interests in relation to their children which cannot be explained away on the basis that they derive only from parental duty. I want to take two topical examples to demonstrate why I prefer the independence thesis to the priority thesis.

My first example is the much-debated, but nonetheless unresolved, question of contact between children and parents.[31] There is an apparently never-ending argument about whether contact is properly described as a right at all and, if so, whether it is the right of the parent or the child. Historically, it was viewed as the former, but since the 1970s the preponderant view has been that it is better described as a right of the child.[32] Certain feminist commentators are particularly hostile to the notion that so-called 'absent fathers' should be able to assert a right

---

[28]   *Ibid*. On the issue of parental responsibility in the context of religion, see further Taylor, this volume.

[29]   Above n 21, 97.

[30]   Above n 18, 119.

[31]   On the issues and controversies surrounding the question of contact between parents and children, see A Bainham, B Lindley, M Richards and L Trinder (eds), *Children and their Families: Contact, Rights and Welfare* (Oxford, Hart, 2003).

[32]   Wrangham J led the way in 1973 in *M v M (Child: Access)* [1973] 2 All ER 81.

of contact[33] and, unsurprisingly, fathers' rights groups are equally insistent that rights are involved in this question.[34] There has also been much discussion about whether there are any meaningful *duties* in relation to contact, which might be seen as the correlative of rights, and sharp disagreement about the extent to which, if at all, it is appropriate for the courts to attempt to enforce contact.[35]

What, then, is the truth of this matter? In order to get to the bottom of the nature of the contact question I want to focus on the position of the divorced, non-resident parent who, I will assume, is the father. It seems likely that many of these men would be the first to recognise that the *most important* interest at stake in maintaining contact following divorce is *the child's* wellbeing. However, it also seems likely that such men will recognise the significance of maintaining contact, not just for the child, but *also for themselves* and for their own future self-esteem and wellbeing. It is unrealistic to assume that the *only* benefit to be derived from contact with a parent is the child's. Surely a much more realistic way of looking at things is that *both* the child and the father will derive independent, or perhaps mutual, benefits from ongoing contact unless there are reasons why this would be harmful. The priority thesis cannot account for post-divorce contact because it is simply not the case that the parent's own interest lies exclusively in discharging a pre-existing obligation to the child. The independence thesis, in contrast, is much more realistic because it acknowledges that *both* child and parent derive benefits from contact. McCall Smith himself used the case of contact as an example of a parent-centred parental right:

> The right to the society of the child is a parental right, and it is appropriately considered as a parent-centred right, and yet it has nothing to do with any consideration of the welfare of the child. This right is accorded to thoroughly disagreeable (though not violent)[36] parents in exactly the same way as it is accorded to those who are more congenial company from the child's point of view.[37]

McCall Smith did not fall into the trap of believing, as many apparently do, that we must jump one way or the other in classifying contact *either* as a right of the

---

[33] See particularly C Smart, 'The ethic of justice strikes back: changing narratives of fatherhood' in A Diduck and K O'Donovan (eds), *Feminist Perspectives on Family Law* (Abingdon, Routledge Cavendish, 2006).

[34] On fathers' rights groups generally, see R Collier and S Sheldon (eds), *Father's Rights Activism and Law Reform in Comparative Perspective* (Oxford, Hart, 2006).

[35] For the view that contact has been over-zealously enforced by the courts, see C Smart and B Neale, 'Arguments against virtue—must contact be enforced?' (1997) *Family Law* 332. The author has expressed the view in 'Contact as a right and obligation' in A Bainham *et al*, above n 31, ch 5, that it is important that attempts should be made to enforce contact and that, indeed, this is required by the European Convention on Human Rights. For the author's view that contact is properly conceptualised as a right and indeed an obligation, see A Bainham, 'Contact as a right and obligation' (1995) 54 *CLJ* 512.

[36] In fact, McCall Smith has turned out to be incorrect about this, at least in England where it is clear that a record of violence by itself does not preclude the courts from (controversially) allowing contact between parent and child. The leading authority is *Re L (Contact: Domestic Violence)* [2000] 2 FLR 334.

[37] Above n 1, 10.

parent *or* as a right of the child. On the contrary, he was at pains to demonstrate that two quite independent rights existed:

> [I]t is true that a child benefits from the society of its parents, but that fact surely is grounds for asserting the *child's* right to parental society, which is another right altogether. In the case of a parental right to a child's society, any infringement of the right deprives the parent of a benefit.[38]

My second example is from the public law and focuses on the recent furore in the media about the young mother whose newborn baby was removed from her (albeit for a very short time as it turned out) in the middle of the night and about two hours after his birth. In *R (G) v Nottingham CC*,[39] Munby J made a peremptory order which required the local authority to reunite mother and child forthwith on the basis that the authority had acted unlawfully in taking the child from the mother without any prior court order. Later that day, the authority did what it should have done in the first place and obtained an interim care order from a judge. How are we to view this unfortunate episode? If we believe in the priority thesis, we are forced into the position that the only legitimate interest at stake here was the baby's interest in not being unlawfully removed from his mother. Any interest or right of the young mother was *exclusively* referable to discharging her duty to her infant son. However, this is not the real world. It is profoundly unattractive to deny that *the mother herself* had independent interests or rights as against the state when threatened with the taking of her child from her. In fact, if the authority had concentrated a little more on assisting the mother with her problems and a little less on taking her child away from her, it might have been better for all concerned, including the baby. The fact that this unlawful practice came to light at all owes much to the fact that the authority was facing an application for judicial review in relation to its statutory 'pathway plan'[40] for the mother on leaving care, which, it was alleged, was so deficient and inadequate as to be unlawful. Could there possibly be a better illustration of the dangers to the fundamental rights of children where the state chooses to ignore the distinctive rights of their parents?

WHY SHOULD THE LAW RECOGNISE PARENTAL INTERESTS?

In the preceding section, I offered the view that there are good reasons for believing that parents have interests in relation to their children which are independent of their children's welfare and which are attributable to their own benefit. One obvious response to this position may be that although it is easy enough to identify parental behaviour which advances a parent's own interests,

---

[38]   *Ibid.*
[39]   [2008] EWHC 152 (Admin).
[40]   As required by Children Act 1989 s 23E, inserted by the Children (Leaving Care) Act 2000.

this does not lead to the conclusion that the law should recognise or support such behaviour unless it is also consistent with the general aim of promoting the child's welfare.[41] I want to suggest that there are perhaps two principal reasons why the law should openly recognise the independent interests of parents.

The first reason relates to honesty and transparency. Of course it would be possible to portray every action which a parent takes, and which the law regards as legitimate, as no more than furtherance of the child's best interests. It could even be said that parents are under a general duty to act at all times with the aim of promoting the welfare of their children, although this immediately runs into the problem that the 'welfare principle' as we know it is of decidedly limited application.[42] However, more importantly, would this be an honest way of looking at things and would it fairly represent the legal position?

Take the central issue of what used to be called the child's 'custody'.[43] It is generally accepted that a most important aspect, perhaps *the* most important aspect, of the powers which parents exercise relates to the physical care and control of the child's movements. The younger the child is, the more obvious this role is. It can be explicitly regulated now by means of a residence order, but more often than not it is subsumed within the wider status of possessing parental responsibility. Are we to believe that in taking decisions relating to such matters as where the child is to live, go on holiday, spend weekends or which friends and relatives the child should visit and when, the parent is legally bound to determine all of these matters with *only* the child's best interests in mind? To characterise these decisions in this way would in my view be at best a distortion of the truth of family life and at worst plainly dishonest. The fact is that decisions like this are *family* decisions and they reflect more often than not the way in which the *parents* wish to spend their time. If the parents decide that Saturday afternoons will be spent shopping and that Sunday lunchtimes will be spent visiting the grandparents, the law supports them in these decisions, however much their objecting children are forced along with them. Only someone with a vivid imagination, surely, could see these decisions as being *just* about the welfare of

---

[41] Dickens rejects any such claim, limiting the general parental duty to the avoidance of harm: above n 23, especially 464.

[42] The welfare or paramountcy principle in the Children Act 1989 s 1 applies only to questions of upbringing or the administration of children's property which are in dispute before the courts. The corresponding provision in Art 3 of the UNCRC is somewhat wider in its application, although the child's welfare is there expressed to be 'a primary consideration' and not the paramount consideration. It is perhaps worthy of note that, whereas the duty to have regard to the child's best interests as a primary consideration applies to 'public or private social welfare institutions, courts of law, administrative authorities or legislative bodies' in their actions concerning children, the imposition of any such duty on parents is conspicuously absent from the list.

[43] 'Custody' was abolished as a concept by the Children Act 1989 to be replaced, at least in the case of court orders, by the new concept of 'residence'. It survives, however, in relation to international child abduction where possessing 'rights of custody' is an essential prerequisite to invoking the Hague Convention. On the old concept of custody and the forms of custody orders which could be made by the courts, see Law Commission, 'Custody' (Law Com WP No 96, 1986) and 'Review of Child Law: Guardianship and Custody' (Law Com No 172, HC 594, 1988).

the children. Therefore, one good reason for the law recognising explicitly that parents are entitled to act in relation to their children in a way which is not constrained entirely by any notion of promoting their best interests, is that this represents reality and is the honest thing to do.

The second reason for legal recognition of the independent interests of parents is ironically grounded in the responsibilities which they undoubtedly have. Essentially, the argument, which has been described as the 'exchange view' of parenthood,[44] is that parents have rights because they have responsibilities and they have responsibilities because they have rights. Birth parents are automatically charged, both by social convention and (more importantly) the law, with the task of caring and providing for their children.[45] Parents are not licensed[46] and neither does the state take the responsibility for the collective upbringing of children from birth. Any idea that children should be automatically raised from birth by anyone other than what Guggenheim has called the 'causal parents' would be completely alien to our thinking in a Western liberal democracy. Guggenheim describes the established process for 'allocation' of responsibility for children as follows:

> First, every child must be associated at birth with some adult who has caretaking responsibility and will make the major life decisions for him or her so that society will know the allocation of their custody when they are born ... As is well known, biological parents are responsible for their children at birth. They have the right, above all others, to raise them in their home or to authorize another to raise them instead ... Under our rules, parents self-identify by putting their names on a child's birth certificate ... [A] myriad of legally significant consequences follow from the formal recognition of parenthood.[47]

So parental status flows from the fact of birth and the establishment of parentage. It gives rise to a 'status responsibility' and many legal consequences which, as McCall Smith has also pointed out, are 'non-negotiable'. As he put it:

> It is not open for a parent to say: I accept that I must feed my child, but I don't accept that I have any duty to educate him or her.[48]

---

[44]   KT Bartlett, 'Re-expressing Parenthood' (1988) 98 *Yale Law Journal* 293.

[45]   Until comparatively recently, it could have been argued that this automatic imposition of parental responsibility (leaving aside the issue of child support) did not apply to fathers who were unmarried to the mother of the child. However, in relation to births since December 2003, the naming of the father on the birth certificate will now lead to these men acquiring parental responsibility: Children Act 1989 s 4(1)(a). There remains a small minority of fathers (about 7% of all fathers and 15% of unmarried fathers) who, although liable for child support, will not acquire wider parental responsibility because they are not identified on the birth certificate.

[46]   Although licensing parents has been mooted from time to time. See particularly H Lafollete, 'Licensing parents' (1980) 9 *Philosophy and Public Affairs* 182. For a more recent suggestion that there should be some attempt to screen out unsuitable parents at birth, which also puts forward a model statute on how this might be done, see J Dwyer, *The Relationship Rights of Children* (Cambridge, Cambridge University Press, 2006) 254 *ff*.

[47]   Guggenheim, above n 14, 20.

[48]   Above n 1, 7.

The argument is therefore that the accommodation of parents' own interests in the legal regime is appropriate because of the extensive burdens, financial, emotional and practical, which are automatically thrust upon them by law and society. These remain in place at least until the child attains adulthood and sometimes, to a limited extent, for some years after that.[49] Neither should we under-value in this equation the burdens and sacrifices associated with pregnancy, the birth itself and the beginnings of life for the child. Quite rightly, these burdens are seen as falling disproportionately on the mother and might be thought to give the mother an especially strong claim to consideration of her interests.[50] However, in many cases (although clearly not all), the father's contribution throughout pregnancy, at the birth and in the immediate nurturing of the child thereafter is far from negligible. The absence of anything approaching satisfactory paternity leave does not assist this contribution, but there are signs that this may be changing, albeit slowly.[51]

How well, then, are we doing in English law in giving appropriate weight to parents' interests or rights? It would be possible to revisit again the debate about the nature and extent of parental autonomy and its relationship with children's welfare and rights. However, it is not my intention to reopen this debate.[52] Instead, I want to concentrate on how effectively we defend the very status of parent. It will be my contention that it is this issue which is most critical to parents and that it is in this area that we are performing spectacularly badly.

THE DEFENCE OF PARENTAL STATUS

The most fundamentally important issue for parents, more important to them than particular questions surrounding upbringing, is the security which is represented by the superior status which they as parents hold over others who claim to have an interest in the child. Furthermore, it is this status which is now being subjected to an unrelenting attack. This is how two academic commentators have recently described the modern approach to the definition of parenthood:

---

[49] Parents may, eg be held financially responsible in divorce or matrimonial proceedings for adult children who are 'receiving instruction at an educational establishment or undergoing training for a trade, profession or vocation' or 'where there are special circumstances which justify the making of an order': Matrimonial Causes Act 1973 s 29.

[50] I argue below, however, that proper consideration of the mother's interests ought not to extend to giving her the sole decision on whether her baby should be adopted or whether the father and wider family should be informed of the birth. The Court of Appeal has, however, effectively upheld the mother's right to decide this in *Re C (A Child) v XYZ CC* [2007] EWCA Civ 1206.

[51] The Work and Families Act 2006 does seek to improve paternity leave by permitting the father to take some of the mother's unused maternity leave, where she elects to forgo it, but it does not embody any principle of *concurrent* maternity and paternity leave beyond the current statutory two weeks' paternity leave.

[52] But for an illuminating discussion of the different political positions on parental autonomy, see Macleod, above n 18.

Who are a child's parents? If one posed this question to a group of passengers on the Clapham omnibus, you [sic] would probably elicit a wide variety of responses. One passenger might respond that it is the man and woman who are linked by blood to the child: the genetic parents. Another passenger might respond that it is the woman who gives birth to the child and her husband and partner: the gestational parents. Yet another passenger might respond that it is the people who love, nurture and care for the child: the social parents. The concept of parenthood and who should be regarded as a child's parents is thus a strongly contested question.[53]

As an academic statement of the law's modern attitude to parenthood, it is difficult to find fault with this, although whether it truly represents how ordinary people would react is perhaps open to question. Is it not just as likely that society in general is capable of keeping in separate compartments the child's biological mother and father and the many other people who, while not being the child's parents, may be acting as parent-substitutes? It is a moot point whether many ordinary people, as opposed to academics, would identify these others as 'parents'. The debate about parenthood is in reality not unlike the debate about cohabitation. Those who are married are readily identified as such by the formality of a marriage certificate. Cohabitants on the other hand are an extremely diverse group who may be cohabiting for a host of differing reasons, for longer or shorter periods of time and with widely different attitudes to commitment and legal regulation of relationships.[54] This is perhaps the principal reason why it has proved so difficult to reach a consensus on what is the appropriate form of legal regulation of cohabitation.[55] Likewise, assuming biological parentage is established, all parents can be defined by reference to their part in procreation. However, this is clearly not the case in relation to so-called 'social parents', which, as a single group, defy any easy definition or identification. It is much more difficult to arrive at an appropriate legal status for such a diverse group; to make them all legal parents is clearly not a desirable or practical option.

Nonetheless, we are increasingly being asked to accept that it is the social role of being a parent which makes someone a parent and which should lead to legal parentage being conferred on that person. Thus, Judith Masson has referred to 'parenting by being' and 'parenting by doing' as alternative bases for the recognition of parental status.[56] The question which is frequently posed is whether the genetic link should carry more weight in the allocation of parenthood than should the assumption of the responsibility for raising a child. This is often

---

[53]   S Harris-Short and J Miles, *Family Law: Text, Cases and Materials* (Oxford, Oxford University Press, 2007) 665.

[54]   See, eg A Barlow and G James, 'Regulating marriage and cohabitation in 21st century Britain' (2004) 67 *MLR* 143.

[55]   This has not, however, prevented the Law Commission from trying to devise a scheme to deal at least with the financial and property issues arising on the breakdown of cohabitation: 'Cohabitation: The Financial Consequences of Relationship Breakdown' (Law Com No 307, Cm 7182, 2007).

[56]   J Masson, 'Parenting by being; parenting by doing—in search of principles for founding families' in JR Spencer and A Du Bois-Pedain, *Freedom and Responsibility in Reproductive Choice* (Oxford, Hart, 2006).

presented as a set of scales in which biology, the 'mere genetic link' as it is often described, is weighed against the burdensome practicalities of raising a child. Yet, this involves a sleight of hand. The point is that the overwhelming majority of biological parents have *much more* than a 'mere genetic link' with their children. They also perform, in most cases at least for a period of time, a psychological or social parenting role. It is true that a small minority of fathers and the very occasional mother can be said to have little or nothing more than the genetic link arising from a single act of intercourse or the donation of sperm (in the case of fathers)[57] or the act of gestating and giving birth (in the case of mothers).[58] However, even in those cases it is worth exploring further *why* they may have no more than that connection before denying them the status normally accorded to biological parents.[59] In any event, we ought not to allow the tail to wag the dog. The definition of parent should be constructed to reflect the more usual circumstances of parenthood and ought not to be driven by an unrepresentative minority. When we are engaging then in this suggested balancing exercise, we ought in most cases to allow for the fact that the biological parent's claim is likely to rest on a good deal more than biology, whereas the claim of other people can *only* be based on a social or psychological contribution and acting as a substitute parent.

Baroness Hale of Richmond brought this out in an illuminating speech in *Re G (Children)*,[60] in which she analysed the separate components of parenthood. She listed the *genetic, gestational* and *social and psychological* contributions. The biological mother would normally make all three contributions. The biological father certainly makes the first and in the majority of cases also the third. Baroness Hale did not credit him with a gestational contribution, although it can be argued that many biological fathers *do* contribute at the gestational stage, albeit of course not in the much more physically and emotionally substantial way that mothers do. In contrast, the lesbian partner in this case had made an undeniably important social and psychological contribution to the welfare of the two children concerned, but she could not claim to have contributed in the other ways which we may associate with being a parent. While the House of Lords denied that this created a legal presumption in favour of primary residence with the biological mother, it did hold that in applying the welfare principle the

---

[57] Licensed sperm donors are accordingly excluded from legal parentage: Human Fertilisation and Embryology Act 2008 s 41(1). Neither do they have 'family life' with the child for the purposes of the ECHR. See *G v The Netherlands* [1990] 16 EHRR 38.

[58] A rare reported case is *Re B (A Minor)* [2001] UKHL 70, where the mother (who had given up a previous child for adoption) did not look at the baby when born and said that she had no maternal instincts.

[59] In a number of reported cases, it has been quite clear that the reason why the father has had no involvement with the child has been either because the mother did not inform him of the pregnancy or birth or because she refused to allow him to have anything to do with the child. See, eg *Keegan v Ireland* (1994) 18 EHRR 342; and *Re H; Re G (Adoption: Consultation of Unmarried Fathers)* [2001] 1 FLR 646.

[60] [2006] UKHL 43.

'special contribution' of the biological parent should be an 'important and significant factor' in the court's determination.

Re G reveals just how far we have come in raising expectations about parental status in those who are not parents. It should be conceded at the outset that the mother's behaviour following her split with her partner was far from impeccable.[61] Even so, the lesbian partner, the so-called 'co-parent', sought (with some success in the High Court and Court of Appeal) not merely parity with the mother through parental responsibility for the children and a shared residence order,[62] but *more than equality* with her in the form of a time-sharing order which broke 70:30 in her favour. The House of Lords, quite rightly in my view, reversed these percentages leaving the mother as the primary, and her former partner as the secondary, carer. The claim of the partner here is just one example of the doubtful argument that doing some of the things which parents do entitles one to be regarded as a parent.

Where will all of this end? We do not appear to be so far away from the position that anyone living with a parent will demand the right to be regarded as a parent. Indeed, the position of the lesbian partner is a very good example of exactly this trend, which began with the equally fictitious attribution of parenthood to non-biological fathers. The Human Fertilisation and Embryology Act 2008, confers legal parentage on lesbian partners in cases of assisted reproduction, automatically in the absence of objection where they are civil partners[63] and where the 'female parenthood conditions' are satisfied if they have not formalised their relationship in this way.[64] These latter conditions essentially require that both partners consent to the acquisition of parental status by the mother's partner and that the consent has not been withdrawn. Parentage here ostensibly turns on consent, but the essence of the claim to parentage is surely the existence of the relationship itself and the joint enterprise to have a child. How long is it going to be before the lesbian partner of a mother who bears a child outside the licensed system, perhaps as in several reported cases after having intercourse with a readily identifiable man,[65] claims that it is discriminatory for her not also to be recognised as the legal parent? After all, her claim is just as strong if we see it as being based on her position as the supportive partner of the mother in their mutual desire to have a child. I have argued at length elsewhere that it is a fundamental error of policy to go further down this road of deliberately creating more instances in which biological and legal parentage do not coincide, notably because of the distortion of kinship which this involves.[66] I will return to this

---

[61]   She had removed the children from Leicester to Cornwall in breach of a court order.
[62]   Under the Children Act 1989 s 12(2), the effect of a residence order in favour of someone who is not a parent is to confer parental responsibility on that person which is held while the order lasts.
[63]   See s 42(1).
[64]   See ss 43 and 44.
[65]   See particularly *Re D (contact and parental responsibility: lesbian mothers and known father)* [2006] EWHC 2 (Fam).
[66]   A Bainham, 'Arguments about parentage' (2008) 67 *CLJ* 322.

issue briefly below since of course it begs the question of exactly what legal status ought to be given to long-term carers of children who are not parents.

Re G also provokes a reassessment of the division between the public and private law relating to parents and children. The central principle governing the public law is that the state may not compulsorily remove a child from the care of a parent unless it can establish that the child is either suffering, or at risk of suffering, significant harm attributable to a standard of care which is not that of the reasonable parent.[67] The Children Act 1989 explicitly rejected the notion that compulsory action leading to the removal of a child from parental care should be based (as it would be if governed by the welfare principle) only on a professional view that someone else can do better than the parent at raising the child.[68] In private disputes, by contrast, the welfare principle *does* apply and it enables individuals who are not parents, like the mother's partner in *Re G*, to argue that the coercive power of the state (exercised through the courts) should be used to deprive a parent of care, or at least primary care, despite the fact that it is not alleged that the parent represents a threat of harm to the child.

This orthodox distinction between the public and private law was recently illustrated in *Re P (Surrogacy: Residence).*[69] In this case, Coleridge J had to adjudicate between the claims of a surrogate mother and those of the biological father whom she had deceived into believing that she had miscarried. In ordering that the child should live with the father and his wife, he quite properly distinguished between the different criteria under the public and private law. He held that it was essential to keep at the forefront of the court's mind that the question was not whether the child had suffered or was likely to suffer significant harm at the hands of either parent. In the private law, when choosing between two competing residential parental regimes, the question was rather 'in which home is he most likely to mature into a happy and balanced adult and to achieve his fullest potential as a human?'[70] This was, however, a case in which the competition was between the two biological parents and, as Coleridge J put it:

> The fact that both sides constitute one of the child's natural parents means that both sides start from the same position, neither side being able to claim that the blood tie should favour their claim.[71]

This is also true, self-evidently, of the much more common instance in which it must be determined which of two parents should be the primary carer following

[67] The so-called 'threshold conditions' in the Children Act 1989 s 31(2). These conditions must also be satisfied under the Adoption and Children Act 2002 s 21(2) where a local authority seeks an adoption placement order in relation to a looked-after child.

[68] See DHSS, *Review of Child Care Law: Report to Ministers of an Interdepartmental Working Party* (London, HMSO, 1985) [15.10].

[69] [2008] 1 FLR 177, upheld by the Court of Appeal in *Re P (Residence: Appeal)* [2007] EWCA Civ 1053.

[70] *Ibid*, at 181.

[71] *Ibid*.

divorce. It is inevitable, in the event of a dispute, that the court must resolve it, and to deprive a parent of care in these circumstances clearly does not entail any judgment that that parent represents a threat of harm to the child. However, we may reasonably question whether the harm principle ought not to play a larger role where the dispute is not between parent and parent, but between parents and others. If we could tear ourselves away from legal theory and concentrate instead on the perception of the parent affected, it may not matter to that parent one jot whether the child is removed from him or her in public law or private law proceedings. In each case, the child will be in the primary care of others under the coercive power of the courts. The difference is that in the former proceedings it is normally necessary to demonstrate that the parent is at risk of harming the child,[72] but in the latter it is not.

Does this in any event truly represent what judges do in private law decisions? A case can be made for saying that practice under the welfare principle is in fact largely consistent with the harm thesis, at least in contexts other than those in which it is necessary to choose a home for the child as between two parents, each of whom could provide this satisfactorily. The case of medical decision-making, so often the site of arguments about parents' versus children's rights, demonstrates that in many cases, although not formulated in this way, the courts are committed to the principle that they ought not to interfere with parental discretion unless the position taken by a parent is considered harmful to the child.[73]

It can be argued more generally that where the dispute is between parent and non-parent, it should be resolved in favour of the parent unless it can be shown that the parent is exposing the child to the risk of harm. Otherwise, the danger is that the state acting through the courts is intervening compulsorily in parenting on the basis of a looser and less exacting standard than Parliament has decreed. In the context of adoption too there are concerns that the child's relationship with the biological family (including the father and the paternal family) may be ignored with impunity where the adoption involves a placement by consent and is therefore characterised by the courts as 'private'. In the case of a public law adoption involving a looked-after child, there is in contrast a statutory duty to explore fully the resources of the birth family.[74] However, if it is important to the child that the potential of the wider family be investigated, it is difficult to see why this is less important simply because proceedings are categorised as 'private'.[75] Further, examined from the perspective of the father or extended family,

---

[72]   This is subject to the qualification that where a child has been harmed, but it is not clear who has perpetrated the harm, a care order may be made even though it has not been possible to attribute the harm to a parent. See *Lancashire CC v B* [2000] 2 AC 147.

[73]   Many examples could be given, but the case of the conjoined twins is perhaps the best: *Re A (Children) (Conjoined Twins: Surgical Separation)* [2001] Fam 147.

[74]   Children Act 1989 ss 22(4) and 23.

[75]   In *Re C (A Child) v XYZ CC* [2007] EWCA Civ 1206 [82], Thorpe LJ said: 'There are good social policy reasons for accepting the option of a private birth' and was concerned that if the mother's

in each case the state, whether in the guise of an adoption agency, the local authority or the court, is taking a decision either to include or exclude them from involvement as possible carers. It does not matter to them one iota whether this is characterised as a private or public issue.

More generally, the parent's position in relation to adoption may be seen as another example of the recent erosion of parents' rights or interests. First, the circumstances under which an adoption may now be granted *without* parental consent essentially depend on an undiluted application of the welfare principle. Despite academic arguments that the 2002 legislation does contain safeguards for the birth families' interests, both in the statutory checklist of factors[76] and in the statutory requirement that 'the welfare of the child *requires* the [parent's] consent to be dispensed with',[77] there remains a strong suspicion that the former test of parental unreasonableness, despite its close association in practice with the professional view of the child's best interests,[78] did provide a stronger safeguard of the parent's position. Indeed, there were reported cases right up to the enactment of the 2002 legislation in which parents were held not to have withheld their consent unreasonably.[79]

If the proposition is accepted that parents should have a priority over, and superior status to, other carers this still leaves open the question of exactly what status it is appropriate to give to these others. I have argued elsewhere[80] that we need to resolve this question by keeping in mind the important distinction between being a parent (parentage) and discharging the functions of a parent (parenting). The former is closely linked to legal kinship, while the latter is closely associated with the legal concept of parental responsibility. The difficulty as I perceive it is twofold. First, there is a strong cultural cachet attached to being accepted as a parent. The fact is that those who are performing a long-term parenting role want to be regarded as parents and are generally not satisfied with a lesser status or with being called something else. This surely in part explains the continued popularity of adoption, the efforts to which some will go to obtain a child through assisted reproduction and the correspondingly low status of foster care. Secondly, we lack an appropriate intermediate status which might be

appeal were dismissed 'we would be effectively precluding private birth as a prelude to fast-track adoption in almost every case'.

[76] Especially factor (c), which refers to 'the likely effect on the child (throughout his life) of having ceased to be a member of the original family and become an adopted person', and factor (f), which refers to the 'relationship which the child has with relatives' and, inter alia, the likelihood of such relationships continuing if adoption were to be granted: Adoption and Children Act 2002 s 1(4).

[77] Adoption and Children Act 2002 s 52(1)(b).

[78] Lord Hailsham started this trend in *Re W (An Infant)* [1971] AC 682, where he expressed the view that a reasonable parent has regard to his or her child's welfare.

[79] An important example being *Re B (Adoption Order)* [2001] EWCA Civ 347, in which Hale LJ (as she then was) emphasised, in the wake of the Human Rights Act 1998, that the Convention requirement of proportionality might mean that adoption was not the proportionate response to the child's long-term needs in some cases and that therefore a parent who appreciated this might not be acting unreasonably in withholding consent.

[80] Bainham, above n 66.

capable of satisfying long-term carers, but which does not involve misrepresenting them as parents. It is possible of course to acquire parental responsibility and it has been legislative policy in recent years to make this easier, most notably by allowing step-parents and civil partners to obtain it by formal agreement with the legal parents.[81] The problem is that although possessing parental responsibility is certainly a status of sorts,[82] it is not an identifiable one in the way that being a parent is. Moreover, the rules on standing for obtaining parental responsibility by court order (should this prove necessary) are perhaps unnecessarily complex.[83]

What we need is a recognisable status, more easily obtained, with a sound pedigree and long-standing social acceptance. The obvious candidate is guardianship.[84] Guardians in legal terms approximate quite closely to parents, but there is no pretence that they are parents[85] and in particular kinship is unaffected by the appointment of a guardian. Guardian is in fact a perfect description of someone who is acting in place of a parent—which, after all, is what all social carers are in fact doing.[86] The new status of 'special guardian' is designed to reflect these concerns and to provide an alternative to adoption, but the omens are not especially good that this will become a mainstream status for long-term carers.[87] In any event, the special guardianship regime may be thought rather too unwieldy to provide a general solution to the status problem. It is a pity in some ways that the term 'guardian' has been so excessively and confusingly over-used. We have had, for example, 'poor law guardians', 'guardians of the estate', 'guardians of the person', 'natural guardians', 'guardians *ad litem*', 'children's guardians', 'guardians' and 'special guardians'. What this does perhaps confirm is the utility of the essential notion of guardianship in different contexts where a legal status is required for those who protect children and defend their interests, but who are *not* parents. It seems unlikely that, for all its merits, guardianship could displace

---

[81]   Children Act 1989 s 4A.

[82]   Notably it confers the right to take or participate in major decisions affecting the child and the right to look after the child unless this is restricted by a residence order.

[83]   The rules are largely contained in the Children Act 1989 s 10 and distinguish between parents, guardians and persons with parental responsibility; step-parents and former step-parents, civil partners and former civil partners, persons who have had the child with them for three years or have the consent of those with parental responsibility; and everyone else. Special rules also apply to local authority foster parents and, under the Children and Young Persons Act 2008, to relatives.

[84]   For detailed discussion of the history of guardianship, which preceded parenthood as a legal status in English law, see Law Commission, 'Review of Child Law: Guardianship' (Law Com WP No 91, 1985). The best account of the current law on guardianship is to be found in N Lowe and G Douglas, *Bromley's Family Law* (10th edn, Oxford, Oxford University Press, 2006) ch 9.

[85]   The Law Commission was concerned that a clear distinction should be drawn between parents and guardians and, accordingly, recommended the abolition of the notion of 'natural guardianship' which had vested in the father of a legitimate child: *ibid* [3.2]–[3.4]. The Children Act 1989 s 2(4) gave effect to this recommendation.

[86]   The Law Commission did moot the possibility of an extension of the existing concept of guardianship to allow the appointment of *inter vivos* guardians (see above n 84, Pt IV), but the idea did not, at the time, capture the imagination of consultees. Perhaps it ought to be resurrected.

[87]   The previous attempt to introduce a status for long-term carers falling short of adoption, custodianship, was very ineffectual and short-lived.

the attractions of parenthood in the popular consciousness. It would nonetheless be better if we were to continue to search for an appropriate status for the many different social carers of children rather than to create ever more instances in which biological and legal parentage do not coincide, with the consequent threat to the special position of biological parents which this poses. In the meantime, the new status of special guardian ought to be welcomed and utilised where possible,[88] and there might also be a case for reforming the current definition of 'child of the family'[89] to recognise *informal*, as well as formal, instances of cohabitation with a parent.

CONCLUSIONS

I have argued here that the debate about parental rights is in simple language an argument about whether parents have independent interests in their children which cannot be accounted for entirely on the basis of their duties or responsibilities towards them. I have further argued that they have and that the law should openly recognise these independent interests, or rights if we prefer to call them that, for two reasons. The first is because in reality the law *does* allow parents to take a host of family decisions which are every bit as much about parents living the kind of lives they wish to live as they are about advancing their children's welfare. Secondly, the automatic status of parenthood, which the law confers or imposes on the birth of a child, justifies respect for parental interests. It is simply not reasonable to take the position that those who bear the legal and moral burdens which society expects of a parent should be denied all recognition of their independent claims or interests.

I have identified protection of the special legal status of parent as the most important issue. When we are considering an appropriate legal status for those who, while not parents, are involved in parenting, we need to remember that the law does *not* automatically impose upon them the responsibilities automatically faced by legal parents on the birth of a child. Liability for child support is perhaps the best example.[90] Therefore, while it is perfectly reasonable for someone who is involved in a major way with upbringing to seek out parental responsibility, to go further and make that person the legal parent muddles kinship and threatens the status of birth parents. This is happening too often in the contexts of assisted reproduction and adoption. While there may well be circumstances under which

---

[88]   Although the early evidence on its use suggests otherwise: see A Hall, 'Special Guardianship: A missed opportunity—findings from research' (2008) *Family Law* 148.

[89]   At present, the definition in Children Act 1989 s 105 covers only those children treated as children of the family by spouses and civil partners, but it must be doubted whether the position of a spouse or civil partner in relation to his or her partner's children is greatly, if at all, different from that of the informal partner.

[90]   This still turns on being the legal parent of the child, which in the overwhelming majority of cases will be the biological parent. For a thorough treatment of the moral and legal basis for child support, see N Wikeley, *Child Support: Law and Policy* (Oxford, Hart, 2006) ch 1.

it is appropriate to reallocate legal parentage, we ought to be strictly confining and not increasing the occasions on which this is done. The search, I have suggested, should rather be for an appropriate intermediate status, like guardianship, which properly recognises *parenting*, but which does not distort *parentage*. The fact is that there is not, and there never can be, true equality or parity as between biological parents and other carers because they are in a materially different position which justifies differential treatment. Parents have a unique role in the creation of the child which can never be true of those who lack this biological contribution.

However, it might be objected that to assert the independent rights or interests of parents, and to place importance on defending the status of biological parents, is to undervalue the commitment to children's welfare or rights. I do not believe this to be the case for two reasons. First, regarding parental autonomy this should be, and clearly is, limited by the harm principle. Where parents cause or threaten harm to their child, this may found a care order or lead to judicial rulings which protect the child in 'single issue' cases, most obviously where a parent is denying the child necessary medical intervention. Secondly, it is surely not in children's interests to pretend that the law is not cognisant of adult claims when in reality clearly it is. Disputes which may be theoretically formulated as being just about children are in reality not just about children. It must be obvious to everyone that the great majority of legal actions concerning children are brought by adults. Truth and transparency are important to children as has been widely recognised, not least by the family judiciary.[91] Therefore, the case for honesty about the legal balance being struck between the interests of children and their parents is a strong one as is the case, increasingly urged by commentators, for reformulation of the welfare principle.[92] We are right to give priority to the rights and interests of children, but we are wrong to imply that no one else, and especially parents, has them too.

---

[91]   For noteworthy judicial statements, see Ward LJ in *Re H (Paternity: Blood Test)* [1996] 2 FLR 65; Sumner J in *Re J (Paternity: Welfare of Child)* [2007] EWHC 2837 at [13]–[14]; and Thorpe LJ in *Re C (Contact: Moratorium: Change of Gender)* [2006] EWCA Civ 1765 at [11].

[92]   Above n 11.

3

Establishing and Ending Parental Responsibility: A Comparative View

JENS M SCHERPE

INTRODUCTION

T
HIS CHAPTER TAKES a comparative look at the way in which parental responsibility is allocated upon a child's birth or established thereafter,[1] and at how parental responsibility can be brought to an end (other than by adoption or death of a parent). The focus is upon the controversial position of the father who is not married to his child's mother.[2] The chapter begins by examining the approach to these issues suggested by the Commission on European Family Law (CEFL), which in 2007 published its *Principles of European Family Law Regarding Parental Responsibilities*.[3] The CEFL is an international group of scholars, established in 2001, which has engaged in some remarkable academic work, producing sets of Principles of European Family Law.[4] The approach taken is inspired by the Restatements of the Law by the American Law Institute and is based on extensive comparative research on a large number of European jurisdictions.

According to their authors, the CEFL Principles represent either the common core of the European family laws or, where no such core was to be found, the 'better law' as determined by the CEFL.[5] In any event, they are based on a

[1] Adoption is not dealt with, and neither are questions of contested filiation.

[2] Hereinafter, somewhat imprecisely but for ease of exposition, referred to as the 'unmarried father'.

[3] K Boele-Woelki, F Ferrand, C González Beilfuss, M Jänterä-Jareborg, N Lowe, D Martiny and W Pintens, *Principles of European Family Law Regarding Parental Responsibilities* (Antwerp, Intersentia, 2007).

[4] For a further description of the working method of the CEFL, see K Boele-Woelki, 'The working method of the Commission on European Family Law' in K Boele-Woelki (ed), *Common Core and Better Law in European Family Law* (Antwerp, Intersentia, 2005) 15–38.

[5] This has been criticised as reflecting 'the value system of a particular world view' and for failing to take the 'crucial' importance of religion into account; cf E Örücü, 'The Principles of European Family Law put to the test: diversity in harmony or harmony in diversity?' in E Örücü and J Mair (eds), *Juxtaposing Legal Systems and the Principles of European Family Law on Divorce and Maintenance* (Antwerp, Intersentia, 2007) 254.

comparative analysis of some 22 European jurisdictions[6] and are meant as a 'frame of reference'[7] for future reforms. In the second and third parts of the chapter, the CEFL Principles are compared with the relevant laws in England and Wales and Germany respectively. These two jurisdictions are chosen for their contrast with the approach suggested by the CEFL Principles, and because they have themselves some different features which are worthy of comparison. Unlike many other European jurisdictions and the approach suggested by the CEFL, neither England and Wales nor Germany automatically grants parental responsibility as a result of filiation, although parental responsibility is granted to a father through marriage to his child's mother. This withholding of parental responsibility from unmarried fathers is controversial and has been criticised by academics and practitioners in both jurisdictions. Yet this differential treatment of the unmarried father has been sanctioned by supreme courts: in 2003 the *Bundesverfassungsgericht* (German Constitutional Court) found this not to be in breach of the German *Grundgesetz* (Basic Law)[8] and the European Court of Human Rights (ECtHR) came to a similar conclusion with regard to the European Convention on Human Rights (ECHR) and English and Welsh law in *B v United Kingdom*.[9] Against the background of the conclusions of the CEFL, therefore, the chapter explores the underlying reasons for withholding parental responsibility from some fathers in both jurisdictions.

Another aspect that will be examined is the ending of parental responsibility. Unlike the law of England and Wales and the CEFL Principles, German law does not allow for acquisition of parental responsibility by an unmarried father *in addition* to that of the mother against her will; therefore, an unmarried father in Germany can only acquire parental responsibility without the consent of the mother if at the same time her parental responsibility is discharged.[10] Hence, the discharge of parental responsibility plays an important role in German family law, in contrast to the more limited legal provision for discharge of parental responsibility in English law. Interestingly, the CEFL Principles also allow for a discharge of parental responsibility.

The final part of the chapter engages in a comparative analysis of the various approaches identified. The role and importance of a legal provision permitting discharge of parental responsibility, as a means of correcting a potentially over-inclusive allocation of parental responsibility, is explored with regard to the legal

---

[6]   Published as K Boele-Woelki, B Braat and I Curry-Sumner (eds), *European Family Law in Action*, Vol III (Antwerp, Intersentia, 2005).

[7]   Boele-Woelki *et al*, above n 3, 5.

[8]   Bundesverfassungsgericht (BVerfG) 29 January 2003, Neue Juristische Wochenschrift (NJW) 2003, 955.

[9]   *B v United Kingdom* [2000] 1 FLR 1.

[10]   The term 'discharge' is used in line with the terminology used by the CEFL. Like the words 'cease' and 'brought to an end' in the Children Act 1989 ss 4(2A) and 4A(3), it denotes the taking away of responsibility in a way that is more than a mere restriction of exercise of parental responsibility, but less than a 'termination' where parental responsibility cannot be restored (see Boele-Woelki *et al*, above n 3, 212 *ff*).

rules governing the exercise of parental responsibility. It is argued that a gender-neutral, child-centred view on parental responsibility is to be preferred, reinforcing the focus on the daily care and support of the child and his or her general welfare.

THE CEFL PRINCIPLES OF EUROPEAN FAMILY LAW REGARDING PARENTAL RESPONSIBILITIES

Terminology is not uniform across Europe: for example, English and Welsh law, the Hague Conference on Private International Law[11] and the European Commission[12] use the term 'parental responsibility'; but the Scots law[13] and the Council of Europe[14] use the plural form, 'parental responsibilities'. The CEFL opted for the latter, despite the fact that (as CEFL acknowledges)[15] some languages (such as French or German) cannot accommodate this form. The reason for preferring the term 'parental responsibilities' was that this expresses more clearly the idea that it comprises 'not only one package of rights and duties but consists of many different rights and duties'.[16] The plural form, it may be argued, also permits a more flexible approach, particularly when attributing such rights and duties to persons other than the parents.

Establishing Parental Responsibilities

Principle 3:8 of the CEFL Principles states: 'Persons, whose legal parentage has been established, should have parental responsibilities for the child.'

This establishes that the legal relationship between parent and child is decisive for the attribution of parental responsibilities—and not the nature of the relationship of the parents. The Principle is based on the CEFL's finding that: 'the majority of the legal systems [in Europe] fully accept that parental responsibilities are a consequence of filiation'; that in those systems this applies 'irrespective of the relationship between the parents'; and that 'joint attribution [of parental responsibilities] is in the best interest of the child'.[17] Where such joint parental responsibilities are not in the best interest of the child, the authors of the

[11]   See, eg Convention of 19 October 1996 on Jurisdiction, Applicable Law, Recognition, Enforcement and Cooperation in respect of Parental Responsibility and Measures for the Protection of Children.

[12]   See, eg Council Regulation (EC) No 2201/2003 of 27 November 2003 concerning jurisdiction and the recognition and enforcement of judgments in matrimonial matters and the matters of parental responsibility (Brussels IIbis).

[13]   Children (Scotland) Act 1995.

[14]   Council of Europe, Committee of Experts on Family Law (CJ-FA), Report on Principles Concerning the Establishment and Legal Consequences of Parentage (the White Paper), 23 October 2006, CJ-FA (2006) 4e.

[15]   Boele-Woelki *et al*, above n 3, 31.

[16]   Boele-Woelki *et al*, above n 3, 30 *ff.*

[17]   *Ibid*, 65.

Principles find that protection is best afforded by a complete discharge of parental responsibilities, or by restricting its exercise.[18]

Automatic attribution of parental responsibilities irrespective of the parents' relationship can indeed be found in many European jurisdictions: Belgium,[19] Denmark,[20] the Czech Republic,[21] Croatia,[22] France,[23] Hungary,[24] Italy,[25] Lithuania,[26] Poland,[27] Russia[28] and Spain.[29] Of those, in Hungary and Italy the acquisition of parental responsibility is only automatic for the father if he still lives with the mother. Many systems, however, still award only the mother parental responsibility automatically on birth if the parents are not married: Austria,[30] England and Wales (see below), Finland,[31] Germany (see below),[32] Ireland,[33] the Netherlands,[34] Norway,[35] Portugal,[36] Sweden[37] and Switzerland.[38] In all of these jurisdictions there are, of course, mechanisms through which the father can

---

[18]   *Ibid.*

[19]   W Pintens and D Pignolet in Boele-Woelki *et al*, above n 6, 265 and 349.

[20]   Since October 2007 the new *forældreansvarslov* (Act on Parental Responsibility) is in force; one of the possibilities for a father to acquire parental responsibility is to acknowledge the child when the parents were registered under the same address for at least 10 months immediately preceding the child's birth, cf § 7 III *forældreansvarslov*. For a brief summary of the new Act, see JM Scherpe, 'Das neue dänische Gesetz über elterliche Verantwortung', *Zeitschrift für das gesamte Familienrecht (FamRZ)* 2007, 1495–6; for a full discussion of the Act, see Udvalget om Forældremyndighed og Samvær (ed), *Barnets perspektiv, Betænkning nr. 1475* (Copenhagen, Nordisk Bog Center A/S, 2006); for its predecessor see I Lund-Andersen, 'Legal Status of Cohabitants in Denmark' in JM Scherpe and N Yassari (eds), *Die Rechtsstellung nichtehelicher Lebensgemeinschaften—The Legal Status of Cohabitants* (Tübingen, Mohr Siebeck, 2005) 467.

[21]   M Hrusaková in Boele-Woelki *et al*, above n 6, 266 and 350.

[22]   D Hrabar, 'Legal Status of Cohabitants in Croatia' in Scherpe and Yassari, above n 20, 409 *ff*.

[23]   F Ferrand in Boele-Woelki *et al*, above n 6, 268 and 353; and F Ferrand, 'Die Rechtsstellung nichtehelicher Lebensgemeinschaften in Frankreich' in Scherpe and Yassari, above n 20, 234.

[24]   Only if the couple lives together; cf E Weiss and Szeibert in Boele-Woelki *et al*, above n 6, 357.

[25]   Only if the couple lives together; cf S Patti, E Bellisario and L Rossi Carleo in Boele-Woelki *et al*, above n 6, 359.

[26]   V Mikelenas in Boele-Woelki *et al*, above n 6, 359 *ff*.

[27]   A Mączyński and J Mączyńska in Boele-Woelki *et al*, above n 6, 362.

[28]   M Antokolskaia in Boele-Woelki *et al*, above n 6, 362.

[29]   Unless the child was conceived by a sexual crime or the father has opposed paternity; cf C González Beilfuss in Boele-Woelki *et al*, above n 6, 362; and C González Beilfuss, 'Spanien und Portugal' in Scherpe and Yassari, above n 20, 267 *ff*.

[30]   M Roth in Boele-Woelki *et al*, above n 6, 349.

[31]   K Kurki-Suonio in Boele-Woelki *et al*, above n 6, 353.

[32]   See also N Dethloff, 'Nichteheliche Lebensgemeinschaft und Kinder' in Scherpe and Yassari, above n 20, 137 *ff*.

[33]   G Shannon in Boele-Woelki *et al*, above n 6, 382.

[34]   K Boele-Woelki, W Schrama and M Vonk in Boele-Woelki *et al*, above n 6, 360 *ff*; and K Boele-Woelki and W Schrama, 'Die nichteheliche Lebensgemeinschaft im niederländischen Recht' in Scherpe and Yassari, above n 20, 324 *ff*.

[35]   T Sverdrup and P Lødrup in Boele-Woelki *et al*, above n 6, 361; and E Ryrstedt, 'Legal Status of Cohabitants in Norway' in Scherpe and Yassari, above n 20, 450.

[36]   G de Oliveira in Boele-Woelki *et al*, above n 6, 362.

[37]   M Jänterä-Jareborg in Boele-Woelki *et al*, above n 6, 363; and E Ryrstedt, 'Legal Status of Cohabitants in Sweden' in Scherpe and Yassari, above n 20, 433 *ff*.

[38]   H Hausheer, C Achermann-Weber and S Wolf in Boele-Woelki *et al*, above n 6, 413 and 433 *ff*.

acquire parental responsibilities by registration (sometimes requiring the consent of the mother), administrative process or court proceedings.

Given the diversity of approaches described above, it is difficult to see how the authors of the CEFL Principles identified a 'common core' which Principle 3:8 (above) is supposed to represent.[39] Nevertheless, irrespective of whether the Principle represents a common core or a better law approach, it still finds ample support in many European jurisdictions.

Ending Parental Responsibilities

Principle 3:32 states that:

> The competent authority should discharge the holder of parental responsibilities wholly or in part, where his or her behaviour or neglect causes serious risk to person or property of the child.

The discharge may be requested by any of the following: a parent having parental responsibilities; the child; any institution protecting the interests of the child; and any competent authority. The competent authority may also order the discharge of parental responsibilities of its own motion (Principle 3:33).[40]

Of the legal systems examined by the CEFL, only one, England and Wales, does not allow for a discharge[41] of the parental responsibilities of all parents,[42] and the CEFL opted to follow the majority of European jurisdictions in this matter. Hence, according to the CEFL Principles, the parental responsibilities of any holder, including those of the child's mother and father, can be fully or partially discharged where he or she puts the child at serious risk: whether or not there is fault is irrelevant. The CEFL did not opt for a list of specific grounds; rather, it decided on a general clause because this was in line with the common core of the jurisdictions examined and 'more in accordance with the interests of the child', as this allows an assessment of the behaviour in question in each individual case.[43]

Parental responsibilities may be restored if the circumstances that led to the discharge no longer exist, provided this is in the best interests of the child (Principle 3:34). The case law of the European Court of Human Rights makes clear that the possibility of restoration is necessary; there is an obligation on the

---

[39] Boele-Woelki *et al*, above n 3, 65.
[40] *Ibid*, 217 *ff*.
[41] Of course, restrictions of the exercise of parental responsibility are possible.
[42] Boele-Woelki *et al*, above n 3, 214 *ff*. The CEFL also lists Denmark as the other exception here, but this appears doubtful because parental responsibility can be transferred to one parent only which discharges the other, see § 11 *forældreansvarslov* and n 20 above.
[43] *Ibid*, 216.

state to work towards reuniting the family (and, where in the best interest of the child, restoring parental responsibilities) as soon as circumstances permit.[44]

GERMAN LAW ON PARENTAL CUSTODY

In Germany, the term 'parental responsibility' ('*elterliche Verantwortung*') is being used increasingly in academic texts[45] and on occasion even in statutes.[46] However, most statutes, including the Civil Code (*Bürgerliches Gesetzbuch*; BGB), still use the term '*elterliche Sorge*', which can be translated as 'parental care'[47] or 'parental custody'.[48] This comprises the care of the child (*Personensorge*) and the care of the child's property (*Vermögenssorge*) (§ 1626 I BGB). In the following discussion, the term 'parental custody' will be used.

Establishing Parental Custody

The BGB does not contain an express provision on parental custody for children born in wedlock. Apparently, it was regarded as self-evident that in such a case both parents would have joint parental custody (*gemeinsame elterliche Sorge*).[49] Despite the lack of an express rule, the existence of this law is not doubted in any way by courts or by academic authors, and is considered the 'general rule'.[50] The rule can be inferred from the wording of § 1626a BGB, the provision dealing with

---

[44]   *Eriksson v Sweden* (1990) 12 EHRR 183; *Andersson v Sweden* (1992) 14 EHRR 615; *Olsson v Sweden (No 1)* 11 EHRR 259; *Olsson v Sweden (No 2)* (1994) 17 EHRR 134; *Hokkanen v Finland* [1996] 1 FLR 289, (1995) 19 EHRR 139; and *K and T v Finland* [2001] 2 FLR 707; see also Boele-Woelki *et al*, above n 3, 223.

[45]   See, eg D Schwab, *Familienrecht* (14th edn, Munich, CH Beck, 2006) 209.

[46]   See N Dethloff and C Ramser, 'Tensions Between Legal, Biological and Social Conceptions of Parentage in Germany' in I Schwenzer (ed), *Tensions Between Legal, Biological and Social Conceptions of Parentage* (Antwerp, Intersentia, 2007) 7. See, eg § 52 of the *Gesetz über die Angelegenheiten der freiwilligen Gerichtsbarkeit (FGG)*, which uses both '*elterliche Sorge*' (parental custody) and '*elterliche Verantwortung*' (parental responsibility)—albeit for different purposes. It should be noted, however, that the FGG is about to be repealed and replaced by the *Gesetz über das Verfahren in Familiensachen und in den Angelegenheiten der freiwilligen Gerichtsbarkeit (FamFG)*, see Bundestagsdrucksache 16/6308.

[47]   Translation used in P Gottwald, D Schwab and E Büttner, *Family & Succession Law in Germany* (Munich, CH Beck, 2001).

[48]   See German translation of Art 2 of the Council Regulation (EC) No 2201/2003 of 27 November 2003 concerning jurisdiction and the recognition and enforcement of judgments in matrimonial matters and the matters of parental responsibility, repealing Regulation (EC) No 1347/2000 (Brussels IIbis).

[49]   Dethloff and Ramser, above n 46, 184; and N Dethloff and D Martiny in Boele-Woelki *et al*, above n 6, 268.

[50]   *Palandt—Bürgerliches Gesetzbuch* (67th edn, Munich, CH Beck, 2007) commentary by U Diederichsen (in the following cited as Palandt-Diederichsen) n 7 to § 1626 BGB and n 1 to § 1626a BGB. Note also that there is no 'escaping' this general rule, so married parents cannot agree that only one of them should have parental custody.

parental custody in the case of parents who are not married to each other at the time of the child's birth.[51] This provision presupposes the general rule, as it states that such parents have joint parental custody only if they subsequently marry[52] or the mother and father, before or after the birth of the child, jointly or separately[53] make a valid[54] and unconditional[55] declaration of joint parental custody (*Sorgeerklärung*) in the form required.[56] In the case of subsequent marriage, the mother's sole parental custody automatically converts into joint parental custody.[57] In both instances, whether the joint parental custody is actually in the best interest of the child is irrelevant,[58] as is whether the parents cohabit or live with different partners.[59] If no such declaration is made and the parents do not subsequently marry, only the mother has parental custody from birth.[60]

In Germany, therefore, a father who is not married to the mother cannot obtain parental custody against her will[61] unless a court orders the *transfer* of the parental custody to him,[62] in which case the mother *loses* parental custody. There is no possibility to obtain parental custody *in addition* to that of the mother without her consent because the German legislature determined that joint parental custody enforced against the will of one parent would be detrimental to the welfare of the child.[63]

Ending Parental Custody

Parental separation or divorce has no impact on parental custody per se.[64] However, in Germany, parental custody can be discharged by a court order.

If the parents have joint parental custody, each of them can, if they live separately, apply to be awarded sole parental custody in part or in full.[65] The court will do so either if the other parent consents and this would not be

---

[51] See references in n 49 above.

[52] § 1626a I No 2 BGB.

[53] See Schwab, n 45 above, 259; and H Grziwotz, *Nichteheliche Lebensgemeinschaft* (4th edn, Munich, CH Beck 2006) 303 *ff*.

[54] See § 1626c BGB.

[55] See § 1626b BGB.

[56] § 1626d BGB—*öffentliche Beurkundung*, ie 'public certification' by a notary or youth welfare office.

[57] Gottwald *et al*, above n 47, 79.

[58] Palandt-Diederichsen, above n 50, n 6 to § 1626a; Bundestags-Drucksache 13/4899, 59, left column; Gottwald *et al*, above n 47, 80; M Lipp and T Wagenitz, *Das neue Kindschaftsrecht* (Stuttgart, Kohlhammer, 1999) 232, n 2 to § 1626a; and Dethloff and Martiny, above n 49, 340 *ff* and 354 *ff*.

[59] Gottwald *et al*, above n 47, 80; Schwab, above n 45, 259 *ff*; and Grziwotz, above n 53, 304.

[60] § 1626 II BGB.

[61] Grziwotz, above n 53, 305, especially fn 29; Dethloff and Ramser, above n 46, 185; and Lipp and Wagenitz, above n 58, 235, fn 13. A transfer *with* the mother's consent is possible according to § 1672 BGB, see below.

[62] Under § 1666 BGB, see below.

[63] See BVerfG 29 January 2003, NJW 2003, 958.

[64] Since 1998; for the situation before see Schwab, above n 45, 314 *ff*.

[65] § 1671 I BGB.

detrimental to the welfare of the child,[66] or if it is to be expected that the ending of the joint parental custody and the transfer of parental custody to one parent would be best for the child's welfare.[67] The threshold for the latter provision is much higher: a transfer against the will of one of the parents with parental custody will only be granted if the court is satisfied that the discharge of joint parental custody *and* replacing it with the sole parental custody of one parent is best for the welfare of the child (ie both must have a *positive* effect),[68] whereas it suffices for the former provision if the transfer is not detrimental to (ie does not have a *negative* effect on) the welfare of the child. Hence, for a transfer without the agreement of the other parent, it is essentially required that the joint parental custody has failed, that other measures like restriction of exercise of parental custody[69] no longer suffice, and that sole parental custody is necessary in order to overcome the problems.[70] This is deemed to be the case when parents disagree about fundamental issues and their disagreement impedes their ability to coordinate and to act in the best interest of the child.[71] Examples include: refusal to communicate after conversion to another religious denomination and relocation with the children without communication;[72] parents having filed criminal charges against each other;[73] continuing disagreements about consultation of doctors and choice of nursery school;[74] and violence.[75]

If the mother has sole parental custody according to § 1626a II BGB and does not live with the father, the latter can obtain sole parental custody by court order in two ways. First, he may make an application under § 1672 I BGB. This requires (i) the consent of the mother and (ii) that sole custody would be in the best interest of the child (ie have a positive effect).[76] Therefore—again—the mother is in a position to 'veto' a transfer and can exclude the unmarried father from

---

[66]   § 1671 II No 1 BGB. On this see Schwab, above n 45, 312 *ff.*
[67]   § 1671 II No 2 BGB.
[68]   Schwab, above n 45, 322 *ff;* and Palandt-Diederichsen, above n 50, fnn 16 *ff* to § 1671.
[69]   See § 1628 BGB and § 1687 BGB.
[70]   *Palandt-Diederichsen,* above n 50, fn 16 to § 1671.
[71]   *Palandt-Diederichsen,* above n 50, fnn 17 *ff* to § 1671; Oberlandesgericht (OLG) Düsseldorf 22 April 1999, NJW 2682; and Kammergericht 8 November 1999, *FamRZ* 2000, 504.
[72]   OLG Celle, 15 December 2003, *FamRZ* 2004, 1667; and *Palandt-Diederichsen,* above n 50, fn 17 to § 1671.
[73]   OLG Nürnberg 20 April 1999, NJWE-FR 1999, 234.
[74]   OLG Celle 14 February 2000, *FamRZ* 2000, 1039; see also OLG Bamberg 26 August 2002, Familie, Partnerschaft, Recht (FPR) 2003, 333.
[75]   OLG Hamm 13 September 1999, *FamRZ* 2000, 501 (reciprocal violence); BVerfG 18 December 2003, *FamRZ* 2004, 354 (violence against the mother); and OLG Brandenburg 29 March 2001, FPR 2002, 15 (violence against step-children).
[76]   The German legislator expressly requires a positive influence on the child's welfare here and not only the absence of a detrimental effect on the child; this is shown clearly by the wording of s 1 of the provision (which can be contrasted with s 2), see Lipp and Wagenitz, above n 58, 259, but see Bundesgerichtshof 29 September 2007, *FamRZ* 2007, 1969. If a transfer of parental custody has been effected according to § 1672 I BGB, joint parental custody can only be re-established by the court according to § 1672 II BGB if one parent makes an application to that effect, if the other parent consents to this, and if this would not be detrimental to the child's welfare.

parental custody. The one exception to this is contained in § 1751 I 6 BGB: if the mother has given her consent to the child being adopted, then the father's application for sole parental custody under § 1672 BGB no longer requires the mother's consent.[77]

Secondly, § 1666 BGB gives the court the power to take measures to protect the child if the welfare of the child is endangered, including discharge of parental custody in part or in full as the most extreme measure.[78] If there was joint parental custody before, the remaining parent with custody becomes the sole holder of parental custody;[79] if the parental responsibility discharged is that of a parent with sole parental custody, the court can award the other parent sole parental custody.[80] However, the conditions for this vary according to the parents' relationship: if the mother and the father were not married and the mother had sole parental custody according to § 1626a II BGB, the transfer of parental custody to the father must serve the welfare of the child (ie have a *positive* effect).[81] In all other cases, it suffices that the transfer is not detrimental to the welfare of the child (ie does not have a *negative* effect).[82]

Hence, the situation of the unmarried father is precarious if the mother does not consent. Without her consent, he cannot obtain parental custody in addition to hers; his only option then is to rely on § 1666 BGB, which allows for a *transfer* of (sole) parental custody to him. However, the threshold for such a transfer is very high: the welfare of the child needs to be endangered and the transfer— which after all includes the mother losing parental custody—must have a positive effect on the child's welfare. Therefore, in effect, the mother has the power completely to prevent the father from obtaining parental custody as long as she exercises her parental custody without endangering the welfare of the child.

LAW OF ENGLAND AND WALES ON PARENTAL RESPONSIBILITY

Establishing Parental Responsibility

In England and Wales, parents married to each other at the time of the child's birth both have parental responsibility automatically.[83] If the parents are not

---

[77] As § 1751 I 6 BGB refers to § 1672 I BGB, the wording of the latter provision in this context has to be interpreted to mean 'not detrimental to the welfare of child', see Bundesgerichtshof 29 September 2007, *FamRZ* 2007, 1969.

[78] See § 1666a BGB for further details regarding proportionality, etc.

[79] § 1680 III, I BGB.

[80] § 1680 III, II BGB.

[81] § 1680 II 2 BGB.

[82] § 1680 II 1 BGB.

[83] Children Act 1989 s 2(1). 'Married to each other at birth', according to Children Act 1989 s 2(3) and Family Law Reform Act 1987 s 1, has to be interpreted to include a child whose parents were

married to each other, only the mother automatically acquires parental responsibility,[84] and the unmarried father can acquire parental responsibility only in accordance with the provisions of the Children Act 1989. Two of the stipulated methods depend on the mother's consent: first, a formal[85] parental responsibility agreement between the parents;[86] and, secondly, the registration of the father on the birth certificate,[87] which in the absence of a relevant court order, depends on the mother giving her authorisation in writing or attending with the father to register the birth.[88] It is interesting to note that neither of these two methods takes the welfare of the child into account in any way.[89]

In the absence of the mother's agreement, the unmarried father can acquire parental responsibility by obtaining a parental responsibility order[90] or residence order;[91] in the latter case an additional parental responsibility order must be made. In both cases, the child's welfare is the court's paramount consideration.[92] However, when making a residence order, this only applies to the decision as to the person with whom the child shall live, whereas in the case of an application for a parental responsibility order the welfare principle is applied specifically to determine whether the father should be granted parental responsibility.[93] In such a case, the following factors have been held to be material according to the leading decision of *Re H (Minors) (Local Authority: Parental Rights) (No 3)*,[94] which has been followed in many decisions since:

married to each other at any time during the period beginning with the insemination or conception and ending with the birth of the child.

[84]   Children Act 1989 s 2(2). If the parents marry after the birth of the child, the father automatically acquires parental responsibility provided the child is still a minor: see Children Act 1989 s 2(3), Family Law Reform Act 1987 s 1(3)(b) and Legitimacy Act 1976 s 10.

[85]   See Children Act 1989 s 4(2) and Parental Responsibility Agreements Regulation 1991, SI 1991/1478, as amended by SI 1994/3157 and SI 2005/2088.

[86]   Children Act 1989 s 4(1)(b).

[87]   Children Act 1989 s 4(1)(a), inserted by Adoption and Children Act 2002 s 111. See P Booth, 'Parental responsibility—What Changes?' [2003] *Family Law* 353; and Lord Chancellor's Department Consultation Paper, *Procedures for The Determination of Paternity and on The Law on Parental Responsibility for Unmarried Fathers* (LCD, 1998). The father can also be appointed as a guardian either by the child's mother or by the court (Children Act 1989 s 5), but this is unusual.

[88]   See Births and Deaths Registration Act 1953 ss 10 and 10A. In 2005, 85% of children born outside of marriage were registered this way: see Department for Work and Pensions, 'Joint birth registration: promoting parental responsibility' (Cm 7160, June 2007) [37], fig 1.

[89]   See, eg *Re X (Minors) (Care Proceedings: Parental Responsibility)* [2000] Fam 156; N Lowe and G Douglas, *Bromley's Family Law* (10th edn, Oxford, Oxford University Press, 2007) 412 ff; and J Wallbank, 'Clause 106 of the Adoption and Children Bill: legislation for the 'good' father?' (2002) 22 *Legal Studies* 288.

[90]   Children Act 1989 s 4(1)(c).

[91]   Children Act 1989 s 12(1).

[92]   Children Act 1989 s 1(1).

[93]   For an interesting comment by Waite J on this 'unusual duality in the character of a parental responsibility order', see *Re CB (A Minor) (Parental Responsibility Order)* [1993] 1 FLR 920, 929.

[94]   [1991] Fam 151, 158.

(1) the degree of commitment which the father has shown towards the child; (2) the degree of attachment which exists between the father and the child; (3) the reasons of the father for applying for the order.[95]

Sometimes it might not be possible to show the required commitment or attachment, for example, if the mother is preventing contact; in such cases it has been considered appropriate to adjourn the application and to see whether commitment and attachment can be established in the future,[96] possibly with the aid of a contact order.[97]

However, even if the *Re H* criteria are satisfied, the court still must apply the paramountcy principle in section 1(1) of the Children Act 1989,[98] so that ultimately an order will only be made if it is best for the child's welfare.[99] In the vast majority of cases, the applications are granted; in 2006 only 148 of 9,674 applications made were refused (1.5 per cent).[100] These very rare refusals often are based on the father's previous violence towards the child or mother.[101] All in all, there seems to be a strong tendency to make an order unless there are good reasons against it.[102]

It is important to note that the father's acquisition of parental responsibility does not lead to the mother losing parental responsibility—the father always acquires his parental responsibility *in addition* to that of the mother.

Ending Parental Responsibility

In England and Wales, parental responsibility cannot be discharged if it is acquired automatically upon birth or through marriage.[103] If, however, parental responsibility was acquired by an unmarried father, the court can order the

---

[95] For a powerful critique of the way in which the courts currently handle parental responsibility orders, see S Gilmore, 'Parental responsibility and the unmarried father—a new dimension to the debate' [2003] 15 *CFLQ* 21; see also Wallbank, above n 89, 283 *ff*.

[96] See *Re D (a child) (IVF treatment)* [2001] EWCA Civ 230; and Lowe and Douglas, above n 89, 418 *ff*.

[97] Indeed, this might be required according to the case law of the ECtHR, see, eg *Görgülü v Germany* [2004] 1 FLR 894 on the importance of genetic fatherhood.

[98] For a debate on whether the welfare principle ought to play a role here, see Gilmore, above n 95.

[99] See *Re RH (A Minor) (Parental Responsibility)* [1998] 1 FLR 855.

[100] 'Judicial and Court Statistics 2006' (Cm 7273, 2007) 88, Table 5.4; 676 applications were withdrawn (7%), 148 orders of no order made (1.5%) and 8,702 parental responsibility orders made (90%). These figures include applications by step-parents, although these are likely to represent a small proportion of the total number.

[101] See Lowe and Douglas, above n 89, 418, for further references and other reasons for refusal.

[102] For a comprehensive discussion of the case law and further references, see Gilmore, above n 95. See also J Eekelaar, 'Rethinking Parental Responsibility' [2001] *Family Law* 426; and H Conway, 'Parental responsibility and the unmarried father' (1996) 146 *New Law Journal* 782.

[103] By contrast the Children (Scotland) Act 1995 s 11 contains such a possibility.

parental responsibility to 'cease'.[104] The child's welfare is the paramount consideration when deciding whether or not such an order should be made.[105] Applications to end paternal parental responsibility can only be made by any person who has parental responsibility for the child or, with leave of the court, by the child him- or herself.[106] These provisions do not allow a court to end parental responsibility of its own motion.

Parental responsibility acquired by way of a residence order ends automatically once the residence order is no longer in force.[107] However, a parental responsibility order accompanying a residence order (ie made pursuant to section 12(1) of the Children Act 1989) continues even where a residence order comes to an end.

COMPARISON

The legal position of the unmarried father has changed quite considerably in many European jurisdictions in the last 50 years. Many reforms were triggered by the desire to end the discrimination against illegitimate children[108] and by the increase of 'non-traditional' family forms, particularly cohabitation outside marriage. The starting point almost universally was that only the mother had parental responsibility[109] and that the unmarried father had no, or very limited, possibilities to acquire it. Nowadays, fathers in all European jurisdictions have that opportunity, one way or another.[110] Three basic types of rule for the inclusion of the unmarried father in European jurisdictions can be identified:[111]

  (i) jurisdictions where the father can only acquire parental responsibility with the consent of the mother—in this chapter represented by Germany;
 (ii) jurisdictions where parental responsibility can be acquired either with the consent of the mother or by court order if that is in the best interest of the child—in this chapter represented by England and Wales; and
(iii) jurisdictions where both parents acquire parental responsibility upon birth of the child, irrespective of their own relationship—which is the situation in

---

[104]   Children Act 1989 s 4(2A). Similar rules for the 'bringing to an end' of parental responsibility apply if a step-parent has acquired parental responsibility according to Children Act 1989 s 4A.

[105]   *Re P (Terminating Parental Responsibility)* [1995] 1 FLR 1048.

[106]   Children Act 1989 s 4(3).

[107]   Children Act 1989 s 12(2). According to s 9(6), residence orders (subject to s 12(5)) usually end when the child reaches the age of 16 unless the court is satisfied that the circumstances of the case are exceptional: see, eg *A v A (Shared Residence)* [2004] EWHC 142 (Fam).

[108]   Greatly furthered by the ECtHR's decision in *Marckx v Belgium* (1979–80) 2 EHRR 330; see also Law Commission, 'Illegitimacy' (Law Com No 118, 1982) [1.3].

[109]   For the comparative part, 'parental responsibility' will be used as an umbrella term unless specifically German law or the CEFL Principles are referred to.

[110]   See the comparative overview in Boele-Woelki *et al*, above n 3, 60 *ff*; and JM Scherpe, 'Rechtsvergleichende Gesamtwürdigung und Empfehlungen zur Rechtsstellung nichtehelicher Lebensgemeinschaften' in Scherpe and Yassari, above n 20, 593 *ff*.

[111]   N Dethloff, 'Das Sorgerecht nicht miteinander verheirateter Eltern aus rechtsvergleichender Sicht', *Das Jugendamt (JAmt)* 2005, 213; see also the national reports in Boele-Woelki *et al*, above n 6.

a large number of European jurisdictions and in this chapter is exemplified by the CEFL Principles.

An argument can be made that it is discriminatory to treat the unmarried father less favourably than both the child's mother and the married father. The potential discrimination against the father has been addressed in the ECtHR cases *B v UK*[112] and *McMichael v UK*,[113] as well as by the German Constitutional Court.[114] In all three cases it was held that the differential treatment was justifiable. However, there is also a further person who might claim to be discriminated against: the child who is placed in a different legal position with regard to his or her parents depending on whether or not they were married.[115]

In the next section, the justifications given for this differential treatment in Germany and England and Wales are examined. Unsurprisingly, the concerns, debates and arguments are quite similar, but do they provide a sufficient case for different treatment?

---

[112] [2000] 1 FLR 1.

[113] (1995) 20 EHRR 205, [1995] 2 FCR 718, [1995] *Family Law* 478 with commentary by J Dewar and by C Barton and A Bissett-Johnson at 507–8. See also G Branchflower, 'Parental Responsibility And Human Rights' [1999] *Family Law* 34 *ff*.

[114] BVerfG NJW 2003, 955. This decision attracted massive criticism by German academia and many authors strongly doubt whether the current legal position is in line with the requirements of the German Basic Law and the ECHR: Lipp, 'Das elterliche Sorgerecht für das nichteheliche Kind nach dem Kindschaftsreformgesetz', *FamRZ* 1998, 65 *ff*, M Coester in J von Staudingers, *Kommentar zum Bürgerlichen Gesetzbuch*, Vol 4 (Berlin, Sellier-de Gruyter, 2007) fnn 3 and 8 to § 1626a BGB; P Huber in Münchener, *Kommentar zum Bürgerlichen Gesetzbuch*, Vol 8 (4th edn, Munich, CH Beck, 2002) fnn 39–42 to § 1626a BGB; case note by M Coester, *FamRZ* 2004, 87; M Coester, 'Verfassungsrechtliche Vorgaben für die gesetzliche Ausgestaltung des Sorgerechts nicht miteinander verheirateter Eltern', *FPR* 2005, 60 *ff*; C Müller, 'Elterliches Sorgerecht des unverheirateten Vaters auch gegen den Willen der Kindsmutter?', *Zentralblatt für Jugendrecht* 2004, 7 *ff*; E Schumann, 'Erfüllt das neue Kindschaftsrecht die verfassungsrechtlichen Anforderungen an die Ausgestaltung des nichtehelichen Vater-Kind-Verhältnisses?', *FamRZ* 2000, 389 *ff*; N Dethloff, above n 32, 145; A Lüderitz and N Dethloff, *Familienrecht* (28th edn, Munich, CH Beck, 2007) 332 *ff*; S Fink, 'Verfassung und das Sorgerecht für nichteheliche Kinder', *JAmt* 2005, 485 *ff*; M Humphrey, 'Das Sorgerecht des nichtehelichen Vaters in rechtsvergleichender Kritik', *FPR* 2003, 578 *ff*; and Scherpe, above n 110, 596 *ff*. However, see Breithaupt, 'Die Alleinsorge der Mutter nach § 1626a II BGB und das Kindeswohl', *FPR* 2004, 488 *ff*. For reform suggestions, see Kinderrechtekommission des Deutschen Familiengerichtstags eV, *JAmt* 2005, 490 *ff*; and M Coester, 'Nichteheliche Elternschaft und Sorgerecht', *FamRZ* 2007, 1137 *ff*.

[115] This point was discussed very briefly—and unconvincingly—in BVerfG NJW 2003, 955 (960). Interestingly, the father in the proceedings had also brought a separate constitutional complaint on behalf of his child which was declared inadmissible as he did not have parental custody and thus was not entitled to do so (at 956).
Art 6(5) of the German *Grundgesetz* (Basic Law, the German constitution) reads as follows: '[c]hildren born outside of marriage shall be provided by legislation with the same opportunities for physical and mental development and for their position in society as are enjoyed by those born within marriage.' In the light of the recent decision BVerfG *FamRZ* 2007, 965 (where differential treatment of mothers because of their marital status was held to be an unjustified discrimination *of the child* and a breach of Art 6(5)), it is not unlikely that the differential treatment of married and unmarried fathers concerning parental custody would also be found to be in breach of Art 6(5). For England, see also A Bainham, 'When is a parent not a parent? Reflections on the unmarried father and his child in English law' (1989) 3 *International Journal of Law and the Family* 208, 215; but see S Sheldon, 'Unmarried Fathers and Parental Responsibility: a case for reform?' (2001) 9 *Feminist Legal Studies* 106.

The Relevance of Consent

England and Wales and Germany have in common that the unmarried father can acquire parental responsibility with the mother's consent. The consent needs to be embodied in some form of formal and express commitment (agreement or registration); for married couples it is deemed to have been given with the formal commitment of marriage.[116] Interestingly, in neither jurisdiction is the child's welfare expressly considered in this process. The underlying assumption seems to be that if the couple agrees, parental responsibility for both parents is always in the best interest of the child and that a further inquiry is therefore unnecessary.[117]

The reason given for the importance attached to the mother's consent is that consent is held to indicate a cooperative (or at least not adversarial) relationship between the parents.[118] It is hoped that in this way acrimonious disputes, which can have a very detrimental effect on the child's welfare, can be avoided.

The consent approach, however, seems somewhat misguided, mainly because the *actual* welfare of the child is of no relevance in the consent approach. It has been said—and been approved by supreme courts[119]—that the aim of not giving all unmarried fathers parental responsibility automatically is to exclude those who are not meritorious. This is not the place to debate what criteria make a father 'meritorious', but it is clear that the decision whether he 'qualifies' at this (consent) stage is placed firmly in the hands of the mother. While there are many good reasons for giving preference to the mother, who after all statistically is most likely to be the primary carer, it is also apparent that her criteria for making her decision will not necessarily be based on what is in the best interest of the child. Therefore, the consent approach amalgamates the interests of child and mother,[120] effectively assuming that whatever is best for the mother in this situation will also be best for the child. It is submitted that this is an untenable position; the interests of mother and child, while often similar, can be distinct and should be treated as such.

Therefore, at best the consent approach can lower the likelihood of detrimental conflicts occurring. However, it neither deals adequately with the situation where there is already conflict between the parents and therefore there is no consent,

---

[116] BVerfG NJW 2003, 955 (956); see also Lord Chancellor's Department Consultation Paper, above n 87, Annex C (Response of the Advisory Board on Family Law to the consultation document on paternity and parental responsibility) [ii]; and Department for Work and Pensions, above n 88.

[117] See, eg Department for Work and Pensions, above n 88; *Palandt-Diederichsen*, above n 50, fn 6 to § 1626a; Bundestags-Drucksache 13/4899, 59, left column; Gottwald *et al*, above n 47, 80; Lipp and Wagenitz, above n 58, 232, fn 2 to § 1626a; and Dethloff and Martiny, above n 49, 340 *ff* and 354 *ff*.

[118] This is the underlying reasoning for the current German law: see Lipp and Wagenitz, above n 58, 232, fn 2 to § 1626a, and this has since been confirmed by BVerfG 29.1.2003, NJW 2003, 955 (referring to, inter alia, BVerfG 24.3.1981, NJW 1981, 1201).

[119] *B v UK* [2000] 1 FLR 1; *McMichael v UK* (1995) 20 EHRR 205; and BVerfG 29.1.2003, NJW 2003, 955; see also Gilmore, above n 95, 29 *ff*.

[120] See also Bainham, above n 115, 208, 211, 227, 231 and 234.

nor with situations where the father represents a risk to the child, but the mother nevertheless consents.

There is, however, a crucial difference between German and English/Welsh law on parental responsibility: while in England and Wales there is at least a court procedure in which the unmarried father can obtain parental responsibility (and thus prove that he is 'meritorious'), this was expressly rejected in Germany.[121] It was deemed that only an express joint commitment would serve as a sufficient basis for a parent–child relationship upon which joint custody should be awarded. If the parents could not agree on joint custody, then it was considered unlikely that they could cooperate in the way necessary and hence joint custody would have more disadvantages than advantages for the child.[122] This may appear curious to the English reader, given the dicta in a number of cases where it was expressly held that a bad relationship between the parents would not preclude awarding the father parental responsibility.[123] Indeed, it has been argued that ordering parental responsibility might lessen the acrimony rather than increase it.[124]

The German position, however, perpetuates the amalgamation of the mother's and the child's interests, with two potential casualties: the father whose interests and indeed merits are of no concern whatsoever, and the child whose— separate—interests likewise are not considered. By contrast, in England and Wales, the criteria for making a parental responsibility order focus on the father–child relationship.[125]

The Relevance of the Exercise of Parental Responsibility

The extent to which the non-resident parent can exercise his or her parental responsibility and the potential for conflict must, one would assume, be an important factor when deciding whether or not to allocate parental responsibility and whether the mother's consent should be a decisive factor. Differences in the legal rules on exercise of parental responsibilities could potentially explain the

---

[121] Bundestags-Drucksache 13/4899.

[122] BVerfG 2003, 955 (957).

[123] See, eg *Re M (Contact: Family Assistance: McKenzie Friend)* [1999] 1 FLR 75; *Re J-S (A Child) (Contact: Parental Responsibility)* [2002] EWCA Civ 1028; *Re H (a child: parental responsibility)* [2002] EWCA Civ 542; *Re P (A Minor) (Parental Responsibility Order)* [1994] 1 FLR 578; *D v S (Parental Responsibility)* [1995] 3 FCR 783; and *Re S (A Minor) (Parental Responsibility)* [1995] 3 FCR 564; see also Gilmore, above n 95, 30 *ff*; and N Lowe, 'The meaning and allocation of parental responsibility—a common lawyer's perspective' (1997) 11 *IJLPF* 205. *Re M (Contact: Parental responsibility)* [2001] 2 FLR 342 is a good example of how to deal with fathers who abuse or might abuse parental responsibility; see also Wilson J in *Re P (A Minor) (Parental Responsibility Order)* [1994] 1 FLR 578 at 585.

[124] *Re P (A Minor) (Parental Responsibility Order)* [1994] 1 FLR 578 at 585 (Wilson J). See also Conway, above n 102.

[125] Although there at least in the past there was a tendency to see the interests of mother and child as synonymous, see Bainham, above n 115, 227 and 234.

differences between the jurisdictions' approaches to allocation of parental responsibility.

In German law, and according to the CEFL Principles, all holders of parental responsibility are free to take day-to-day decisions for the child, but they have to agree on decisions of 'significance'[126] or of 'importance'.[127] If an agreement cannot be reached, the parties have to seek a decision by the competent authorities or courts. Thus, there is some potential for interference, for example, by the non-resident unmarried father. Surprisingly, this leads to diametrically opposite conclusions in Germany and under the CEFL Principles: German law excludes the unmarried father in order to avoid interference, whereas the CEFL Principles automatically include him upon birth of the child in spite of this problem. The CEFL Principles maintain that the restriction of exercise or the discharge of parental responsibilities is sufficient as a safeguard. While German law possesses the same safeguards, they were not considered to be satisfactory: the potential conflict between parents and its possible effects on the child were held to justify giving parental custody only to the mother.[128] Apart from the continuous—and misplaced—equation of the mother's and the child's interests, this argument is rather weak, given that once the father has acquired parental custody with the mother's consent (for which, it must be remembered, the individual welfare of the child is irrelevant), the same problems can and indeed do arise. Moreover, the absence of a possibility for the unmarried father to obtain parental custody without the consent of the mother, aggravated by the fact that the individual circumstances and the father's interests are not considered at any point, leaves Germany very vulnerable to a challenge under the ECHR.[129]

As was laid out above, England and Wales hold the middle ground between Germany and the CEFL Principles by allowing the unmarried father to acquire parental responsibility by court order without the mother's consent. With regard to exercise, section 2(7) of the Children Act 1989 clearly states that each holder of parental responsibility may act alone unless there is an enactment which requires the consent of the other holder(s) of parental responsibility.[130] Further, the exercise of parental responsibility must not be inconsistent with any order under the Children Act 1989.[131] However, these are very narrowly confined exceptions. Therefore, notwithstanding recent attempts by the courts to establish a 'duty to consult',[132] the primary carer (still most of the time the mother) is in fact barely

---

[126]   § 1628 BGB.
[127]   CEFL Principle 3:12. This also contains a non-exhaustive list of matters which are considered to be important, namely education, medical treatment, child's residence and administration of child's property.
[128]   BVerfG 29 January 2003, NJW 2003, 955; see also *Zaunegger v Germany* (Appl no 22028/04).
[129]   See references in n 114 above.
[130]   See, eg Children Act 1989 s 13.
[131]   Children Act 1989 s 2(8).
[132]   *Re G (A Minor) (Parental responsibility: Education)* [1994] 2 FLR 964; *Re J (Specific Issue Orders: Child's Religious Upbringing and Circumcision)* [2000] 1 FLR 571; *Re PC (Change of Surname)*

restricted by law in the exercise of her parental responsibility.[133] Indeed, on the face of it, as Lowe and Douglas have put it, the mother loses relatively little if the father acquires parental responsibility.[134]

The Relevance of Concerns about the Exercise of Parental Responsibility

Many of the concerns in the debate—in one way or another—stem from the fear that the unmarried father might misuse his parental responsibility, for example, by intervening if the child is taken into care, or by harassing or even blackmailing the mother (and potentially her new partner who is *in loco parentis*).[135] The debate (again) very much focuses on parent-centred (and mostly mother-centred) concerns, and not child-centred ones; once more, the child's welfare is merely an appendix rather than an issue in its own right.

Since in England there is, legally, little room for interference,[136] the concerns mostly relate to the psychological effect of the father's acquisition of parental responsibility: mothers may be intimidated by the father having a 'right', and fathers encouraged to (unduly) interfere.[137] While these are very real and unfortunately often justified concerns, one may question whether they are sufficient to rationalise that all unmarried fathers as a matter of principle should not acquire parental responsibility automatically. The overwhelming majority of unmarried fathers—if one sees the number of registrations, agreements and successful applications to court as meaningful indicators—apparently are 'meritorious'(or at least not unmeritorious); why, therefore, should a minority's lack of merit determine the law? In addition, is it not likely that fathers who are

[1997] 2 FLR 730; and *Re B (A Child) (Immunisation)* [2003] 3 FCR 156; for a discussion see J Eekelaar, 'Do Parents have a Duty to Consult?' (1998) 114 *LQR* 337 and above n 102.

[133] See J Herring, *Family Law* (3rd edn, Harlow, Pearson Education Ltd, 2007) 288 *ff*; Lowe and Douglas, above n 89, 421; and Eekelaar, above n 102.

[134] Lowe and Douglas, above n 89, 421; see also Eekelaar, above n 102.

[135] See Law Commission, 'Illegitimacy', above n 108, [4.26]. Of course there are other concerns, particularly legal certainty and the 'rapist father' (irrespective of whether or not married to the mother). Space precludes a full discussion in this comparative chapter, see generally Herring, above n 133, 343 *ff*; Lowe and Douglas, above n 89, 426 *ff*; Scottish Law Commission, 'Parental responsibilities and Rights, Guardianship and Administration of Property' (Discussion Paper No 88, 1990) and 'Family Law' (Report No 135, 1994); and A Bainham, 'Reforming Scottish Children Law—sense from North of the border' (1993) 5 *Journal of Child Law* 3; for Germany, see Bundestags-Drucksache 13/4899; BVerfG 29 January 2003, NJW 2003, 955; and Lipp and Wagenitz, above n 58, 235. As usually the same concerns have been raised in the debates in other countries, it would be highly interesting to see an empirical study of whether the concerns have actually materialised in those jurisdictions where both parents automatically acquire parental responsibility upon birth. The national reports in Boele-Woelki *et al*, above n 6, at least do not seem to indicate major problems.

[136] See *Re S (A Minor) (Parental Responsibility)* [1995] 3 FCR 564; *D v S (Parental Responsibility)* [1995] 3 FCR 783; *Re J (Specific Issue Orders: Child's Religious Upbringing and Circumcision)* [2000] 1 FLR 571; *Re C (Welfare of Child: Immunisation)* [2003] 2 FLR 1054; Lowe and Douglas, above n 89, 421; and Herring, above n 133, 390.

[137] *Ibid*; M Hayes, 'Law Commission Working Paper No. 74: Illegitimacy' (1980) 43 *MLR* 299, 301; Eekelaar, above n 102; and Sheldon, above n 115, 109 *ff.*

inclined to pester the mother will do so irrespective of whether or not they have parental responsibility?[138] Moreover, does the exclusion from parental responsibility actually lead to mothers feeling more secure and fathers less inclined to intervene? Should the feelings of a parent—rather than the facts and the individual welfare of the child—determine the content of the law?[139] The Children Act 1989 provides ample tools to deal with undue interference or the consequences of the fear of such interference, which—it seems—are deemed sufficient for the majority of cases, namely children born in wedlock. However, on top of those tools there is even the possibility to remove the unmarried father's parental responsibility by court order. That is the most extreme measure available—but apparently that still is not enough to allow automatic parental responsibility for unmarried fathers. Are English and Welsh unmarried fathers as a group so much more volatile, dangerous or socially deviant[140] when compared with their European counterparts, with married fathers, or indeed with mothers, that England and Wales cannot follow the example of many European jurisdictions and 'reverse' the current approach, from selection to deselection?

Selection Or Deselection?

The current system in England and Wales is one of selection: 'meritorious' fathers can 'graduate'[141] to parental responsibility if they prove they are 'meritorious' (either by having the consent of the mother or by being 'approved' by the court). By contrast, the system of the CEFL Principles and a large number of European jurisdictions is one of deselection: the parental responsibility of 'unmeritorious' fathers (whether married or unmarried) and of mothers can be discharged if it is necessary for the child's welfare. The underlying rationale is clear: gender or marital status should not matter when the child's welfare is endangered, and there are cases where a restriction of the exercise of parental responsibility simply will not suffice. In a way, therefore, holders of parental responsibility are permanently 'on probation'—which is not necessarily a bad thing.

In England and Wales, the parental responsibility of mothers and married fathers cannot be discharged. They can be as irresponsible or 'unmeritorious' as they like, but they cannot lose parental responsibility (other than by adoption). This approach is held to be appropriate for the child-abusing mother or the wife-beating husband and apparently not inconsistent with the welfare of the child. One wonders what possible additional dangers could emanate from unmarried fathers to justify their inferior legal position, especially given the lack

---

[138]   See Herring, above n 133, 344.
[139]   Scottish Law Commission, 'Parental responsibilities and Rights, Guardianship and Administration of Property' (Discussion Paper No 88, 1990) [2.4] *ff* and 'Family Law' (Report No 135, 1994) [2.38] *ff*; Bainham, above n 135, 5 *ff*; and Lowe and Douglas, above n 89, 426.
[140]   See Wallbank, above n 89, 279 *ff.*
[141]   Bainham, above n 115, 228.

of any general duty to seek the consent of or consult with other holders of parental responsibility. Not only do they not get parental responsibility automatically, but once they have it they face the possibility of discharge and having to demonstrate to a court's satisfaction that they are not 'unmeritorious'. In a way, therefore, the law of England and Wales is overly restrictive in comparison with the other legal rules examined in this chapter, and it seems questionable whether it gets the balance right.[142]

CONCLUSION

Both German law and the law of England and Wales operate a system of 'selecting' unmarried fathers for parental responsibility. The attribution of parental custody under German law is solely based on the mother's consent. There is thus a focus on the mother's perception into which the welfare of the child is absorbed. This in itself probably violates the ECHR; but coupled with the complete disregard for the father's interests and hence his Convention rights, Germany is undoubtedly vulnerable to a challenge in the ECtHR. German law, therefore, is in dire need of reform.

In comparison, the law of England and Wales at least allows for the acquisition of parental responsibility of an unmarried father without the mother's consent and, therefore—at least according to *B v UK*[143] and *McMichael v UK*[144]—is not in breach of the ECHR. Nevertheless, there are good reasons to reform the law in England and Wales as well. The CEFL Principles and the research on which they are based, together with the experiences of those European jurisdictions that give all parents parental responsibility upon birth (about one-half of the European jurisdictions) and that allow a discharge of parental responsibility of both parents (virtually all European jurisdictions) might prove very fruitful here.

It appears that the available instruments for protecting the mother and the child's welfare—which should be the central concern when considering parental responsibility—are sufficient to allow the allocation of parental responsibility upon birth to all parents; at least the safeguards in England and Wales are fairly similar to those of the European jurisdictions that do so. While a deselection of 'unmeritorious' parents might put additional strain on the other 'meritorious' one who will have to instigate proceedings accordingly, an automatic allocation is

---

[142] See Eekelaar above n 102; Lowe and Douglas, above n 89, 426 *ff*; Lowe, above n 123, especially 207 *ff*; Gilmore, above n 95; Bainham, above n 115; Conway, above n 102; and R Pickford, 'Unmarried Fathers and the Law' in A Bainham, S Day Sclater and M Richards (eds), *What is a Parent?* (Oxford, Hart Publishing, 1999) 143 *ff*; but cf Sheldon, above n 115; R Deech, 'The Rights of Fathers: Social and Biological Concepts of fatherhood' in J Eekelaar and P Šarčević, *Parenthood in a Modern Society* (London, Martinus Nijhoff, 1993) 19 *ff*; and Wallbank, above n 89, 276 *ff*.

[143] [2000] 1 FLR 1.

[144] (1995) 20 EHRR 205.

much more in line with social reality. After all, the majority already obtain parental responsibility, one way or the other.

Moreover, having the possibility to 'deselect', ie to discharge the parental responsibility of all parents and not merely to restrict its exercise, could further the focus on the actual care and support given to the child, emphasising the importance of parental responsibilities and the relationship with the child— while at the same time abolishing differential and potentially discriminatory treatment of parents. As outlined above, England and Wales is the only jurisdiction that does not have that possibility.[145] Combined with giving all parents parental responsibility upon birth, it would allow a truly gender-neutral and non-discriminatory approach to parental responsibility, reinforcing the importance of the daily care and support of the child and his or her general welfare. This is what the CEFL Principles suggest[146] and it is an approach supported by many academic authors.[147] Under English law, the holder of parental responsibility (typically still the mother) who undertakes these tasks is—rightly—privileged and should remain so. However, the other parent also has a role to play, which should be recognised by the law as long as that is in line with the child's welfare.[148] That, and not the interests of individual parents, must be the principal focus.

---

[145]   eg Scots law, also contains such a provision in the Children (Scotland) Act 1995 s 11; for other jurisdictions see Boele-Woelki *et al*, above n 3, 212 *ff* (and fn 42); and the national reports in Boele-Woelki *et al*, above n 6.

[146]   Boele-Woelki *et al*, above n 3, 59 *ff*.

[147]   For England and Wales, see references in n 142; for Germany, see references in n 49.

[148]   The importance of having a responsible father in a child's life has continuously been emphasised by the government and academic authors, see, eg Department for Work and Pensions, above n 88; Law Commission, above n 108; Scottish Law Commission, above n 135; Gilmore, above n 95, at 38; Bainham above nn 115 and 135; and Eekelaar, above n 102.

4

The Limits of Parental Responsibility

STEPHEN GILMORE*

INTRODUCTION

Q UESTIONS CONCERNING THE nature of parental responsibility raise difficult and important issues, and are quite rightly the subject of academic inquiry. The chapter in this volume examining the complex question of whether parental rights are derived merely from duty (entirely child-centred), or whether they also comprise parents' independent interests, provides an excellent example.[1] But whatever the answers to such questions, or whatever the legal terminology employed to describe 'parental decision-making', there will perhaps be a more fundamental question within any legal system (at least from a practical point of view): where do the boundaries of the bundle of jural relations we call 'parental responsibility' lie? In other words, what are the limits to parental decision-making? In this chapter I attempt an answer to this question as a matter of English law at the level of general principle, focusing on the relationship between parental autonomy and children's interests.

The chapter begins by examining the complex and uncertain issue of the impact of the child's autonomy interest upon parental decision-making. Following the House of Lords decision in *Gillick v West Norfolk and Wisbech AHA and Department of Health and Social Security*[2] (hereinafter *Gillick*), a popular view emerged that English law had given legal recognition to a child's autonomy interest.[3] On this view, upon a child's acquisition of full capacity to decide an issue, any relevant parental rights were 'eclipsed'.[4] The strength with which this interpretation took hold is perhaps in part evidenced by the hostile academic reaction to subsequent Court of Appeal decisions which held that a child's refusal

* I should like to thank Liam D'Arcy Brown, Jonathan Herring and Rebecca Probert for their helpful comments on an earlier draft, and all who have discussed this subject with me over the years, in particular Beverley Brown, John Eekelaar, Hilary Lim and Stuart Vernon. The usual caveats apply.

[1] See Bainham, this volume.
[2] [1986] 1 AC 112.
[3] See, eg J Eekelaar, 'The Emergence of Children's Rights' (1986) 6 *OJLS* 161.
[4] J Eekelaar, 'The Eclipse of Parental Rights' (1986) 102 *LQR* 4.

of consent to medical treatment could be overridden by the exercise of parental responsibility,[5] and which were seen as signalling a retreat from *Gillick*.[6] More recently, *Gillick* was interpreted and developed in the post-Human Rights Act era by Silber J in *R (Axon) v Secretary of State for Health (Family Planning Association intervening)*[7] (hereinafter *Axon*), prompting academic comment that his Lordship's interpretation of Article 8 of the European Convention for the Protection of Human Rights and Fundamental Freedoms 1950 (ECHR) might indicate a reversal of this so-called retreat.[8]

In what follows, I examine whether a children's autonomy rights reading of *Gillick* is the most plausible interpretation. I shall suggest that the claim that *Gillick* recognised a competent child's autonomy—in the sense of a child's general right to act contrary to his or her own interests—may exaggerate the impact of the decision. I shall seek to show that *Gillick* was essentially a case about children's welfare, in which their Lordships were seeking to resolve the potentially conflicting claims of adults to know what is in a child's best interests. I shall attempt to demonstrate that their Lordships recognised a socially constructed, socially changing parent/child relationship, which is not regulated simply by reference to a child's empirically ascertainable abilities. I shall argue that the solution adopted by their Lordships suggests that parental discretion is regulated by reference to child welfare, taking account of the child's abilities, and that the boundary of that discretion lies at the point at which the parent's protective role can be safely abandoned.

In the light of this analysis, the chapter moves on to consider more generally the scope of parental discretion, together with an examination of the emphasis

---

[5]   *Re R (A Minor) (Wardship: Consent to Treatment)* [1992] Fam 11; and *Re W (A Minor) (Medical Treatment: Court's Jurisdiction)* [1993] Fam 64.

[6]   Perhaps most explicitly in G Douglas, 'The Retreat from *Gillick*' (1992) 55 *MLR* 569. See also A Bainham, 'The Judge and the Competent Minor' (1992) 108 *LQR* 194; E Lawson, 'Are *Gillick* rights under threat?' (1991) 80 *Childright* 17; J Masson, 'Adolescent Crisis and Parental Power' [1991] *Fam Law* 528; J Murphy, 'Circumscribing the Autonomy of "*Gillick* Competent" Children' (1992) 43 *NILQ* 60; J Eekelaar, 'White Coats or Flak Jackets? Doctors, Children and the Courts—Again' (1993) 109 *LQR* 182; J Masson, '*Re W*: appealing from the golden cage' (1993) 5 *Journal of Child Law* 37; J Bridgeman, 'Old enough to know best?' (1993) 13 *Legal Studies* 69; L Edwards, 'The Right to Consent and the Right to Refuse; More Problems with Minors and Medical Consent' [1993] *Juridical Review* 52; A Grubb, 'Treatment decisions: keeping it in the family' in A Grubb (ed), *Choices and Decisions in Health Care* (Chichester, John Wiley, 1993) 37; and J Murphy, 'W(h)ither Adolescent Autonomy?' [1992] 2 *JSWFL* 529. The few commentators who have injected some balance include: J Montgomery, 'Parents and children in dispute: who has the final word?' (1992) 4 *Journal of Child Law* 85, 87 (describing Lord Donaldson's reasoning as 'not without merit'); N Lowe and S Juss, 'Medical Treatment—Pragmatism and the Search for Principle' (1993) 56 *MLR* 865 ; JK Mason, 'Master of the Balancers; Non-Voluntary Therapy under the Mantle of Lord Donaldson' [1993] *Juridical Review* 115 (supporting Lord Donaldson's reasoning on Family Law Reform Act 1969 s 8); C Hamilton, 'Editorial' (1993) 5 *Journal of Child Law* 1, 1–2; and P Bromley and N Lowe, *Bromley's Family Law* (8th edn, London, Butterworths, 1992) 295 (viewing subsequent case law merely as a narrow interpretation of *Gillick*).

[7]   [2006] EWHC 37 (Admin).

[8]   R Taylor, 'Reversing the retreat from *Gillick*? *R (Axon) v Secretary of State for Health*' [2007] 19 *CFLQ* 81.

given to parents' views when the courts are called upon to take decisions on matters of parental responsibility. In the next section, the analysis begins with brief accounts of *Gillick* and *Axon* as a foundation for the arguments that follow.

PARENTAL RESPONSIBILITY AND CHILDREN'S AUTONOMY

Gillick v West Norfolk and Wisbech AHA and Department of Health and Social Security

In *Gillick*, the House of Lords, by a majority of three to two,[9] upheld the lawfulness of official Guidance[10] to doctors on the provision of contraceptive advice and treatment.[11] Rejecting Mrs Victoria Gillick's arguments, the House held that a girl under 16 could provide a valid consent to contraceptive treatment, and a doctor could lawfully prescribe such treatment without her parents' knowledge and consent. In reaching this conclusion, the majority eschewed any rule of absolute parental authority[12] as well as the view that a child's intellectual ability is irrelevant. Instead, their Lordships approved Lord Denning's opinion in *Hewer v Bryant*[13] that parental custody is a 'dwindling right which the courts will hesitate to enforce against the wishes of the child, and the more so the older he is'.[14]

Once the rule of parents' absolute authority was abandoned, Lord Fraser saw the solution in the appeal as depending 'upon a judgment of what is best for the welfare of the particular child':[15]

[the] only practicable course [was] to entrust the doctor with a discretion to act in accordance with his view of what is best in the interests of the girl who is his patient.[16]

---

[9] Lord Fraser of Tullybelton, Lord Scarman and Lord Bridge of Harwich; Lord Brandon of Oakbrook and Lord Templeman (dissenting).

[10] HN(80)46, Section G (as revised). See [1986] 1 AC 112, 179–80.

[11] For more detailed accounts and commentary on the decision, see A Bainham, 'The Balance of Power in Family Decisions' (1986) 45 *CLJ* 262; A Bainham, *Children, Parents and the State* (London, Sweet & Maxwell, 1988) ch 3; S de Cruz, 'Parents Doctors and Children: the *Gillick* Case and Beyond' [1987] *JSWL* 93; J Devereux, 'The Capacity of a Child in Australia to Consent to Medical Treatment—*Gillick* Revisited?' (1991) 11 *OJLS* 283, 289–94; M Jones, 'Consent to Medical Treatment by Minors after *Gillick*' (1986) 2 *Professional Negligence* 41; I Kennedy, 'The Doctor, the Pill and the 15-year-old Girl' in I Kennedy, *Treat me Right, Essays in Medical Law and Ethics* (Oxford, Oxford University Press, 1988) ch 5; S Lee, 'Towards a Jurisprudence of Consent' in J Eekelaar and S Ball (eds), *Oxford Essays in Jurisprudence* (3rd Series, Oxford, Oxford University Press, 1987) ch 9; J Montgomery, 'Children as Property?' (1988) 51 *MLR* 323; P Parkinson, 'The *Gillick* Case—Just What has it Decided?' [1986] *Fam Law* 11; GL Peiris, 'The *Gillick* Case: Parental Authority, Teenage Independence and Public Policy' [1987] *Current Legal Problems* 93; and G Williams, 'The *Gillick* Saga' [1985] *NLJ* 1156–8 and 1179–82.

[12] As suggested in *Re Agar-Ellis* (1883) 24 Ch D 317.

[13] [1970] 1 QB 357.

[14] *Ibid*, at 369.

[15] [1986] 1 AC 112 at 173D–E.

[16] *Ibid*, at 174B–C.

He enumerated five conditions on which the doctor would need to be satisfied if he were to be justified in proceeding without a parent's consent or knowledge:

(1) that the girl (although under 16 years of age) will understand his advice; (2) that he cannot persuade her to inform her parents or to allow him to inform the parents that she is seeking contraceptive advice; (3) that she is very likely to begin or to continue having sexual intercourse with or without contraceptive treatment; (4) that unless she receives contraceptive advice or treatment her physical or mental health or both are likely to suffer; (5) that her best interests require him to give her contraceptive advice, treatment or both without the parental consent.[17]

Lord Scarman agreed with Lord Fraser's opinion. While acknowledging that parental rights 'clearly do exist, and they do not wholly disappear until the age of majority', Lord Scarman went on to declare more explicitly than Lord Fraser that the underlying principle of the law, as exposed by Blackstone and acknowledged in the case law, is that:

parental right yields to the child's right to make his own decisions when he reaches a sufficient understanding and intelligence to be capable of making up his own mind on the matter requiring decision.[18]

Applying this approach to the medical context, he set a stringent test for competence,[19] and held that:

as a matter of law the parental right to determine whether or not their minor child below the age of 16 will have medical treatment terminates if and when the child achieves a sufficient understanding and intelligence to enable him or her to understand fully what is proposed.[20]

R (Axon) v Secretary of State for Health (Family Planning Association intervening)

Over 20 years later, in *Axon*, the High Court addressed similar questions in judicial review proceedings in respect of an updated version of the relevant Guidance,[21] this time in the context of abortion advice and treatment. A mother, Ms Susan Axon, sought a declaration that medical professionals are under no

---

¹⁷   *Ibid*, at 174D–E.

¹⁸   *Ibid*, at 186D.

¹⁹   *Ibid*, at 189D: 'There are moral and family questions, especially her relationship with her parents; long-term problems associated with the emotional impact of pregnancy and its termination; and there are the risks to health of sexual intercourse at her age, risks which contraception may diminish but cannot eliminate. It follows that a doctor will have to satisfy himself that she is able to appraise these factors before he can safely proceed upon the basis that she has at law capacity to consent to contraceptive treatment.'

²⁰   [1986] 1 AC 112 at 188H–189B.

²¹   Guidance for Doctors and other Health Professionals on the Provision of Advice and Treatment to Young People under 16 on Contraception, Sexual and Reproductive Heath (29 July 2004), gateway reference No 3382. Relevant parts of the Guidance are set out at [2006] EWHC 37 (Admin), [22]–[24].

obligation to maintain confidentiality in relation to such matters unless disclosure might prejudice the child's physical or mental health. She argued (and sought declarations to the effect) that the Guidance misrepresented *Gillick*, and failed to discharge the state's positive obligation to give practical and effective protection to her rights under Article 8(1) of the ECHR. Rejecting her claim, Silber J concluded that there was no such misrepresentation, and that the approach in *Gillick* 'was and is of general application to *all* forms of medical advice and treatment', including therefore abortion advice and treatment. These situations could also be dealt with by way of Lord Fraser's guidelines, which Silber J clarified were legal preconditions[22] and to be strictly observed. His Lordship then re-wrote Lord Fraser's guidelines to include within his first guideline (ie that the child understands the advice) the stringent test for capacity set out by Lord Scarman in *Gillick*, and explained that 'all relevant matters' were included within the meaning of 'understanding'.[23]

Silber J cited Articles 16(1) and 12(1) of the United Nations Convention on the Rights of the Child and the judgment of Thorpe LJ in *Mabon v Mabon*[24] as illustrations that:

the right of young people to make decisions about their own lives by themselves at the expense of the views of their parents has now become an increasingly important and accepted feature of family life.

And he concluded:

In the light of this change in the landscape of family matters, in which rights of children are becoming increasingly important, it would be ironic and indeed not acceptable now to retreat from the approach adopted in the *Gillick* case … and to impose additional new duties on medical professionals to disclose information to parents of their younger patients.[25]

Addressing Ms Axon's argument based on Article 8(1) of the ECHR, Silber J opined that:

any right to family life on the part of a parent dwindles as their child gets older and is able to understand the consequence of different choices and then to make decisions relating to them.[26]

And that 'this autonomy must undermine any Article 8 rights of a parent to family life'.[27] Accordingly:

---

[22] Above n 7, at [110] and [111].
[23] *Ibid*, at [154]. See also the passage from Lord Scarman's opinion set out at n 19 above.
[24] [2005] EWCA Civ 634.
[25] Above n 7, at [80].
[26] *Ibid*, at [129].
[27] *Ibid*, at [130].

parents do not have Article 8 rights to be notified of any advice of a medical professional after the young person is able to look after himself or herself and make his or her own decisions.[28]

Given that the guidance has the additional safeguard that the advice/treatment must be in the child's best interests, in his Lordship's view there was nothing in the Guidance which interferes with a parent's Article 8 rights.[29] Even if the Guidance did so interfere, Silber J held that the infringement could be justified under Article 8(2). The legislative objective (of reducing unwanted pregnancies and addressing sexually transmitted diseases) is sufficiently important to justify limiting parents' Article 8 rights; Lord Fraser's guidelines were rationally connected to that objective and impaired freedom no more than necessary to achieve it.[30]

To What Extent Has English Law Recognised Children's Autonomy?

Rachel Taylor, in an illuminating commentary on the *Axon* case,[31] argues that Silber J's repeated emphasis on children's autonomy, especially his highlighting the increased importance of allowing young people to make decisions about their own lives at the expense of their parents' views, might be interpreted as signalling that the basis of decision-making about competent children is their autonomy, not their welfare. Thus, there would need to be respect for the decisions of mature children, even if the consequences are difficult to accept.[32] This would indeed be a principled approach. Taylor acknowledges, however, that whether the decision will be viewed as a case promoting child autonomy remains to be seen.

For three reasons, I doubt whether it will. First, and perhaps most importantly, Silber J's judgment makes it more difficult to argue an autonomy rights interpretation of *Gillick* since he re-writes the Fraser guidelines so that they now require both a very high level of understanding *and* a conclusion that it is in the child's best interests to have the treatment *without parental consent*. Any argument that *Gillick* recognised that the child's interests (other than the autonomy interest) were protected simply by the child's achievement of a high level of understanding seems more difficult now.

Secondly, recent case law cited by Silber J, such as *Mabon v Mabon*,[33] while acknowledging an increased focus on children's autonomy, also has a strong focus on child welfare. Indeed, Thorpe LJ in *Mabon* says:

---

[28]   *Ibid*, at [132].
[29]   *Ibid*, at [134].
[30]   *Ibid*, at [150]–[152].
[31]   Taylor, above n 8.
[32]   *Ibid*, at 93–4.
[33]   Above n 24.

In testing the sufficiency of a child's understanding I would not say that welfare has no place. If direct participation would pose an obvious risk of harm to the child arising out of the nature of the continuing proceedings and, if the child is incapable of comprehending that risk, then the judge is entitled to find that sufficient understanding has not been demonstrated.[34]

Furthermore, it is perhaps unlikely that Court of Appeal decisions on children's rights to freedom of expression and participation will have much impact on long-standing Court of Appeal authorities on the approach to children's refusal of medical treatment where such refusal risks irreparable harm or death.

Thirdly, with respect, Silber J may be wrong in his interpretation of Article 8. In reaching his view of Article 8 as a dwindling right, his Lordship relied on Lester's and Pannick's observation that: 'As the child matures, the burden of showing on-going family life by reference to substantive links or factors grows.'[35] However, as Taylor observes, this passage is not directed to the question of parental control, but 'whether a parent can enjoy "family life" with adult children who are no longer dependent or resident with her'.[36] Furthermore, Silber J refers throughout his judgment to the right to family life. In fact, Article 8 provides a right to *respect for* family life. It may be doubted whether respect for an aspect of family life within Article 8 ought to be, and is, extinguished simply upon a child's acquisition of capacity. It is certainly arguable that respect for a parent's personal interest in protecting a child against harm requires that the child's autonomy interest ought to be weighed against that aspect of the parent's existing family life with the child, rather than being automatically extinguished upon the child's acquisition of capacity. All of this, however, rather begs the question, which was not addressed by Silber J, whether the *Gillick* case recognised that parental responsibility was usurped simply by the child's acquisition of capacity.

Gillick has certainly attracted a children's autonomy rights discourse. The Children's Legal Centre proclaimed *Gillick* as a 'landmark decision for children's rights',[37] describing it as:

> the first legal judgment which unequivocally recognises the right of young people to make decisions about their lives and their bodies if they are old enough to have a mature appreciation of the issues and to make up their own minds.[38]

Perhaps most influentially, at least within academic writing, John Eekelaar's interpretation, in an article[39] and case commentary[40] respectively, announced 'the emergence of children's rights' and 'the eclipse of parental rights'. Drawing upon

---

[34] Above n 24, at [29].
[35] A Lester and D Pannick, *Human Rights Law and Practice* (2nd edn, London, LexisNexis UK, 2004) [4.8.48].
[36] Taylor, above n 8, 90.
[37] (1985) 22 *Childright* 11.
[38] *Ibid.*
[39] Above n 3.
[40] Above n 4.

parts of Lord Scarman's speech, and arguing that Lord Fraser's opinion should be read to the same effect,[41] he suggested that:

> The significance of Lord Scarman's opinion with respect to children's autonomy interests cannot be over-rated. It follows from his reasoning that, where a child has reached capacity, there is no room for a parent to impose a contrary view, *even if this is more in accord with the child's best interests*. For its legal superiority to the child's decision can rest only on its status as a parental right. But this is extinguished when the child reaches full capacity.[42]

On this view, the law reconciled the child's autonomy interest with the need to protect the child's other interests 'through the empirical application of the concept of the acquisition of full capacity',[43] namely intellectual understanding supplemented by emotional maturity.[44] Children had thus been given:

> in wider measure than ever before, that most dangerous but most precious of rights: the right to make their own mistakes.[45]

There have, of course, been more moderate interpretations. Andrew Bainham, for example, suggested that the case represented 'a small but significant shift towards the thinking of the child liberationist school',[46] while cautioning that one should not 'equate this with a policy of legal autonomy or independence for children'.[47] For Bainham, the case supported 'a participatory model of decision making',[48] its true value being in highlighting the 'independent interests of parents and children and the need for the law to find a means of accommodating their potentially conflicting claims'.[49]

Despite this more moderate interpretation, however, the children's autonomy rights reading of *Gillick* has had considerable force in the literature, perhaps because it coheres with a general trend of greater acknowledgment of children's rights and with the approach to adult autonomy. The medical context, in which the notions of consent and autonomy are often equated, may also have played its part. But is that interpretation the most plausible? I shall begin to answer this question by examining the public portrayal of the *Gillick* case, and how the issue was characterised by counsel and the judiciary. As I shall seek to show, these features of the case provide some reasons for viewing with caution the suggestion

---

[41] *Ibid*, 6–7.
[42] Above n 3, 181.
[43] *Ibid.*
[44] The case would thus apparently require a re-orientation of the court's approach to custody disputes on divorce (see J Eekelaar, 'Gillick in the divorce court' (1986) 136 *NLJ* 184); and in wardship (see Eekelaar, above n 3, 181).
[45] Above n 3, at 182.
[46] Bainham, 'The Balance of Power in Family Decisions', above n 11, 275.
[47] *Ibid.*
[48] Bainham, *Children, Parents and the State*, above n 11, 72.
[49] *Ibid*, 74.

that *Gillick* accorded to competent children a general right to act contrary to their own interests.

Public Portrayal of the Gillick Debate

Mrs Gillick's 'crusade',[50] as Lord Templeman described it in the course of his opinion, 'provoked great controversy which is not legal in character',[51] and there are many indications that the House of Lords' judgments in *Gillick* were influenced by the case's perceived social consequences. It has been observed that their Lordships' disagreement was 'largely, perhaps entirely, brought about by divergent views on policy'.[52] Given these observations, the public portrayal of the *Gillick* debate warrants careful consideration, as an important background against which their Lordships' opinions may be understood.

As early as July 1983, when Mrs Gillick's campaign first made front-page news in *The Times*, it was reported that she wanted 'to retain her duty as a mother to the exclusion of any other person',[53] seeing the issue as a matter of whether there was a 'right of the state or doctors, or outside interfering authorities to meddle with the sacred duties of parents'.[54] For Mrs Gillick, therefore, the case was a battle between doctors and parents for the right to determine children's welfare, and she launched a three-pronged attack on doctors, arguing that the availability of contraception involved a social not a clinical judgment, that doctors were encouraging illicit sex, and that they had a vested (commercial) interest in providing birth control,[55] which was harmful to children.

Mrs Gillick's opponents adopted different views, but the arguments inhabited the same terrain: organisations representing the medical profession urged that 'doctors had to act in their patient's best interests'.[56] A *Times* editorial, following the House of Lords decision, summed up the arguments of each faction:

---

[50] [1986] 1 AC 112 at 206G–H.

[51] *Ibid*, at 202G–H.

[52] Williams, above n 11, 1157. And see: [1986] 1 AC 112 at 166 (Lord Fraser), 176 (Lord Scarman), 195 F–G (Lord Brandon) and 207 (Lord Templeman).

[53] *The Times* (19 July 1983) 3. See also her letter to *The Times*, 13 January 1984. See also F Cannell, 'Concepts of parenthood: the Warnock Report, the Gillick debate, and modern myths' (1990) 17 *American Ethnologist* 667 (examining both broadsheet and tabloid press coverage, and concluding that the debate 'mainly concerned the attempt to draw a line between "orderly" and "disorderly" sexuality'). See also [1986] 1 AC 112 at 202D–E (Lord Templeman).

[54] Interview with Mrs Gillick reported in *The Guardian* (19 November 1984) 12. Cannell, above n 53, 680, comments: 'The press often described the atmosphere of the Gillick family home as "Victorian"' and 'portrayed the family as a little fortress of self-sufficiency, doing without television and modern gadgets and relying instead on family music, games of charades, and their own cooperative labor power'.

[55] J Lewis with F Cannell, 'The Politics of Motherhood in the 1980s: Warnock, Gillick and Feminists' (1986) 13 *Journal of Law and Society* 321, 326.

[56] Dr Havard, Secretary of the British Medical Association, *The Times* (2 December 1983) (a view supported by the General Medical Council and the DHSS). Some doctors, however, supported Mrs Gillick's position. See, eg 'Rebel GP opposes pill for youngsters' *The Times* (12 November 1983) 3.

The main contention on one side is that the law ought to be arranged so as to lend support to those parents who are conscientiously doing their duty to care for the health and morals of their children in their upbringing ... The main contention of the other side is that the law ought to be arranged so as to permit effective help to be brought to girls under the age of 16 who have fallen into the practice of sexual intercourse.[57]

Each side thus sought protection for children according to their own perceptions of the potential harmful consequences of under-age sexual intercourse. Whilst Mrs Gillick's strong position on family autonomy certainly left scope for the implication that, on her defeat, children would be freed from her allegedly restrictive modes of child-rearing, there is evidence that generally neither those involved in the debate, nor those reporting it, perceived the issue as one of children's autonomy rights. The rare newspaper articles of the time that took a children's rights perspective either focused on the 'child's right to medical welfare'[58] or had a rather narrow origin in the Children's Legal Centre.[59]

Counsel's Arguments

A focus on children's welfare is also evident in counsel's submissions. Mrs Gillick's counsel explicitly argued that the appeal was 'not about parents' rights against children's rights', but about 'doctors' rights'.[60] The arguments of counsel for the Department of Health and Social Security (DHSS) had a similar focus. Rather than taking a children's rights perspective or inviting the court to investigate the relationship between the generations, counsel focused much more narrowly on the potential commission of a tort or criminal offence by a doctor[61] and consent as a necessary prerequisite to the lawful performance of the doctor's professional duty. Indeed, counsel asserted that 'the cases on the age of discretion are of no assistance on the issue of the child's capacity to consent',[62] and stated:

It is not necessary for the department to submit that a girl under 16 has the wisdom of an adult. It merely has to be shown that a girl of that age has capacity to consent to medical treatment ... The concern in the end is about how a doctor is to perform his professional duty.[63]

---

[57]   Leading article, 18 October 1985, 17.

[58]   See D Pannick, 'A Bitter Pill to Swallow' *The Guardian* (22 December 1984) 15 (arguing that the Court of Appeal decision in *Gillick* was 'incompatible with children's rights').

[59]   See, eg P Newell, 'One law for parents, another for children' *The Guardian* (5 October 1983) 13 (writer connected with the Children's Legal Centre); 'Children's Rights: Gillick's gift to the kids' *The Economist* (26 October 1985) 65–6 (drawing on the views of the Children's Legal Centre). An extremely rare example among general writers in the press is the comment of P Toynbee, *The Guardian* (19 November 1984) 12, that 'it is a matter of the rights of children to make important decisions for themselves, if they choose'.

[60]   [1986] 1 AC 112 at 159.

[61]   *Ibid*, at 151.

[62]   *Ibid*, at 155.

[63]   *Ibid*, at 153.

On this view there was no conflict in law between the duties of parents and doctors since they were both duties to act in the best interests of the child. Thus, in the submission of counsel for the DHSS, the question for the court was:

whether a doctor should have a discretion to act in the best interests of the child without having resort to the court.[64]

Judicial Perception of the Issue

Not surprisingly, judicial perception of the issue bears a striking resemblance to how the case was argued. Lord Fraser held that the guidance which was the subject matter of the appeal conveyed the message that, in the last resort, the decision whether or not to prescribe was a matter for the clinical judgment of the doctor.[65] The central issue in the appeal, therefore, was whether such prescription could ever be lawful.[66] There are also frequent pointers that Lord Scarman perceived the issue as one of resolving potential conflict between parental 'right' and doctor's duty. Early in his opinion, he acknowledged that Mrs Gillick:

performed a notable public service in directing judicial attention to the problems arising from the interaction of parental right and a doctor's duty.[67]

For Lord Scarman, the guidance clearly implied that in exceptional cases the parental right could be *overridden in exercise of clinical judgment.*[68] He character-ised the question in the appeal as the extent and duration of *parental right* and the circumstances in which it can be *overridden by the exercise of medical judgment,*[69] and made an explicit link between this perception of the issue and his search for principle when he explained that the difficulty in the search for principle is that parental right and doctor's duty may point in different direc-tions.

While, therefore, the House of Lords' opinions make passing references to teenage independence,[70] the central issue as perceived by the majority was not whether a child had a *right* to make his or her own decisions. Rather, in line with the public portrayal of the debate, the focus was on resolving the potentially conflicting claims of doctors and parents to know what was in a child's best interests.[71]

---

[64] *Ibid*, at 154A–B.
[65] *Ibid*, at 164F–G.
[66] *Ibid*, at 165E–F.
[67] *Ibid*, at 176C–D (emphasis added).
[68] *Ibid*, at 180H–181A.
[69] *Ibid*, at 184G–H.
[70] *Ibid*, at 199 (Lord Templeman) and 182H (Lord Scarman).
[71] A perception entirely consistent with their Lordships' earlier rejection of an application by the Children's Legal Centre to make submissions or instruct counsel as *amicus curiae* on behalf of children in general. See (1985) May *Legal Action* 3. The DHSS consented, but Mrs Gillick did not. No reasons were given by their Lordships. Note also Eekelaar's comment that '[t]he public debate which

It is certainly difficult to see *Gillick* as a binding precedent for the view that children have been given such autonomy rights, given that its *ratio decidendi* must at least bear some relation to judicial perception of the material facts and issues in the case. The case could be narrowly construed as confined to contraceptive treatment,[72] or only to NHS treatment as Lord Fraser appeared to indicate,[73] or more plausibly simply to medical treatment.[74] Even in the latter case, the most *Gillick* could represent as a binding precedent would be the child's power to consent to medical treatment offered in the child's best interests. Putting the case at its most abstract, far from declaring a child's unqualified right to make his or her own mistakes, it would appear only to endorse a child's power to accept someone else's bona fide, yet possibly mistaken, view of what is in a child's interests.

Analysis of the Majority Opinions in Gillick

Given the similarity of sources on which Lords Fraser and Scarman draw, and indeed the similarity in their reasoning, it is not unreasonable to suggest that both adopted Lord Scarman's principle that parental right yields to the child's right. However, it is necessary to examine carefully how their Lordships understood this principle, in particular what they envisaged as the point at which 'parental right yields'. One must be careful not to make an unjustified jump from the fact that the law treats a child as a person with capacities and rights, and that intellectual ability is not irrelevant, to the conclusion that such ability is determinative of the relationship between parents and children.

It is unlikely that either Lord Fraser or Lord Scarman adopted a simple child-development model of the parent/child relationship. Their Lordships were concerned to ensure that the law retains capacity for development, Lord Scarman commenting that this is 'an area where the law must be sensitive to human development *and social change*'.[75] For the law to defer simply to the child's empirically ascertainable capacities would, in the event of marked social change, risk placing upon it the very mark of obsolescence that Lord Scarman was at pains to avoid. It is more likely, therefore, that Lords Fraser and Scarman recognised a socially constructed, socially changing parent/child relationship. As Lord Fraser explained:

> Social customs change, and the law ought to, and does in fact, have regard to such changes when they are of major importance.[76]

---

surrounded the litigation tended to revolve around the competing claims of parents and doctors to determine children's interests': above n 3, 178.

[72] See de Cruz , above n 11, 100–1.

[73] [1986] 1 AC 112 at 165H–166A.

[74] The case has, of course, been cited in other contexts: see, eg *Re Roddy (A Child) (Identification: Restriction on Publication)* [2003] EWHC 2927 (Fam).

[75] *Ibid*, at 186B (emphasis added).

[76] *Ibid*, at 171F. See also Munby J in *Re Roddy*, above n 74, at [51]–[52], who set out passages from Lord Scarman's opinion, including his general principle, and indicated that 'precisely the same

Explaining current perceptions of the parent/child relationship, he said that 'most wise parents relax their control gradually as the child develops and encourage him or her to become increasingly independent' and:

> the degree of parental control actually exercised over a particular child does in practice vary considerably according to his understanding and intelligence.[77]

This passage supports a social construction of the parent/child relationship, which gives greater recognition to children's independence in the light of their abilities than in former times, but it is difficult to see it as support for the view that competent children now possess absolute autonomy. The presumably careful choice of the word 'hesitate' in Lord Denning's dictum in *Hewer v Bryant* suggests no more than that the child's wishes will carry more weight the older he or she is, and does not preclude the view that, where necessary, they could be overridden in a child's interests.

The difficulty with simply taking at face value Lord Scarman's statements that parental right 'yields' or 'terminates' upon a child's acquisition of capacity to make his or her own decision is that there are other statements in his judgment which, if also taken at face value, are inconsistent with that view. For example, Eekelaar's position (at least in theory) leads to the conclusion that where a child is competent in all spheres of his or her life, parental powers (as far as the common law is concerned) are extinguished. Yet this does not sit easily with Lord Scarman's statement that parental rights 'do not wholly disappear until majority'. Furthermore, as Lee has usefully pointed out, Lord Scarman's 'quest for principle yields several different formulations'[78] which, linguistically, are capable of connoting different emphases to autonomy and paternalism. It becomes important, therefore, not simply to view Lord Scarman's statement of general principle in isolation, but to seek an understanding of it in the context of the reasoning from which it emerged. In particular, Lord Scarman did not reject all of the old case law. He suggested that earlier 'age of discretion'[79] cases, and specifically *R v Howes*,[80] may afford 'a clue to the true principle of the law'.[81]

Lord Scarman explained that the principle underlying the habeas corpus cases was that 'an order would be refused if the child had *sufficient intelligence and*

---

principles must articulate the court's decision-making'. He then cited in support Lord Upjohn's opinion in *J and Another v C and Others* [1970] AC 668 at 723, that the law and practice relating to children must 'develop by reflecting and adopting the changing views, as the years go by, of reasonable men and women, the parents of children, on the proper treatment and methods of bringing up children'.

[77] [1986] 1 AC 112 at 171D–F.

[78] Lee, above n 11, 203.

[79] Lord Scarman explained that these cases were ones in which a father issued a writ of habeas corpus to secure the return of his child who had left home without consent. The courts would refuse an order if the child had attained an age of discretion. By analogy with the Abduction Acts, the first of which appeared in the sixteenth century, the age of discretion was set at 14 for boys and 16 for girls.

[80] (1860) 3 E & E 332.

[81] [1986] 1 AC 112 at 183F.

understanding to make up his own mind.[82] Given that these italicised words are
effectively the ones used by Lord Scarman in his general principle, and that that
principle is said to have been expounded by Blackstone and acknowledged in case
law, Lord Scarman's analysis of the reasoning in *R v Howes* is an important
indication of the sense in which he uses those words. Whilst rejecting the fixed
age limits in the earlier case law, he cited the following passage from *R v Howes*
and intimated that the reasoning and principle on which such limits were based
remain relevant today:

> Now the cases which have been decided on this subject shew that, although a father is
> entitled to the custody of his children till they attain the age of 21, this court will not
> grant a habeas corpus to hand a child which is below that age over to its father, provided
> it has attained an age of sufficient discretion to enable it to exercise a wise choice for its
> own interests. The whole question is, what is that age of discretion? We repudiate
> utterly, as most dangerous, the notion that any intellectual precocity in an individual
> female child can hasten the period which appears to have been fixed by statute for the
> arrival of the age of discretion; *for that very precocity, if uncontrolled, might very probably
> lead to her irreparable injury.* The legislature has given us a guide, which we may safely
> follow in pointing out 16 as the age up to which the father's right to the custody of his
> female child is to continue; and short of which such a child has no discretion to consent
> to leaving him.[83]

This reasoning reveals that the prerequisite to declaring an age of discretion was
adequate protection of the child, with the age set at a point which aimed to
ensure that the child would not take decisions that would lead to his or her
irreparable harm. Drawing on this reasoning, and adopting an approach which
was implicit in Lord Fraser's speech,[84] Lord Scarman explained the current law
thus:

> While it is unrealistic to treat a 16th century Act as a safe guide in the matter of a girl's
> discretion, and while no modern judge would dismiss the intelligence of a teenage girl
> as 'intellectual precocity', we can agree with Cockburn CJ as to the principle of the
> law—the attainment by a child of an age of sufficient discretion to exercise a *wise choice
> in his or her interests.*[85]

In the light of the emphasis in *R v Howes* on child protection, it is submitted that
it is unlikely that Lord Scarman envisaged that children should be declared to

---

[82]   *Ibid*, at 187D (emphasis added).

[83]   Above n 80, at 336–7 (Cockburn CJ, emphasis added).

[84]   Parker LJ, in the Court of Appeal, had preferred parental rights to a fixed age rather than what
he saw as the 'singularly unattractive and impractical' alternative of determining 'in relation to a
particular child and a particular matter, whether he or she is of sufficient understanding to make a
responsible and reasonable decision' (see [1986] 1 AC 112 at 124F–G). Whilst indicating that, with
respect, he had reached a different conclusion as to parental rights to a fixed age, Lord Fraser did not
question Parker LJ's formulation of the alternative, which appears entirely in line with Cockburn CJ's
principle (see [1986] 1 AC 112 at 171).

[85]   [1986] 1 AC 112 at 187H–188A (emphasis added).

have capacity and then permitted to carry through decisions which would seriously prejudice their interests.

On the above analysis of Lord Scarman's general principle, parental power is not usurped simply by an empirical finding of a child's intellectual ability and emotional maturity. Rather, whilst those factors are of importance, the child's power to take a decision is ultimately acknowledged in the absence of the need for parental powers of protection. It may be objected that this leaves redundant the process of determining competence, for why should one bother to determine competence if ultimately the question is whether or not the actions are beneficial for the child?[86] However, the child's competence remains important for a number of reasons. It will be important as a defence to a charge of battery. Practically it may be a prerequisite to the proposed activity. Taking the facts of *Gillick* as an example, it would be difficult to see the provision of contraceptives to a child as a credible intervention unless the child understands the 'workings' of the contraceptive pill. More generally, the child's capacity will be an important factor in determining where the child's interests lie.

Far from asserting an unqualified acquiescence to the competent child's wishes, Lord Scarman's aim, in his own words, was:

> to keep the law in line with *social experience*, which is that many girls are fully able to make *sensible decisions* about many matters before they reach the age of 16,[87]

and 'to establish a principle flexible enough to enable justice to be achieved by its application to the particular circumstances'.[88] As Austin observes:

> Lords Scarman and Fraser did not portray children as isolated individuals. Rather, they required evidence of sensible and honest thinking that locates the child within relationships.[89]

With this analysis it becomes possible to understand why Lord Fraser saw the solution in the appeal as depending on welfare, and why Lord Scarman was able to agree with him.

Eekelaar has sought to underplay the potential that this part of Lord Fraser's opinion and his guidelines have to conflict with his interpretation of Lord Scarman's opinion. He has suggested that the part of Lord Fraser's opinion dealing with parental rights 'is placed firmly within the context of medical

---

[86] A point made by John Eekelaar in correspondence with the author dated 18 February 2002.
[87] [1986] 1 AC 112 at 191B–C (emphasis added).
[88] *Ibid*, at 186C–D.
[89] G Austin, 'Righting a Child's Right to Refuse Medical Treatment, Section 11 of the New Zealand Bill of Rights Act and the *Gillick* competent child' (1992) 7 *Otago Law Review* 578, 594. See also J Bridgeman, 'Because we care? The medical treatment of children' in S Sheldon and M Thomson (eds), *Feminist Perspectives on Health Care Law* (London, Cavendish, 1998) 106, arguing that in case law on children's refusal of consent, the search for a legal basis for providing treatment may be 'motivated by the circumstances of existing relationships, a sense of responsibility and sentiments of care and affection'.

treatment, whereas Lord Scarman discusses parental rights on a general level'.[90] In addition, he has argued,[91] along with other commentators,[92] that conditions (2) to (5) are matters for professional discipline only and have no reference to legal liability. However, at least three objections may be raised to this approach.

First, it may be observed that Lord Scarman agreed with Lord Fraser's opinion, not the reverse. Accordingly, Lord Fraser's opinion should be the starting point of any analysis, and Lord Scarman's opinion should be read in the light of his agreement with it.[93] By contrast, a radical interpretation of *Gillick* is forced to discount the significance of certain passages of Lord Fraser's opinion to correspond with such an interpretation.

Secondly, it is not immediately apparent why the medical context of Lord Fraser's discussion should invalidate any inferences that could be drawn therefrom as to the nature of parental rights in general. Lord Fraser's more general observations on the nature of parental rights, drawing on Blackstone, do not appear to be tainted by the fact that they appear in a section of his opinion headed 'The parents' rights and duties in respect of medical treatment of their child'. Furthermore, Lord Scarman discussed parental rights under the heading 'Parental rights and the age of consent' (clearly referring to consent to medical treatment), so it would appear difficult to extricate his discussion wholly from the medical context.

Thirdly, as we now know from *Axon*, Lord Fraser's guidelines are legal preconditions. The fact that conditions (2) to (5) have no reference to legal *liability* does not mean that they are devoid of legal significance and can be simply ignored. Lord Fraser's guidance is clearly influenced by the role parents have to play in their child's life.[94] It will be observed that condition (5) is not simply a requirement that treatment be in the child's best interests, but rather that it be in the child's interests to have such treatment *without parental consent.*[95] The legal significance of Lord Fraser's guidelines is that they demonstrate the scope of parental privilege and how, in the context of medical practice with its

---

[90] Above n 4, 6.

[91] *Ibid*, 7.

[92] Montgomery, above n 11, 339 ('they are obiter, and if they have force it is as the content of the doctor's duty of care in negligence'); and A Grubb, 'Contraceptive Advice and Medical Treatment for Children' [1986] 45 *CLJ* 3, 5.

[93] The facility with which Eekelaar has been able to focus on Lord Scarman's speech has arguably been aided by the tendency amongst commentators to identify differences in the majority opinions. There is a range of views as to the nature and extent of the divergence: SM Cretney, 'Family Law' [1995] *All ER Annual Review* 173, 175; Parkinson, above n 11, 13–14; Kennedy, above n 11, 96; and K McK Norrie, 'Gillick again: the House of Lords decides' (1986) 10 *SLT* 69; cf Lee, above n 11, 206; A Grubb and D Pearl, 'Medicine, Health, the Family and the Law' (1986) 16 *Fam Law* 227, 238–9; and de Cruz, above n 11.

[94] See McK Norrie, *ibid*, 70.

[95] cf Williams, above n 11, 1179, who in setting out what he terms Lord Fraser's five ethical precepts leaves out the words which refer to parental consent in ethical precept number five. Williams' omission is hardly surprising, however, since he views the parental rights issue in *Gillick* as a misdirection of judicial effort (at 1182).

special feature of patient confidentiality, that privilege is to be negotiated with children's interests in decision making. The guidance illustrates that the doctor must ensure, in what is an extension[96] of his clinical judgment, that the parents' duty of protection can be safely abandoned.[97] There is no reason to suppose that this does not reflect their Lordships' earlier conclusions as to the general principles of the law.

The difference of emphasis in the majority opinions does not compel the conclusion that their Lordships are not united as to the general approach. Lord Bridge fully agreed with the reasoning in both speeches,[98] and while he could have agreed with opinions with different emphases, it is unlikely that he could have agreed with two fundamentally opposed positions.

As noted earlier, Lord Scarman introduced a more stringent test for the child's capacity, going beyond mere understanding of the nature of the advice given. The necessity that the girl be able to appraise these factors appears to require that she be able to justify (beyond the obvious fact that treatment is being prescribed in her medical interests) that what she proposes is in her interests. From the doctor's perspective, it entails a judgment of the child's capacity to make a wise choice. In line with the analysis of Lord Scarman's opinion above, this translates into a judgment of what is in the child's interests. As Williams has pointed out, the theoretical distinction 'between having the capacity to make a wise decision and actually making it' may be 'too fine for forensic use'.[99] It is likely, therefore, that Lords Fraser and Scarman reached substantially the same conclusion by different routes.

THE SCOPE OF PARENTAL DISCRETION

The foregoing analysis suggests that parental decision-making should be guided by the welfare of the child, taking due account of the role that a child's capacity may play in indicating where the child's welfare lies.[100] In practice, however, parents have considerable discretion as to how parental responsibility is exercised. Beyond any specific parental duty, and in the absence of any court order, the law does not require parents to act in particular ways which positively advance a child's welfare or best interests,[101] nor is the scope of parental

---

[96] For detailed arguments supporting the view that Lord Fraser extends the doctor's role, see Kennedy, above n 11, 94–5.

[97] cf Kennedy, above n 11, 94, who suggests that Lord Fraser takes this view as a matter of public policy.

[98] [1986] 1 AC 112 at 195B.

[99] Williams, above n 11, 1180.

[100] See, eg in the context of medical treatment, *Re J (a minor) (wardship: medical treatment)* [1991] Fam 33 at 41: 'The parents owe the child a duty to give or to withhold consent in the best interests of the child and without regard to their own interests.'

[101] BM Dickens, 'The Modern Function and Limits of Parental Rights' (1981) 97 *LQR* 462, 464.

discretion drawn in such a way as to avoid all harm to the child.[102] This approach probably reflects at least two considerations: the fact that welfare is a vague concept within which there is scope for legitimate differences of opinion as to what might positively promote a child's welfare;[103] and that there are limits to what the law is capable of enforcing with regard to the day-to-day private lives of parents and children. The law therefore permits parents' discretion in matters of parental responsibility provided the discretion does not conflict with any parental duties, nor violate children's interests in such a way that the law has declared unacceptable.[104] As discussed in the introductory chapter to this volume, the boundaries of acceptable behaviour are drawn by the criminal law and criteria by which the state may intervene in family life to protect a child.

In addition, Bainham has cogently argued by reference to *R v D*[105] (upholding a father's conviction for kidnap of his five-year-old son) and *R v Rahman*[106] (upholding a father's conviction for false imprisonment of his teenage daughter) that parental powers are bounded by reasonableness, in the sense that they must not be exercised unreasonably.[107] In the former case, a majority of the House of Lords appeared to indicate that the unlawfulness of the father's act turned upon a presumed lack of consent on the part of the child, which may be equated with the reasonableness of the act. In the latter, the detention was in such circumstances 'as to take it out of the realm of reasonable discipline'.[108] Bainham argues that it follows from these adjudications that the fathers exceeded their lawful authority, that parents' powers are automatically so qualified, and that in dealings with a child a third party may need to have regard to the reasonableness of a parent's view.[109] However, other than perhaps in cases requiring confidentiality, cases of necessity, or those requiring the child's very short-term protection, a third party should perhaps exercise caution in seeking to override the perceived unreasonable views of a parent with parental responsibility without seeking court approval. In *Glass v United Kingdom*,[110] for example, the European Court of Human Rights found that the Article 8 right of a 12-year-old severely mentally and physically disabled child to respect for private life had been breached when

---

[102]   I should like to thank Jonathan Herring for this observation.

[103]   Bainham, *Children, Parents and the State*, above n 11, 59.

[104]   Whether or not the law actually intervenes is another question.

[105]   [1984] AC 778.

[106]   (1985) 81 Cr App R 349.

[107]   This may also be supported by reference to the defence of reasonable chastisement in the Children and Young Persons Act 1933 s 1, although this no longer provides a defence to a charge of assault occasioning actual bodily harm or a more serious offence against the person (see Children Act 2004 s 58).

[108]   See the discussion in Bainham, above n 103, 54–7.

[109]   *Ibid*, 57.

[110]   (Application No 61827/00) [2004] 1 FLR 1019; and see in relation to medical treatment *Re J (a minor) (wardship: medical treatment)* [1991] Fam 33 at 41: 'if time permits, [doctors] must obtain the consent of the parents before undertaking serious invasive treatment.'

doctors administered morphine against his parent's wishes. The court held that the onus was on the NHS trust to seek court authority for the treatment.

Another way, therefore, in which parental discretion may be limited is when a court is charged with the decision. In this context, the question is not whether the parent's view is reasonable. In deciding a matter with respect to a child's upbringing, the court must apply the child's welfare as its paramount consideration.[111] What weight is given to a parent's views in such decision-making? In *Re Z (a minor) (freedom of publication),*[112] Bingham MR said:

> I would for my part accept without reservation that the decision of a devoted and responsible parent should be treated with respect. It should certainly not be disregarded or lightly set aside. But the role of the court is to exercise an independent and objective judgment. If that judgment is in accord with that of the devoted and responsible parent, well and good. If it is not, then it is the duty of the court, after giving due weight to the view of the devoted and responsible parent, to give effect to its own judgment.[113]

In *Re T (A Minor) (Wardship: Medical Treatment)*[114] (*Re T*), Waite LJ indicated that each case must be decided on its facts and that generalisations are 'wholly out of place'. He commented in the context of a parent's decision about a child's medical treatment:

> It can only be said safely that there is a scale, at one end of which lies the clear case where parental opposition to medical intervention is prompted by scruple or dogma of a kind which is patently irreconcilable with principles of child health and welfare widely accepted by the generality of mankind; and that at the other end lie highly problematic cases where there is genuine scope for a difference of view between parent and judge. In both situations it is the duty of the judge to allow the court's own opinion to prevail in the perceived paramount interests of the child concerned, but in cases at the latter end of the scale, there must be a likelihood (though never of course a certainty) that the greater the scope for genuine debate between one view and another the stronger will be the inclination of the court to be influenced by a reflection that in the last analysis the best interests of every child include an expectation that difficult decisions affecting the length and quality of its life will be taken for it by the parent to whom its care has been entrusted by nature.[115]

In *Re C (A Child) (HIV Testing),*[116] Wilson J collected from this case the proposition that:

---

[111] Children Act 1989 s 1(1). Discussion of whether current interpretation of this provision must be reformulated in the light of the Human Rights Act 1998 is beyond the scope of this chapter.

[112] [1996] 2 WLR 88.

[113] *Ibid,* at 113.

[114] [1997] 1 All ER 906.

[115] *Ibid,* at 917–18.

[116] [2000] Fam 48.

the views of parents, looked at widely and generously, are an important factor in the decision, even to some extent irrespective of the validity of the underlying grounds for their views.[117]

His Lordship explained that parents' views were important because any intervention might be unworkable without the parents' consent, and also because to go against the parents' wishes may disable them (by emotional stress caused) from caring for the child. Accordingly, a court invited to override the wishes of parents must move extremely cautiously.

In some cases, therefore, the child's welfare has been seen as consistent with the parents' wishes. In *Re T*, for example, the Court of Appeal held that it was not in the child's interests to undergo a possibly life-saving liver transplant operation against the child's mother's wishes. In other cases, parents' views are overridden: in *Re C (A Child) (HIV Testing)*, for example, a mother who was HIV positive rejected conventional views as to the source of AIDS and appropriate treatments for it. In the light of these views, the mother (with the support of the child's father) refused consent to the child being tested for the presence of the virus. Upon a local authority's application for a specific issue order, Wilson J held that the case for testing in the child's best interests was overwhelming. In yet other cases, the courts may be faced with deciding between parents' opposing views. In *Re C (Welfare of Child: Immunisation)*,[118] for example, non-resident fathers with parental responsibility sought, and were granted, specific issue orders that their respective children were to receive vaccinations against the views of the children's mothers.

CONCLUSION

Analysis of the limitations placed on the exercise of parental responsibility suggests that the exercise of parental responsibility is controlled by child welfare. Parents have considerable discretion, however, in exercising parental responsibility. Parental discretion is acknowledged in so far as it does not conflict with parental duty, nor exceed the boundaries of acceptable behaviour as drawn by the criminal law or the criteria by which the state may intervene in family life to protect children. Beyond this, in the absence of court proceedings, the law does not require parents to act in particular ways which positively promote a child's welfare. The law on parental discretion is drawn, therefore, in such a way that not all parental harm to children is precluded.

---

[117]   *Ibid*, at 58.
[118]   [2003] EWHC 1376 (Fam), affirmed by the Court of Appeal in *Re B (A Child) (Immunisation)* [2003] EWCA Civ 1148. For criticism, see K O'Donnell, '*Re C (Welfare of Child: Immunisation)*— Room to refuse? Immunisation, welfare and the role of parental decision making' [2004] 16 *CFLQ* 213, 225–6.

When disputes as to the exercise of parental responsibility are brought before a court, while parents' views are overridden only with caution, the child's welfare is the court's paramount consideration.

In addition, English law has yet to recognise that parents' powers to decide matters relating to a child's upbringing are extinguished simply upon a child's acquisition of capacity to take a decision. *Gillick* was essentially a case about children's welfare, in which their Lordships were seeking to resolve the competing claims of doctors and parents to know what is in a child's interests. In finding a solution to these competing claims, their Lordships articulated the scope of parental discretion. They concluded that, in relation to a competent child, parental decision-making could be usurped once the parents' function of protecting the child could safely be abandoned. Their Lordships recognised a socially constructed, socially changing parent/child relationship, which in modern times increasingly takes account of children's capacities, but which is not regulated simply by reference to a child's empirically ascertainable abilities.

No doubt children's rights advocates would wish the law to aspire to what they would see as a more principled approach to children's autonomy. However, it may be important that that aspiration should not lead the interpretation of the case law and distract from the most plausible interpretation. Otherwise there is a risk of thinking that something has been achieved which has not. There is arguably still much work for children's rights campaigners to do if the child's autonomy interest is to be recognised in law.

5

The Degradation of Parental Responsibility

HELEN REECE*

INTRODUCTION

I
N THIS CHAPTER I argue that the concept of parental responsibility in the
Children Act 1989 has moved further and further away from its predecessor,
parental rights. First, I look at this in general, focusing on the background to
the introduction of the term 'parental responsibility'. Then I turn to an examination of the allocation of parental responsibility. In this context, I suggest that
parental responsibility has moved away from meaning *parental authority* towards
meaning *legitimation*. I illustrate this with a recent case, *Re D (contact and
parental responsibility: lesbian mothers and known father)*,[1] which I argue is
indicative of three trends away from parental authority, namely the proliferation
of parental responsibility, the degradation of parental responsibility and the shift
in the reasons given for granting parental responsibility. In my conclusion, I
query whether this is merely a staging post on the way to parental responsibility
meaning nothing whatsoever.

THE CHANGING MEANING OF PARENTAL RESPONSIBILITY

Although parental rights still form an aspect of the definition of parental
responsibility,[2] there is no doubt that with the advent of the Children Act 1989,
parental responsibility ousted parental rights as the dominant legal conception of
the parent–child relationship.[3] Writing about the United States, Martha Fineman

---

* I am grateful to John Gillott and to the participants at the 2008 seminar that preceded this
book for helpful comments on earlier drafts of this chapter.
  [1] [2006] EWHC 2.
  [2] Children Act 1989 s 3(1).
  [3] H Reece, 'From Parental Responsibility to Parenting Responsibly' in M Freeman (ed), *Law and
Sociology: Current Legal Issues 2005* (Oxford, Oxford University Press, 2006).

has given an explanation for this development[4] that is far more elegant than, but substantively similar to, one that I have previously given.[5] Fineman notes that the 'charge often leveled is that the law treats children as though they are the property of their parents'.[6] Her rejection of equality in the context of the family enables her to take a robust attitude to this charge. While Fineman recognises that the parent–child relationship is inherently unequal,[7] she suggests that nothing follows from this inherent inequality as to the extent to which we value children.[8] Nor does it follow that the parent–child relationship is exploitative: it is wrong to equate the lack of a legal voice with the lack of an actual voice.[9] Not only is exploitation not a necessary consequence of inequality, but Fineman also posits that, in practice, relationships between caretakers and dependants are interactive, with caretakers typically considering dependants' needs.[10]

Accordingly, she believes that the charge that the law treats children as though they are the property of their parents is 'an inflammatory characterization that does more to obscure than to illuminate the issues'.[11] Nonetheless, she explains that this charge has resulted in suggestions for recasting the relationship between parent and child, for example by substituting concepts such as stewardship or trusteeship for the more traditional notion of parental authority, in order to level out the relationship.[12]

Fineman's description of US developments maps very well onto the United Kingdom. In the United Kingdom, the charge that the law treated children as though they were the property of their parents was levelled at parents' rights: the concept of parents' rights was accused of treating children as though they were the property of their parents. For example, Jonathan Herring interprets the shift from parental rights to parental responsibility as demonstrating that 'children are not possessions to be controlled by parents, but instead children are persons to be cared for'.[13] Writing in 1991, Michael Freeman expressed the accusation vividly:

> The shift from parental rights and duties (a property concept, almost) to parental responsibility, with parents as trustees for their children, the beneficiaries, has to be welcomed. We clearly have to get away from the notion of children as consumer durables, completing a family after the C.D. player and video recorder.[14]

---

[4]   MA Fineman, *The Autonomy Myth: A Theory of Dependency* (New York, The New Press, 2004).
[5]   Reece, above n 3.
[6]   Fineman, above n 4, 301.
[7]   *Ibid*, 304–5.
[8]   *Ibid*, 304.
[9]   *Ibid*, 305.
[10]   *Ibid*, 305.
[11]   *Ibid*, 301.
[12]   *Ibid*, 301.
[13]   J Herring, *Family Law* (3rd edn, Harlow, Pearson Education, 2007) 376. See also NV Lowe, 'The Meaning and Allocation of Parental Responsibility—A Common Lawyer's Perspective' (1997) 11 *IJLPF* 192, 192 for the association between parental responsibility and parental care.
[14]   M Freeman, 'In the Child's Best Interests? Reading the Children Act Critically' (1992) 45 *Current Legal Problems* 173, 185.

Despite characterising the consensus, this charge is a caricature of the role of parents' rights. In living memory, the idea that children are their parents' possessions has never been legally endorsed; nor has the idea that children are persons to be cared for ever been legally doubted. When I read Michael Freeman's depiction, I cannot help bringing to mind the old joke:

Question: What is the difference between an elephant and a post-box?

Answer: I don't know. What is the difference between an elephant and a post-box?

Riposte: Well, if you don't know I won't ask you to post my letters.

There is no danger of confusing children with CD players, no comparison between the way in which children and video recorders complete a family. Indeed, parents commonly lament children's lack of an off switch, volume control or even a pause button.

More seriously though, the charge was wrong because it was crystal clear that, far from parental rights' treating children as property, the law treated parental rights as existing for the benefit of the child, not the parent. This approach was entrenched in the law by the House of Lords in the celebrated case of *Gillick v West Norfolk and Wisbech AHA* in the mid 1980s.[15] Thus, according to Lord Fraser:

[P]arental rights to control a child do not exist for the benefit of the parent. They exist for the benefit of the child and they are justified only in so far as they enable the parent to perform his duties towards the child, and towards other children in the family.[16]

The House of Lords made quite clear that they were making explicit a long-standing principle, which they traced back to *Blackstone's Commentaries* of 1830.[17] Accepted on all sides, this was not one of the points of contention in *Gillick*.[18]

Despite the fact that the principle that parental rights existed for the benefit of children was settled beyond peradventure, it was concern to emphasise this principle further that provided both the initial and main impetus for switching from parental rights to parental responsibility.[19] However, originally, the shift was conceived of as 'largely a change of nomenclature',[20] the Law Commission assuring that it 'would make little difference in substance'.[21] The strong connection with parental rights is evident in the definition given in the Children Act

---

[15] [1986] AC 112. See SM Cretney, JM Masson and R Bailey-Harris, *Principles of Family Law* (7th edn, London, Sweet & Maxwell, 2003) 522; and Herring, above n 13, 377.

[16] [1986] AC 112 at 170. See also *ibid*, at 184 (Lord Scarman).

[17] *Ibid*, at 170 and 184–5.

[18] *Ibid*, at 170.

[19] See further Reece, above n 3, 462–3.

[20] Lord Mackay, 'Perceptions of the Children Bill and beyond' (1989) 139 *NLJ* 505, 505.

[21] Law Commission, 'Family Law: Review of Child Law, Guardianship and Custody' (Law Com No 172, 1988) 6. See also Cretney, Masson and Bailey-Harris, above n 15, 522.

1989 itself,[22] which 'immediately throws one back to the rights and duties concept which "responsibility" was supposed to replace',[23] the first word used to describe parental responsibility being 'rights'.[24] So in other words, parental responsibility originally had a lot of parental rights left in it. Accordingly, in 1991 John Eekelaar could quite plausibly describe 'parental responsibility' as synonymous with 'parental authority', embodying ideas of freedom of parents from government.[25]

Fineman warns, though, that the ideals embodied in the substitution of egalitarian concepts for parental authority:

> amorphously appealing on a rhetorical level, seem harmless enough as aspirations. The problems arise when they are implemented into laws that can be used at the relatively unfettered discretion of various state actors to undermine, even usurp, parental decision-making authority.[26]

This is what we have witnessed in the United Kingdom. The shift from parental rights to parental responsibility set the stage for the current approach, which has switched from the idea that parental authority exists purely for the benefit of children to the idea that parental authority *itself* is antithetical to children's welfare. I have previously looked at this shift in relation to parental responsibility for children's crimes and misdemeanours and I have argued that in this context parental responsibility now means parental accountability to external agencies.[27] In the remainder of this chapter, I look at this shift in relation to the allocation of parental responsibility.

ALLOCATION OF PARENTAL RESPONSIBILITY

Since most of the legal disputes concerning parental responsibility are over its acquisition as opposed to its exercise, examining the allocation of parental responsibility takes us right into the heart of the legal meaning of the concept.

The dominant view among commentators who have investigated the meaning of parental responsibility in the context of allocation is that it is 'a confused, contradictory concept'.[28] There is much force in this view. The allocation of parental responsibility performs a diverse array of different roles, and the case law

---

[22]   Children Act 1989 s 3(1).
[23]   Lowe, above n 13, 195.
[24]   Herring, above n 13, 376.
[25]   J Eekelaar, 'Parental Responsibility: State of Nature or Nature of the State?' (1991) 13 *JSWFL* 37. See further Reece, above n 3, 460–61.
[26]   Fineman, above n 5, 301.
[27]   Reece, above n 3.
[28]   J Bridgeman, 'Parental Responsibility, Responsible Parenting and Legal Regulation' in J Bridgeman, C Lind and H Keating (eds), *Responsibility, Law and the Family* (London, Ashgate, 2008) 237. See also Herring, above n 13, 385; and S Gilmore, 'Parental Responsibility and The Unmarried Father—A New Dimension to the Debate' [2003] 15 *CFLQ* 21, 38.

reflects these many meanings. One enduring strand of the meaning of parental responsibility in this context is undoubtedly parental authority: the law still needs to delineate who has the power to decide which school a child will go to or which medical treatment the child will have.

However, I would not wholly endorse the chaotic account. I believe that, even among the many strands of meaning, it is possible to discern a dominant trend, *away from* parental responsibility as parental authority *towards* parental responsibility as legitimation. In relation to the allocation of parental responsibility, an increasingly significant element of the meaning of parental responsibility is 'a pat on the back, official confirmation'.[29]

I want to illustrate this with the case of *Re D*.[30] This case concerned a lesbian couple, Ms A and Ms C, who advertised for a man interested in fathering a child: Mr B responded. From an early stage it transpired that the three adults had different expectations of Mr B's involvement with the child:

> Mr B was expecting something of the role of the absent parent after divorce who might share the child's leisure time equally with the child's mother and participate in decisions about the child whereas Ms A and Ms C intended that he should complement their primary care of the child by being a real father but by doing so through no more than relatively infrequent visits and benign and loving interest.[31]

These differing expectations led Mr B to apply for parental responsibility.

The court granted him parental responsibility hedged with conditions, the specific ones being that unless he had the prior written consent of the primary carers, he was not allowed to visit or contact the child's school or any of her health professionals for any purpose. Black J made plain to Mr B that these were by no means the only situations from which he was excluded:

> The court has power to regulate others, should they arise, through Children Act orders. Given that Mr B will know, following this judgment, the sort of context that the court anticipates there will be for his involvement in D's life, he will be able to forecast the likely consequences of attempts to become involved in areas of her life not covered by the proposed conditions and it is my judgment that that ought to be a brake upon his conduct.[32]

Black J decided that 'the fundamental nature of these restrictions on Mr B's parental responsibility'[33] would be reflected by setting out in the parental responsibility order that the order was made in reliance upon them.[34] Arguably *de trop*, Black J added that Mr B had no role in D's day-to-day care, 'whether in relation to decision making or otherwise'.[35]

---

29 Herring, above n 13, 384.
30 [2006] EWHC 2, [2006] 1 FCR 556.
31 [2006] 1 FCR 556 at 557 (Black J).
32 *Ibid*, at 582.
33 *Ibid*, at 582.
34 *Ibid*, at 582.
35 *Ibid*, at 583.

I would regard the approach taken in *Re D* as fundamentally inconsistent with the granting of parental responsibility.[36] It is a 'now you see it, now you don't' approach to parental responsibility. Rather than Mr B having any authority or decision-making power over D, he has actually been ordered to keep away. In a sense, he has even fewer powers over the child than 'the man on the Clapham omnibus', who has not been barred from the sites of decision making about her. Mr B has degraded parental responsibility, with the courts telling him exactly how much he has and precisely what he can do with it.

Clearly, *Re D* is highly atypical. Black J commented:

> None of the authorities has so far dealt … with the sort of situation that exists in this case where a same sex couple has deliberately decided to create a family and, with the knowledge of all concerned that it is their intention that they should be the primary carers, involves a man to father a baby.[37]

However, this only strengthens the point that I am making: the fact that even Mr B could be granted parental responsibility shows that parental responsibility has become debased. Moreover, although the case itself is unusual, I want to suggest that *Re D* is indicative of three aspects of the trend away from parental responsibility as parental authority, namely the proliferation of parental responsibility, the degradation of parental responsibility and a shift in the reasons given for granting parental responsibility.

Proliferation of Parental Responsibility

The categories of people who have parental powers automatically and who may acquire parental powers have been expanded at regular historical intervals. The Children Act 1989 represented a significant extension; nevertheless, the categories have been further stretched since, particularly in relation to unmarried fathers and step-parents.[38]

The Family Law Reform Act 1987 allowed unmarried fathers to acquire parental powers for the first time ever.[39] The Children Act 1989 maintained this position, but diversified the ways in which this could happen.[40] The Adoption and Children Act 2002 extended parental responsibility to all unmarried fathers who sign the birth register.[41] The recent government White Paper, 'Joint birth registration: recording responsibility', proposes to make joint birth registration

---

[36]   See J McCandless, 'Status and Anomaly: *Re D (contact and parental responsibility: lesbian mothers and known father)* [2006] EWHC 2 (Fam), [2006] 1 FCR 556' (2008) 30 *JSWFL* 63, 67.

[37]   [2006] 1 FCR 556 at 561. But see *Re B* [2007] EWHC 1952 (Fam), [2008] 1 FLR 1015.

[38]   In what follows, the term 'step-parent' refers to a partner of a parent who has taken on a parenting role in relation to the parent's child, irrespective of whether he or she has married or entered into a civil partnership with the parent.

[39]   Family Law Reform Act 1987 s 4(1).

[40]   Children Act 1989 s 4.

[41]   Adoption and Children Act 2002 s 111.

for unmarried parents compulsory unless it is impossible, impracticable or unreasonable, so that almost all unmarried fathers would have parental responsibility.[42] The Adoption and Children Act 2002 also introduced acquisition of parental responsibility by step-parents, defined as those persons who are either married to or in a civil partnership with one of the parents.[43]

By judicial fiat, *Re G (shared residence order: parental responsibility)*[44] stretched parental responsibility still further so as to include step-parents who are no longer or never have been married to or in a civil partnership with one of the parents. This case concerned the breakdown of a lesbian relationship, and specifically an application by the non-biological parent, W, for a shared residence order in order to gain parental responsibility for the couple's two children. Thorpe LJ explained that it was common ground in the hearing that:

> A significant feature of the fact that the parties to this appeal had been in a same-sex relationship was that the appellant could only achieve parental responsibility in relation to these two children if she succeeded in her application for a residence order.[45]

With respect, this explanation is misleading. It is true that the only way in which W could gain parental responsibility was through a residence order, but it is not true that this was because she was in a same-sex relationship. Rather, the reason was that she was not in a civil partnership with the children's biological mother. W thus had this feature in common with heterosexual step-parents who are not married to one of the parents.

From the fallacious premise that it was because W was in a same-sex relationship that she could only achieve parental responsibility through a residence order, the Court of Appeal drew the conclusion that it would be unfair not to grant W parental responsibility, their reasoning being that she would have been granted parental responsibility had she been an unmarried father:

> Although [counsel for W] has not asserted discrimination against his client he has made the general observation that, had the case concerned the two children of a heterosexual couple who had cohabited between 1995 and 2003 and the father, being the absent parent, had sought the parental responsibility order on the strength of the same degree of past and proposed future commitment as has been demonstrated by Miss W, the outcome would have been evident.[46]

Accordingly, the Court of Appeal treated her application for a shared residence order as an application for parental responsibility, so much so that they applied the threefold test developed in *Re H (minors) (local authority: parental rights) (No 3)*[47]

---

[42] Department for Work and Pensions, 'Joint birth registration: recording responsibility' (Cm 7293, 2008); see now cl 44 of the Welfare Reform Bill 2009.
[43] Adoption and Children Act 2002 s 112; and Civil Partnership Act 2004 s 75(2).
[44] [2005] EWCA Civ 462, [2005] 2 FLR 957.
[45] [2005] 2 FLR 957 at 959.
[46] *Ibid*, at 964–5.
[47] [1991] Fam 151.

for determining whether or not to grant a parental responsibility order to an unmarried father, namely the degree of commitment shown to the child, the degree of attachment with the child and the reasons for applying for the order.[48]

However, the correct comparator in *Re G* was not the unmarried father, but the unmarried heterosexual step-parent. While the precedents established that an intact couple consisting of a cohabiting parent and step-parent might be granted shared residence primarily or even solely as a means for the step-parent to gain parental responsibility,[49] at that time the precedents suggested that slightly more stringent criteria applied when the couple had separated, as was the case in *Re G*.

Re WB (minors) (residence orders)[50] concerned the relationship breakdown of a heterosexual couple who had lived together for about 10 years, during which time the mother had given birth to two children. N had brought up the children believing them to be his biological children, but after the couple separated blood tests revealed that this was not the case. Like W 10 years later, N applied for a shared residence order as his only route to parental responsibility. Thorpe J, as he then was, described N's appeal against the justices' refusal to grant his application as 'devoid of any merit'.[51] Once the justices had reached the unchallengeable conclusion that shared care was inappropriate, it would have been:

> quite wrong had they expressed their conclusion in the shape of a shared residence order for no other reason than to arrive at a finding of parental responsibility in the appellant.[52]

Re WB was distinguished in *Re H (shared residence: parental responsibility)*.[53] Here the husband met the mother when she was pregnant with her eldest child, whom he accepted as his own. They later had a child together. When the couple separated, the trial judge made a shared residence order in relation to both children, which the mother appealed. Ward LJ distinguished *Re WB* on the basis that there the making of a shared residence order would have been 'quite artificial and unreflective of the reality'.[54] In contrast:

> This is a case where a shared residence order is not artificial but of important practical therapeutic importance. This is a case where its making does reflect the reality of the father's involvement ... Here it was important that the boys retain the perception that they lived with their father when they did not live with their mother. ... Here it was necessary for the boys to know they lived with the respondent and that they did not just visit him.[55]

---

[48]   *Ibid*, at 158.
[49]   See, eg *Re AB* [1996] 1 FLR 27.
[50]   [1995] 2 FLR 1023.
[51]   *Ibid*, at 1026.
[52]   *Ibid*, at 1027.
[53]   [1995] 2 FLR 883.
[54]   *Ibid*, at 889.
[55]   *Ibid*, at 889. See also in the context of a lesbian relationship *G v F* [1998] 2 FLR 799.

In the light of these precedents, it seemed that, after a couple had separated, a shared residence order might be made primarily in order to confer parental responsibility on the step-parent, so long as shared care was otherwise considered appropriate. Accordingly, it may well be that shared residence was justifiable on the facts of *Re G*. However, the case was not decided by examining whether shared care was otherwise suitable, but on the legally incorrect basis that a lesbian co-parent should be treated equivalently to an unmarried father when awarding parental responsibility.

Although neither the specific precedents nor the general comparator of heterosexual step-parents was mentioned in *Re G*, the case has already been held to apply in this wider context. In *Re A (a child) (joint residence: parental responsibility)*,[56] as in *Re WB*, A had brought up the child on the assumption that he was the biological father, but during contact proceedings it emerged that this assumption was false. At first instance, despite the fact that shared care was not considered appropriate, the recorder made a shared residence order with regard to the child, in order to give A parental responsibility. Dismissing the mother's appeal against the shared residence order in a unanimous Court of Appeal judgment, Sir Mark Potter P. drew from *Re G* the following, unqualified, legal principle:

> it is ... clear the making of a residence order is a legitimate means by which to confer parental responsibility on an individual who would otherwise not be able to apply for a free-standing parental responsibility order.[57]

By judicial fiat, parental responsibility has thus been extended to step-parents who are not married to or in a civil partnership with one of the parents.

The proliferation of parental responsibility has become more significant as a result of another recent body of case law. Despite the fact that the Children Act 1989 s 2(7) provides that a person with parental responsibility is allowed to act alone and without the other or others in meeting his or her responsibility, the courts have developed a group of what they regard as important decisions that may only be taken with the agreement of everyone with parental responsibility. In *Re J (specific issue orders: child's religious upbringing and circumcision)*,[58] in which the issue was whether the child should be circumcised given the parents' disagreement on this matter, Butler-Sloss LJ considered that the group included sterilisation, change of surname[59] and circumcision itself.[60] In *Re C (welfare of child: immunisation)*,[61] the Court of Appeal added immunisation to the list.[62] Although one view is that this case law has augmented the authority aspect of

---

56 [2008] EWCA Civ 867, [2008] 2 FLR 1593.
57 [2008] 2 FLR 1593 at 1613.
58 [2000] 1 FLR 571.
59 See *Re PC* [1997] 2 FLR 730.
60 [2000] 1 FLR 571 at 577.
61 [2003] EWCA Civ 1148, [2003] 2 FLR 1095.
62 [2003] 2 FLR 1095 at 1099.

parental responsibility, the better view is that these precedents have further diluted parental authority, since they are likely to lead to more decisions being taken by courts, as opposed to parents.

The watering down of parental responsibility perhaps provides an explanation for the recent liberalisation of the circumstances in which shared residence orders may be made.[63] Part of the hope behind the Children Act 1989 was that after separation or divorce the endurance of parental responsibility would lead orders about children to be made less frequently than had been the case.[64] As parental responsibility has been diluted, shared residence orders have arguably come to represent the new way of giving separated parents equal authority.[65]

Current ease with the proliferation of parental responsibility presents a marked contrast with historical unease: the Guardianship of Infants Act 1925 rejected equal parental authority for mothers primarily on the basis that any splitting of parental authority at all would be divisive.[66] This contemporary ease indicates that parental responsibility has shifted away from its origins in parental authority. When the meaning of parental responsibility is closely tied to parental authority, it is important for external agencies to limit the holders of parental responsibility so that everyone knows who is in charge. Conversely, the proliferation of parental responsibility demonstrates that parental responsibility is no longer predominantly about parental authority or decision-making. The fact that the law is quite relaxed about giving parental responsibility to an ever-widening circle, even the father in *Re D*, strongly suggests that parental responsibility no longer represents a buffer against the law; no longer to the same extent does parental responsibility signify parental freedom from legal intervention.[67]

Degradation of Parental Responsibility

As I have already recognised, *Re D* is an extreme case. However, in this section I suggest that *Re D* is the nadir of a line of cases in which parental responsibility has been given only a minimal connection with parental authority. This line of cases, about the circumstances in which parental responsibility should be awarded, have all been concerned with unmarried fathers because until recently they were the only group entitled to apply for parental responsibility.[68]

Much of the case law dealing with unmarried fathers' applications for parental responsibility makes plain that their parental responsibility has little to do with authority. This is apparent in *Re D*, but it is also apparent in the cases that form

---

[63]   See *Re D* [2001] 1 FLR 495; and S Gilmore, 'Court decision-making in shared residence order cases: a critical examination' [2006] 18 *CFLQ* 478.

[64]   See Law Commission, above n 21, 7–8 and 14.

[65]   I am grateful to Jonathan Herring for this point.

[66]   S Cretney, *Law, Law Reform and the Family* (Oxford, Clarendon Press, 1998) ch 7.

[67]   See Herring, above n 13, 343.

[68]   See above, text at nn 39 *ff.*

the foundations of *Re D*. Unlike *Re D*, it would be fair to describe *Re P (a minor: parental responsibility order)*[69] as a run-of-the-mill unmarried father case. In *Re P*, the magistrates refused to grant the father a parental responsibility order because they felt that he would be able to use such an order to question aspects of the child's upbringing, to the child's detriment. However, Wilson J allowed the father's appeal, stating:

> It is important to be quite clear that an order for parental responsibility to the father does not give him a right to interfere in matters within the day-to-day management of the child's life.[70]

It is true that Wilson J continued:

> There is, of course, an order for residence in favour of the mother under the Act and that invests the mother with the right to determine all matters which arise in the course of the day-to-day management of this child's life.[71]

This meant that the father's use of his parental responsibility was in any case restricted, given the provision in the Children Act 1989 s 2(8) that parental responsibility does not entitle the holder to act incompatibly with a Children Act order. However, in *Re S (parental responsibility)*,[72] a Court of Appeal decision the following year that confirmed and extended Wilson J's reasoning, the mother did not have a residence order. The Court of Appeal placed no significance on this distinction.

In *Re S*, the mother objected to the unmarried father's application for parental responsibility because he had been convicted of possessing child pornography. The Court of Appeal overrode this objection and granted parental responsibility, not because of any newly found permissiveness about child pornography, Ward LJ describing it inter alia as an 'appalling activity',[73] but rather on the basis that granting the father parental responsibility really did not entitle him to do very much. Ward LJ emphasised:

> It is wrong to place undue and therefore false emphasis on the rights and duties and the powers comprised in 'parental responsibility' and not to concentrate on the fact that what is at issue is conferring upon a committed father the status of parenthood.[74]

Despite the Law Commission's earlier assurance that the shift from parental rights to parental responsibility would make little substantive difference, *Re S* marks a significant break with parental rights. According to Ward LJ, the decision in the Children Act 1989[75] to define parental responsibility with reference to parental rights gave 'outmoded pre-eminence'[76] to rights, exhibiting:

---

[69] [1994] 1 FLR 578.
[70] *Ibid*, at 584.
[71] *Ibid*, at 585.
[72] [1995] 2 FLR 648.
[73] *Ibid*, at 649.
[74] *Ibid*, at 657. See also *Re C and V* [1998] 1 FLR 392 at 397.
[75] Children Act 1989 s 3(1).
[76] [1995] 2 FLR 648 at 657.

a most unfortunate failure to appreciate the significant change that the Act has brought about where the emphasis is to move away from rights and to concentrate on responsibilities.[77]

Butler-Sloss LJ agreed with Ward LJ's judgment, adding a short judgment of the same tenor if less forcefully expressed, in which she referred to a parental responsibility order as one of 'duties and responsibilities as well as rights and powers'.[78]

In both *Re S* and *Re P*, it was emphasised that to the extent that parental responsibility did give fathers rights, any misuse could be controlled by the granting of specific issue or prohibited steps orders.[79] In neither of these cases were such orders deemed necessary. However, in the later case of *Re H (a child: parental responsibility)*,[80] Thorpe LJ granted the father parental responsibility, hedged by both a specific issue order giving the mother sole responsibility for decisions about the child's medical treatment and a prohibited steps order preventing the father from trying to find out the child's address. Following *Re S*, he confirmed that giving this father parental responsibility was 'essentially an acknowledgment and declaration of his parental status'.[81]

These cases were relied upon in *Re D*,[82] but *Re D* also takes them further. McCandless explains that while attaching section 8 orders to parental responsibility orders seems similar to the decision in *Re D* to make the parental responsibility order in reliance on certain restrictions, there are 'subtle but important differences'[83] between the methods. If circumstances changed so that limitations on parental responsibility were no longer called for, in *Re H* the section 8 orders could be removed to leave the parental responsibility order intact, but in *Re D* parental responsibility itself would have to be reviewed. Relatedly, regulating parental responsibility with section 8 orders implies that the father is prima facie entitled to parental rights, but current circumstances dictate particular restrictions; there is no equivalent implication of entitlement in *Re D*.[84]

It is right to recognise that there is other case law that ascribes more potency to unmarried fathers' parental responsibility. In the recent case of *Re B (role of biological father)*,[85] in which a man who had fathered a child for a lesbian couple applied for parental responsibility, the court declined to grant the order in what were apparently similar circumstances to *Re D*. Hedley J's brief reasoning on this point seems to have been that the father should not be granted parental

---

[77]   *Ibid*, at 657.
[78]   *Ibid*, at 659.
[79]   *Ibid*, at 657; and *Re P* [1994] 1 FLR 578 at 585. See also *Re C and V* [1998] 1 FLR 392 at 397.
[80]   [2002] EWCA Civ 542.
[81]   *Ibid*.
[82]   [2006] 1 FCR 556 at 582.
[83]   Above n 36, 69.
[84]   *Ibid*.
[85]   [2007] EWHC 1952 (Fam), [2008] 1 FLR 1015.

responsibility precisely because it was inappropriate for him to exercise parental responsibility in this situation; if the father were granted parental responsibility, he would inevitably seek to use it.[86] Another instructive example is *M v M (parental responsibility)*.[87] In this case, the father had very severe learning difficulties. Wilson J refused him a parental responsibility order, mainly on the basis that he was incapable of exercising parental responsibility:

> for example to weigh up the merits of rival schools or to balance the potential benefits and risks of a surgical operation.[88]

Wilson J stressed that parental responsibility was not trivial, following Butler-Sloss LJ[89] in emphasising its weight.[90] Even so, this was a highly unusual case, in which the father's disability unsettled the presuppositions on which parental responsibility is based.[91]

Moreover, the current government proposal to make parental responsibility compulsory for almost all fathers is inextricably linked to the diminishing parental authority element of parental responsibility.[92] Compelling almost all fathers to have parental responsibility would inevitably mean that those fathers who are unwilling, unavailable or seen as unsuitable to make decisions about the child's upbringing or otherwise exercise parental authority would be endowed with parental responsibility. The fact that the government regards this as a desirable outcome indicates the dwindling authority aspect of parental responsibility.

Indeed, if almost all unmarried fathers are compelled to hold parental responsibility, their parental responsibility will no longer even imply official approval of them,[93] at least as individual fathers.[94] Nevertheless, parental responsibility as legitimation will remain an important strand in the meaning of the term. Since the case law so far exclusively concerns unmarried fathers, it would be possible to regard this conceptualisation of parental responsibility as specific to unmarried fathers. However, I believe it is more general. Even if the government proposal is implemented, I expect a similar account of parental responsibility to emerge in step-parents' future applications for parental responsibility.

---

[86] [2008] 1 FLR 1015 at 1022–3.
[87] [1999] 2 FLR 737.
[88] *Ibid*, at 743.
[89] *Re S* [1995] 2 FLR 648 at 659.
[90] [1999] 2 FLR 737 at 743.
[91] *Ibid*, at 743.
[92] Department for Work and Pensions, above n 42.
[93] I am grateful to Kathryn Hollingsworth for this point.
[94] On the status of fatherhood generally, see R Collier, 'A Hard Time to Be a Father? Reassessing the Relationship Between Law, Policy and Family (Practices)' (2001) 28 *Journal of Law and Society* 520.

The Shift in Reasons for Granting Parental Responsibility

Since the Children Act 1989, there has been a shift in the reasons given by the courts for granting unmarried fathers parental responsibility. In the earlier cases, the main reason for giving an unmarried father parental responsibility was to give him decision-making power. In the more recent cases, the reasons are less to do with decision-making and more to do with feelings and emotions.

In 1991, in the leading case of *Re H*,[95] which set out the criteria for granting parental responsibility orders, the question to be determined was the extent to which the father's parental rights needed to be enforceable for them to be granted. The Court of Appeal found no difficulty in disagreeing with the trial judge's view that parental rights should only be given if all the rights were immediately capable of being exercised.[96] However, the stronger argument against granting parental rights was that since the judge had already decided on the merits that the children would be freed for adoption irrespective of the father's opposition, there was little point in making a parental rights order just to give the father *locus standi* to oppose the freeing order: all that this would mean was that his parental rights and duties would be given and then immediately taken away. The Court of Appeal accepted the force of this argument. Their reason for rejecting it was to point to certain limited rights that a parent still had even after a child had been freed for adoption, for example to receive progress reports and to apply to revoke the freeing order in certain circumstances.[97] It was these residual rights that could later become of benefit to the father that justified making a parental rights order.[98] Feelings and emotions played no part in the Court of Appeal reasoning, not even warranting a mention in the judgment.

The following year, in *Re C (minors)*,[99] the Court of Appeal confirmed that unmarried fathers should be granted parental rights even if those rights were unenforceable, partly on the basis that married fathers with automatic parental rights might also be unable to exercise their rights for a variety of reasons. Although the court did make passing reference to the father's 'peace of mind'[100] as a hypothetical factor, their main reason for giving parental status to a father who could not exercise it was that this parental status would have 'real and tangible value … as a status carrying with it rights in waiting':[101]

> Though existing circumstances may demand that his children see or hear nothing of him, and that he should have no influence upon the course of their lives for the time being, their welfare may require that if circumstances change he should be reintroduced

---

[95]   [1991] Fam 151.
[96]   *Ibid*, at 159–60.
[97]   *Ibid*, at 160.
[98]   *Ibid*, at 161.
[99]   [1992] 2 All ER 86.
[100] *Ibid*, at 89.
[101] *Ibid*, at 89.

as a presence, or at least an influence, in their lives. In such a case a PRO, notwithstanding that only a few or even none of the rights under it may currently be exercisable, may be of value to him and also of potential value to the children.[102]

In the 1994 case of *Re G (a minor) (parental responsibility order)*,[103] the emphasis was still very firmly on decision-making. Balcombe LJ regarded the father's reason for seeking parental responsibility, that the father wanted to have 'the ability to have a say in the life of his child',[104] as a perfectly proper reason and wholly appropriate factor to take into account. He viewed it as clearly in the interests of the child that 'her natural father should be given a proper part to play in her life by being given a *locus standi*'.[105] Beldam LJ similarly based his judgment on decision-making:

> It must ... be in a child's interest that a devoted father should have the degree of involvement in her future given by a parental responsibility order, which would enable him to contribute to the promotion of her welfare and to play the natural part of her father in the future.[106]

The turning point came in 1995 with *Re S*,[107] which we have already seen marked a significant rupture between parental responsibility and parental rights.[108] In this case, Ward LJ introduced an entirely new reason for granting parental responsibility, which had never been given in any previous case. This was to confer upon the father a *stamp of approval*:

> I have heard, up and down the land, psychiatrists tell me how important it is that children grow up with good self-esteem and how much they need to have a favourable positive image of the absent parent. It seems to me important, therefore, wherever possible, to ensure that the law confers upon a committed father that stamp of approval, lest the child grow up with some belief that he is in some way disqualified from fulfilling his role and that the reason for the disqualification is something inherent which will be inherited by the child, making her struggle to find her own identity all the more fraught.[109]

Ward LJ also suggested that emphasis should be:

> placed upon children growing up in the knowledge that their father is committed enough to wish to have parental responsibility conferred upon him.[110]

---

[102]   *Ibid*, at 89.
[103]   [1994] 1 FLR 504.
[104]   *Ibid*, at 508.
[105]   *Ibid*, at 508–9.
[106]   *Ibid*, at 510.
[107]   [1995] 2 FLR 648.
[108]   See above, text at nn 71 *ff*.
[109]   *Re S* [1995] 2 FLR 648 at 657. See also *Re H* [1995] 2 FLR 883 at 889; and *Re C and V* [1998] 1 FLR 392 at 397.
[110]   *Re S* [1995] 2 FLR 648 at 659.

Later that year in *Re H*,[111] Ward LJ adopted similar reasoning, describing it as important, given the child's shock on discovering the truth about his paternity,[112] that:

> the benefits of the parental responsibility order ... be impressed upon the boy to give him the confidence that he has not suffered some life-shattering blow to his self-esteem.[113]

Likewise, in *Re M (contact: family assistance: McKenzie friend)*,[114] Ward LJ emphasized that:

> the important thing to recognize is that it is essential for the well-being of the children ... to begin to know that their father was concerned enough to make an application to be recognised as their father, and that his status as their father has the stamp of the court's approval.[115]

In the subsequent case of *Re H*,[116] Thorpe LJ took the same approach, granting the father parental responsibility, hedged with conditions, in the hope that this would benefit the child 'in years to come so that she knows she has two parents'.[117]

The stamp of approval reason in *Re S* marks the start of a process of psychologising the reasons for granting parental responsibility, of granting parental responsibility for therapeutic purposes. At this juncture, the therapeutic reasoning focuses on the child's needs. However, the extent to which a child's feelings and emotions would be affected by a legal order with no tangible effect on him or her is highly questionable.[118] Certainly, in the cases just mentioned, there was no hard evidence that granting or refusing parental responsibility to the father would affect the child's feelings in the manner depicted.[119] As Herring rightly points out, 'the order is more likely to affect the father's image of himself than his child's'.[120]

Therefore, there seems to be a certain logic in the main reason for granting parental responsibility in *Re D*[121] being that the *father* needed recognition:

> For Mr B, to be D's father is simply not enough; he wishes to be recognised as a father and a parent and he perceives that a parental responsibility order would bring this recognition.[122]

---

[111]   [1995] 2 FLR 883.
[112]   See above, text at n 53.
[113]   [1995] 2 FLR 883 at 889.
[114]   [1999] 1 FLR 75.
[115]   *Ibid*, at 80.
[116]   [2002] EWCA Civ 542.
[117]   *Ibid.*
[118]   See Herring, above n 13, 339.
[119]   *Re S* [1995] 2 FLR 648; *Re H* [1995] 2 FLR 883 (CA); and *Re H* [2002] EWCA Civ 542.
[120]   Herring, above n 13, 339.
[121]   [2006] EWHC 2, [2006] 1 FCR 556.
[122]   [2006] 1 FCR 556 at 561.

Mr B's motives for applying for a parental responsibility order are complex and I do not insult him by attempting to reduce their sophistication to a list for this judgment. I am quite satisfied that they do not include any trace of malice but have at their root his feelings for and about D and his wish to be recognised as belonging to her and to do all that he can towards securing her welfare.[123]

Once we have realised that the courts are on occasion deciding parental responsibility on the basis of adults' need for recognition, a hypothesis emerges as to why the apparently similar case of *Re B*[124] was decided differently. Arguably, in both *Re D* and *Re B*, the courts balanced the father's and the lesbian couple's need for recognition. In *Re D*, the balance came down in favour of granting Mr B parental responsibility partly because Black J was confident of the couple's robustness.[125] In contrast, in *Re B*, Hedley J found that granting the father parental responsibility would lead the couple to 'feel assailed and undermined in their status as parents'.[126]

It is highly regrettable that 'recognition' switches to considering adults' feelings and emotions in deciding whether to grant parental responsibility.[127] I have previously argued that adults' interests should be taken into account in deciding disputes about children,[128] and no doubt on occasions their needs should also be considered. However, in this instance the argument for granting parental responsibility is not that an adult needs the *effects* of a legal order, but that an adult needs the *legal order itself*, irrespective of any tangible effect. Truly, this is parental responsibility as legitimation.

In a different context, Andrew Bainham has aptly described this need to be recognised as 'status anxiety', a term he attributes to de Botton.[129] Bainham notes that while one prevalent view is that status is of decreasing importance, with a new emphasis on contract and the private ordering of family affairs,[130] the opposite is in fact the case, reflecting a contemporary desire to secure for family relationships the 'imprimatur of the law'.[131] In *Re D*, the father's need to be recognised was an illegitimate basis for giving him parental responsibility. Parental responsibility should not be granted in order to prevent adults feeling that the law has emotionally neglected them: parental responsibility should be awarded to adults if and only if they deserve parental responsibility.

---

[123] *Ibid*, at 581.
[124] [2007] EWHC 1952 (Fam), [2008] 1 FLR 1015.
[125] [2006] 1 FCR 556 at 575.
[126] [2008] 1 FLR 1015 at 1023.
[127] See McCandless, above n 36, 69.
[128] H Reece, 'Paramountcy Principle: Consensus or Construct?' (1996) 49 *Current Legal Problems* 267.
[129] A Bainham, 'Status Anxiety? The Rush for Family Recognition' in F Ebtehaj, B Lindley and M Richards (eds), *Kinship Matters* (Oxford, Hart Publishing, 2006) 47.
[130] *Ibid*, 47.
[131] *Ibid*, 48.

CONCLUSION

In this chapter I have argued that, so far as the allocation of parental responsibility is concerned, there is a trend away from parental responsibility as parental authority towards parental responsibility as nothing more than official approval, at least in some cases. While I have argued against the view that parental responsibility is at present an incoherent concept, it may be that the process of degrading parental responsibility will continue until parental responsibility is not so much incoherent as completely devoid of any meaning.[132] Certainly, some commentators have seen the decision in *Re D*[133] as being the first case to award 'pure status',[134] blurring the distinction between parenthood and parental responsibility by awarding parental responsibility simply on the basis of biological fatherhood.[135] Perhaps, if the government proposals to make parental responsibility compulsory for almost all unmarried fathers are implemented,[136] we will see parental responsibility come full circle to Eekelaar's original description of it as meaning nothing more than 'acting responsibly'.[137] However, if this happens, this phrase will not return to the meaning ascribed to it by Eekelaar, that parents are expected to behave responsibly.[138] Rather, 'acting responsibly' will have acquired the New Labour meaning that parents are regarded as needing support to behave responsibly.[139]

---

[132]   See Bridgeman, above n 28, 242.
[133]   [2006] EWHC 2.
[134]   McCandless, above n 36, 67.
[135]   C Lind, 'Responsible Fathers: Paternity, the Blood Tie and Family Responsibility' in Bridgeman, Lind and Keating, above n 28, 192. See also Herring, above n 13, 339.
[136]   See above n 42.
[137]   Above n 25.
[138]   *Ibid.*
[139]   See Bridgeman, above n 28, 242. See further V Gillies, 'Meeting parents' needs: discourses of "support" and "inclusion" in family policy' (2005) 25 *Critical Social Policy* 70; and V Gillies, 'Perspectives on Parenting Responsibility: Contextualizing Values and Practices' (2008) 35 *JLS* 95.

Part II

The Content of Parental Responsibility

6

The Shaming of Naming: Parental Rights and Responsibilities in the Naming of Children

JONATHAN HERRING

INTRODUCTION

Out of the ground the Lord God formed every beast of the field and every bird of the air, and brought them to Adam to see what he would call them. And whatever Adam called each living creature that was its name.[1]

I N THE JUDEO-Christian creation story God gives to Adam the power to name the creatures of the earth. This is seen to symbolise God giving humankind authority over animals. Indeed, generally the ability to name is seen as synonymous with superiority and dominion.[2] Much political control is currently exercised through the power to label a person as a terrorist, as disabled or as a criminal. Much feminist writing has highlighted the ways in which names and labels are used to hide women from public debate and to structure arguments or concepts in a male way.[3] In the law, named categories are created and legal consequences flow from them. As Friedrich Nietzsche stated:

> The lordly right of giving names extends so far that one should allow oneself to conceive the origin of language itself as an expression of power on the part of the rulers: they say 'this is this and this,' they seal every thing and event with a sound and, as it were, take possession of it.[4]

This chapter will consider the power parents are given to name their child and the court resolution of cases where parents are in dispute over what name a child

---

[1] *The Bible*, Genesis 2, v 19.
[2] J Kaplan and A Bernays, *The Language of Names* (New York, Simon & Schuster, 1997).
[3] See, eg D Spender, *Man Made Language* (2nd edn, New York, Routledge, 1994) 183–90.
[4] F Nietzsche, *On the Genealogy of Morals*, trans. W Kaufmann (New York, Random House, 1989)

should have. It will be argued that these cases reveal disputes over names that reflect complex personal and political issues. The way in which the law deals with them raises several issues about the nature of parental responsibility.

NAMES

Having a name is important, as is recognised by the fact that several international conventions express a child's right to a name.[5] Parents often agonise over the names given to their children. When Jordan and Peter Andre announced the name of their daughter, Princess Tiáamii, they felt it necessary to justify their decision.[6] The name Princess was said to convey the meaning that the child was 'their princess' and the name 'Tiáamii' was a combination of the names of their mothers: Amy and Thea. Although Jordan explained: 'We've put an accent over the first A to make it more exotic and two Is at the end just to make it look a bit different'. The couple explained that they had considered using the name Tinkerbell, but decided not to use it because too many celebrities used that name for their dogs. As this exotic example shows, a host of factors can play a part in choosing a name for a child. Many parents attempt to find a name which reflects family ties, which has positive associations to the couple (and will not have negative connotations to others), or is perhaps 'a bit different'—although few couples' negotiations are likely to lead to the same result as Jordan's and Peter's.

HISTORY OF SURNAMES

Until fairly recently in historical terms surnames[7] were unknown in England, although names of some kind seem to have been used from earliest times.[8] Until the mid-part of the Middle Ages, people generally only had given names. Surnames appear to have grown from the difficulty of there being too many people with the same given name and performed the role of distinguishing between them.[9] In the earliest times the surname was bestowed by the community. It might refer to some characteristic of the person or the place where they lived. Hence, 'Hill' and 'Short' are some of the earliest names. The person's job or personality was another popular choice. Hence names such as 'Carpenter' or 'Hardy' were developed. Therefore, in their origins surnames were personal descriptions, rather than a reference to a family tie. It appears to have been the

---

    [5]   eg UN Convention on the Rights of the Child Art 7.
    [6]   BBC News Online, 'Jordan decides on daughter's name' (24 July 2007).
    [7]   There is no consensus on the correct term for names. Here the terminology 'surname' and 'given name' will be used.
    [8]   R McKinley, *A History of British Surnames* (London, Longman, 1990).
    [9]   R Thornton, 'The Controversy Over Children's Surnames: Familial Autonomy, Equal Protection and the Child's Best Interests' (1979) *Utah Law Review* 303, 305.

Normans who first introduced the custom of naming sons after fathers to Britain.[10] But that did not become a universal practice until much later.

As Western societies developed, surnames came to express kinships, but not necessarily on the paternal side. Matronymics have consistently been followed in Spain and were used in England certainly up until the fourteenth century. Some time after the early fourteenth century surnames started to become hereditary family names based on the father's line. The establishment of the Parish Registry System during the reign of Henry VIII, recording births, marriages and deaths, reinforced the practice of using the father's surname. This was seen as greatly assisting in recording identity for taxation purposes. The position of the surnames of children born to unmarried parents was more complex. Early on they were said to be 'nullius filius', so did not acquire a surname from any parent and their name was developed by reputation.[11] Later, they were given the mother's or supposed father's name.

In very recent times, naming practices have again been under scrutiny. It is becoming increasingly common both for women not to take their husband's name and for children to be born outside marriage. This has led to a range of alternatives in selecting surnames. Further, with increasing rates of relationship break-up and repartnering, children's names are increasingly open to change, whether formally or informally.

LAW OF NAMES

What follows will be only a brief summary of the law on children's names.[12] The focus of this chapter will be a consideration of what the law on children's surnames reveals about parental responsibility.

What is a Person's Name?

English law on surnames is astonishingly unregulated. *Re T (Otherwise H) (An Infant)*[13] makes it clear that a person's surname in law is simply that by which she or he is customarily known. This does not have to be the registered name on the birth certificate. It is possible through a deed poll to provide formal evidence of a change from the registered surname, although it is not essential. If a deed poll is used to recognise a child's new surname, it must be signed by all those with parental responsibility.[14]

---

[10] *Ibid.*
[11] Thornton, above n 9, 312.
[12] See S Gilmore, 'The Nature, Scope, and Use of the Specific Issue Order' [2004] 16 *CFLQ* 367 for a useful discussion of the courts' approach in cases of disputes over names.
[13] [1962] 3 All ER 970.
[14] *Practice Direction (Minor: Change of Surname: Deed Poll)* [1995] 1 All ER 832.

The English position on names is remarkable in two ways. First, there is a complete lack of any requirement of formal recording of one's name or change of name. This, one might have thought, would produce all kinds of administrative difficulties for the government. However, in practice it seems not to. In part this may be due to officialdom's use of numbers to identify people (for example, a National Insurance number). Secondly, even if a person does register a name or change it by formally executing a deed poll, this can be changed by common usage.[15] Therefore, not only is there no need for a formal record of a name, where there is a formal record this may not be the name in the eyes of the law.

Registration of Birth

A child's birth must be registered within 42 days[16] and the person registering the birth can declare 'the surname by which at the date of the registration of the birth it is intended that the child shall be known'.[17] The birth can be registered by both parents together or the mother alone; a father can only register the birth by himself if he is married to the mother, if there is a parental responsibility agreement in respect of the child or if he has one of the court orders listed in section 10(1)(e) or 10(1)(f) of the Births and Deaths Registration Act 1953.[18] In the absence of an agreement or a court order evidencing paternity, where the parents are unmarried the choice of registered surname lies with the mother.[19] Where both have the entitlement to register the birth with their preferred name, whoever registers first will make the selection. Once a name has been registered, it can only be changed in the case of clerical error.[20] Although it may be possible to change the name of the child later, this will not alter the name on the birth certificate.

There is no restriction on what names parents can select, although it must consist of letters in Roman script. The child's surname does not need to be one of their own. Their imagination can run riot. I am reliably informed[21] that Bud Weiser, Iona Frisbee, Lou Zar, Shanda Lear and Abbie Birthday all exist and have their parents to thank for their names. Some celebrities' children rebel. Zowie

---

[15] A Bond, 'Reconstructing Families—Changing Children's Surnames' [1998] 10 *CFLQ* 17.

[16] Births and Deaths Registration Act 1953 s 2.

[17] Registration of Births and Deaths Regulations 1987 reg 9(3).

[18] See also *Dawson v Wearmouth* [1997] 2 FLR 629.

[19] It has been claimed that this unfairly discriminates against unmarried fathers: N Gosden, 'Children's Surnames—How Satisfactory is the Current Law?' [2003] *Fam Law* 186. However, if the law wants to grant unmarried fathers parental responsibility only with the consent of the mother, then using registration provides an easy and convenient way to restrict access to parental responsibility.

[20] See M Hayes, 'What's in a Name? A Child by any other Name is Surely just as Sweet?' [1999] 11 *CFLQ* 423, 430 for a discussion of whether it is possible to mount a legal challenge to the registration.

[21] <http://www.ethanwiner.com/funnames.html>; and <http://www.namehumor.com>.

Bowie has let it be known that he wishes to be known as Duncan.[22] In other countries there is far greater control over the names selected, with a requirement for a name to be chosen from an approved list, or at least a discretion for the Registrar to refuse to accept a particular name.[23]

Changing a Name Unilaterally

It is, in fact, rare for a dispute over a surname to arise at the point of registration. Generally it is some time later, when the parents' relationship has broken down, that the issue arises. I will address two key questions: first, whether it is permissible for one parent to change the child's name on their own or whether they need the consent of the other parent or a court order to change the name; and secondly, if there is a dispute which is brought to court, how the court resolves that dispute.

In relation to the first question, the law distinguishes several scenarios.[24]

Where a Residence Order in Respect of the Child Is in Force

Here the law is clear. Section 13(1) of the Children Act 1989 states:

Where a residence order is in force with respect to a child, no person may—

(a) cause the child to be known by a new surname; . . .

without either the written consent of every person who has parental responsibility for the child or the leave of the court.

This provision is self-explanatory. It is notable that the consent of the child, even if *Gillick* competent, is not required for the change to take effect. Of course, in fact, this is not unusual. Parents make all kinds of decisions concerning children without their 'permission'. Schools, places of residence and even country of domicile can all be changed without the child's consent.

Where No Residence Order Is in Force

The Children Act 1989 provides no explicit guidance on the legal position concerning changing names where there is no residence order. The courts have drawn a distinction between cases where a person has parental responsibility and where they do not. Where both parents have parental responsibility, it appears from the Court of Appeal decision in *Dawson v Wearmouth*[25] and *Re T (Change of*

---

[22] A Swedish couple is currently in dispute with the authorities over their wish to name their daughter Elvis (http://news.uk.msn.com/odd-news/article.aspx?cp-documentid=8461839).

[23] See, eg the scheme in Finland: *Johansson v Finland* [2007] 3 FCR 420.

[24] Bond, above n 15.

[25] [1997] 2 FLR 629.

Surname)[26] that a change of name is only permitted if either both parents agree or if the court approves it. If each parent with parental responsibility were able to change the name unilaterally, this might lead to an absurd situation where each parent could unilaterally and repeatedly change the name of the child. A child could have 10 names before breakfast!

Where only one parent has parental responsibility, the legal position is less clear. The view with the most support in the case law is that the parent with parental responsibility does have the right unilaterally to change the name of the child.[27] However, the courts[28] have stated that they should consult with the other parent and that if there is no agreement the matter should be taken to court. That, however, is less a legal obligation than a statement of desirable practice.

Child in Care

Under section 33(7) of the Children Act 1989, if a child is in care then his or her name can only be changed if all those with parental responsibility consent in writing or the court gives leave. It is open for children in care, if sufficiently competent, to apply to have their name changed.[29] In such a case, the court will make the decision applying the welfare principle.[30]

Given Names

In *Re H (Child's Name: First Name)*,[31] it was held that the rules in relation to surnames do not apply to forenames. A court will not stop the resident parent from using whatever forename he or she wishes. The father had registered the child with one first name and it was decided that this would remain the registered name, but for all practical purposes the mother could choose the name she wished. It was explained that children often have a number of different given names during their life. No order was necessary to allow a parent to use a different first name from the one the child was registered with.

Making Decisions Where There Is a Dispute

If a dispute over a child's name is brought to court, the welfare principle in section 1 of the Children Act 1989 applies.[32] This is so whether the application is

---

26   [1998] 2 FLR 620.
27   *Re PC (Change of Surname)* [1997] 3 FCR 544; and *Re W, Re A, Re B (Change of Name)* [1999] 2 FLR 930.
28   *Re R (A Child)* [2002] 1 FCR 170 at [9].
29   *Re S (Change of Surname)* [1999] 1 FLR 672.
30   Children Act 1989 s 1.
31   [2002] 1 FLR 973.
32   *Dawson v Wearmouth* [1999] 1 FLR 1167.

brought as an application under section 8 or 13.[33] The welfare principle provides the court with a broad discretion to determine whether the change of name will promote the welfare of the child. In *Re W (A Child) (Illegitimate Child: Change of Surname); Re A (A Child); Re B (Children)*,[34] Butler Sloss LJ provided the following as a non-exhaustive list of factors to be considered:

> Among the factors to which the court should have regard is the registered surname of the child and the reasons for the registration, for instance recognition of the biological link with the child's father. Registration is always a relevant and an important consideration but it is not in itself decisive. The weight to be given to it by the court will depend upon the other relevant factors or valid countervailing reasons which may tip the balance the other way . . . The relevant considerations should include factors which may arise in the future as well as the present situation . . . Reasons given for changing or seeking to change a child's name based on the fact that the child's name is or is not the same as the parent making the application do not generally carry much weight. The reasons for an earlier unilateral decision to change a child's name may be relevant . . . Any changes of circumstances of the child since the original registration may be relevant . . . In the case of a child whose parents were married to each other, the fact of the marriage is important and I would suggest that there would have to be strong reasons to change the name from the father's surname if the child was so registered . . . Where the child's parents were not married to each other, the mother has control over registration. Consequently on an application to change the surname of the child, the degree of commitment of the father to the child, the quality of contact, if it occurs, between father and child, the existence or absence of parental responsibility are all relevant factors to take into account.

DISCUSSION OF THE LAW

What Are Important Issues in Family Law?

It is striking that we have case law on surnames at all. There are many important issues which generate arguments between parties on family breakdown, but with which the courts or lawyers do not want to get involved. We have, for example, very few cases at all on what should happen to family pets when relationships end, but this is an issue that may well be of great importance to children and adults. Similarly, it is common for one parent to object to the other parent's way of raising a child. As practitioners are all too aware, on family breakdown huge importance can be attached by the parties to the most insignificant of matters. Much family law practice is taken up trying to persuade clients to focus on the more important issues and to settle less important ones. Where cases are brought concerning 'day-to-day' issues relating to child rearing, the courts have tended to

---

[33] Technically, where the application is brought under s 13 the checklist of factors in s 1(3) does not apply, but it is difficult to imagine that this will be of any practical significance.

[34] [1999] 2 FLR 930 at 933.

regard these as decisions for the resident parent, about which the non-resident parent cannot object.[35] There is not even a need for the resident parent to consult the other parent with parental responsibility over child-rearing issues unless it is of fundamental importance.[36] However, the courts have held that changing a surname is one such issue, as are issues over education, circumcision and important medical decisions.[37] Therefore, it is important to ask why naming is deemed worthy of litigation, and is not a matter on which unilateral action is allowed.

The judiciary has not been consistent on whether the issue of names should be regarded as so important. Thorpe LJ in *Re R (A Child)*[38] described naming as 'a comparatively small issue', but in *Re T (Minors)*[39] the same judge referred to 'the clear principle that children's names are important'. The fact that the House of Lords has been willing to hear a case on children's surnames[40] indicates that among the judiciary the issue must be regarded as of sufficient importance that significant judicial resources are spent on it. The number of cases heard indicates that people are certainly willing to spend significant sums of money litigating them.

This still leaves the question of why the judiciary and litigants appear to see the issue of the naming of children as important. It seems that the current view is that names are of significance because of their symbolic significance. In the House of Lords in *Dawson v Wearmouth*,[41] Lord Jauncey elaborated on the significance of a surname:

> A surname which is given to a child at birth is not simply a name plucked out of the air. Where the parents are married the child will normally be given the surname or patronymic of the father thereby demonstrating its relationship to him. The surname is thus a biological label which tells the world at large that the blood of the name flows in its veins. To suggest that a surname is unimportant because it may be changed at any time by deed poll when the child has attained more mature years ignores the importance of initially applying an appropriate label to that child.

This quotation is interesting for several reasons. One is that the blood in the child's body is described as 'the blood of the [father's] name', rather than being simply the child's blood or, even if one wanted to see the issue in his terms, the blood of both parents.

Nevertheless, it is clear that quite a number of people would echo Lord Jauncey's views, although none of the other Law Lords in the case did. To the non-resident parent, the change of name to that of the resident parent's new

---

[35]   *Re P (A Minor) (Parental Responsibility Order)* [1994] 1 FLR 578.
[36]   Children Act 1989 s 2(7).
[37]   See J Herring, *Family Law* (Harlow, Pearson Education Ltd, 2007) 388–9 for a discussion of the law on this.
[38]   [2001] EWCA Civ 1344 at [1].
[39]   CCFMI 98/0035/2 19 May 1998.
[40]   *Dawson v Wearmouth* [1999] 2 WLR 960.
[41]   [1999] 2 WLR 960.

partner's name symbolises the eclipse of him from the child's life. It conveys the message that he is no longer the father, and never was the father. However, this view that names should be regarded as symbolising the child's link with the father is not by any means universally held. Hale LJ states in *Re R (A Child)*:[42]

> I return to the issue of names. It is also a matter of great sadness to me that it is so often assumed, and even sometimes argued, that fathers need that outward and visible link in order to retain their relationship with, and commitment to, their child. That should not be the case. It is a poor sort of parent whose interest in and commitment to his child depends upon that child bearing his name. After all, that is a privilege which is not enjoyed by many mothers, even if they are living with the child. They have to depend upon other more substantial things.

Bob Geldof has responded to these comments with characteristic vigour:

> 'A poor sort of parent' is what this unfortunate was called, whose child would at least know who she and her father were before the past and her identity were stripped, like a Stalinist photograph out of her family's history. He was not allowed even to give her his name. Her family name. So a man is to be stripped of even that. He is to be utterly expunged from the past.[43]

It may be that the question of whether or not names *should* be important is beside the point. Lord Hobhouse noted that the surname of a child 'is among the questions' which give rise to the most deeply felt disputes between parents'. That being so, whether parents should feel strongly may not matter; it is an issue which requires resolution by the courts.

But are names important? Jacques Lacan[44] has argued that names have a dual effect. On the one hand, they enable the child to identify as an individual, while on the other hand, the fact that the name is given to the child, rather than chosen for him or her, demonstrates the extent to which a child's ego is formed socially. The name places the child, and attributes to the child social information about the child's kinship, ethnicity, religion and race. Certainly Lacan is right to emphasise the role of identification with a name. We might feel mildly uncomfortable when we meet someone with our name, and if there are two people with the same given name among a social group it is common for one person to amend a name so that a distinction of identity is preserved. Notably, when the singer Prince changed his name to one that could not be spoken, he became known as 'the artist formerly known as Prince', demonstrating the unacceptability of being someone who could not be named.

---

[42]   [2001] EWCA Civ 1344 at [13].
[43]   B Geldof, 'The Real Love that Dare not Speak its Name' in A Bainham, B Lindley, M Richards and L Trinder (eds), *Children and their Families* (Oxford, Hart, 2003) 185.
[44]   J Lacan, *Écrits: A Selection* (New York, WW Norton & Company, 1977).

But do names do any more than identify?[45] This has been an issue of much debate.[46] The point is that the name may not simply be an identifier, but may also convey a message about that individual.[47] John Stuart Mill clearly argues to the contrary:

> Proper names are not connotative; they denote the individuals who are called by them; but they do not indicate or imply attributes as belonging to those individuals.[48]

However, others disagree and argue that through a surname a child will be marked as having ties to families, communities and groups within our society.[49] This, with respect, seems doubtful. There can no longer be any assumption that children will take on their parents' religious, cultural or political beliefs.[50] Even if this were so, the courts are not able to determine (except in unusual cases) whether the associations and groups marked by the name X are going to be any better or worse for the child than being marked by the name Y, any more than the court would wish to decide whether a child is better brought up by parents who generally vote Conservative or those who generally vote Labour.

Therefore, it is argued that, given the fluidity within society, a surname cannot be said itself to connote that the child will have particular attributes or belong to a specific group. So, to individual children the issue of whether they bear surname A or B at birth is of little importance. However, it will be argued later that surnaming practices are not trivial in that they send some powerful messages about family life. Their symbolic and cultural significance is important.

Avoiding Litigation

Mary Hayes[51] explains that on relationship breakdown there is often animosity and that the parties will seek out issues on which to fight. She concludes:

> It is surely better, therefore, to try to avoid creating the opportunity for the parents' personal hostility to be vented in litigation about their children's names if at all possible.[52]

Therefore, the law should seek a rule with which to deal with these disputes to prevent them coming to court. Her proposed solution is that the law should place weight on the registered name, and only if there is a very strong case not to

---

[45]   R Nelson, *Naming and Reference: the Link of Word to Object* (New York, Routledge, 1992).
[46]   Bond, above n 15.
[47]   S Soames, *Beyond Rigidity: The Unfinished Semantic Agenda of Naming and Necessity* (Oxford, Oxford University Press, 2002).
[48]   JS Mill, *A System of Logic* (New York, Longmans, 1990) 20.
[49]   R Jayaraman, 'Personal Identity in a Globalized World: Cultural Roots of Hindu Personal Names and Surnames' (2005) 38 *Journal of Popular Culture* 476.
[50]   See Taylor, this volume.
[51]   Hayes, above n 20.
[52]   *Ibid.*

uphold the registered name should there be consent to depart from it. While agreeing that it is beneficial to have a clear rule to avoid litigation, her suggestion that this would be provided by the registered name is problematic, as we shall see.

However, first, we will consider what weight the courts have placed on the registered name. The courts have regarded the registered name as a factor in applying the welfare test, but not one of overriding importance. The person seeking to change the child's name from the registered one has the burden of persuading the court that the change of name is in the child's welfare. Ward LJ in *Re C (Change of Surname)*[53] stated that the person seeking to change the name must provide 'good and cogent reasons' to support the change. On the other hand, it would be wrong to state that registration should be regarded as decisive.[54] Indeed, at the heart of the House of Lords' decision in *Dawson v Wearmouth* is the finding that the Court of Appeal had put too much weight on the registered name and regarded it as the 'all important issue'.[55]

What is not entirely clear from the case law is why the courts think that the registered name is of significance at all. One possibility is that this is no more than shorthand for the principle in section 1(5) of the Children Act 1989. There is, in other words, no more to the relevance of the registered name than the normal principle that the court needs to be persuaded that making an order is better than not. This appears to be the explanation adopted by the then Lord Chancellor Lord McKay of Clashfern in the case of *Dawson v Wearmouth*:[56]

> ... the right course, in my opinion, must be to apply the criteria in s 1 of the 1989 Act including s 1(5) and not make an order for the change of name unless there is some evidence that this would lead to an improvement from the point of view of the welfare of the child.

If this is the explanation, it will mean that the registered name is of significance purely as it constitutes the status quo. However, Lord Hobhouse seemed to indicate that it had an independent importance, stating that the registered name:

> is a relevant factor which must be taken into account and may, in certain cases, like any other relevant factor make the difference between whether an order is made or not.[57]

An alternative explanation would seek to put weight specifically on the registration. It might be argued that litigation over this issue should be discouraged and so there needs to be a general principle to be applied which the courts will follow, in the absence of strong evidence that a child is being harmed. In such a case the registered name of the child is as good a principle as any. Seen in this way, as a deterrence to litigation, weighty evidence would be required to justify displacing the name.[58]

53   [1999] 1 FCR 318.
54   *Re W, Re A, Re B (Change of Name)* [1999] 2 FLR 930.
55   *Dawson v Wearmouth* [1999] 1 FLR 1167 at 1180 (Lord Hobhouse).
56   [1999] 1 FLR 1167 at 1173H.
57   [1999] 1 FLR 1167 at 1180.
58   Hayes, above n 20.

Neither argument, it is submitted, should be regarded as convincing. First, it should be recalled that all the registered name is meant to be is the name the parents intend to use for the child. The courts are attaching greater significance to the name at registration than seems justified by the Registration of Births and Deaths Regulations 1987.[59] If the registered name is taken to be the name that the child should have unless there are good reasons otherwise, this should be made clear to the parents at the time of registration. Secondly, arguing that the registered name represents the status quo is inaccurate. Where a parent has changed a child's name and this is objected to by the other party, the child's current name is in English law the name by which the child is generally known.[60] As already mentioned, the registered name is not significant in ascertaining a person's name. Therefore, the status quo is the name by which the child is generally known, not their registered name. It is therefore submitted that the registered name should carry no weight when the court is resolving a dispute over names.

Therefore, it is submitted that the courts are wrong to place even the little weight they do on the registered name. Further, Hayes' argument that it should be given even greater weight fails for the same reason. Added to this is the argument that shall be developed later, that supporting registered names, in effect, means supporting patronymy (the use of male surnames for children), a practice which should be challenged, rather than reinforced. A preferable solution is that where there is a dispute between parents over the name, a child should have two surnames, one selected by each parent.[61] Therefore, in *Dawson v Wearmouth*, the child should have the surname Dawson Wearmouth.[62] This will recognise the link to both parents and does not convey a message that one parent is more important than the other.[63] It has the benefit of providing a ready solution which should leave neither side feeling it has 'lost'. There is some mild judicial support for this. In *Re R (A Child)*,[64] it was suggested that using a combination of both surnames was to be encouraged because it would recognise the importance of both parents to the child.[65] It is argued here that the courts should be bolder and

---

[59]   SI 1987/2088.

[60]   I am grateful to Stephen Gilmore for demonstrating to me that this is not beyond dispute. As he points out, in *Re PC (Change of Surname)* [1997] 3 FCR 544, changing a name without the consent of all those with parental responsibility has been described as 'unlawful'. However, I do not think that that means the change of name is ineffective. The principle in English law is that one's name is the name one uses and is generally known by. Where a parent without consent causes their child to be known by a different name, they have acted unlawfully, but the name of the child has indeed changed.

[61]   There may be some cases where melding of the surnames of both parents would be effective.

[62]   I would suggest that no hyphen be used, but have no strong views on this.

[63]   No doubt those desperate for a fight will want to argue about which name goes first. If a resolution is required, alphabetical order or the tossing of a coin are suitably arbitrary.

[64]   [2002] 1 FCR 170. The option did not appeal to HHJ Tyrer in *A v Y (Child's Surname)* [1999] 2 FLR 5, who thought that only the mother's half (the latter half) of the name would be used.

[65]   One factor which may have influenced the court was that the family were moving to Spain where the use of double surnames is the normal practice.

require a two-surname solution unless there is an extreme case where a different solution might be preferred (for example, where a name change is necessary to avoid a feared abduction).[66] It might be said that double surnames are cumbersome, embarrassing or even posh. However, any harm resulting from these is arguably outweighed by the avoidance of litigation and antagonism surrounding the issue.

Acknowledging the Limits of the Courts' Power

There have been quite a number of cases where courts have held that the child should keep the registered name for formal purposes (for example, medical records; passport), but the day-to-day name (ie the name the law regards as the actual name) should be kept as the one requested by the resident parent.[67] This will occur particularly where the child's surname has been changed and the child has used the new name for some time before the matter is brought before the court. In such circumstances, the court may easily be persuaded that it would be harmful for the child to have the name changed back to the original name.[68]

One justification for this approach is that it is simply acknowledging the limits of the courts' powers. Wilson J in *Re B (Change of Surname)* accepted that, in practice, there is little the law can do to control the name by which a child is to be known on a day-to-day basis. The court can only control the name by which the child will be known in formal documents, such as a birth certificate or formal medical record.[69] An alternative justification is that the law is respecting the rights of the resident parent. To force them on a daily basis to use for their child a name they object to could be regarded as a serious invasion of their right to respect for their family life. However, if the obligation only arises on rare formal occasions, the degree of interference will be much less.[70]

Despite the convenience of the courts' approach, it has serious disadvantages. The occasions on which the formal name will be required—hospital appointments, meetings with educational authorities, court hearings and the like—will be fraught with tension for the child. For the child then to be called by a name he or she is unfamiliar with or to require the child to explain any inconsistency with names seems undesirable. At those formal times everything should be done to put the child at ease. At the very least that should mean referring to the child by the name with which he or she is familiar. It is therefore submitted that the name by which the child is generally known (ie their name in the eyes of the law) should be the one used on formal documents. It might be argued that this can

---

[66] *F v M* [2007] EWHC 2543 (Fam).
[67] See, eg, *Bucknell (formerly Hallas) v Hallas*, unreported, 2 April 1990.
[68] See, eg *Re C (Change of Surname)* [1998] 2 FLR 656.
[69] [1996] 2 FCR 304.
[70] This kind of argument was influential in *Guillot v France* [1996] ECHR 48.

only lead to problems with identification, although with medical documents, for example, patient numbers, rather than names, are more commonly used.

Parental Responsibility and Children's Views

The child's views will be important, but not the sole consideration, when a court applies the welfare principle in a naming case. Wilson J in *Re B (Change of Surname)*[71] ordered that three children (two of them teenagers) keep their father's surname, despite their opposition, in order to maintain the link with their father. However, it might be thought that little more could be done to damage the relationship between a father and teenagers than forcing them to keep his name.[72] Despite this decision, it was made clear in *Re S (Change of Surname)*[73] that the views of a *Gillick*-competent child over a surname should be given careful consideration. In *Re M, T, P, K and B*[74] it was held that a court should be 'particularly loathe' to refuse applications to change names which are supported by mature children, although the Court added that such wishes are 'neither paramount nor determinative'.

The fact that children's rights to choose their names are not permitted in these cases illustrates how little weight the notion of children's autonomy rights actually has in UK law. This is a situation where there is an extremely strong case for allowing a competent child to choose their own name. The following points can be emphasised. First, the name by which a person is known is a highly personal matter of daily import. Children's interests in what they are called must surely be regarded as weightier than the parents' interest. Secondly, this is an issue where children cannot really suffer harm as a result of exercising their right to choose, except in extreme cases.[75] Some commentators are understandably concerned about letting children make decisions for themselves where that decision will severely impede their wellbeing. However, this is not an issue where that is likely to occur. Thirdly, this is an issue where views on what is best for children differ and there is no clearly correct answer. In such a case it is particularly apt to allow children to make decisions for themselves. The fact that it is not shows that the law has a long way to go before properly acknowledging that children have autonomy rights.

---

[71]   *Re B (Change of Surname)* [1996] 2 FCR 304.
[72]   See for further extra-judicial comment on this decision: Sir N Wilson 'The ears of the child in family proceedings' [2007] *Fam Law* 808, 817–8.
[73]   [1999] 1 FLR 672.
[74]   [2000] 2 FLR 645.
[75]   eg where the child's name can lead to them being identified and then abducted.

Step-Families

Many of the cases concerning disputes over surnames involve a battle over whether the child should be integrated into a new step-family by taking on the surname adopted by the mother and her new family or whether the surname should be used to retain a link between the child and the father. The courts have accepted the argument that the surname retains an important link with the birth father, but much less attention has been paid to the role that it can play in integrating the child into the step-family. In general, where there is a poor relationship between the child and father, this is seen as an argument in favour of changing the child's name from his.[76] In the B case in *Re W, Re A, Re B (Change of Name)*,[77] approval was given to a change of name from the father's after the father had been imprisoned. One reason for this was because there was not likely to be a meaningful relationship between the child and her father in the future. In cases involving children in care, the link with the birth family provided by the name has been seen as generally important. Foster carers and special guardians are not permitted to change the child's name from that selected by the birth parents without the leave of the court or consent of all with parental responsibility,[78] although, of course, on adoption the child generally takes the name of the adoptive family.

It is interesting how rarely the court sees these name disputes in the context of this tension between social and biological parenting. It is a useful reminder of the ways in which a dispute may in fact disguise broader issues between the parties than the apparent one raised in the case. An example in a slightly different context is *Re L (A Child)*,[79] where it was interesting that the special guardians, who were taking over the care of a deeply troubled child, wanted the child to have their surname in an attempt to normalise the situation. The dispute in that case over the surname appears to have been a symptom of the insecurity of the special guardians in their status, given some rather heavy-handed social work intervention during the case.

Parental Responsibility and Wider Social Issues

Exercises of parental responsibility are often seen as essentially private matters of little significance outside the context of the family. However, it is submitted that surnames do have important social significance. The 'standard' approach for the last few centuries, at least in the United Kingdom, is that on marriage the wife takes her husband's surname and that any children produced likewise take on his

---

76 *Re P (Parental Responsibility: Change of Name)* [1997] 3 FCR 739.
77 [1999] 2 FLR 930.
78 Children Act 1989 s 14B. See further *Re L (A Child)* [2007] EWCA Civ 196; and *Re D, L and LA (Care: Change of Forename)* [2003] 1 FLR 339.
79 [2007] EWCA Civ 196.

name.[80] The vast majority of disputes involving children's surnames concern a father seeking to prevent the child losing his name. Surnames have been used, and to a degree continue to be used, as a way of perpetuating patriarchy.[81] Patronymy often reflects and reinforces a number of gender stereotypes. It is claimed that:

> By the rules of patronymy, therefore, the woman is symbolically compelled into a posture of existential derivation, dependence, and submission.[82]

The taking by the wife and children of the husband's name might be seen as sending a message that the husband is the head of the household and the wife and children are subject to his control,[83] and that the wife on assuming her husband's name becomes subsumed behind his identity.[84] This is most apparent in the, now admittedly less common, practice of referring to a wife as, for example, Mrs Gordon Brown. Patronymics reflect the well-known legal dictum that on marriage the husband and wife become one and 'the husband is that one'.[85] Of course there is an irony here for women who seek to break free from the tradition by selecting to keep their own names, since in doing so they often retain the names of their fathers.[86] On divorce, some see the issue of naming as sending a clear message to children. Priscilla Ruth MacDougall claims that retaining their father's surname 'tells children that their mother's importance remains secondary to that of their fathers even after their parents are divorced'.[87]

The practice of patronymy has led some commentators to suggest that women's attitudes towards, and understandings of, their names are different.[88] Women grow up realising that they may well change their name. For many women, therefore, the surname is temporary, a symbol of their current status rather than being central to their identity. Indeed, the use by women of different surnames in different contexts appears increasingly common,[89] while for men the surname will be a life-long constant, which through children may continue in history. It has, therefore, a sense of immutability which gives it a different context

---

[80]   Although there are historical examples of a man taking his wife's name, especially when marrying an heiress (L Stone and J Fawtier Stone, *An Open elite? England 1540–1880* (Oxford, Clarendon Press, 1984). I am grateful to Rebecca Probert for referring me to this.

[81]   M Daly, *Beyond the Father: Toward a Philosophy of Women's Liberation* (Boston, Beacon Press, 1973) 8–10 and 47–9.

[82]   O Morgenstern Leissner, 'The Problem that has no Name' (1998) 4 *Cardozo Women's Law Journal* 321.

[83]   M Arichi, 'Is it radical? Women's right to keep their own surnames after marriage—Yesterday and today' (1999) 22 *Women's Studies International Forum* 411.

[84]   S Kupper, *Surnames For Women: A Decision-Making Guide* (Jefferson NS, McFarland, 1990) 23.

[85]   Sir William Blackstone, *Commentaries on the Laws of England*, Vol 1 (first published 1765–69, 21st edn, 1844) 442.

[86]   M Omi, 'The Name of the Maiden' (1997) 12 *Wisconsin Women's Law Journal* 253.

[87]   P MacDougall, 'The Right of Women to Name Their Children' (1985) 3 *Law & Inequality Journal* 91, 99.

[88]   Omi, above n 86, 270.

[89]   L Scheuble and D Johnson, 'Women's Situational Use of Last Names' (2005) 53 *Sex Roles* 3.

from the position of some women. Some claim that the courts are following male rather than female understandings of naming.[90]

Even if this argument is accepted, it may be said that this should be of no relevance for the law. There are all manner of sexist practices which reinforce patriarchy and we might wish did not happen, but the law cannot be expected to deal with all of them. Parents may raise their children to believe in gender stereotypes, but we cannot regulate that. While the law should not enforce these attitudes by requiring women and children to take men's names, the current system leaves it to couples to make their own minds up. Education may lead to wider awareness of the issues, but it is not suggested that at birth registration couples are compelled to use a non-patronymic surname.[91] However, where the court is called upon to resolve a dispute, it should legitimately take into account the wider social ramifications of the decision. This can be achieved by the courts adopting the dual-name form suggested above.

The broader social significance of naming is well revealed by looking at the way in which lesbian couples have taken to giving surnames to children they intend to raise together. This is particularly interesting as here there is no preconceived idea of names.[92] What is notable from one leading survey is the range of surnaming practices. Of 20 couples interviewed, eight different approaches were taken. However, a consistent theme was the wider social significance of their practice. One couple changed their name to a new third surname and gave their child that name too. They wanted to make it clear to society that they were starting a new family together. Many couples interviewed were attracted by versions of double-barrelled names to reflect the equal status of both parents and refute negative portrayals about lesbian motherhood. As this shows, the decision to name cannot be made in a social vacuum. The debates between these women reflect wider debates in society over the role of surnames.

CONCLUSION

This chapter has considered and critiqued some of the law on the naming of children. It has proposed some reforms to the law, in particular that in cases of dispute the child should have two surnames, one selected by each parent. However, the discussion has also raised some broader points concerning parental responsibility. First, there is the broad discretion in English law left to parents over parenting decisions, and over names in particular. Unlike in other countries, there is no restriction on what name a child can be given. Secondly, we have seen

---

[90] M Weiner, 'We Are Family: Valuing Associationalism in Disputes Over Children's Surnames' (1997) 75 *North Carolina Law Review* 1625.

[91] In *Johansson v Finland* [2007] 3 FCR 420, the court confirmed that the selection of a child's name should be protected as part of respecting the right to private and family life.

[92] K Almack, 'What's in a Name? The Significance of the Choice of Surnames Given to Children Born within Lesbian-parent Families' (2005) 8 *Sexualities* 239.

the difficulty in separating out issues which relate to parents' interests and those that relate to children's. All too easily, because an issue is seen as important to an adult, it is seen as important to a child. Although whether a child has one name or another matters a huge deal to some parents, it is not obvious that it matters enormously to children's welfare. Much of the case law exhibits power struggles between parents rather than attempts to ascertain what will be in a child's best interests. Thirdly, although parental decisions, such as those involving names, are often seen as being essentially private matters, in fact they reflect and reinforce wider social attitudes and can have wider social repercussions.[93] In this chapter we have seen how surnaming has been used to normalise and symbolise male power over women and children. That can be avoided by the courts advocating the use of double surnames.

[93] Morgenstern Leissner, above n 82.

7

Parental Responsibility and Religion

RACHEL TAYLOR

INTRODUCTION

And these words which I command you today shall be in your heart.
You shall teach them diligently to your children, and shall talk of them
when you sit in your house, when you walk by the way, when you
lie down, and when you rise up.[1]

Religion is the one field in our culture about which it is absolutely
accepted, without question—without even noticing how bizarre it is—that
parents have a total and absolute say in what their children are going
to be, how their children are going to be raised, what opinions their children
are going to have about the cosmos, about life, about existence. Do you see
what I mean about mental child abuse?[2]

T HE QUESTION OF whether it is best for a child to be brought up within
a particular religion, or in none, is one on which reasonable people deeply
disagree. The state has no tools by which to resolve this disagreement,[3]
and instead leaves the question almost entirely in the hands of the individual
parent. Whilst there is no duty on a parent to bring a child up with religious
knowledge, the right to determine a child's religious upbringing is unquestionably an aspect of parental responsibility.[4] Indeed, for devout parents this is often
one of the most important aspects of parental responsibility, setting the context
in which they bring up their children and organise their family life. Further, many

---

[1] *The Bible*, Deuteronomy 6, v 6–7.
[2] R Dawkins, 'Is Science a Religion?' (*The Humanist*, 1997) <http://www.thehumanist.org/
humanist/articles/dawkins.html>.
[3] *Re Carroll* [1931] KB 317 at 336.
[4] *Re J (Specific Issue Orders: Muslim Upbringing and Circumcision)* [1999] 2 FLR 678. In this
chapter the determination of a child's 'religious upbringing' includes the determination that the child
is brought up without a religion.

religions place obligations on parents to bring their child up with knowledge of the principles and rituals of that religion. Parents may, therefore, see their responsibility for determining a child's religious upbringing both as of benefit to the child and as a manifestation of their own religious beliefs. The law does little to regulate the decisions made by parents concerning their children's religious upbringing, only interfering in those decisions in rare cases of a serious threat of harm to the child or where a dispute between those with parental responsibility is brought to the courts. In this sense, parental responsibility for the religious upbringing of the child is primarily concerned with freedom from state interference.

Children have a widely recognised right to freedom of thought and religion, as recognised, for example, in Article 14 of the United Nations Convention on the Rights of the Child:

> 1. States Parties shall respect the right of the child to freedom of thought, conscience and religion.
>
> 2. States Parties shall respect the rights and duties of the parents and, when applicable, legal guardians, to provide direction to the child in the exercise of his or her right in a manner consistent with the evolving capacities of the child.

This Article raises, but does not resolve, the tension between the evolving capacity of the child to freedom of thought, conscience and religion and the rights of parents to provide direction to her in that freedom. Arguably, the Article fails to give children an independent right to freedom of thought and religion, but instead predicates that right on the right of the parent to provide direction.[5] Certainly, English law can be seen as following such a model; the child's freedom is rarely seen behind the parent's right to determine his or her religious upbringing.

The right to determine a child's religious upbringing raises two of the key questions for parental responsibility: first, how far parental responsibility has moved beyond traditional notions of parental rights; and, secondly, whether the interests of children can be separated from those of their parents in a pluralistic society where the state is unable to determine the 'best' upbringing for a child.

PARENTAL RIGHTS AND RELIGIOUS UPBRINGING AT COMMON LAW

The modern law of parental responsibility in this area has its roots in the common law right of a father to determine the religious upbringing of his child.[6] Although the religious conflicts of the sixteenth and seventeenth centuries saw

---

[5] For discussion, see C Hamilton, *Family Law and Religion* (London, Sweet & Maxwell, 1995) 144; J Fortin, *Children's Rights and the Developing Law* (2nd edn, Cambridge, Cambridge University Press, 2005) 42–3; SE Mumford, 'The Judicial Resolution of Disputes Involving Children and Religion' (1998) 47 *ICLQ* 117; and S Langlaude, *The Right of the Child to Religious Freedom in International Law* (Leiden, Nijhoff, 2007) ch 4.

[6] Save in cases of illegitimacy, where the mother held such rights.

draconian state intervention to restrict the ability of parents to bring their children up outside the established church,[7] by the early nineteenth century the father had almost complete control over his child's religious upbringing. The potential strength of paternal rights is perhaps best illustrated in the well-known case of *Agar-Ellis*.[8] In that case, a father, wishing his children to be brought up as Protestants, removed his children from all contact with their mother, who had secretly educated them as Roman Catholics. The court refused to interfere with exercise of the father's rights, despite the fact that there had been an agreement at the time of marriage that the children would be brought up as Roman Catholics and that the children's own wishes were that they would continue to be brought up in that faith. In the view of the court, the question was not one of the children's welfare or conflict between parents, but whether the father had forfeited or abandoned his paternal rights. As he had not done so, the court 'could not interfere with him in his honest exercise of the jurisdiction which the law had confided to him'.[9]

In *Agar-Ellis*, the question of the religious upbringing of the child was not clearly distinguished from the father's right to custody and control of education. The right to determine a child's religious upbringing was, nevertheless, more than simply an attribute of the right to custody. This is clearly seen from the fact that the father's religion would continue to dominate the child's religious upbringing even following the father's death and even where the father had not given express direction as to the child's religion. This led to harsh cases such as *Hawksworth v Hawksworth*,[10] in which the religion of a Roman Catholic father, who had died leaving no instructions as to the upbringing of his then six-month-old daughter, prevailed over the express wishes of her Protestant mother, who had brought her up in that religion for the eight years following his death.[11]

This paternal right was, however, not absolute. There were some circumstances in which a father would be adjudged to have forfeited his rights to determine the religious upbringing of his children. Most famously, the poet Shelley was deprived of the custody of his children on the grounds that he professed and acted upon irreligious and immoral principles.[12] Further, a second strand of cases considered that the dominant question for the court was the welfare of the children, although this would usually be secured by following the wishes of the father.[13]

---

[7]   LM Friedman, 'The Parental Right to Control the Religious Education of the Child' (1916) 29 *Harvard Law Review* 485.

[8]   *Re Agar-Ellis* (1878–79) LR 10 Ch D 49; (1883) LR 24 Ch D 317.

[9]   *Re Agar-Ellis* (1878–79) LR 10 Ch D 49 at 75.

[10]   *Hawksworth v Hawksworth* (1871) LR 6 Ch App 539.

[11]   See also *Re Scanlan* (1888) LR 40 Ch D 200.

[12]   *Shelley v Westbrooke* (1817) Jac 266. See also *Wellesley's Case* (1827) 38 ER 236; (1828) 4 ER 1078. Other undesirable aspects of Shelley's parenting may have influenced the court: J Todd, *Death and the Maidens* (London, Profile Books, 2007).

[13]   See, eg *Stourton v Stourton* (1857) 8 DeG M&G 760. For discussion, see JC Hall, 'The Waning of Parental Rights' (1972) 31 *CLJ* 248; and Friedman, above n 7.

Legislative change,[14] culminating in the Children Act 1989, has altered the right to determine religious upbringing: it now belongs to parents, rather than fathers, and is subject to the principle that the child's welfare is paramount. Nevertheless, this right has its roots in the common law paternal right and grants a wide ambit of discretion to parents to decide their children's religious upbringing free from state intervention.

PARENTAL RESPONSIBILITY AND THE CHILDREN ACT 1989

The modern law of parental responsibility continues to give parents a remarkably broad discretion to determine the religious upbringing of their children.[15] The position under the Children Act 1989 was summarised by Wall J in *Re J* as follows:

> The Children Act 1989 does not impose any obligation on parents in respect of religious upbringing or instruction. Section 3, which defines parental responsibility, describes it as 'all the rights, duties, powers, responsibilities and authority which by law a parent of a child has in relation to the child and his property.' Parental responsibility thus clearly includes the right to bring up children in a particular religious faith, or in none.[16]

It is clear that the right to bring a child up within a particular religion survives as an aspect of parental responsibility under the Children Act 1989. It is also clear that there is no obligation to give a child any form of religious upbringing or education. There is, however, no clear definition of the content, nature and limitations of this 'right' in the case law or legislation. It is to this question of definition that we now turn.

A Right to Determine a Child's Religion?

In the quotation above, Wall J was concerned with the parental right to decide upon a child's religious upbringing. By contrast, in their well-known list of the attributes of parental responsibility, the authors of *Bromley's Family Law* refer to a right to determine the *religion* of the child and not merely his or her religious *upbringing*.[17] In fact it seems that no case to date has determined the religion of a child as opposed to his or her religious upbringing.[18] It is suggested that the

---

[14] See especially the Guardianship of Infants Act 1925.
[15] For the position of local authorities acquiring parental responsibility through a care order, see below.
[16] *Re J (Specific Issue Orders: Muslim Upbringing and Circumcision)* [1999] 2 FLR 678 at 685.
[17] N Lowe and G Douglas, *Bromley's Family Law* (10th edn, Oxford, Oxford University Press, 2007) 377.
[18] *Re J (Specific Issue Orders: Child's Religious Upbringing and Circumcision)* [2000] 1 FLR 571 at 575.

current state of the law is correct and that it is better to regard parents as having the right to determine a child's religious upbringing rather than his or her religion.

It is difficult to see what the legal significance of a right to determine a child's *religion* might be. In this jurisdiction, there is no process by which a formal declaration of a person's religion is made. There are few situations in which a person's religion affects their legal rights or obligations, and where those situations do arise the person's religion is best determined as a matter of fact in the context in which it is raised.[19]

A parental right to determine a child's religion would also be problematic as each religion has discretion as to the grounds on which it recognises members of its own faith. There is no one model of religious belonging: it may be formed through birth into a religious family; participation in the rituals, traditions and activities of a religion; and personal belief in the tenets and doctrines of that religion.[20] The extent to which each of these interlinked components is regarded as important will vary between religions and individuals. A parent may have a strong influence over each of these components, but cannot determine the actions and beliefs of a child. Even a child who is not yet *Gillick* competent may question his or her religious upbringing and begin to construct his or her own religious identity.[21] A parent may have a significant influence over their child's religion, but this falls short of the ability to determine that religion.

A focus on the determination of a child's religion may also raise problems in the resolution of disputes between parents. This is illustrated by *Re J*,[22] in which a five-year-old boy living with his non-practising Christian mother was essentially receiving a secular upbringing. His non-practising Muslim father wanted him to receive aspects of Muslim upbringing, including circumcision. The father argued that J was a Muslim by birth under Islamic law and that, as a Muslim, his welfare required such an upbringing. The court rejected this approach, focusing instead on the child's upbringing to date and relations with the wider community. Affirming this decision, Thorpe LJ considered that:

> Some faiths recognise their religion as a birthright derived from either the child's mother or the child's father. Some recognise religion by some ceremony of induction or initiation, but the newborn does not share the perception of his parents or of the religious community to which the parents belong. A child's perception of his or her religion generally depends on involvement in worship and teaching within the family. From this develops the emotional, intellectual, psychological and spiritual sense of

---

[19] A rare example would be that a Sikh wearing a turban is exempt under the Road Traffic Act 1988 s 16(2) from laws on protective headgear.

[20] See Langlaude, above n 5, ch 1 for discussion of research on the development of religious identity in children.

[21] Y Ronen, 'Redefining the Child's Right to Identity' (2004) 18 *IJLPF* 147. See the chapters by Gilmore and Hagger, this volume, on *Gillick* competence.

[22] *Re J (Specific Issue Orders: Muslim Upbringing and Circumcision)* [1999] 2 FLR 678; [2000] 1 FLR 571.

belonging to a religious faith. So far, for all practical purposes, the courts have been right to focus upon religious upbringing and it is no surprise to me that there is no reported case focusing on a child's religion.[23]

It is submitted that this is correct. Each faith is free to determine its own rules on religious affiliation and a court attempting to adjudicate on those rules risks becoming unnecessarily embroiled in inter- and intra-religious disputes, which it is ill equipped to resolve.[24] Further, although religious considerations will often be important in considering welfare, the focus should be on the realities of the child's life rather than the religious label attached to him or her.

For these reasons, it is suggested that it is legally correct and desirable to regard parents as having a right to determine a child's religious upbringing rather than to determine the child's religion itself.

Content of the Right to Determine Religious Upbringing

It is clear that parental responsibility gives parents the right to determine their child's religious upbringing, should they wish to do so, but also that it does not place parents under a duty to provide any form of religious instruction. There is, however, no definition of the content of this parental 'right' in the case law, and barely any legislative regulation of its exercise. Further consideration must be given to exactly what is meant by a parental right to determine religious upbringing.

Religious motivation may be present in making decisions on many aspects of parental responsibility such as the naming of children[25] and the consent to medical treatment of minors.[26] Our concern here, however, is with those aspects of parental responsibility that are directly related to a child's religious education and experience. Religious upbringing may involve restriction or obligation in a wide range of aspects of the child's life, such as his or her diet and clothing. It may also involve attendance at or participation in services, rituals, collective worship and festivals and the provision of religious education. Parents have a broad discretion, within the boundaries of the general law and the welfare principle, to determine these matters.

It may, however, be asked whether there is anything unusual about the religious context. Parents have a broad discretion to determine a child's diet, dress and attendance at events and classes, whether or not the exercise of that discretion has a religious motivation: is the 'right' to determine a child's religious upbringing anything more than a particular manifestation of general freedom of

---

[23]   *Re J (Specific Issue Orders: Child's Religious Upbringing and Circumcision)* [2000] 1 FLR 571 at 575.
[24]   S Van Praagh, 'Religion, Custody and a Child's Identities' (1997) 35 *Osgoode Hall Law Journal* 309, 343 and 363–4.
[25]   See, eg *Re S (change of names: cultural factors)* [2001] 3 FCR 648.
[26]   See, eg *Re O (a minor) (medical treatment)* [1993] 2 FLR 149.

parents to bring their children up as they think best?[27] However, whilst many of the decisions that a parent might make concerning a child's religious upbringing could be classed as falling within this general parental freedom, this is not the case with all aspects of religious upbringing. In addition to a broad freedom, the law also grants parents some unusual rights, suggesting that particular weight is given to the religious decisions of parents. This is illustrated by the law on religious education and circumcision.

Removal from Religious Education and Collective Worship

Parents have a long-standing and absolute right to remove their children from religious education and collective worship that would otherwise form part of the child's compulsory education even, it appears, if the child him- or herself wishes to attend such classes.[28] The only comparable right is the similar, and more recent, parental right to remove a child from sex education.[29] A parent[30] is not obliged to give any reason for the exercise of this right and the school is obliged to give effect to the parent's decision.[31] This is an important right, emphasising the rights of parents, rather than the state, to determine the religious education of the child.

Importantly, this is clearly a parental right, not the right of the child concerned. Although a recent change in the law now allows sixth-form students to remove themselves from religious worship,[32] mature teenagers below the minimum school leaving age are not granted such a choice. This focus on the rights of parents to determine their child's religious education reflects a narrow reading of the text and case law concerning Article 2 of Protocol 1 of the European Convention on Human Rights (ECHR). As Fortin comments, this approach seems to rest 'on the assumption that although the state must not indoctrinate children, their parents can'.[33] The Joint Committee on Human Rights has recommended a change to the law to allow all children of 'sufficient maturity, intelligence and understanding' to themselves elect to withdraw from religious education and worship.[34] Such an approach would recognise that children themselves have rights under Article 9 ECHR and that a *Gillick*-competent child

---

[27] J Eekelaar, 'What Are Parental Rights?' (1973) 89 *LQR* 210, 221.

[28] This right is currently contained in School Standards and Framework Act 1998 s 71.

[29] Education Act 1996 s 405. This right only applies to sex education that does not form part of the National Curriculum.

[30] The term 'parent' includes all those with parental responsibility and those with care of the child whether or not they have parental responsibility: Education Act 1996 s 576.

[31] Department for Education and Skills, Circular 1/94 [83]–[87].

[32] Education and Inspections Act 2006 s 55.

[33] J Fortin, *Children's Rights and the Developing Law* (2nd edn, Cambridge, Cambridge University Press, 2005) 356.

[34] Joint Committee on Human Rights, 'Nineteenth Report' (2006–2007) 1.40–45. Presumably a child reaching this standard should also be entitled to attend religious education and worship despite the objection of his or her parents.

is able to form his or her own beliefs, protected by this right. At present, the law allows parents to dictate the religious education received by their children.

Circumcision

A further unusual right granted to parents is the right to consent to the circumcision of sons. Although male circumcision[35] has long been practised within the United Kingdom, the legality of performing the operation on minors for non-therapeutic reasons was merely assumed[36] until the decision in *Re J*[37] in 1999. In *Re J*, Wall J found that parental responsibility includes the right to consent to the circumcision of boys, whether or not the procedure is medically indicated. The exercise of this right, however, requires the agreement either of all of those with parental responsibility or of the court. This is an exception to the usual rule that one parent with parental responsibility may act alone.[38]

The right to consent to circumcision gives parents an unusual right: the right to submit their child for a surgical procedure involving permanent change to the child's body, despite the lack of medical need for such a procedure.[39] The law does not usually allow parents to submit children to the inherent risks, however small, of surgery unless it is in the child's best interests.[40] The gravity of the right involved is evident both from the requirement of joint consent and from the reluctance of the courts to allow circumcision in cases of disagreement.[41] Nevertheless, where parents do agree, they have the right to consent to an act with potentially profound implications for the moral and physical integrity of the child. Whether parents should possess such a right has been the subject of intense debate.[42] Arguably, circumcision at a young age can promote a child's best interests by allowing his full acceptance into the community in which he will be brought up.[43] Against this it can be contended that the infliction of painful and irreversible surgery on a person without their consent is an example of inhuman treatment that cannot be justified on the basis that it will be in that person's best

---

[35]   Female circumcision is prohibited under the Female Genital Mutilation Act 2003.
[36]   *R v Brown* [1994] 1 AC 212 at 231. Law Commission, 'Consent in the Criminal Law' (Law Com No 139, 1995).
[37]   *Re J (Specific Issue Orders: Child's Religious Upbringing and Circumcision)* [1999] 2 FLR 678; [2000] 1 FLR 571. For criticism, see H Gilbert, 'Time to Reconsider the Lawfulness of Ritual Male Circumcision' [2007] *European Human Rights Law Review* 279.
[38]   Children Act 1989 s 2(7); and J Eekelaar, 'Do parents have a duty to consult?' (1998) 114 *LQR* 337.
[39]   Although circumcision may confer health benefits, the right to consent to such a procedure is not dependent on showing that such benefits will arise.
[40]   M Fox and M Thomson, 'Short Changed? The Law and Ethics of Male Circumcision' (2005) 12 *International Journal of Children's Rights* 161.
[41]   *Re J*, above n 37; and *Re S (Children)* [2004] EWHC 1282 (Fam); [2004] EWCA Civ 1257.
[42]   Fortin, above n 33, 331–2; and Hamilton, above n 5, 148–9.
[43]   *Re J*, above n 37.

interests.[44] Whether or not circumcision can be justified as being in the best interests of the child, it is clear that the law protects the interests of parents. It allows parents to fulfil their own religious obligations by permanently marking the child with the symbol of their religion at an age where he is not capable of accepting that religion for himself.

Parental Responsibility, Local Authorities and Adoption

Whilst individuals with parental responsibility have considerable discretion concerning a child's religious upbringing, this discretion is entirely removed from local authorities with parental responsibility. A local authority acquiring parental responsibility through a care order[45] shall not:

> cause the child to be brought up in any religious persuasion other than that in which he would have been brought up if the order had not been made.[46]

This restriction is one of a very limited set of important statutory restrictions on the parental responsibility of local authorities acquired under a care order; other restrictions are concerned with adoption and the child's name and country of residence.[47] These restrictions go to the core of children's identities and connections to their parents. By reserving the question of religious upbringing to the parents themselves, the law views this as one of a limited number of matters that are fundamentally those of parents. This suggests that the religious upbringing of a child is seen as a bond between child and parents that a local authority should not be permitted to break. It also suggests that the law on the determination of a child's religious upbringing is, at least in part, concerned with protecting the parents' own interests in the child's religious upbringing.

Local authorities are also under a positive obligation to have regard to the child's religious persuasion in making decisions concerning him or her.[48] This focus of the statutory wording is on the child, rather than his or her parents, and on his or her current religious persuasion rather than merely his or her religious background. If the views of a competent child diverge from those of his or her parents, it seems that it is the child's religious persuasion that is to be considered. However, for most children, particularly younger children, this section means that the religious views of the parents will remain significant, although not

---

[44]   D Feldman, *Civil Liberties and Human Rights in England and Wales* (2nd edn, Oxford, Oxford University Press, 2002) 272.

[45]   Children Act 1989 s 33(3)(1).

[46]   Children Act 1989 s 33(6)(a).

[47]   A local authority may not agree to, or refuse to agree to, an adoption order and may not appoint a special guardian: Children Act 1989 s 33(6)(b). Further, whilst a care order is in force, a decision to change a child's surname or remove him or her from the United Kingdom requires the written consent of everyone with parental responsibility: Children Act 1989 s 33(7).

[48]   Children Act 1989 s 22(5)(c).

determinative, in local authority decision-making.[49] The obligation on the local authority is particularly relevant in the placing of children with foster carers.[50] Although there is no longer a rule that foster carers must be of the same religion as the child,[51] local authorities will endeavour to find a placement with a family of the same religious persuasion as the child as this is likely to provide continuity and so promote the child's welfare.[52] Similarly, in placing a child for adoption, the child's religious persuasion must be considered by the adoption agency.[53] Again, in practice, this is likely to mean that the parents' religious views will be significant in placing a child. Indeed, the guidance accompanying the Act requires adoption agencies to ascertain the wishes of birth parents as to the religious upbringing of the child.[54]

Although the right to determine religious upbringing is a part of parental responsibility, the fact that it is removed from local authorities suggests that it is primarily a parental right. While there is increasing statutory recognition of the importance of the child's religious persuasion, in practice the parents' views on the religious upbringing of the child are likely to be influential even in extreme situations in which parents are unable to care for their children.

Conclusions: The Content of Parental Responsibility

For most parents, the right to determine religious upbringing will be experienced as part of a general freedom to raise a child without state interference. Nevertheless, this right is more than a mere freedom. Significant rights, such as the right to consent to circumcision, attach to it. The extensive power granted to parents to determine a child's religious upbringing is capable of supporting the child's welfare by building strong links to family, community, culture and belief. Nevertheless, the rights and freedoms granted to parents are also concerned with protecting the interests of the parents themselves. The parents' interest is preserved even when day-to-day care of the child is transferred elsewhere. Further, the rights granted to parents can often be exercised without regard to the views of the child him- or herself, as can be seen in the right of parents to remove a child

[49]   See *Re P (A Minor) (Residence Order: Child's Welfare)* [1999] 3 WLR 1164 for influence of parental religion in determining that of the child.

[50]   Care homes are also under an obligation to accommodate the child's religious persuasion where possible: the Children's Homes Regulations 2001, SI 2001/3967.

[51]   Local authorities were previously required, where possible, to place a child with a family of the same religious persuasion or to obtain an undertaking that the child would be brought up in that religious persuasion: the Foster Placement (Children) Regulations 1991, SI 1991/910 reg 5.

[52]   Fostering Service Regulations 2002, SI 2002/57; The Children Act 1989 Guidance and Regulations, Vol 3 [2.40]–[2.42]; and Department of Health, Local Authority Circular (98)20, [11]–[18].

[53]   Adoption and Children Act 2002 s 1(5). The previous law contained in the Adoption Act 1976 s 7 required regard to be had (so far as practicable) to the wishes of the child's parents concerning religious upbringing.

[54]   Department for Education and Skills, *Adoption Guidance: Adoption and Children Act 2002*, ch 2, [21].

from religious education and worship. This may be unsurprising, since the religious rights of parents are widely recognised in national and international law; there is, however, a danger that the child's evolving rights to determine his or her own beliefs will be lost in the focus on parents.

RESTRICTIONS ON PARENTAL RESPONSIBILITY: HUMAN RIGHTS ACT 1998

Parents have a broad freedom to determine their children's religious upbringing, but this is not an unrestricted freedom. Whilst legal intervention specifically aimed at limiting a parent's religious freedom is rare, parents may find their freedom curtailed by the application of general legal standards which, although not specifically aimed at limiting parental religious freedom, do so by imposing restrictions or obligations on parents that conflict with their religious beliefs. 'Religious freedom is not the solvent of legal obligation':[55] parents cannot claim exemption from generally applicable law simply on the grounds of religious belief.

A diverse range of laws may have the incidental effect of interfering with parental religious freedom. Banning corporal punishment in schools restricts those who view an education involving the possibility of such punishment as a Biblical obligation.[56] Restrictions on child labour may prevent children from distributing religious literature with their parents.[57] Those parents who treat their sick child through faith healing alone may be prosecuted for child neglect.[58] A decision to ban knives in schools may affect Sikhs who wish their children to wear the kirpan at all times.[59] Parents who find their religious freedom curtailed in this way may turn to the human rights legislation to protect that freedom. In this jurisdiction parents are likely to turn to Article 9 of the ECHR, which protects the right of parents to direct their children's religious upbringing, but also recognises that the state may be justified in interfering with parental rights to pursue particular aims.[60]

Although freedom of thought, conscience and religion is absolute under Article 9, freedom to *manifest* that religion or belief may be limited under Article 9(2). To bring a successful claim under Article 9, a parent would have to establish that: (i) the matter concerned a religion or belief that engaged Article 9; (ii) there was a manifestation of that belief; (iii) there was an interference with that manifestation of belief; and (iv) the interference was not proportionate to a

---

[55] *Church of the New Faith v Commissioner of Pay-Roll (Victoria)* (1986) 154 CLR 120 at 136 (Mason ACJ and Brennan J).

[56] *Williamson v Secretary of State for Education and Employment* [2005] UKHL 15; and *Christian Education South Africa v Minister of Education* (2000) 9 BHRC 53.

[57] *Prince v Massachusetts* (1944) 321 US 158.

[58] Hamilton, above n 5, 151–6.

[59] *Singh-Multani v Marguerite-Bourgeoys* [2006] SCC 6.

[60] In the context of education, Art 2 of Protocol 1 of the ECHR may also play a significant role.

legitimate aim under Article 9(2).[61] The potential of Article 9 to strengthen parental rights depends on the courts' approach to each of these questions. The most significant domestic decision on Article 9 is the House of Lords' decision in *Williamson*.[62] In that case, the applicants claimed that the prohibition of corporal punishment in schools[63] was an unjustified interference with the manifestation of their religious beliefs: namely that they were under a Biblical obligation to use corporal punishment as an integral part of the children's education. The House of Lords, in common with the courts below, rejected that claim, but its reasons for doing so are significant for parental rights. The case sets a relatively low hurdle for each of the first three questions under Article 9, meaning that parents will find it relatively easy to show that a law that affects their parental responsibility for religious upbringing will interfere with a manifestation of their beliefs and require consideration of whether that interference is proportionate. This means that the courts will increasingly be faced with the challenge of deciding when the restriction of parental religious rights may be justified.

It is first necessary to ask whether the case involves a belief protected by Article 9.[64] In *Williamson*, the House of Lords drew on Strasbourg jurisprudence in holding that an applicant would need to show that the belief was coherent, met an 'adequate degree of seriousness and importance' and was 'consistent with basic standards of human dignity and integrity'.[65] There was concern that the court should take care not to apply these standards in a manner that deprived genuine belief of protection. Lord Nicholls was concerned to stress that, whilst the belief should be intelligible, religious belief was not always capable of rational justification or precise explanation. Lord Walker suggested a similar approach, taking the view that the court was not equipped to assess the coherence, seriousness and importance of a belief and finding the idea that it might enquire closely into these matters alarming.[66] Further, the test of compatibility with human dignity was passed, provided that there was no actual violation of the protected rights of the children in question. This was the case even though the court recognised that corporal punishment would adversely affect the physical and moral integrity of the child.[67] These 'modest threshold requirements' will be easily satisfied in the case of most religious beliefs.

The second question is whether there is a manifestation of a belief. It is clear from Strasbourg jurisprudence on Article 9 that not every action motivated or

---

[61] Lord Walker in *Williamson* (above n 56, at [66]) expressed doubts as to whether a rigid analytical approach is useful in adjudication. This method will be used here as a means of assessing the scope of the Article.

[62] *Williamson*, above n 56.

[63] Education Act 1998 s 548.

[64] There is no requirement that this belief is a religious belief: *Kokkinakis v Greece* (1993) 17 EHRR 397 at [31].

[65] *Williamson*, above n 56, at [23] (Lord Nicholls). These standards are relevant where the case concerns the manifestation of a belief. The right to freedom of thought is absolute.

[66] *Ibid*, at [60].

[67] *Ibid*, at [27].

influenced by a belief is protected as a manifestation of that belief,[68] only those that are intimately connected to the belief in question.[69] This raises a difficult question of how one is to determine whether an act is core to a religious belief or merely inspired by it. In the Court of Appeal, Buxton LJ had tried to resolve this question by objectively considering whether the act was a constitutive part of the religion, finding that it was not possible to characterise the use of corporal punishment as a 'clear, uniform and agreed' requirement of Christianity.[70] This approach has been widely criticised as requiring the court to assess what is core to a religious belief rather than considering the subjective views of the applicants themselves.[71] The House of Lords rejected this approach, focusing instead on whether the applicants were acting under a perceived obligation. If they were, this would be sufficient to constitute a manifestation of belief.[72]

The third question is whether there had been an interference with the manifestation of the parents' beliefs. Article 9 does not protect the right to manifest belief at the time and place of one's choosing: the state may restrict the circumstances in which a belief is manifested without infringing Article 9.[73] In a significant line of cases, the European Court of Human Rights has adopted a strict interpretation of 'interference', stating that a restriction will only interfere with a belief if it makes manifestation of the belief 'impossible', not merely more inconvenient.[74] The Court of Appeal used this line of cases to hold that there was no interference with the rights of the parents in *Williamson*: the law only restricted the punishment by the teachers, there was nothing to prevent the parents home schooling or punishing the child at home or at the school. Whilst this approach is reconcilable with the European Court of Human Rights decisions, the House of Lords rejected it, suggesting that 'impossible' was too high a standard and that instead the court should consider whether the restriction was 'significant in practice'.[75] As the options suggested in the Court of Appeal did amount to significant restrictions on the right of the parents to choose an educational environment which used corporal punishment, there was an interference with the parents' rights.

The approach of the House of Lords to these first three questions sets a relatively low bar for parents with a genuine religious belief. A law that imposes significant restrictions on a perceived obligation will be sufficient to require the courts to turn to the core question of justification under Article 9(2). This

---

[68]   *Arrowsmith v United Kingdom* (1980) 19 DR 5.
[69]   *X v United Kingdom* (1977) 11 DR 55.
[70]   *Williamson v Secretary of State for Education* [2002] EWCA Civ 1926 at [35].
[71]   J Eekelaar, 'Corporal Punishment, Parents' Religion and Children's Rights' (2003) 119 *LQR* 370.
[72]   *Williamson*, above n 56, at [32] (Lord Nicholls) and [63] (Lord Walker). The existence of a perceived obligation is a sufficient but not necessary condition for a manifestation of a belief.
[73]   *R (Begum) v Denbigh High School* [2006] UKHL 15 at [50].
[74]   *Jewish Liturgical Association v France* (2000) 9 BHRC 27.
[75]   *Williamson* above n 56, at [39]. See also *Begum*, above n 73, at [24] and [52].

exercise requires the courts to confront the tension described by Sachs J in the case of *Christian Education*:

> The underlying problem in any open and democratic society … is how far such democracy can and must go in allowing members of religious communities to define for themselves which laws they will obey and which not. Such a society can cohere only if all its participants accept that certain basic norms and standards are binding. Accordingly, believers cannot claim an automatic right to be exempted by their beliefs from the laws of the land. At the same time, the state should, wherever reasonably possible, seek to avoid putting believers to extremely painful and intensely burdensome choices of either being true to their faith or else respectful of the law.[76]

In *Williamson*, the House of Lords addressed this tension by deferring to the decision of Parliament on this contested matter of broad social policy. The ban on corporal punishment pursued a legitimate aim: the protection of all school children. Parliament had considered the evidence with care and was entitled to take the decision that a total ban was preferable to a partial ban designed to accommodate religious beliefs.[77] In this context, the court was not required to assess the evidence itself.

Nevertheless, the decision in *Williamson* is significant: it gives parents a tool to challenge restrictions on their broad freedom to determine religious upbringing. Experience in other jurisdictions illustrates that the courts have been willing and able to subject restrictions on religious freedom to close scrutiny and, at times, to require decision-makers to accommodate the beliefs of parents.[78] For example, the US Supreme Court famously struck down laws on compulsory education as incompatible with the religious rights of Amish parents to remove their adolescent children from formal education.[79] While such cases must be treated with care given the difference in constitutional and cultural background, *Williamson* provides the potential for strengthened protection of parental religious freedom.

RELIGIOUS UPBRINGING AND THE CHILD

It is striking that the House of Lords' decision in *Williamson* was framed as a question of the limitations placed on parental rights rather than the need to protect the rights and interests of the children concerned. It was only Baroness Hale who considered the children's perspective, noting:

> this is, and has always been, a case about children, their rights and the rights of their parents and teachers. Yet there has been no one here or in the courts below to speak on behalf of the children. No litigation friend has been appointed to consider the rights of

---

[76]   *Christian Education South Africa v Minister of Education* (2000) 9 BHRC 53 at [35].
[77]   *Williamson*, above n 56, at [42]–[52] (Lord Nicholls) and [86] (Baroness Hale).
[78]   *Singh-Multani v Marguerite-Bourgeoys* [2006] SCC 6; *Christian Education South Africa v Minister of Education* (2000) 9 BHRC 53; and *Wisconsin v Yoder* (1972) 406 US 205.
[79]   *Yoder, ibid.*

the pupils involved separately from those of the adults. No non-governmental organisation, such as the Children's Rights Alliance, has intervened to argue a case on behalf of children as a whole. The battle has been fought on ground selected by the adults. This has clouded and over-complicated what should have been a simple issue.[80]

This focus on adult rights is not confined to the circumstances of rights-based litigation. The law on parental responsibility in this area is largely concerned with parental freedom. Unless the exercise of that freedom is a matter of dispute between parents, or risks harm of a severity that meets the threshold for state intervention, the religious upbringing of the child will remain a private matter, leaving parents to decide how far to take the views of their children into account. This focus on parental rights can also be seen in the specific rights granted to parents, for example, the right to remove a child from religious education and worship without consulting him or her.

Where the courts do consider the child's religious upbringing, for example, in a residence dispute, the child's perspective and interests have often been hidden from view behind those of the parents. In resolving such disputes, the court is obliged to apply the welfare principle,[81] including consideration of the 'ascertainable wishes and feelings of the child concerned'[82] and his or her religious heritage.[83] As discussed above, the religious identity of a child is a complex matter influenced by questions of his or her religious heritage, involvement in the religion and his or her own beliefs. Children are increasingly able to determine their own religious identity as they mature.[84] There has been a tendency in some cases to simplify this question and treat the child's religious identity simply as a matter of his or her 'birth religion'. So, for example, in *Re S*, children aged 13 and 11 were told that they had been born Roman Catholics and were too young to decide that 'their religion' was no longer for them.[85] At the other end of the spectrum, in *Re P*, an eight-year-old child with Down's syndrome was treated as an Orthodox Jew despite the fact that the expert evidence showed that she was unlikely to have any real perception of what that might mean.[86] In neither of these cases did the label attached to the child determine the outcome, although it remained a significant factor within the welfare assessment. A similar blindness to the child's independent position is evident from the decisions of the European Court of Human Rights, where the religious rights of children rarely receive

---

[80]   *Williamson*, above n 56, at [71]. A similar point was made in the powerful dissent of Mr Justice Douglas in *Yoder, ibid*, at 242–6.

[81]   Children Act 1989 s 1(1).

[82]   Children Act 1989 s 1(3)(a). See *Re R (A Minor) (Residence: Religion)* [1993] 2 FLR 163.

[83]   Children Act 1989 s 1(3)(d). See *Re P (A Minor) (Residence Order: Child's Welfare)* [1999] 3 WLR 1164.

[84]   See J Eekelaar, 'Children Between Cultures' (2004) 18 *IJLPF* 178 for discussion of the broader question of children's cultural identity.

[85]   *Re S (Minors) (Access: Religious Upbringing)* [1992] 2 FLR 313.

[86]   *Re P*, above n 83. Identity as a Jew has racial, cultural and religious elements. The focus of the court decision was on the religious aspects of her identity. In particular, stress was placed on the father's position as an Orthodox Jewish Rabbi.

independent consideration from those of their parents, even in cases where it is the child's actions that form the basis of the alleged rights violation.[87]

THE CHILD'S RIGHT TO FREEDOM OF THOUGHT, CONSCIENCE AND BELIEF

Despite the law's focus on adults, it is clear that children possess their own rights to thought, conscience and belief, both under Article 9 ECHR and in international law.[88] To give full realisation to these rights, it is essential to consider both how far children who are not yet competent can enjoy religious rights, and how the child's religious rights can be reconciled with the parents' right to manifest their religion in the upbringing of their children. As noted above, Article 14(2) of the United Nations Convention on the Rights of the Child requires states to respect the right of parents to:

> provide direction to the child in the exercise of his or her right in a manner consistent with the evolving capacities of the child.

This focus on the evolving capacity of the child provides the key to understanding children's religious rights.[89] Children's experience of religion may develop very differently from that of adults. Analysis of children's rights must take into account the fact that children tend to develop their religious identity in the context of their family's beliefs and customs and involvement in the practices of the religion in question. For younger children, protection of these aspects of religious experience may be more important than consideration of the child's actual beliefs, which may be in a process of transition.[90] As the child evolves the capacity to develop his or her own beliefs, the rights of the parent to provide direction reduce. This approach to the parents' diminishing right can be seen, in a different context, in the decision of Silber J in *Axon*.[91] While the parents retain their right to practise their own religion as they wish, once the child reaches competence the parents have no right to force the child to act contrary to his or her own conscience.

---

[87]   See, eg *Valsamis v Greece* (1996) 24 EHRR 294 at [37]. Similarly, *Re J (Specific Issue Orders: Muslim Upbringing and Circumcision)* [1999] 2 FLR 678 contains a brief reference to the child's rights with no attempt to define the content of those rights.

[88]   See, eg *Valsamis, ibid*; and *R (Begum) v Denbigh High School* [2006] UKHL 15. See Langlaude, above n 5, for detailed discussion of children's religious rights in international law.

[89]   This is a particular example of the general principle contained in Art 5 of the United Nations Convention on the Rights of the Child.

[90]   See Langlaude, above n 5, ch 1; Van Praagh, above n 24, 358; and *Begum*, above n 88, at [93] (Baroness Hale).

[91]   *R (Axon) v Secretary of State for Health* [2006] EWHC 37 (Admin). See also R Taylor, 'Reversing the Retreat from *Gillick*?' [2007] 19 *CFLQ* 81.

This recognition of the child's evolving capacity is similar to the approach of dynamic self-determinism developed by John Eekelaar.[92] This approach recognises children's ability to develop their own identity. In this case, the ultimate aim is for a child to achieve the capacity to form his or her own beliefs, including his or her Article 9 right to change his or her religion or beliefs. This does not mean that the child's wishes should necessarily be determinative in a dispute concerning them, particularly where there is fear that the child's beliefs may not be freely formed. To allow the wishes of an immature child to determine a decision may well reduce his or her capacity to develop his or her own beliefs in the future.[93] Similarly, the recognition that children develop their own understanding of their religious identity does not require their parents to bring them up in a 'neutral' environment with equal access to different religious choices. Such an approach would deny the parents' own religious freedom to teach their children about their beliefs. It would also be an impossible standard to reach. Further, children may find it difficult to achieve full participation or acceptance within a religion unless they have been educated within a religion or experienced certain rites, such as circumcision. Preventing a child from receiving a religious upbringing may well deny him or her the ability to choose that religion in the future.

This approach is particularly useful in resolving disputes concerning religious upbringing. A good example is the decision of Baron J in *Re S (Specific Issue Order: Religion: Circumcision)*.[94] In that case the children, aged almost 10 and eight-and-a-half had been brought up with exposure to Islam through their mother, with whom they were now living, and to Jainism through their father. Baron J found the children to be too old for the court to seek to favour one religion over the other. Instead, each parent was free to involve the children in their religion, but not to take steps to covert them to that religion, for example, by circumcising the child before the child was competent to make that decision himself. Baron J was clearly influenced by the evidence that the children had been brought up within the two religions in the past, but that full conversion to Islam would be incompatible with Jainism and would affect the children's relationship with their father. The children's continued contact with both religions left them free to make their own choices in the future, without preventing the parents from manifesting their own beliefs. The mother in *Re S* had argued that the court should follow the approach taken in relocation cases,[95] and effectively adopt a presumption that the child's religion should follow that of the resident parent. This is a misguided comparison: children may only have one country of primary residence, but may have exposure to different religions without necessarily

---

[92]   J Eekelaar, 'The Interests of the Child and the Child's Wishes: The Role of Dynamic Self-determinism' (1994) 8 *IJLPF* 42, and above n 84.

[93]   *Re R (A Minor) (Residence: Religion)* [1993] 2 FLR 163. In this case the child wished to remain in the closed community of the Exclusive Brethren.

[94]   [2004] EWHC 1282 (Fam); [2004] EWCA Civ 1257.

[95]   *Payne v Payne* [2001] EWCA Civ 166; and J Herring and R Taylor, 'Relocating Relocation' [2006] 18 *CFLQ* 517.

suffering harm.[96] While the court should not force a parent to raise a child against their own beliefs and conscience,[97] there is no need to restrict the child's experience of other beliefs, unless there is clear evidence of harm.[98]

Recognition of the child's own evolving right to thought, conscience and belief, rather than a focus on the religious identity of the parents, should be a significant factor in court decisions concerning a child's residence and upbringing. Children's rights can also play an important role in considering how far the state is permitted to restrict parents' religious rights in order to protect the children's interests. While children's rights are particularly important in court resolution of disputes, their recognition is also important outside that context. Children's rights can be a powerful means of challenging the current legal focus on the freedom of parents, allowing recognition of children's evolving capacity to form their own beliefs.[99]

CONCLUSIONS

The law on parental responsibility for religious upbringing is largely concerned with parents' freedom to raise their children as they wish without state interference. Whilst in some areas parents are increasingly regulated by the state,[100] in the religious sphere it is parents' freedom that is most striking. This freedom, with its roots in nineteenth-century common law, is subject to very little regulation, save where the child is at risk of serious harm or there is a dispute between those with parental responsibility. Where regulations are imposed, parents have the potential to challenge restrictions on their parental responsibility through Article 9 ECHR. This freedom is further supported by specific rights, such as the right to remove a child from religious teaching and worship, which further enhance parental control of religious upbringing.

The law's focus on religious upbringing is on the parent. Parental rights are usually regarded as existing for the benefit of the child.[101] However, in the context of religion, parental rights also serve wider interests, including parents' interests in meeting their own religious obligations and the interests of religious communities in transmitting their beliefs and practices between generations. These interests mean that, while the child is young, it is perhaps best to characterise

---

[96]   *Zummo v Zummo* (1990) 574 A 2d 1130.

[97]   *Re J (Specific Issue Orders: Muslim Upbringing and Circumcision)* [1999] 2 FLR 678.

[98]   As there arguably was in *Re S (Change of Names: Cultural Factors)* [2001] 3 FCR 648, in which allowing the child to be brought up in both the Sikh and Muslim faiths posed a serious risk that he would be rejected by the Muslim community in which the mother was based. See also *Young v Young* (1994) 108 DLR (4th) 193.

[99]   See, eg the use made of Art 9 by the Joint Committee on Human Rights in recommending changes to the law on religious education and worship in schools: above n 34 and accompanying text.

[100]   H Reece, 'From Parental Responsibility to Parenting Responsibly' in M Freeman (ed), *Law and Sociology* (Oxford, Oxford University Press, 2005).

[101]   *Gillick v West Norfolk and Wisbech AHA* [1986] AC 11.

parental responsibility for religious upbringing as a parent-centred right, valued for preserving parental freedom of belief.[102] This approach can also be supported by the fact that the state has no means of preferring one form of religious upbringing to another, unless there is a risk of actual harm to the child. This parent-centred approach provides children with the context in which they may come to understand and develop their own beliefs. As children develop their own beliefs, the parent-centred focus of the law becomes inappropriate. As children develop their religious identity, so they develop the capacity to enjoy their right to live according to their own freedom of thought, conscience and belief.

[102] A McCall Smith, 'Is Anything Left of Parental Rights?' in E Sutherland and A McCall Smith (eds), *Family Rights: Family Law and Medical Ethics* (Edinburgh, Edinburgh University Press, 1990).

8

Parental Responsibility and Education: Taking a Long View

DANIEL MONK

INTRODUCTION

PARENTAL RESPONSIBILITY AND education is a vast subject. Like the (still relatively new) legal category of Education Law, while the single word 'education' suggests a discrete and highly specialised area, in reality it is one that covers a whole gamut of legal fields. Private law actions under the Children Act 1989 arise when parents disagree about their child's education; public welfare and, increasingly, criminal law sanctions exist to ensure that parents fulfil their legal duties; conversely, administrative law (judicial review and the ombudsmen) provides remedies for parents to protect their rights against public authorities and negligence claims to claim redress for local authority failures. These cases provide a rich source for exploring the inherent tensions and multiple meanings of the concept of parental responsibility, as they portray parents as at times uniquely privileged and trusted to have a particular insight and knowledge of their children; and at other times they dismiss their views, choices and actions and treat them as quasi and 'real' criminals.

Parents are, of course, far from monolithic and, consequently, these contrasting images, arguably, merely reflect the full gamut of 'responsible' and 'irresponsible' parenting practices. However, law rarely, if at all, ever simply reflects reality; rather, law has a productive role. Revealing this role is aided by reading law as narrative rather than doctrine. Gewirtz, drawing on a variety of post-structuralist ideas, has argued that this means:

> looking at facts more than rules, forms as much as substance, the language used as much as the idea expressed, it sees laws as artifacts that reveal a culture, not just policies that shape culture.[1]

---

[1] P Gewirtz, 'Narative and rhetoric in the law' in P Brooks and P Gewirtz (eds), *Law's Stories* (New Haven, Yale, 1996) 3.

The complexity of parental responsibility in this field reflects the extent to which education policies are, and always have been, contested and inherently political. In law, this is reflected by the fact that education is both a key civil and political right and, at the same time, a social and welfare right.[2] Framed in this way, these—often competing—rights discourses legitimise different representations, demands and investments in parental responsibility. As a civil and political 'right' (or negative right), parental responsibility is characterised within liberal political thinking as a bulwark against the dangers of unfettered state control. This representation is most explicit in Cold War Western narratives where Soviet history books were presented as exemplars of the dangers of state control over education.[3] This rights paradigm also underlies and legitimises more recent discourses of parental choice.[4] Yet as a social and welfare right (or positive right), the role of the state is more complex and in this context parental responsibility is represented not so much in opposition to state intervention, but more as a joint enterprise, as evidenced by the imposition of compulsory education and parental duties to enforce it (the power relationship underlying this 'joint enterprise' is, of course, critical). However, the binary paradigm of the civil/political versus the social/welfare has its limits: state intervention can be justified as protecting the civil and political rights of children vis-à-vis their parents and, conversely, parental rights can be understood as being in the interests of children's developmental rights as much as essential for the 'liberal state'.

This chapter examines these ambivalent understandings of parental responsibility by tracing the shifting ways in which law has regulated the relationship between parents and schooling at different points in history. As noted above, parental responsibility in education is central to a much wider variety of claims and disputes,[5] but it is in relation to the law relating to parental choice and school attendance that the tensions are most explicit; for it is in this context that 'parental responsibility' has allowed the greatest freedom and imposed the most demanding requirements. Taking the long view on these provisions serves both to support and, at the same time, to challenge progressive narratives which claim that parental rights have been replaced by a more 'child-centered' notion of parental responsibility. For while parents originally had a choice as to *whether* to educate their children and now have an (increasingly circumscribed) choice as to *how* their children should be educated, the historical perspective reveals the extent to which legal intervention has always been mediated through calculations

---

[2] For a detailed overview of international and regional legal provisions, see D Hodgson, *The Human Right to Education* (Aldershot, Ashgate/Dartmouth, 1998).

[3] See J White, 'Two National Curricula—Baker's and Stalin's. Towards a Liberal Alternative' (1988) 36 *British Journal of Educational Studies* 218.

[4] N Harris, *Law and Education: Regulation, Consumerism and the Education System* (London, Sweet & Maxwell, 1993); and N Harris, *Education, Law and Diversity* (Oxford, Hart, 2006).

[5] For a general account of the law in all aspects of education, see J Ford, M Hughs and D Ruebain, *Education Law and Practice* (2nd edn, Bristol, Jordans, 2005).

and assumptions premised primarily on social class, but also religion and gender, and in doing so it reveals a remarkable degree of continuity.

COMPULSORY EDUCATION AND THE EDUCATION ACT 1870

The most radical and critical shift in understanding of parental responsibility was the imposition on parents in 1870 of a legal duty to educate their children. Section 74 of the Education Act 1870 required that unless a child aged between five and 12 was receiving 'efficient education in some other manner', parents had a duty to 'cause such children to attend school'. While the age limits have changed over time, as have the means of enforcing it, the basic duty is the same now. And while now largely unquestioned, the imposition of this parental duty represented the reversal of a long-standing principle that education was a private matter within the sole discretion of parents.

This principle was clearly stated in *Hodges v Hodges*.[6] This case held that while a deserted wife was entitled to financial support from her husband for the maintenance of their children, the obligation of support did not stretch to providing for the children's education. According to Lord Kenyon:

> A father was bound by every social tie to give his children an education suitable to their rank, but it was a duty of imperfect obligation, and could not be enforced in a court of law. The richest man in the kingdom might say to his heir apparent, 'go and earn your daily bread by your daily labour' and the law could not interfere. There is no further obligation than that which nature has implanted in his breast. The law obliged him to nothing but nurture, which duty expired when the child reached the age of seven.[7]

That the 'imperfect' nature of the parental obligation was perceived as a fundamental principle is also evident from JS Mill's observation in *On Liberty*, over 60 years later, that while the educating of one's child 'is unanimously declared to be the father's duty, scarcely anybody, in this country will bear to hear of obliging him to perform it'.[8]

The reasons why the imposition of a legal duty was considered 'unbearable' in 1859, but enshrined in law in 1870, are multiple and complex.[9] Two key factors, both of which resonate with contemporary debates about education, were social class and religion. However, while the former legitimised state action, concerns about the latter supported a less interventionist approach.

Religion and education are both aspects of parental responsibility that are perceived not simply as matters of child welfare, but as touching upon significant parental civil rights. The interconnectedness of the two issues is such that early

---

[6]   (1796) Peake Add. Cas 79; 170 ER 120.
[7]   *Ibid*, at 80.
[8]   *On Liberty* (first published 1859, London, JM Dent, 1983) 175.
[9]   J Murphy, *The Education Act 1870* (Newton Abbot, David and Charles, 1972); and E Rich, *The Education Act 1870: A Study of Public Opinion* (Harlow, Longmans, 1970).

family law texts discuss them under the same heading.[10] While it is possible, in terms of current law, to distinguish education from religion, to the extent that the former is perceived as a universal right of the child and the latter as a parental right,[11] in the nineteenth century the distinction was far less clear.

The point here is that the fundamental common-law principle of absolute paternal rights in education can partly be explained as reflecting the historical political settlement that emerged after the protracted carnage of the religious civil wars of the seventeenth century; religious communities other than the established Anglican church were tolerated, but this settlement required education to be located firmly within the private sphere.[12] Further, perhaps the separation of education and religion in terms of law's understanding of parental responsibility has been one of the ways—imperfectly of course—by which parental rights in education have become more easily perceived as 'neutral', 'politically unproblematic' parental responsibilities.

The religious basis of the reluctance to interfere with educational matters is clear from *Stourton v Stourton*.[13] Here the court held—with great reluctance and after what appears from the judgment to be much agonizing—that a nine-year-old boy should remain in a Church of England school, as wished for by his mother, despite the objection of his deceased father's aristocratic Catholic family on the basis that: 'the distinctive doctrines of that church had taken a strong hold on his mind' and that a change of school now would be 'dangerous' as it might confuse him and 'leave him with no religious principles at all'.[14]

The effort which the court went to in this case to justify educating a child in a religion different from his patrilineal family attests to the interconnectedness of religion and education. Further, it reflects the fact that, prior to 1870, educational provision was almost exclusively—and unproblematically—perceived as falling legitimately within the preserve, directly or indirectly, of religious bodies. In other words, and to a certain extent mirroring developments in family law, state intervention in education could be perceived as a challenge to ecclesiastical as much as parental influence.[15] In debates leading to the 1870 Act, concerns were expressed about the dangers of uneducated children having no faith, which echo those expressed in *Stoughton*. This, in part, explains why, in contrast to developments in family law, religious bodies' influence over education was protected, since the 1870 Act, famously, merely 'filled in the gaps' and extended provision by developing schools in areas where there was no existing provision, rather than taking over the running of existing religious schools. And this settlement laid the

---

[10]   See, eg PM Bromley, *Family Law* (London, Butterworths, 1957).

[11]   See Taylor, this volume.

[12]   See P Hirst, 'J.N.Figgis, Churches and the State' in D Marquand and RL Nettler (eds), *Religion and Democracy* (2000) *The Political Quarterly* 104.

[13]   (1857) 8 De G M&G 760; 44 ER 583.

[14]   *Ibid.*

[15]   J Murphy, *Church, State and Schools in Britain 1800–1970* (London, Routledge and Kegan Paul, 1971).

foundations for future debates and tensions about the role of religion in admission criteria and about faith schools generally.[16]

In the much quoted case of *Kjedsen v Denmark*,[17] the European Court of Human Rights (ECtHR) justified compulsory sex education by making a distinction between 'information' and 'indoctrination'. However, detaching doctrine from education was, as *Stoughton* indicates in the nineteenth century, and for many still remains, meaningless and contradictory. 'Indoctrination' had none of the negative connotations it has now, but was rather a legitimate aim of education. While this may offend liberal individualistic views of education, it simultaneously reveals their inherent contradictions, as it questions the possibility of education ever being in any way politically, or spiritually, neutral.

In explaining the reversal in 1870 of the long-standing common-law principle of absolute parental rights over education, the most significant factor is social class. To a certain extent, this overlapped with the focus on religion and morality in the context of concerns about the effects of urbanisation and juvenile delinquency. However, there was also a more explicit political dimension. The 1870 Act followed the extension of the franchise by the Electoral Reform Act 1867, leading Robert Lowe, the then Chancellor of the Exchequer, to make the much-quoted observation that 'it is time to educate our masters'.[18] However, the more dominant motivations for state intervention were concerns about economic competitiveness that highlighted the necessity of a trained work force. Moral, political and economic considerations, while distinct, all pointed to the necessity of educating the working classes. Consequently, while in *Hodges v Hodges* Lord Kenyon had stated that:

> The richest man in the kingdom might say to his heir apparent, 'go and earn your daily bread by your daily labour' and the law could not interfere[19]

the 1870 Act curtailed this option even for the poorest man.

That the focus of the 1870 Act was principally on the working classes was enshrined in law by the defence provided in section 74 that a reasonable excuse for failing to secure attendance at school was 'efficient instruction in some other manner'. Case law makes clear that in practice this exempted middle and upper classes families from the attention of local education boards (the precursors of Local Education Authorities) attempting to enforce school attendance. For example, in the Edwardian cases of *R v West Riding of Yorkshire Justice, ex p Broadbent*[20] and *Bevan v Shears*,[21] the courts upheld the right of parents to educate their children at home by governesses. Moreover, in *Bevan*, Alverstone CJ made clear

---

[16]   See Harris, *Education, Law and Diversity*, above n 4.
[17]   (1976) 1 EHRR 711.
[18]   See AJ Marcham, 'Educating Our Masters: Political Parties and Elementary Education 1867 to 1870' (1973) 21 *British Journal of Educational Studies* 180.
[19]   See above, text at n 7.
[20]   [1910] 2 KB 192.
[21]   [1911] 2 KB 936.

that private education was beyond the remit of the school boards established by the 1870 Act. In that case, he rejected arguments by a school board that 'efficient education' had to be the same as that provided by a school board or in accordance with curriculum guidance provided by the Central Board of Education, observing that the difference was precisely the reason why parents might choose to send their children to Eton! These cases and the debates surrounding the enactment of the 1870 Act suggest that one can reasonably question whether the parental right vis-à-vis education would ever have been transformed into a legal duty had it not been for concerns and calculations about the working classes.

The 1870 Act required a reconstruction of working-class childhood from one of 'wage-earner' to 'school pupil'.[22] Consequently, it did far more than simply construct a legal duty, but represents a key moment whereby modern childhood becomes increasingly understood and defined by spatial boundaries. As James *et al* argue, '[c]hildhood is that status of personhood which is by definition often in the wrong place',[23] and it is no coincidence that the 1870 Act coincided with Factory Acts which gradually restricted child labour. For working-class parents, this required a fundamental shift in their relationship with their children; no longer a source of income, they became economic dependants. Conceptualising childhood through education was critical for the modern Western construction of them as 'not-yets' and as investments for the future.[24] However, the legal duty was also critical in the modern definition of parental responsibility. For while the universal right to education is now seen as unproblematic, the impact on parents is less frequently explored—and as schooling became seen as 'natural' and a norm of childhood, so too does this aspect of parental responsibility. In other words, while the legal duty was imposed for national economic calculations, the economic impact on families was, and remains, frequently overlooked as the duty becomes seen as natural—and this tension is particularly apparent now in developing countries where often well-intended initiatives to move children from factories into schools without addressing the impact on family economics frequently have a serious detrimental impact.[25]

As the 1870 Act did not provide parents with additional resources to comply with the new duty, for many it was a clear burden, and this resonates, to a certain extent, with the position now whereby 'choice' is a privilege only of the middle classes, an issue explored below. The co-existence of the 'duty' with a 'choice'

---

[22]   H Hendrick, 'Constructions and Reconstructions of British Childhood: An Interpretative Survey, 1800 to the Present' in A James and A Prout (eds), *Constructing and Reconstructing Childhood* (2nd edn, London, Routledge Falmer, 1997).

[23]   A James, C Jenks and A Prout, *Theorising Childhood* (Cambridge, Polity, 1997) 39.

[24]   See NM Lee, *Childhood and Society: Growing Up in an Age of Uncertainty* (Buckingham, Open University Press, 2001).

[25]   J Boyden, 'Childhood and the Policy Makers: A Comparative Perspective on the Globalization of Childhood' in A James and A Prout (eds), *Constructing and Reconstructing Childhood* (2nd edn, London, Routledge, 2002).

masks how the duty has always been experienced in different ways, and the origins of the duty in the nineteenth century remind us of the centrality of class.

Not surprisingly, this radical shift in parental responsibility was far from immediate, and the case law in the early years following the 1870 Act demonstrates sensitivity to the position of parents when interpreting what could be considered an 'unavoidable cause' for non-attendance at school. In *The London School Board v Duggan*,[26] the court held that this was the case where a girl was working to support her family, in the words of the judge Stephen J, 'discharging the honourable duty of helping her parents'.[27] Similarly, in *The School Attendance Committee of Belper Union v Bailey*,[28] where a boy was not attending through his own choice, or 'wandering' as the case describes it, the justices held that 'a labouring man could not be expected to employ a servant to conduct his child to school'.[29]

These nineteenth-century cases can be read as failing to uphold the universal right to education and equality of opportunity. This is borne out by the matter-of-fact assumption—expressed with remarkable and disquieting ease as a matter of unproblematic common sense—that the social background dictates the child's opportunities. However, as we shall see, their sympathy for the parents coheres with contemporary commentaries that critique the current increasingly punitive approach to enforcing attendance for failing to take account of the socio-economic realities of parents' lives. The explicit acceptance of class has been replaced with relative silence.

'A BETTER START IN LIFE'? THE EDUCATION ACT 1944

Contemporary accounts of the current education system frequently take the 1944 Education Act—'Butler's Act' or 'The Great Act'—as the starting point. Within progressive accounts, it represents a new beginning—both in terms of children's right to education and of the welfare state more generally. Indeed, as Chitty argues, it has become 'entrenched in folklore as benevolent and accommodating'.[30] However, using this Act as a starting point is problematic. A number of education historians have demonstrated the extent to which the 1944 Act represented continuity as much as change.[31] Cocks reminds us that it effectively saved the private sector and introduced the expression 'independent schools':

---

[26] (1884) XIII QBD 176.
[27] *Ibid*, at 178.
[28] (1882) IX QBD 259.
[29] *Ibid*, at 260.
[30] C Chitty, *Understanding Schools and Schooling* (London, Routledge Falmer, 2002) 11.
[31] M Barber, *The Making of the 1944 Education Act* (London, Cassell, 1994); and K Jones, *Education in Britain 1944 to the present* (Cambridge, Polity, 2003).

a shrewd change to make in a society which was less respectful of private property than it had been: 'independent' had all the right political connotations.[32]

Similarly, Harris argues that it also protected denominational schools, as 'state support was critical for their long term future'.[33] More generally, Ransom argues that it ensured that 'in exchange for the retention of liberal capitalism the working class would be offered the opportunity of social mobility'.[34]

While the saving of the independent sector protected the *rights* of privileged parents, in keeping with the pattern established by the 1870 Act, the 1944 Act also heralded a shift in understandings of parental *responsibility* that would impact primarily on working-class parents. This was not by statute—the legal duty in the 1944 Act was almost identical to that in 1870—but by the judiciary: for after 1944, the excuses for non-attendance accepted by the courts in the cases noted above are firmly and consistently rejected.[35]

An example of this is *Jenkins v Howells*.[36] This case concerned the non-attendance at school of a 14-year-old girl who was living on an isolated farm with her widowed and infirm mother and older brothers and undertaking domestic work to support them. In rejecting her circumstances as a defence for non-attendance, Goddard CJ held as follows:

> We think that the words 'unavoidable cause' must be construed in relation to the child . . . The unavoidable cause in this case affects the mother and not the child. Parliament has not seen fit to provide that family responsibilities or duties can be used as an excuse for a child not attending school. If we allowed the facts in this case, which certainly arouse great sympathy, to afford a defence, it would mean that this child would not go to school at all. How the domestic affairs of this farm and this small family are to be carried on, I do not pretend to know, and I quite understand the justices taking the view that they did, but I think we are bound to hold that the reason for the child's absence does not amount to a defence. I think that 'unavoidable cause' in this sub-section must be read as something in the nature of an emergency. If, for instance, the house where the child lived were burnt down that would be regarded, at any rate for a day or two, as an unavoidable cause.[37]

Why Goddard CJ felt 'bound' to take this course has much to do with shifting views about education; for Parliament in 1870 had also 'not seen fit to provide that family responsibilities or duties can be used as an excuse for a child not attending school', rather it had been left to the courts' discretion. The 1943 White Paper on Educational Reconstruction stated that the purpose of education was to

---

[32]   R Cocks, 'Ram, Rab and the civil servants: a lawyer and the making of the "Great Education Act 1944"' (2001) 21 *Legal Studies* 15, 28.

[33]   Harris, *Education, Law and Diversity*, above n 4, 239.

[34]   S Ransom, *Towards the Learning Society* (London, Cassell, 1994).

[35]   See, eg *Shaxted v Ward* [1954] 1 All ER 336 (which indicates the rejection of the *Belper* judgment above); and *Spiers v Warrington Corp* [1954] 1 QB 61; and *Hinchley v Rankin* [1961] 1 WLR 421.

[36]   [1949] 1 All ER 942.

[37]   *Ibid*, at 220.

'secure for children a happier childhood and a better start in life'.[38] This is a notably distinct shift from the political language that informed the 1870 Act. For while the 1944 Act enshrined continuity with the past, it also heralded a new direction; and many of its supporters clearly envisaged the Act as a tool for the creation of a classless and more democratic society. In 1870, a farm girl would not have been considered to need any other skills for her life, which would, in the eyes of a Victorian or Edwardian judge, have remained on a farm: class mobility was explicitly not the aim in 1870. The decision in *Jenkins*, consequently, can be read as supporting the progressive narrative surrounding the 1944 Act. After 1944, children, and as the case indicates, this includes girls, are perceived not simply as wage earners, but as having, potentially, an independent destiny. Yet the case also clearly reveals the limits of the new political ideals. By refusing to acquit the mother, Goddard CJ upholds the child's independent right to education, but in doing so acknowledges that he does not know how the family will manage. The child's right here represents an almost abstract individualistic ideal; an attempt to uncouple welfare and civil rights to education from economics—an unresolved tension that is well documented in wider critiques of liberal human-rights discourses.[39]

In this way, the 1944 Act cohered with the developing universalist claims of human rights and this required a further shift in parental responsibility. For while in 1870 they were required to rely no longer on their children's wages and instead support them financially, after 1944 parents are required to support the political aspirations of a better life—regardless of whether they were compatible with personal practicalities or expectations. In *Hodges v Hodges*, the judgment referred, rhetorically, to the 'richest man in the country' and contrasted him with the labourer;[40] after 1944 the labourer is expected to treat the education of his children with as much seriousness as the richest man. As the aims of education change, so too does parental responsibility.

Historians of childhood such as Hendrick see the post-war period as a time when we see the shift from the 'factory child' to the 'pupil' taking a further development towards the 'psychological child'.[41] As the 1943 White Paper notes, their *happiness* is now desired; thus the welfare state gives birth to the welfare child. This focus on the psychological development of the child—which universal education and equality of opportunities support—requires parents to take on this role. Failure to secure school attendance becomes, consequently, not just a failure to comply with the law, nor a question of reckless, even immoral, parents, nor even a matter of unfortunate circumstances, but, rather, a *pathological* failure.

---

[38] Cmd 6458, [1].

[39] See, eg R Fine and S Picciotto, 'On Marxist Critiques of Law' in Ian Grigg-Spall and P Ireland (eds), *The Critical Lawyers Handbook*, Vol 1 (London, Pluto Press, 1992); and C Douzinas, *The End of Human Rights: Critical Legal Thought at the Fin-de-Siecle* (Oxford, Hart, 2000).

[40] See above, text at n 7.

[41] Hendrick, above n 22.

This cultural shift coheres with the understandings of John Bowlby and Donald Winnicott, leading and influential child psychologists in the post-war era, whose impact on family law has been documented elsewhere.[42] In different ways, they both spoke of school attendance as necessary for healthy child development. In their work, school phobia and truancy are explained as indicators of psychological disorders of the parents: too attached emotionally in the case of school phobia or too detached in the case of truancy. The significance of their work is that they indicate the extent to which after 1944 ensuring school attendance becomes not just a legal duty, but a psychological norm of responsible parenting. In so doing, it served to depoliticise this cultural shift in the same way as feminist theorists have demonstrated that contemporaneous theories of child development depoliticised post-war norms of 'motherhood' through equally essentialist and psychological discourses.[43] The emergence of a psychological role in legal understandings of parental responsibility resonates with more recent criminal-law initiatives and it is to the present day that this chapter now turns.

THE PRESENT DAY: 'CHOICE' AND 'CRIMINALITY'

Having sketched the historical background, what of more recent developments? The dominant discourses that frame understandings of parental responsibility remain those of 'choice' and 'criminality', but since 1979 both have been emphasised and recast in radical new ways.

Enhancing Choice

Much has been written about enhancing parental choice in education. Harris' ground-breaking monograph documented the attempt by the Conservative governments to impose a market model on the education system and also how the rhetoric of 'parent power' legitimised the removal of powers from local education authorities (LEAs) and local accountability, the right to express a preference, league tables, publication of information by schools, admissions appeals and the establishment of the Special Educational Needs (SEN) tribunal.[44] All of these measures radically changed the education system, reconfiguring the welfare state, significantly by the juridification of a system that had previously been local,

---

[42]   See M Freeman, 'Feminism and Child Law' in D Monk and J Bridgeman (eds), *Feminist Perspectives on Child Law* (London, Cavendish, 2000) 29, who writes of 'the days when Bowlbyism reigned'.
[43]   For a more detailed analysis of this, see D Monk, 'Problematising Home Education: Challenging "Parental Rights" and "Socialisation"' (2004) 24 *Legal Studies* 568.
[44]   Harris, *Law and Education*, above n 4.

largely bureaucratic and paternalistic. Parents were reconstructed as 'active citizens' rather than 'passive recipients'.[45]

The trend has continued under New Labour. As Harris notes, in the 2005 General Election:

both parties seemed keen to give the impression of not only attaching ideological importance, but also of having a real commitment, to placing more power into the hands of ordinary citizens in relation to core public services.[46]

Yet despite the rhetoric of enhancing choice, once again, the reality is that parental rights serve to support the privileged. Harris argues that:

there is little evidence to suggest that real parental empowerment has occurred . . . Indeed the transfer of power away from elected local authorities has weakened still further local democratic accountability for educational provision

and that in practice it 'reinforces social divisions . . . with disproportionately more middle class children going to the highest achieving schools'.[47] Similarly, Stephen Ball's work documents in great detail how middle-class parents are able to take full advantage of 'the market' to sustain or re-assert their class advantage.[48]

At the same time, however, 'parental choice' impacts on all parents—the requirement to express a preference becomes a form of parental responsibility. The House of Commons Education and Skills Select Committee reported in 2004 that 'parental preference places the responsibility for securing a place in a good enough school on parents' shoulders'; that it:

distracts attention from the responsibility of Government and LEAs to ensure that all schools are good enough while creating an environment of, sometimes frenzied, competition between parents for places in the most popular schools;

and that:

far from being an empowering strategy the school admissions process, founded on parental preference, can be a time-consuming cause of much distress in the lives of many families.[49]

Despite the importance of the decision, parental disputes about choice of school rarely reach the courts. For most parents, it is not something over which either parent has much control, and so it is not surprising that the case law dealing with

---

[45] For critiques of this, see L Bash and D Coulby (eds), *The Education Reform Act: Competition and Control* (London, Cassell, 1989); Jones, above n 31; and A Barron, 'The Governance of Schooling: Genealogies of Control and Empowerment in the Reform of Public Education' (1996) 15 *Studies in Law, Politics and Society* 167.

[46] N Harris, 'Empowerment and State Education: Rights of Choice and Participation' (2005) 68 *MLR* 925, 930.

[47] Harris, *Education, Law and Diversity*, above n 4, 315.

[48] See SJ Ball, *Education Policy and Social Class* (London, Routledge, 2006).

[49] Quoted in Harris, 'Empowerment and State Education', above n 46, 955–6.

these disputes all involve, in some way, the possibility of private education.[50] The case law in this area is important because it raises questions about the respective rights of resident and non-resident parents, and the approach of the courts demonstrates ambivalence about the purpose of education and responsible decision-making.

In *Re A (children) (specific issue order: parental dispute)*,[51] the Court of Appeal dismissed the appeal of an English mother against the High Court's decision to send her two children to the fee-paying French Lycee school in South Kensington—the preferred choice of the French father. Her preference was for them to remain at the private schools in the countryside where she lived. Losing her appeal in effect required her to relocate to London. In making his decision, Robert Walker LJ praised the excellent education provide by the Lycee and held that:

> Frenchness and Englishness are abstract and somewhat amorphous concepts but it is very important that these two children should keep closely in touch with their father—there is no dispute about that—and that should if possible include keeping closely in touch with the father's language, his family and his home country (para 28).

Living in England and being educated in French appeared, to the court, to be an ideal solution. That the court made no reference to the impact on the day-to-day life of the mother resonates with fathers' rights campaigns in relation to contact. For attempting to ensure that the children remain both 'French' and 'English' to a certain extent mirrors the '50:50' assumption about residence unsuccessfully campaigned for by the fathers' rights movement.[52] The case also demonstrates a remarkable degree of continuity with the nineteenth-century case of *Stoughton* discussed above, to the extent that the court identifies education as a means of ensuring the continuation of paternal identity. In that case, it was considered too late for the child to become a Catholic and the option of being brought up in two religions was not considered at all (although it is an option taken by some parents of different religious faiths or backgrounds). In this case, national culture through education represents something akin to the father's name—something that must if at all possible be continued.[53]

A different approach was taken in *Re W (children) (education: choice of school)*.[54] Here the father wished his son to remain at a fee-paying school. However, there were questions about whether the family could afford it and the

---

[50] About 7% of the children of compulsory school age attend non-maintained schools, an increase of approximately 50,000 since 1970: *Social Trends 38* (London, Office for National Statistics, 2008) Table 3.3.

[51] [2001] 1 FLR 210.

[52] S Sheldon and R Collier (eds), *Father's Rights Activism and Law Reform in Comparative Perspective* (Oxford, Hart, 2006).

[53] See also *Re T and M (Minors)* [1995] ELR 1; and *Re Z (a child) (specific issue order: religious education)* [2002] EWCA Civ 501, where disputes about religious education are decided in favour of the fathers, albeit in very different and particular circumstances.

[54] [2002] EWCA Civ 1411.

mother wished to relocate and for her son to move to a state school near to her new home along with his siblings. Hale LJ held in favour of the mother. Significantly, while she makes clear that the decision is not one for the resident parent alone, unlike the previous case the day-to-day reality was an important factor:

> she has decided to move to the city of Wells. She has actually now, I am told, done so. The children live with her on most of their school days. It makes good practical commonsense for the children to have much shorter travelling distances (para 19).

Another key factor was that the mother appeared to the court to be more realistic than the father about the fees and thus more responsible. According to Hale LJ, it was unrealistic to expect the mother to contribute towards the fees and she held that:

> Both parents have now to accept that their standard of living, circumstances, everything about their lives will have to be downsized. That includes the education of their children (para 38).

That state education is represented here as a form of unfortunate 'downsizing' rather than an equal alternative is regrettable, albeit not explicit and perhaps unintended. However, it is interesting to query whether, had the family finances been different, the mother's choice of the local state school would still have been perceived as 'responsible'. Would a private school in those circumstances have been considered more in the child's interests?[55] The case makes clear that education remains an indicator of a family's 'station in life' now as much as in 1870. Despite the radical ideals that informed the 1944 Act, 'parental responsibility' legitimately serves to institutionalise privilege, continuing to reinscribe the significance of birth rather than transgressing it.[56]

In the latest recorded parental dispute case, *M v M (Specific Issue: Choice of School)*,[57] the facts were very similar: a father preferring a private school against the mother's choice of a local state school, when funds were limited, meant the only way in which it would be possible would be by sending the child for a voice test at a cathedral school to be eligible for a scholarship. The court ordered the mother to send the child for the voice test—against the child's wishes and contrary to the advice of the boy's teachers. The mother claimed that the father's insistence on upholding his parental rights vis-à-vis education was simply part of a campaign to undermine her role and force her to move home. This claim is not unusual in these cases, as the education dispute is often part of a more complex

---

[55] Another question raised by the case, but on which law is currently silent, is whether parental responsibility requires siblings to be treated equally. Anecdotal evidence suggests that it is not unusual in some families, as in this case, for only the boys to be educated privately.

[56] For a theoretical attempt to reconcile the tension between social justice and parental rights in education, see A Swift and H Brighouse, 'Family Values and Social Justice' in G Craig, D Gordon and T Burchardt (eds), *Social Justice and Public Policy* (Bristol, Policy Press, 2008).

[57] [2005] EWHC 2769 (Fam).

acrimonious conflict between the parents about a variety of matters. Standing argues that judicial respect for the non-resident father's parental responsibility in relation to education strengthens his position within the broader conflict in ways similar to contact disputes.[58] The gendered aspect of parental responsibility also has a significant impact in the context of 'criminality'.

Enhancing Criminality

From choice we move to look at criminality—the 'other side of the coin' of parental responsibility in education. The contrast is immense. Whereas parents have very limited powers against the state to enforce their preferences, the reverse is true as the state has increasingly invasive powers to enforce parental duties. Whereas 'choice' benefits middle-class parents and non-resident fathers, in the context of criminality it is mothers and underprivileged families that bear the brunt.

New Labour has altered little in relation to admissions procedures and parental choice. Where it has been extremely active is in relation to enforcing attendance and behaviour in schools. Truancy and exclusions was the topic of one of the first reports by the Social Exclusion Unit[59] and was followed by extensive statutory reform. Under the legal framework established by the 1944 Act, failure to ensure school attendance was addressed by School Attendance Orders—which could result in criminal prosecutions. While the courts' approach to the defences has changed—and narrowed over the years, as shown above—this procedure remains largely unchanged from that established in 1870. Alongside this are Education Supervision Orders created by the Children Act 1989, which take a less punitive approach.[60] These all remain in place, but alongside them are new measures— parenting contracts, parenting orders and penalty notices—created by the Anti-Social Behaviour Act 2003 and the Education and Inspections Act 2006.[61] A key document that provides an insight into the shifting understanding of parental responsibility and the intended use to be made of these provisions is the 'Guidance on Education-Related Parenting Contracts, Parenting Orders and Penalty Notices'.[62]

The guidance states that:

---

[58]   K Standing, 'Reasserting fathers' rights? Parental responsibility and involvement in education and lone mothers families in the UK' (1999) 7 *Feminist Legal Studies* 33. See also Wallbank, this volume.

[59]   *Truancy and Social Exclusion* (London, SEU, 1998).

[60]   See Ford *et al*, above n 5.

[61]   See Harris, *Education, Law and Diversity*, above n 4.

[62]   Department for Children, Schools and Families (Revised edn, September 2007).

These measures will help parents to fulfill their responsibilities to ensure their children regularly attend school and behave well when they get there, providing support as appropriate.[63]

It is suggested, however, that the provisions do more than simply 'help' parents: they create and expand parental responsibilities, and in so doing limit parental rights. To support this, five aspects of the guidance are examined below.

Extending Parental Responsibility to School Behaviour

The reference above to behaviour 'when they get there' represents a significant extension of parental responsibilities, as misbehaviour by children within school can now trigger parental orders and penalty notices. In earlier debates, in particular surrounding both the 1870 and 1944 Acts, one of the explicit benefits of school attendance was that it would raise children's aspirations beyond those in the home and would compensate for parental attitudes. This is evident from cultural narratives about the authority and status of teachers, as in many ways 'social betters'—the assumption being that teachers were not simply there to teach the curriculum, but also 'aspirational' appropriate behaviour.[64] In 1870, of course, the vast majority of working-class parents would not have attended school themselves. In contrast, the assumption now is that parents will themselves have been 'educated', or more critically as Gewirtz argues, behave according to a particular 'ideal-typical middle-class', which assumes that parents will adopt a policing role in relation to the school as well as in relation to their own children.[65] Where they are deemed to have failed, then, as we shall see, the new measures effectively serve to 'educate' them accordingly.

This extension of parental responsibility represents a 'criminalising' discourse in two ways. Misbehaviour in school is effectively treated as a 'crime' (the exclusions process attests to this) and parents and children are both held to account and found culpable. There is also a degree of continuity here, as the language used in policy documents now echoes the moral justifications for education in 1870—but, as with attendance, there are now to be 'no more excuses'.

SEN or Crime?

Alongside the penal discourse exists the SEN and disability framework. Here, behaviour is explained in a radically different way. Put simply, a child who misbehaves because of a SEN is constructed as 'ill', whereas a child whose

---

[63] *Ibid*, 5, [2].

[64] P Gardner, 'Teachers' in R Aldrich (ed), *A Century of Education* (London, Routledge Falmer, 2002).

[65] S Gewirtz, 'Cloning the Blairs: New Labour's programme for the re-socialization of working class parents' (2001) 16 *Journal of Education Policy* 365.

behaviour cannot be explained in this way is constructed as 'bad'.[66] This categorisation is implicitly adopted in the 2007 guidance, which states that: 'Behaviour
and attendance problems could, in some instances, relate to a child's special
educational needs'; and that:

> Parenting contracts, parenting orders and penalty notices are not, and should not be
> used as, alternatives to taking appropriate action to meet a pupil's special educational
> needs (paras 15 and 17).

Despite this 'reassurance', the guidance fails to provide any advice as to how
schools should determine whether misbehaviour or non-attendance is a result of
a SEN or disability. This is important because extensive research has repeatedly
indicated that the binary SEN/disciplinary offence paradigm is a highly artificial
and social, rather than medical, categorisation, and that, in practice, gender, race
and especially social class play a crucial role—albeit one masked through the
'neutral' scientific discourse of psychological development. This has significant
implications for parental responsibility: a parent whose child misbehaves for a
reason attributed to a SEN is, according to the guidance, a blameless and
potentially responsible parent. Yet, as the research repeatedly demonstrates,
accessing the SEN framework effectively requires parents to be persistent, articulate and, frequently, able to afford legal expertise.[67] Parents without those
capabilities and resources are therefore doubly disadvantaged and stigmatised.

There is an irony in the way in which law 'colonises' psychology here and uses
it for its own purposes.[68] For where a child is not deemed to have a SEN and the
penal approach to misbehaviour is adopted, one of the outcomes of parenting
contracts and orders is counselling and psychological support for parents. In
other words, a child's moral, as opposed to pyschological, culpability for misbehaviour appears to be attributed to the psychological failings of the parent. Yet,
unlike with children, there is nothing in the guidance that suggests that the penal
approach is inappropriate where this is the case.

Voluntary?

In relation to parenting contracts, the guidance repeatedly emphasises that
'[e]ntry into a parenting contract is voluntary' and that '[c]ontracts are *supportive
interventions and should not be seen or used as a punitive measure against the
parent*' (paras 38 and 40, emphasis added). Parent–school contracts are not
totally new: Home-School contracts were introduced in the 1990s for all parents,
and commentators have questioned the degree of voluntarism and the extent to

---

[66] For a more detailed examination of this binary construction, see D Monk, 'Theorizing
Education Law and Childhood: Constructing the Ideal Pupil' (2000) 21 *British Journal of Sociology of
Education* 355.
[67] Harris, above n 4, 326; and M King and D King, 'How the Law Defines the Special Educational
Needs of Autistic Children' [2006] 18 *CFLQ* 23.
[68] M King and C Piper, *How Law Thinks About Children* (Aldershot, Arena, 1991).

which they function as a form of control over parents.[69] What is new here is the use of them for particular parents who have been deemed to be failing in their role as parents; and in this context the voluntary nature of the contracts is even more questionable.

The assumption in the guidance is that responsible parents will want to work with schools and will agree to the contract. Moreover, while the guidance states:

> 77. Failure, by parent, school or LA, to keep to the terms of the parenting contract cannot lead to action for breach of contract or for civil damages. There is no sanction for a parent's failure to comply with, or refusal to sign, a parenting contract.

– it goes on to add that:

> [I]f the pupil's misbehaviour continues or escalates to such a level that the school or LA considers an application for a parenting order is appropriate, the court will be required to take any failure by the parent to comply with, or enter into, the contract into account in deciding whether to make the order. Similarly, if the pupil's irregular attendance continues or escalates to the point where a prosecution is deemed appropriate, any failure or refusal should be presented as evidence in the case.

Further, in relation to grounds for making a parental order, the guidance states that:

> 112. The applicant should also provide evidence of any experience of trying to engage the parent through a parenting contract. Magistrates are obliged to take into account any parental refusal to enter into, or failure to comply with, a parenting contract. This evidence is relevant to the consideration of whether the order is desirable in the interests of preventing further poor behaviour in school which may trigger an exclusion. If the parent will fully engage with support offered on a voluntary basis, a parenting order would not usually be desirable.

The incentives to comply and cooperate are clear and the reality of the ever-present threat of coercion later, and the unequal 'bargaining' position, mean that use of the language of contract is highly problematic.[70]

Infantilising Parents

What is clear from the above is that what is repeatedly in question is the behaviour *of the parent* as much as that of the child. In the context of parenting orders, this is explicit as parents can be required to attend a parenting pro-gramme, in effect compulsory education in parenting skills. The extent to which this form of education mirrors the education of children in terms of 'non-attendance' provisions is clear from the statements below:

---

[69] A Blair, 'Home-school agreement: A legislative framework for soft control of parents' (2001) 2 *Education Law Journal* 79.

[70] This in many ways mirrors the failure of 'voluntarism' in provisions in the Children Act Pt III: see J Tunstill, 'Family Support Clauses of the 1989 Children Act' in M Parton (ed), *Child Protection And Family Support: Tensions, Contradictions And Possibilities* (London, Routledge, 1997).

139. Monitoring compliance with a requirement to attend a parenting programme will be straightforward. Any failure by the parent to attend should be immediately reported . . . Where a parent has failed to fully comply with the requirement to attend the programme as directed by the responsible officer, the responsible officer can direct the parent to attend enough sessions to make up the missed sessions or, if that is impractical, a whole new programme . . .

141. If a parent fails to comply with a requirement of the order the responsible officer should contact the parent within one working day by visit, telephone or letter. . . .

142. What constitutes a reasonable excuse will depend on the circumstances and the responsible officer will need to make a judgement on each occasion . . . In some cases it may be reasonable to expect the parents to provide evidence to support their explanation—for instance a doctor's note where illness prevents them from complying.

The infantilising of parents here is similar to the language used in debates at the time of the 1870 Act. Yet then it was precisely because large sections of working-class parents were deemed incapable of educating their children. Once again, now, the assumption is that if they cannot they are irresponsible parents.

Who Is the Parent?

An important question raised by these new measures is: which parent should be held responsible? As family lawyers know, there are many ways of answering the question: who is a child's parent?

The guidance addresses this issue as follows:

27. 'Parent' means all natural parents, whether they are married or not; and includes any person who, although not a natural parent, has parental responsibility (as defined in the Children Act 1989) for a child or young person; and any person who, although not a natural parent, has care of a child or young person. Having care of a child or young person means that a person with whom the child lives and who looks after the child, irrespective of what their relationship is with the child, is considered to be a parent in education law. For further information see *Schools, 'Parents' and 'Parental Responsibility'* DfEE 0092/2000.

The document referred to states that:

Everyone who is a parent, whether they are a resident or non-resident parent, has the same right to participate in decisions about a child's education and receive information about the child. However for day to day purposes, the school's main contact is likely to be the parent with whom the child lives on school days . . .

School and LEA staff must treat all parents equally, unless there is a court order limiting an individual's exercise of parental responsibility.

The critical question left unanswered is to what extent a non-resident parent should be held responsible for non-attendance or misbehaviour. In theory, there is nothing to stop them being subject to parenting orders. In practice, however, it is the parent with residence who is subject to them. Consequently, while the rights of a non-resident parent—most often the father—to be informed about school progress are explicitly upheld by the guidance, it is silent about his responsibilities. This is all the more problematic when, as noted above, the non-resident parent's right to be involved in the choice of school is protected. Significantly, when we turn to look at the cases about non-attendance, there is a markedly disproportionate number of mothers being prosecuted. In this way, the *practice* of law appears to reinforce gendered understandings of parental responsibility: that for fathers it is more a question of status, whereas for mothers, it is more an activity.[71]

Enforcing Attendance: The Role of the Courts

A number of recent school attendance cases demonstrate an ambivalent response to the increasingly penal approach. There are two possible offences under the Education Act 1996 (as amended). Under section 444(1), the LEA need only show that the child failed to attend regularly at the school without authorisation. The only evidence which the LEA needs to produce to the court in this instance is the certificate of attendance. Section 444(1A) contains a more serious offence and the LEA must show not only that the child failed to attend regularly at school without authorisation, but that the parent knew and failed without reasonable justification to cause the child to do so.

Section 444(1) is an offence of strict liability, and consequently the parents' attempts to secure school attendance are irrelevant. In some cases, this has been seen to be problematic. For example, in *Bath and North East Somerset DC v Warman (Jennifer)*,[72] the pupil in question was almost aged 16 and living with her boyfriend. The mother, who was not aware of her daughter's whereabouts, was convicted. However, the magistrates were sympathetic to her and suggested an absolute discharge. Similarly, in *London Borough of Bromley v C*,[73] the magistrates had acquitted a mother who had been prosecuted under section 444(1) for taking her children on two unauthorised holidays[74] and repeated lateness. The court held that the strict liability nature of the offence meant that they ought to have convicted her: the acquittal was accordingly quashed and the case remitted to the magistrates' court. However, because of the family history, the fact that the mother and children were living in temporary accommodation after repossession of their home as a result of divorce proceedings and had been re-housed further away from the school; and, significantly, that she appeared to the court to be a 'good mother', Auld J chose to:

---

[71] C Smart, B Neale and A Wade, *The Changing Experience of Childhood: Families and Divorce* (Cambridge, Polity Press, 2001).

[72] (1999) ELR 81.

[73] [2006] EWHC 1110 (Admin).

[74] 'Responsible' parents sometimes argue that these holidays are 'educational': there is no legal basis or case law on this point, and the matter rests with the individual schools.

express the view that it does not consider that it is in the public interest, in the particular circumstances of this case, that any form of disposal other than one by way of absolute discharge would be appropriate.[75]

Few cases will reach the higher courts, and this is an area where further research is needed. The decisions of magistrates and LEAs here provide an interesting insight into what is considered 'responsible' or 'irresponsible' parenting and of 'blameworthy' or 'innocent' parents. Determining the failure or compliance with a legal duty in effect becomes a moral judgment about parenting.

A particularly interesting case is *Barnfather v London Borough of Islington Education Authority and the Secretary of State for Education and Skills*.[76] The case considered whether the strict liability was compatible with Article 6 of the ECHR. The court held—with notable reluctance—that strict liability offences do not per se infringe Article 6. Elias J commented:

> [T]here is nonetheless a real stigma attached to being found guilty of a criminal offence of this nature. It suggests either indifference to one's children, or incompetence at parenting, which in the case of the blameless parent will be unwarranted . . . justice is not served by prosecuting the innocent . . . it was disproportionate to the objective to be achieved.[77]

In response to the government's claim that a prosecution would be unusual where parents were *not* to blame, he noted that it:

> comes very close to a submission that in fact there will be no prosecution unless there is a fault on behalf of the defendant.[78]

This judicial criticism reflects concerns about reforms in youth justice generally. As Hollingsworth has argued:

> it should be recognised that where parents are held accountable in an evaluative and explanatory sense this is not a form of criminal legal liability, but a way of enforcing the parent's responsibility to their child. Parental responsibility should not be used as a mask to control and police the activities of children but to support them. As such, it is inappropriate to use the criminal justice sphere to coerce or encourage certain types of parenting.[79]

Taking the long view, what is striking about the cases where the courts respond sympathetically to the parents is the extent to which they resonate with the earlier Victorian cases, discussed above, where the courts acquitted parents for failing to comply with the 1870 Act. However, there is a very significant difference. The earlier cases excuse the parent because of their economic conditions or status or

---

[75]   *Ibid*, at 30.
[76]   [2003] ELR 263.
[77]   *Ibid*, at [57].
[78]   *Ibid*, at [55].
[79]   K Hollingsworth, 'Responsibility and Rights: Children and their Parents in the Youth Justice System' (2007) 21 *IJLPF* 190, 192.

class. In recent cases, these excuses, however relevant, are unacceptable, notwithstanding that research indicates significant links. What the courts appear to consider a legitimate excuse now is the *attitude* of the parent and the extent to which they can demonstrate to the court that they have cooperated with the authorities. For example, in *London Borough of Sutton v S*,[80] the court was sympathetic to the parents because they had 'done their best'. However, different benches and judges clearly take very different views. This is critical, because it means that it is not at all clear what exactly is required by parents: in other words, it is impossible to define with any certainty 'parental responsibility'.[81]

This is clear from *R (P) v Liverpool City Magistrates*.[82] In this case, the magistrates convicted the mother (it is worth noting again that the reported cases all relate to mothers) on the basis that there was no evidence of her having made any attempt to contact the child's father (her ex-husband) in order to ask him for support, of having inquired of social services to see if support was available, or of having asked the LEA about alternative forms of education. On appeal, the court quashed the conviction, holding that there was no burden of proof on the mother to have to demonstrate these attempts and that there was no evidence that the father was someone who would be of any assistance. The court was particularly sympathetic to the mother because, in attempting to get her teenage son to school, she had had a number of physical fights with him (the head of year in court gave evidence that physical force would be the only way to get that particular boy to school). In concluding that she could not have done anything more, she was acquitted (even though as the prosecution was under section 444(1), technically this was incorrect).

As Hollingsworth has commented in relation to youth justice, what is clear here is that 'there is no diminution in parental responsibility as the child gains responsibility',[83] although this indicates that some courts may take into account the decision of a child who clearly does not wish to attend school. However, there is clearly a conflict here with children's rights understandings of autonomy. It would appear that school attendance, like life-saving medical treatment, is not something that a 'responsible' child will refuse. As proposals to extend compulsory education are enacted, it is likely that this issue will prove increasingly problematic.

CONCLUSIONS

When law speaks of 'parental responsibility', it appeals to an abstract universal construct. Yet locating the ways in which it has been understood in history to the

---

[80] [2005] ELR 276.
[81] H Reece, 'From Parental Responsibility to Parenting Responsibly' (2006) *Current Legal Issues* 459, and see also chapter five, this volume.
[82] [2006] EWHC 887 (Admin).
[83] Hollingsworth, above n 79.

present day demonstrates that its uses and meanings have always been contingent, ambivalent and directed at shifting problem populations.

In many respects, we find ourselves in a position remarkably similar to that in 1870. Parental responsibility enables and legitimises those with real choices to exercise them in a sphere of remarkably unregulated freedom (in relation to private education) and in such a way that reinforces their privileges (in relation to the maintained sector). For those parents unable, or unwilling, to take advantage of these freedoms or to perform in accordance with the desired ideal, parental responsibility operates increasingly as a burden and legitimises increased surveillance and control.

The utopian, albeit romanticised, ideals that informed the 1944 Act live on not primarily through the desire to create a more equal society, but more powerfully by the extent that it gave voice to a pathologising of parents who do not 'behave responsibly'. This has been given full rein now and needs to be seen as a logical outcome of the inevitable failures of the post-war ideals. It would seem that the shift in parental responsibility has responded to the failure to create a more just society by holding those who have been failed by society responsible. As Finch argues:

> If the principle of citizenship rights is to be applied without challenging the economic order, the aim of the right to unlimited education for every citizen cannot be sustained.[84]

It is with this historical and political legacy that attempts to define and apply parental responsibility must grapple.

---

[84]   J Finch, *Education as Social Policy* (Harlow, Longman, 1984) 87.

9

Parental Responsibility and Corporal Punishment

SHAZIA CHOUDHRY

INTRODUCTION

THIS CHAPTER WILL explore the issue of corporal punishment as an aspect of parental responsibility within the context of what is expected of a 'responsible parent' in the international human rights arena. The development of the law on corporal punishment prior to the impact of the decisions of the European Court of Human Rights and other international bodies will be outlined. A further analysis will be conducted of the law after the implementation of the Human Rights Act 1998 and of whether current English law is compliant with it. English law on corporal punishment is a good case study of how far the state can resist its international obligations concerning the rights of its individual citizens and of the subsequent conflict this may cause with regard to domestic interpretations of the law. This chapter will thus demonstrate how the exercise of parental responsibility at the individual level has been considerably reduced by the United Kingdom's obligations under various international human rights treaties and conventions. In particular, it will illustrate how the issue has evolved from a question of parental rights to a question of parental responsibility and, more recently, to a question of compliance with human rights standards.

THE DEVELOPMENT OF THE ENGLISH LAW ON CORPORAL PUNISHMENT PRIOR TO INTERNATIONAL INTERVENTION

Historically, as Smith[1] has noted, support for the absolute right of parents to physically discipline their children could be found in a number of religious texts, including the Bible: 'he that spareth his rod hateth his son'.[2] However, by 1860, in

---

[1] R Smith, '"Hands off parenting?"—towards a reform of the defence of reasonable chastisement in the UK' [2004] 16 *CFLQ* 261.

[2] *The Bible*, Proverbs 13, v 24.

the seminal case of *R v Hopley*,[3] it was clear that the right to administer corporal punishment was not an unfettered one, but, in fact, subject to some regard for proportionality:

> If it [the punishment] be administered for the gratification of passion or rage or if it be immoderate or excessive in its nature or degree, or if be protracted beyond the child's power of endurance or with an instrument unfit for the purpose and calculated to produce danger to life and limb [then] the punishment is unlawful.[4]

By 1933, advances in child protection had led to the passage of the Children and Young Persons Act and the creation of criminal offences concerning the abuse and neglect of children. Nonetheless, the right of parents to 'administer punishment to their child' remained and was preserved by the same statute.[5]

The situation, however, soon changed following a series of challenges at the European Court of Human Rights concerning the use of corporal punishment outside the home.[6] As a direct result of these cases, legislation was finally enacted in 1986 to remove the right of teachers in state schools in England and Wales to physically chastise children.[7] Corporal punishment was finally banned from all schools in England and Wales in 1998[8] following the decision of the Court in *Costello-Roberts v UK*.[9]

The 1986 ban was recently challenged, and upheld by the House of Lords in *Williamson v Secretary of State for Education and Employment and Others*,[10] which sought to challenge its application within the voluntary aided school system. In contrast to other cases brought before the courts concerning corporal punishment, the parents in this case *wanted* corporal punishment to be administered to their children whilst in school as an expression of their Christian belief, the aim being 'to help form godly character'. As such, they claimed that the statutory ban was incompatible with their Article 9 rights to freedom of religion and freedom to manifest their religion in practice by delegating the administration of corporal punishment to teachers at these schools. There was also discussion of the proposed punishment and whether the applicants' argument, presumably in reliance upon *Costello-Roberts*, that it would not contravene Article 3[11] was correct. In a unanimous judgment, the applicants' arguments were rejected and the House of Lords had no difficulty in applying the case law of the European

---

[3] (1860) 2 F&F 202.

[4] *Ibid*, at 206 (Chief Justice Cockburn).

[5] Children and Young Persons Act 1933 s 1(7) provided that 'the [crime of wilful assault, ill treatment or neglect in s 1(1)] does not affect the right of any parent to administer punishment to their child'. Section 1(1) stated that it is an offence to assault or ill-treat a child in a manner likely to cause him or her unnecessary suffering or injury to health.

[6] See, eg *Tyrer v UK* [1978] 2 EHRR 1.

[7] Education (No 2) Act 1986 s 47.

[8] Education Act 1996 ss 548–9 as inserted by Schools Standards and Framework Act 1998 s 131.

[9] [1995] 19 EHRR 112.

[10] [2005] UKHL 15.

[11] See *Williamson v Secretary of State for Education and Employment and Others* [2005] UKHL 15 at [10] and [27] (Lord Bingham) and [77] and [80] (Baroness Hale).

Court of Human Rights to conclude that, although the Article 9 rights of the claimants were engaged, and were plainly being interfered with by the existence of the ban, such interference was necessary in a democratic society for the protection of the rights and freedoms of others. The state was entitled, therefore, to limit the practice of corporal punishment in all schools, in line with its positive obligations under Article 3, to protect the rights and freedoms of all children. Prohibiting only such punishment as would violate their rights under Article 3 would bring difficult problems of definition, demarcation and enforcement and would not meet the authoritative international view of what other international instruments required.[12] Even if it could be shown that a particular act of corporal punishment was in the interests of an individual child, it was clear, Baroness Hale said, that a universal or blanket ban may be justified to protect a vulnerable class; it was the vulnerability of the class which provided the rationale for the law in question.[13] What was particularly striking about this case, therefore, was the lack of consideration for the point of view of children. As Baroness Hale observed:

> This is, and has always been, a case about children, their rights and the rights of their parents and teachers. Yet there has been no one here or in the courts below to speak on behalf of the children. No litigation friend has been appointed to consider the rights of the pupils involved separately from those of the adults. No non-governmental organi-sation, such as the Children's Rights Alliance, has intervened to argue a case on behalf of children as a whole. The battle has been fought on ground selected by the adults.[14]

In summary, the parental right to delegate the administration of corporal punishment to schools was, over time, overridden as a result of the Convention obligations which the state[15] has towards all citizens: parents *and* children. Baroness Hale's point is also well made: English case law on the matter had largely been conducted within the context of the parental right to decide what was in the best interests of the child; the interests of children were considered incidentally. A separate consideration of the rights and interests of the child has only occurred either at the European Court of Human Rights or as a direct result of the obligations upon the courts under the Human Rights Act. These obliga-tions are thus highly significant to the hierarchy of responsibility towards children. The state is reconfigured within these obligations as a 'national parent' enjoined, therefore, to exercise a higher level of parental responsibility in doing so with regard to matters that were in the remit of the state. The message was loud and clear: a responsible state and, therefore, by implication, a responsible parent could not allow a child to be subjected to the possibility of 'institutional violence' because of the risk that it may breach the Article 3 rights of the child even if this

---

[12]   Such as the UN Convention on the Rights of the Child—see Baroness Hale in *Williamson,* above n 11, at [86].

[13]   *Ibid,* at [80].

[14]   *Ibid,* at [71].

[15]   The so-called 'vertical effect'.

meant that parental rights would be limited. The right of the parent to administer physical chastisement within the home, however, remained.

A V UNITED KINGDOM AND THE EFFECT OF INTERNATIONAL LAW

With the passage of the Children Act 1989 came the new concept of 'parental responsibility', which, in addition to a number of other provisions, signalled the symbolic move away from regarding children in the same terms as property and towards the centralisation of the concept of child welfare. Parental rights were replaced by 'parental responsibility', custody was replaced by 'residence' and access was replaced with 'contact.' However, the Act did nothing to alter the position regarding the use of physical chastisement within the home. Significantly, the concept of parental responsibility had no effect upon the common law defence of 'reasonable chastisement'[16] statutorily confirmed by section 1(7) of the Children and Young Persons Act 1933:

> Nothing in this section shall be construed as affecting the right of any parent, or (subject to section 548 of the Education Act 1996) any other person, having the lawful control or charge of a child or young person to administer punishment to him.

Thus, any 'parent' charged with *any* offence under the Offences Against the Persons Act 1861 (ranging from section 18, wounding with intent, to section 39, common assault) could seek to rely on this defence, albeit subject to the requirement of reasonableness. However, it is of some significance that the term 'parent' was not limited to those who held parental responsibility alone—it was available to those acting in *loco parentis*. There was also evidence that 'reasonable' was being 'interpreted by juries and the courts to cover a range of behaviour that many people would consider went beyond a "loving smack".[17]

It was, however, again, decisions by the European Court of Human Rights and other international pressure that paved the way for further reform. For, once it had been decided that a responsible parent ought not to allow corporal punishment of their child at school, sufficient to engage Article-3-type treatment, it was not such a great leap to the next logical conclusion that a responsible parent ought not to administer the same kind of corporal punishment to the same child within the home. In 1995, the UN Committee on the Rights of the Child, after examining the United Kingdom's first report under the UN Convention on the Rights of the Child (UNCRC), expressed concern at the existence of the 'reasonable chastisement' defence and the level of violence against children in the United Kingdom and recommended the prohibition of all corporal punishment in the family.[18]

---

[16]   *R v Hopley* (1860) 2 F&F 202 (Cockburn CJ).
[17]   See Joint Committee on Human Rights, 'Report on the UN Convention on the Rights of the Child', 10th Report of Session 2002–3, [99].
[18]   15 February 1995, CRC/C/15/Add.34, [16], [31] and [32].

The United Kingdom has, of course, ratified but not incorporated the UNCRC, but nevertheless its influence is still strong, particularly within the European Court of Human Rights. Article 19 of the UNCRC, for example, which provides that states are enjoined to take all appropriate measures 'to protect the child from all forms of physical or mental violence, injury or abuse', was specifically referred to by the European Commission in its decision in the case of *A v UK*.[19] Here, a nine-year-old child applicant complained that the government had failed to protect him from degrading treatment carried out towards him by his stepfather. The applicant had been beaten with a garden cane on two or more occasions in the course of one week and at least some of the strokes were inflicted directly onto the bare skin, causing him significant bruising. The stepfather was subsequently charged with assault occasioning actual bodily harm pursuant to section 47 of the Offences Against the Persons Act 1861, but had not, however, been held liable for his actions due to his successful use of the defence of reasonable parental chastisement.

While acknowledging that, unlike the cases concerning corporal punishment administered by a teacher, no direct responsibility could attach to the United Kingdom under the European Convention for the acts of the applicant's step-father, the Commission recalled that it had previously held that, even in the absence of any direct responsibility for the acts of a private individual under Article 3 of the Convention, state responsibility may nevertheless be engaged through the obligation imposed by Article 1 of the Convention 'to secure ... the rights and freedoms defined in Section 1 of this Convention'. The European Court subsequently followed the reasoning of the Commission when it upheld its decision. They held that it was due to the availability of the 'reasonable chastise-ment' defence to a charge of assault on a child and the fact that the burden of proof was on the prosecution to establish beyond reasonable doubt that the assault went beyond the limits of lawful punishment, that, despite the fact that the applicant had been subjected to treatment of sufficient severity to fall within the scope of Article 3, the jury had acquitted his stepfather.-As a result, the Court found that the law did not provide adequate protection to the applicant against treatment or punishment contrary to Article 3 and that the applicant's Article 3 rights had been breached.

The reaction of the UK Government, unlike after *Costello*, was *not*, however, to effect an immediate change in the law. Although the UK Government had, during the course of *A v UK*, accepted that the law currently failed to provide adequate protection to children and should be amended, it did nothing towards achieving further change other than publishing a consultation document upon the issue[20]

[19]   (1999) 27 EHRR 611.
[20]   This ruled out the possibility of an outright ban of corporal punishment by parents. See the consultation paper issued by the Department of Health, 'Protecting Children, Supporting Parents: A Consultation Document on the Physical Punishment of Children' (2000) [1.5], <http://www.dh.gov.uk/en/Consultations/Closedconsultations/DH_4083513>.

and, arguably, passing the Human Rights Act in 1998. In particular, section 2 of the Human Rights Act required courts, when determining a question which had arisen in connection with a Convention right, to take into account Convention law, which includes the judgments and declarations of the European Court of Human Rights, opinions of the European Commission of Human Rights and decisions of the Committee of Ministers of the Council of Europe. Further, section 3 provides that all legislation must, as far as it is possible to do so, be read and given effect in a way that is compatible with the Convention rights. This applies to all legislation whenever enacted.

Regardless of whether the government had intended the Human Rights Act to form the catalyst for a change in the law, it soon became clear that the courts had decided to comply with their duties under it before it had even come into force. In *R v H (Assault of Child: Reasonable Chastisement)*,[21] the Court of Appeal took the opportunity to take into account the decision in *A v UK* and, more specifically, the criteria that were referred to by the European Court of Human Rights in order to establish whether or not the treatment administered crossed the threshold of entry into Article 3:

> The assessment of this minimum level of severity depends on all the circumstances of the case. Factors such as the nature and context of the punishment, the manner and method of its execution, its duration, its physical and mental effects and, in some instances, the sex, age and state of health of the victim must all be taken into account.[22]

However, as has been noted by a number of authors,[23] the Court erroneously went further than the European Court of Human Rights in seemingly extending the criteria to include the reasons for the punishment. Although questions of motive or reason for parental chastisement could lead to a higher likelihood of conviction if the punishment appeared disproportionate to the 'wrong' being chastised or if they could be regarded as generally unworthy, they could also easily water down the protection afforded by the decision of the European Court of Human Rights in *A v UK*. In particular, there were concerns that it could lead to acquittals from juries sympathetic to the reasons given, even where the threshold of treatment had crossed that of Article 3. More importantly, however, while questions of motive are, as far as the European Convention is concerned, irrelevant when considering whether the treatment comes within the ambit of Article 3, what is of most concern under Article 3 are questions that relate directly to the severity of the punishment. The confidence in which the Court of Appeal professed this 'incremental development' of the law as being compatible with Convention case law was seemingly misplaced.

---

[21]   [2002] 1 Cr App R 7.
[22]   The Court referred to para 30 of the judgment in *Tyrer v UK* [1978] 2 EHRR 1.
[23]   J Rogers, 'A criminal lawyer's response to chastisement in the European Court of Human Rights' [2002] *Crim LR* 98; Smith, above n 1; and H Keating, 'Protecting or Punishing Children: Physical Punishment, Human Rights and English Law Reform' [2006] 26 *Legal Studies* 394.

It soon became clear, therefore, that the development of the common law in this manner would not, even if it was correct, be enough to satisfy the obligations created by a number of international treaties and conventions. In 2002, the UN Committee on the Rights of the Child, after examining the United Kingdom's second report under the UN Convention on the Rights of the Child, stated that:[24]

> In light of its previous recommendation, the Committee deeply regrets that the State party persists in retaining the defence of 'reasonable chastisement' and has taken no significant action towards prohibiting all corporal punishment of children in the family. The Committee is of the opinion that governmental proposals to limit rather than to remove the 'reasonable chastisement' defence do not comply with the principles and provisions of the Convention and the aforementioned recommendations, particularly since they constitute a serious violation of the dignity of the child.

The Committee further recommended that the United Kingdom urgently adopt legislation to remove the reasonable chastisement defence and prohibit all corporal punishment in the family and in any other contexts not covered by existing legislation. More international pressure for change came in 2004 when the Parliamentary Assembly of the Council of Europe adopted the recommendation that:

> The Assembly considers that any corporal punishment of children is in breach of their fundamental right to human dignity and physical integrity. The fact that such corporal punishment is still lawful in certain member states violates their equally fundamental right to the same legal protection as adults.[25]

The government's response to the pressure was, however, to resist amendments[26] that would have introduced a complete ban on the physical chastisement of children and instead to support an amendment which would limit the availability of the reasonable chastisement defence for parents to common assault alone. This was despite the fact that the Joint Committee on Human Rights[27] issued a report urging a complete abolition of the defence of 'reasonable chastisement' in order to meet human rights obligations under three international treaties (the UN Convention on the Rights of the Child, the International Covenant on Economic, Social and Cultural Rights and the European Social Charter). However, regardless of such objections, the Children Act 2004 was passed with the amendment intact and contained in section 58, but, significantly, with a commitment that the government would review the practical consequences of the section and seek parents' views on smacking two years after its commencement. Of particular note is that the definition of 'parents' within the context of section 58 remained the same, ie parents and adults acting in *loco parentis*, excluding those expressly

---

[24] 4 October 2002, unedited version CRC/C/15/Add.188, [35] and [36 (a and b)].
[25] Recommendation 1666 (2004) adopted by the Assembly debate on 23 June 2004 (21st Sitting).
[26] For a comprehensive account of the passage of the Bill, see Keating, above n 23.
[27] Joint Committee on Human Rights (2004) Children Bill, 19th report of Session 2003–4, HL Paper 161, HC 537, [118]–[177].

prohibited (such as teachers and childminders). Thus, there is no requirement that the 'parent' exercising the corporal punishment should hold parental responsibility for the child. Further changes in the practical application of the law came shortly after the passage of the Act when the Crown Prosecution Service amended the Charging Standard on offences against the person. The standard now states that the vulnerability of the victim, such as being a child assaulted by an adult, should be treated as an aggravating factor when deciding the appropriate charge. Injuries that would normally have led to a charge of common assault will now be charged as assault occasioning actual bodily harm under section 47 of the Offences against the Person Act, under which the defence of reasonable punishment will not be available.

The campaign for the complete abolition of the reasonable punishment defence did not, however, slow down. In 2005, the Committee of Ministers of the Council of Europe, the body responsible for monitoring conformity with the European Social Charter, issued its conclusion on the latest UK report (submitted in June 2004) and found UK law in breach of human rights obligations.

In January 2006, the United Kingdom's four Children's Commissioners called upon the government and the Scottish Executive to introduce legislation that would ban the defence of reasonable chastisement/punishment throughout the United Kingdom.[28] In June 2006, the UN Committee on the Rights of the Child issued a 'General Comment'[29] on 'the right of the child to protection from corporal punishment and other cruel or degrading forms of punishment'. The comment emphasises:

> that eliminating violent and humiliating punishment of children, through law reform and other necessary measures, is an immediate and unqualified obligation

for states which have ratified the Convention on the Rights of the Child. Finally, in August 2006, the report of a four-year study on violence against children was published by the United Nations Secretary-General.[30] The report called on all countries to prohibit all corporal punishment in the family, at school and everywhere else by 2009.

It has now been two years since section 58 of the Children Act 2004 came into force and the government recently published its promised review of the section following a consultation exercise. The review[31] notes at the outset that a substantial majority of the respondents said that section 58 had not improved legal protection for children and that the defence of reasonable punishment should be

---

[28]   Letter to Ruth Kelly, then Secretary of State for education, *The Times* (21 January 2006).
[29]   The General Comment is available at <http://www.unhchr.ch/tbs/doc.nsf/(Symbol)/CRC.C. GC.8.En?OpenDocument>.
[30]   See The United Nations Secretary General's Study on Violence against Children at <http://www. violencestudy.org/r25>.
[31]   Department for Children, Schools and Families, 'Review of Section 58 of the Children Act 2004' (Cm 7232, 2007), <http://www.dfes.gov.uk/publications/section58review/>.

removed in its entirety. However, these responses were rather summarily dismissed on the basis that no evidence was offered for these views and that they were simply statements of belief.[32] Some concessions were made: 'much of the evidence gathered suggests that there is a lack of understanding about the law',[33] which referred, it is presumed, to evidence contained in the review that the Crown Prosecution Service (CPS) had in some cases allowed the defence to be raised where it should not have been made available and that a number of agencies said that the legal position on physical punishment was not well understood by parents and made it difficult for practitioners to work with them.[34] In order to rectify this, the government states in the review that the CPS will issue a bulletin to its staff reminding them of section 58 and will ask them to continue to monitor the use of the defence. Ultimately, the review concludes that, through the enactment of section 58, the United Kingdom has met its international obligations under Article 3 of the European Convention on Human Rights (ECHR) and will retain the current law in its present form in the absence of evidence that it is not working satisfactorily.

In short, despite considerable domestic and international opposition, the government is sticking to its guns on the preservation of the parental right to administer 'reasonable punishment', albeit in a much more limited form. Moreover, its conduct since *A v UK* has demonstrated that it is not interested in the philosophical, theoretical or sociological arguments for and against the smacking of children or whether it can ever be in the interests of children. It resists a change in the law in pure doctrinal reliance of the fact that the current state of the law does not represent any problems of incompatibility. The next section will examine in detail if this is the case and, if so, how this can be possible and for how long.

IS THE PARENTAL DEFENCE OF REASONABLE PUNISHMENT COMPATIBLE
UNDER INTERNATIONAL LAW?

It is of significance that when the government talked of compatibility in its recent review of section 58, it did so in relation to the ECHR alone. As detailed above, the current law on corporal punishment could be said to be in breach of a number of other international conventions that the United Kingdom has entered into, these being the UNCRC, the International Covenant on Economic, Social and Cultural Rights (ICESCR) and the European Social Charter (ESC). Indeed, the Joint Committee on Human Rights stated as much when it concluded that:

> Although clause 49 [the predecessor of s 58] achieves a greater degree of compatibility with the UK's obligations under the CRC by restricting the scope of the reasonable

32 *Ibid*, [20]–[26].
33 *Ibid*, [48].
34 *Ibid*, [25]–[26] and [37]–[38].

chastisement defence, by preserving it as a defence to common assault it does not achieve full compatibility with the UK's obligations under the CRC as interpreted by the UN Committee on the Rights of the Child, or under the ICESCR, as interpreted by the Committee on Economic, Social and Cultural Rights, or under the European Social Charter, as interpreted by the European Committee of Social Rights.[35]

However, none of these instruments, although significant, has been incorporated and thus the United Kingdom is under no legal obligation to change its law. It is the ECHR alone which is binding upon the United Kingdom. Therefore, it is to the Convention that questions of compatibility must be addressed.

The Applicability of Article 3

Article 3 of the ECHR provides, in absolute terms, that '[n]o one shall be subject to torture or to inhuman or degrading treatment or punishment'. No provision is made for exceptions and no derogation from it is permissible, even in times of war or other national emergency.[36] The proportionality exercise is therefore irrelevant. The development of a number of general principles can, however, be discerned from an examination of the reasoning of the European Court of Human Rights on Article 3.[37] The Court has referred to the need for the alleged 'ill-treatment' to attain a minimum level of severity[38] if it is to fall within the scope of Article 3. Treatment involving actual bodily injury or intense physical or mental suffering will generally qualify as 'ill treatment'.[39] Treatment which humiliates or debases an individual; shows a lack of respect for, or diminishes human dignity; or arouses feelings of fear, anguish or inferiority capable of breaking an individual's moral and physical resistance, may also be characterised as degrading and fall within the prohibition of Article 3.[40] In considering whether treatment is 'degrading', the Court will have regard to whether its object was to humiliate and debase the person concerned and whether, as far as the consequences are concerned, it adversely affected his or her personality in a manner incompatible with Article 3.[41]

The Court has also made it clear that the assessment of treatment is relative and will depend upon all the circumstances of the case. Factors that have been taken into account by the Court have included the nature and context of the

---

[35] See Joint Committee of Human Rights, above n 27, [161].

[36] See *Chahal v UK* [1997] 23 EHRR at [79].

[37] For a comprehensive analysis of these principles, see D Feldman, *Civil Liberties and Human Rights in England and Wales* (2nd edn, Oxford, Oxford University Press, 2006) ch 5.

[38] *Ireland v UK* [1979] 2 EHRR 25 at [162]; *Tyrer v UK* [1979–80] 2 EHRR 1 at [30]; and *A v UK* [1999] 27 EHRR 61 at [20].

[39] See *Ireland v UK, ibid*, at [167]; and *Pretty v United Kingdom* (2002) 35 EHRR 1 at [52].

[40] See amongst recent authorities, *Price v UK* [2002] 34 EHRR 53 at [24]–[30]; and *Valašinas v Lithuania*, no 44558/98, [117], ECHR 2001-VIII.

[41] Even the absence of such a purpose cannot conclusively rule out a finding of a violation of Art 3: *Valašinas v Lithuania, ibid*, at [101].

treatment; its duration; its physical and mental effects; and, in some cases, the sex, age and state of health of the victim.[42] Thus, just because a form of conduct is not degrading treatment for one person does not mean that it cannot be so for another. The Court, which views the Convention as a living instrument,[43] has also stated that it will be possible to reclassify its definition of ill-treatment in the light of developments in policy of the Member States.[44] Generally speaking, Article 3 imposes primarily a negative obligation on states to refrain from inflicting serious harm on persons within their jurisdiction. Most cases involving Article 3 and the infliction of corporal punishment had, therefore, prior to the decision in *A v UK*, involved state agents or public authorities inflicting treatment on individuals.[45] However, the Court had been developing a certain level of flexibility in addressing the application of Article 3 within the 'private context'[46] and this flexibility was further developed by the court in *A v UK* (detailed above) in recognising that the state can be under positive obligations to protect one individual from having their rights under Article 3 infringed by another individual. It was for this reason that, in *A v UK*, the Court held that not only was the level of severity of the child's punishment sufficient to constitute inhuman or degrading treatment, but also that the responsibility of the state was engaged under Article 3 in respect of the acts of private individuals. However, it is also clear that although Article 3 is drafted in absolute terms, the *duties* imposed by these positive obligations are not. It is for this reason that the Commission in *A v UK* was able to explicitly state that corporal punishment of children is not per se a violation of Article 3:

> The Commission would emphasise that this finding does not mean that Article 3 is to be interpreted as imposing an obligation on States to protect, through their criminal law, against any form of physical rebuke, however mild, by a parent of a child.[47]

Further, in *Z and Others v UK*[48] and in *E v UK*,[49] two cases decided after *A v UK*, the Court set out further guidance as to the nature and extent of positive obligations under Article 3 in relation to claims under English civil law. In its judgments, the Court reiterated the principle that states should provide effective protection in relation to children and vulnerable adults, particularly where the authorities had or ought to have had knowledge of abuse.[50]

---

[42]   See among other authorities *Costello-Roberts v UK* [1995] 19 EHRR 112.
[43]   *Tyrer v UK*, Series A 2 EHRR 1 at [31].
[44]   *Selmouni v France* [2000] 29 EHRR 403.
[45]   See *Tyrer v UK* [1979–80] 2 EHRR 1 at [31].
[46]   See *D v UK* [1997] 24 EHRR 423 at [49].
[47]   *A v UK*, Commission Opinion, [55], (1999) 27 EHRR 611, 624.
[48]   [2002] 34 EGRR 3.
[49]   [2003] 36 EHRR 31.
[50]   See *E v UK* [2003] 36 EHRR 31 at [88]; *Z v UK* [2002] 34 EGRR 3 applied. See also *Stubbings v UK* [1997] 23 EHRR 213 at [64].

The test under Art.3 however does not require it to be shown that 'but for' the failing or omission of the public authority ill-treatment would not have happened. *A failure to take reasonably available measures which could have had a real prospect of altering the outcome or mitigating the harm* is sufficient to engage the responsibility of the State[51] (emphasis added).

Thus, if the state can show that it has taken all reasonably available measures to provide effective protection against a breach of the Article 3 rights of children, liability for any breach may not, as a result, attach to it. It is here that the new Charging Standard issued in conjunction with section 58 is of crucial significance, for it was argued by the government that its very existence would mean that in all cases concerning treatment which crosses the Article 3 threshold, a more serious offence than common assault would be charged. This would, in turn, result in the fact that the reasonable chastisement defence would not be available in relation to such treatment. If this is indeed the case, the conclusion of the Joint Committee on Human Rights[52] may well be correct:

[T]he combination of the new clause and the new charging standard may well be considered sufficient to satisfy the UK's obligation to comply with the judgment of the European Court of Human Rights in *A v UK*, because it makes the defence unavailable in relation to treatment or punishment which is contrary to Article 3.

It is certainly arguable, however, that the charging standard may not adequately protect children from treatment that crosses the threshold of the degrading elements of Article 3. In other words, the focus of the charging standard upon the physical nature of the punishment may mean that in instances where the Article 3 threshold is crossed by virtue of psychological or emotional harm, the charging standard does not ensure that a charge higher than common assault will be brought against the defendant. This is despite the fact that it is clearly established within criminal law that psychological illnesses could, under section 47 of the Offences against the Person Act 1861, be included in the term 'actual bodily harm' as long as the harm was a medically defined illness and not a mere emotion, such as fear or panic.[53] If this is the case, the section 58 defence may still be available in cases that breach the Article 3 rights of the child.

The government review of section 58 notes that the Charging Standard has clarified the boundary between what constitutes common assault and what constitutes assault occasioning actual bodily harm and takes into account the particular seriousness of an adult assaulting a child.[54] It also records the fact that the standard may have resulted in the removal of a certain amount of discretion from the police, which has had the added effect of providing *more* protection for children:

---

[51]   *E v UK* (2003) 36 EHRR 31 at [99].
[52]   Joint Committee on Human Rights, above n 27, [137].
[53]   *R v Chan-Fook* [1994] 2 All ER 552; and *Ireland v Burstow* [1998] AC 147.
[54]   'Review of Section 58', above n 31, [45].

However, it (the charging standard) means that the police sometimes have to record as assault occasioning actual bodily harm a crime which is not perceived as being particularly serious, best dealt with by children's social care rather than the criminal justice system, and which previously would have been recorded as common assault.[55]

However, no information is given with regard to how many cases involving psychological as opposed to physical injury are charged under section 39 or 47 of the Offences Against the Persons Act. It is therefore difficult to assess whether the government's claim that current UK law on the parental defence of reasonable punishment in relation to common assault is compatible with Article 3, in the absence of a further decision on the matter from the European Court of Human Rights.

The Applicability of Article 8

Thus far, questions of compatibility that have arisen before the European Court of Human Rights have concerned Article 3 alone, despite the fact that rights under Article 8 may also be claimed: for example, the right to administer physical punishment to one's child as an aspect of family life. However, the Court has expressly declined to consider Article 8 cases in such cases. In *A v UK*, the applicant invited the court to rule also on the merits of his Article 8 complaint, which he argued was necessary in order to provide guidance for the government and protection for children against all forms of deliberate violence. However, the Court declined to do so, holding that having found a violation of Article 3 it was not necessary to examine whether the inadequacy of legal protection was also in breach of Article 8.[56] This does not, however, preclude the future application of Article 8 to such cases; nor does it preclude, necessarily, that a breach of it will not be found. We will now turn to an examination of the applicability of Article 8 to the parental right to reasonable chastisement of a child.

Article 8 provides that:

1. Everyone has the right to respect for his private and family life, his home and his correspondence.

2. There shall be no interference by a public authority with the exercise of this right except such as in accordance with the law and is necessary in a democratic society in the interests of national security, public safety or the economic well being of the country, for the prevention of disorder or crime, for the protection of heath or morals, or for the protection of the rights and freedoms of others.

---

[55] *Ibid.*
[56] However, one member of the Commission in *A v UK* would have preferred to deal with that case under Art 8 rather than Art 3: see Concurring Opinion of EA Alkema (1999) 27 EHRR 611 at 628–9.

It has been held that Article 8 provides for the right to respect for both privacy (including a person's physical and mental integrity) and family life. The right to private life is wide-ranging. Of particular relevance to the corporal punishment context are three points. First, 'the concept of private life covers the physical and moral integrity of the person'.[57] Mental health and stability is said to be part of a person's moral integrity.[58] In *X and Y v The Netherlands*,[59] the lack of effective protection under the criminal law against sexual assault for a mentally ill woman was said to amount to an infringement of her right to private life. The state, it was said, is required under Article 8 to protect one person's right to private life against unwanted contact or infringements to moral integrity. The state may thus be required to protect a vulnerable person from violence under Article 8.[60] Secondly, the European Court of Human Rights has stated that Article 8 is concerned with protecting a person's physical and psychological integrity[61] and their right to identity and personal development.[62] Thirdly, the Court is increasingly referring to the Convention on the Rights of the Child in the course of its judgments in cases concerning children and their right to physical integrity. In *Sahin v Germany*,[63] for example, the Court recently said that:

> [T]he human rights of children and the standards to which all governments must aspire in realizing these rights for all children are set out in the Convention on the Rights of the Child.[64]

These three points form the basis, therefore, for the argument that the existence of a parental right to reasonable chastisement, at any level, would in fact breach the child's Article 8 right to personal integrity and private life.

However, Article 8 will also require a consideration of the right to family life. Once the question of whether or not family life is in existence has been established,[65] there may be, in addition, positive obligations inherent in effective 'respect' for private or family life.[66] These obligations may involve the adoption of measures designed to secure respect for family life in relations between private individuals, including both the provision of a regulatory framework of adjudication and enforcement to protect individual rights.[67] Most cases concerning these rights have concerned alleged interference with the right for a parent and a child

---

[57]   *X and Y v the Netherlands* [1986] 8 EHRR 235.
[58]   *Bensaid v UK* [2001] 33 EHRR 10.
[59]   *Ibid.*
[60]   *Costello-Roberts v UK* [1995] 19 EHRR 112.
[61]   *Pretty v UK* (2002) 35 EHRR 1 at [61].
[62]   *Bensaid v UK* [1995] 19 EHRR 112 at [45].
[63]   [2003] 15 BHRC 84.
[64]   *Ibid*, at [39]–[41] and [64].
[65]   The existence or non-existence of 'family life' for the purposes of Art 8 is essentially a question of fact depending upon the real existence, in practice, of close personal ties—see *K and T v Finland* [2003] 36 EHRR 18 at [150].
[66]   See *X and Y v Netherlands* [1986] 8 EHRR 235.
[67]   *Glaser v UK*, no 32346/96, [63], 19 September 2000.

to enjoy each other's company.[68] However, can a parent claim a right to administer punishment to his or her child as an aspect of their right to family life? This question, as the Joint Committee on Human Rights noted,[69] has already been answered by the European Commission of Human Rights in *Seven Individuals v Sweden.*[70] This case concerned a Swedish amendment to criminal law, which equalised the legal position of children and adults in the context of assault. Parents who claimed that the scope of the criminal law of assault failed to respect their right to respect for private and family life challenged this extension of the law of assault. In rejecting the complaint as manifestly ill-founded and therefore inadmissible, the Commission found that:

> The fact that no distinction is made between the treatment of children by their parents and the same treatment applied to an adult stranger cannot, in the Commission's opinion, constitute an 'interference' with respect for the applicant's private and family lives since the consequences of an assault are equated in both cases. Nor does the mere fact that legislation, or the state of the law, intervenes to regulate something which pertains to family life constitute a breach of Article 8(1) unless the intervention in question violates the applicants' right to respect for their family life. The Commission finds that the scope of the Swedish law of assault and molestation is a normal measure for the control of violence and that its extension to apply to the ordinary physical chastisement of children by their parents is intended to protect potentially weak and vulnerable members of society.[71]

If we add to this the observation made above, that the European Court of Human Rights is increasingly influenced by the Convention on the Rights of the Child, adopted by the United Kingdom since the decision, it is not difficult to see why the Joint Committee on Human Rights thought it likely that:

> the Court of Human Rights would today reach the same conclusion in any similar Article 8 challenge to a law which removed the defence of reasonable chastisement.[72]

However, the question of whether the parental defence of reasonable punishment is incompatible with Article 8 is not, it is submitted, completely answered by the above analysis. It is of particular noteworthiness that the case above is a fairly old admissibility decision of the Commission and concerned a case where parents sought to challenge the *removal* of the right to physically chastise a child brought in by the state and, therefore, as the analysis below will demonstrate, was an entirely different structural argument. At present, the UK Government has made it clear that it does not intend to equalise the position of children and adults under the law of assault and, as a result, supports a limited right of parental chastisement. We must therefore consider an alternative use of Article 8, ie a

---

68 See, amongst others, *Johansen v Norway* [1997] 23 EHRR 33 at [52].
69 Above n 27, [173]–[175].
70 (1982) 29 DR 104 (E Comm).
71 *Ibid*, at [114].
72 See the Joint Committee on Human Rights, above n 27, at [174].

claim brought by a child that his or her right to private life is being breached by the existence of section 58.

Unlike Article 3, Article 8 is not an absolute Article and therefore allows for a balancing exercise for which in particular the second paragraph of Article 8 contains explicit criteria. Further, even in cases where Article 8 implies a positive obligation for the state, the second paragraph 'may be of certain relevance'[73] and offers the basis for testing the proportionality of legislation seeking to protect children against abuse. This means that, unlike in Article 3, an assessment of all the conflicting rights will occur within the context of paragraph 2. Specifically, in the case of a challenge to current UK law, the right of the parent wishing to preserve the right to administer corporal punishment as an aspect of family life will have to be balanced against the right of the child to not be subject to a breach of his or her right to privacy and personal integrity. Integral to the 'balancing exercise' will undoubtedly be the type and level of punishment that is being proposed, and if we consider that the combination of section 58 and the current charging standard may not be sufficient to breach Article 3, it is not immediately apparent that what amounts to the ability to administer 'common assault' upon a child by a parent will automatically be regarded as disproportionate. However, what of the much-quoted influence of the Convention on the Rights of the Child, and where exactly does its influence lie in the process?

The key area in which arguments based on the provisions of the UNCRC and other international instruments will operate is in relation to the margin of appreciation (or area of discretion at the national level): a certain level of discretion for the state is indispensable where the state's responsibility is an indirect one, as in the case between a conflict of rights between private individuals. The margin of appreciation is closely connected to the proportionality exercise and, further, it is apparent that where there is little or no consensus amongst contracting states on the rights in question and where the decision of the Court concerns the balancing of those rights against social interests, a wide margin of appreciation will be accorded to the state[74]—the so-called European consensus standard. Moreover, the extent of the positive obligations upon the state in relation to those rights will also be narrowed. The impact of the doctrine of the margin of appreciation is therefore of real significance in terms of assessing how the European Court of Human Rights is likely to interpret any claim, founded in Article 8, that section 58 may breach the right to personal integrity. In order to examine the effect of the doctrine in this particular context, we must look to its application in analogous circumstances.

As stated above, where little or no consensus exists among contracting states, a wide margin of appreciation will be accorded, and it may be thought that the opposite would therefore be true, ie that where such consensus exists, the margin

---

[73] See *Rees v UK*, judgment of 17 October 1986, at 15, at [37].
[74] See *Evans v UK* (2006) 43 EHRR 21 at [77]–[82] amongst others.

will be narrowed. However, as the transgender cases that have come before the European Court of Human Rights demonstrate, this is not always the case. At first sight it would appear that the issue of European consensus was integral to the decision as to whether there was a breach of Articles 8 and 12, both in those cases that found that no breach had occurred[75] and then in finding, finally, that a breach *had* occurred.[76] In the latter cases, it was the recognition of an international trend in favour of an increased social acceptance of transsexuals and of the legal recognition of the new sexual identity of post-operative transsexuals that seemingly persuaded the court. It may be thought, therefore, that the considerable evidence of a growing European and international consensus on the removal of the parental right to chastise would be decisive in narrowing the margin of appreciation accorded, particularly when we consider that more than one-third of European countries now afford children equal protection from assault.[77] However, as these cases will demonstrate, the margin of appreciation does not operate in a straightforward manner.

In *Sheffield and Horsham v UK*,[78] the Court disregarded clear evidence of a European consensus on the official treatment of transsexuals on the fairly tenuous ground that the evidence did not demonstrate a common European approach as to how to address the repercussions that the legal recognition of a change of sex may entail for other areas of law such as marriage, filiation, privacy or data protection. However, by the time that *Goodwin v UK*[79] and *I v UK*[80] were heard, no further statistical evidence of a European consensus could be provided by Liberty; rather, it was further evidence provided by Liberty[81] on a continuing *international* trend towards legal recognition of transsexuals that seemed to render previous concerns as to the wider repercussions of official recognition in the *European* signatory states suddenly irrelevant.

These cases demonstrate two points: first, that the use of the European consensus principle can be highly selective and illustrates the Court's willingness to *disregard* clear evidence of a consensus, if necessary, if the desired result is that of a wide margin of appreciation; and, secondly, that there might be the beginnings of the emergence of a new *international* consensus standard, more influential than a European consensus standard. These two points mean that the claim that section 58 breaches a child's Article 8 right to physical integrity is not

---

[75] In relation to birth and marriage—*Rees v UK* [1987] 9 EHRR 56. See also *Cossey v UK* (1990) 13 EHRR 622 at [38]–[40]; *Sheffield and Horsham v UK* (1998) 27 EHRR 163 at [57]–[61]; and *X, Y and Z v UK* (1997) 24 EHRR 143 at [44] and [52] (in relation to parental rights and transsexuality).

[76] *Goodwin and I v UK* (2002) 35 EHRR 18 at [84]–[86].

[77] Countries where children have equal protection are: Sweden (1979), Finland (1983), Norway (1987), Austria (1989), Cyprus (1994), Denmark (1997), Latvia (1998), Croatia (1999), Bulgaria (2000), Germany (2000), Iceland (2003), Hungary (2004), Romania (2004) and Ukraine (2004), and Italy and Portugal (2005).

[78] *Sheffield and Horsham v UK* (1998) 27 EHRR 163.

[79] *Goodwin v UK* (2002) 35 EHRR 18.

[80] *I v UK* (2002) 35 EHRR 18.

[81] *Ibid*, at [55]–[56].

in any way secure and is therefore highly dependent upon how the European Court of Human Rights wishes to proceed. If the court favoured the abolition of the defence of reasonable punishment, it could easily do so on the apparent existence of a European consensus on the issue, in addition to its apparent regard for the vulnerability of children. Equally, however, if the Court wished to allow the United Kingdom a wider margin of appreciation on the issue, the apparent European consensus on the issue could easily be circumvented, as demonstrated by the transsexual cases. The transsexual example in itself demonstrates how the Court has, in the past, shown a certain willingness to allow the United Kingdom to move towards the European consensus on an issue in its own time, it having taken some 15 years for the European Court of Human Rights to hold the United Kingdom in violation of transsexuals' rights under Articles 8 and 12.

CONCLUSION

This chapter has demonstrated that what was initially regarded as a parental right to chastise a child had, in reality, prior to international intervention, been subject to some form of reasonableness and proportionality even where this right was delegated to others. The effect of international law upon this right has been to turn the issue from a question of parental right to one of how this particular right can, if ever, be exercised responsibly. It is in relation to this question that advances under international law have had the most effect.

However, we have also seen that despite the fact that a number of international conventions and treaties have advocated the banning of the parental defence of reasonable punishment, one Convention in particular has had the most effect—the European Convention on Human Rights. First, by its 'vertical effect' on the state, which led to the removal of the right to delegate reasonable punishment to schools; and, secondly, by its 'horizontal effect', which led to the removal of the defence of reasonable punishment in all criminal charges excepting common assault. Finally, the jurisprudence of the European Court of Human Rights demonstrates that because of the operation of the margin of appreciation and the structure of certain Articles within the Convention, this now limited parental defence of reasonable punishment may not necessarily be incompatible with its provisions.

It seems, therefore, in the absence of a sudden decision of the European Court of Human Rights to the contrary, that those seeking an abolition of the defence of reasonable chastisement will have to wait for a change in government policy. What is particularly ironic, however, is that although the development of the law on this issue has included a great deal of debate as to whether a responsible parent can ever 'reasonably' administer physical punishment to his or her child it has been conducted without any reference to the apparent 'status' that was conferred upon certain parents by the concept of parental responsibility first introduced under the Children Act 1989. It is time that the two conceptions of responsibility were more closely aligned.

10

Parental Responsibility and Children's Health Care Treatment

LYNN HAGGER

INTRODUCTION

A S PROXY DECISION-makers for children, those with parental responsibility[1] have the capacity to consent to medical treatment on behalf of a child.[2] However, this simple statement raises a whole multitude of questions. Parental responsibility, as we know, encompasses both rights and duties, and parents enjoy discretion in this area of the law as well as others. How, then, is the responsible parent to exercise his or her rights and carry out the necessary duties? In addition, in individual cases there will always be the question of how far the child's views should be taken into account: the exercise of parental responsibility may be limited by the wishes of a mature adolescent, while even younger children may have distinct views that the responsible parent will take into account.

This chapter looks first at what a parent with parental responsibility is *required* to do in this context, and then at the more difficult question of what he or she is *allowed* to do. It then goes on to examine how the law has constructed the concept of the responsible parent, how much weight is given to a parent's own religious or cultural views, and how a responsible parent takes the child's views into account. It concludes with an examination of the case law on mature minors and the relationship between children's autonomy and parental responsibility.

WHAT DOES PARENTAL RESPONSIBILITY REQUIRE?

The law imposes obligations on those with parental responsibility in the context of medical care for their children. Not seeking appropriate medical treatment can

---

[1] Children Act 1989 s 3(1).
[2] See, eg *Re Z* [1997] Fam 1 at 26.

amount to a criminal offence or lead to care proceedings;[3] similarly, seeking *inappropriate* medical treatment may also be the basis for care proceedings.

However, once parents take the step of seeking medical treatment, they are neither required nor entitled to demand a particular form of treatment. As Lord Scarman noted in *Gillick v West Norfolk and Wisbech AHA*:

> parental rights must be exercised in accordance with the welfare principle and can be challenged, even overridden, if it is not.[4]

Of course, it is only if the matter is brought before the court that the parent's decision will be challenged as being contrary to a child's welfare. Where agreement cannot be reached between parents, carers and health professionals, it will be necessary to seek a court authorisation from the High Court under its inherent jurisdiction or for a specific issue order under section 8 of the Children Act 1989 to determine the appropriate way forward.[5] The Court will make its order based on what it determines is in the child's welfare. The courts have adopted a broad reading of best interests, which encompass medical, emotional and other welfare factors,[6] including the psychological and social benefits to the child.[7] The Court must have regard to the wishes and feelings of the child concerned as far as they can be ascertained according to their age and understanding.[8] Recently, the courts have been enthusiastic about adopting a balance-sheet approach whereby a list is drawn up of benefits and burdens of proposed courses of action and following the approach which has the greatest overall benefit.[9]

The parents' views will also be taken into account as part of the assessment of a child's welfare. What is expected of the responsible parent is considered further below, but we must first consider the types of medical treatment to which a parent with parental responsibility may consent.

WHAT DOES PARENTAL RESPONSIBILITY ALLOW?

Where more than one person has parental responsibility, the consent of one will usually suffice,[10] although there are some procedures that should not be carried out where parents disagree unless specific approval has been given by the Court.[11]

---

3   See, eg Children and Young Persons Act 1933 s 1(1) and (2).
4   [1986] AC 112 at 184.
5   Judicial sanction is a legal requirement where a child is a ward of court when important steps are being considered: see, eg *Re J* [1991] Fam 33.
6   *Re A (Male Sterilisation)* [2000] 1 FLR 549 at 555 (Butler-Sloss P).
7   *Re Y* [1997] 2 WLR 556 at 562.
8   Children Act 1989 s 1(3)(a).
9   See, eg *Wyatt and another v Portsmouth Hospital NHS Trust and another* [2005] EWCA Civ 1181.
10   Children Act 1989 s 2(7).
11   Sterilisation, male circumcision and immunisation would constitute such procedures: see, eg *Re C (a child) (immunisation: parental rights)* [2003] 2 FLR 1095 at [15]–[17].

Although the courts have said that parents should act in their child's best interests,[12] they have also stated that medical interventions may be permissible provided they are not *against* the child's best interests.[13] Changing the test from 'best interests' to 'not against best interests' could be criticised as a dilution of the welfare principle,[14] but it could render non-therapeutic interventions lawful, provided they do not cause significant harm.

Clearly, medically necessary therapeutic interventions are likely to be viewed as being in the child's best interests and this could include so-called 'cosmetic' procedures where these can be justified on the basis of emotional wellbeing. This could range from relatively simple 'ear-pinning' to the rather more significant limb-lengthening treatment for those suffering from restricted growth. Limb-lengthening may be viewed as necessary by parents who are only too aware of the adversity that may be faced by their child with a substantially diminished stature.[15]

A more difficult issue concerns ritual circumcision where there is no clinical need for the operation.[16] Male circumcision is, increasingly, a matter of debate.[17] The current British Medical Association (BMA) guidance[18] suggests that both parents should consent, that competent children should decide for themselves and that, even if incompetent, children's views should be considered. So-called 'female circumcision' is prohibited under the Female Genital Mutilation Act 2003, but male circumcision is generally available for religious purposes, as well as those situations where it is medically advisable. Despite some evidence that it does provide protective effects from certain diseases,[19] a number of surgeons nevertheless consider it to be unnecessary, if not positively harmful. Given the level of concern that the procedure is irreversible, medically unnecessary and performed on a child who cannot consent, it seems unlikely that the matter is settled. Is this religious concession to minority groups coherent when other procedures are forbidden, despite being regarded as acceptable in some cultures?

While so-called 'female circumcision' is abhorrent to most and is not physically equivalent to the male procedure, the degree of physical intrusion is only a

---

[12] *Gillick v West Norfolk and Wisbech AHA* [1986] AC 112 at 127.

[13] *S v S* [1972] AC 24, where it was considered that to allow paternity testing against the mother's wishes would not be against the child's interests and was justifiable in the general public interest.

[14] M Fox and J McHale, 'In Whose Best Interests?' (1997) 60 *MLR* 700–9.

[15] Cf TW Shakespeare, *Disability Rights and Wrongs* (London, Routledge, 2006) for an exposition of the need for society to accommodate the disabled rather than the latter feeling the need to conform to societal norms.

[16] See JM Hutson, 'Circumcision: A Surgeon's Perspective' (2003) 30 *Journal of Medical Ethics* 238, who discusses the possible protective effects of circumcision and its alternatives.

[17] See also Taylor, this volume.

[18] BMA, *The Law and Ethics of Male Circumcision: Guidance for Doctors* (2006).

[19] See, eg DT Minniberg, 'Circumcision' and AKM Rickwood, 'British Attitudes to Circumcision' in B O'Donnell and SA Koff (eds), *Paediatric Urology* (Oxford, Butterworth-Heineman, 1997); and personal communication from Mr J Roberts, paediatric surgeon at Sheffield Children's NHS Foundation Trust. See also D Baker, 'The unkindest cut of all?' *The Times* (24 March 2008), for a discussion about the advantages and disadvantages of the procedure.

question of degree. There are of course differences. As traditionally carried out, female genital mutilation is a more painful procedure than male circumcision (even if carried out under anaesthetic), carries higher risks of complications and reduces sexual pleasure.[20] Further, while the majority of women who have undergone female genital mutilation as minors may wish they had not had it when they grow up and feel strongly about this, only a minority of circumcised males seem to regret having had the procedure, if the media coverage of these topics is any indication.[21] Despite these differences, further cogent ethical arguments are required to justify male circumcision on children.[22] There seems to be a legal anomaly in that the court will allow parents to arrange a procedure as harmful as circumcision and yet prohibit such procedures as tattooing for those under the age of 18, even with parental consent. The courts may be reluctant to pursue this line of thought given the cultural significance of male circumcision under Jewish and Muslim traditions. Further, there are practical considerations. Even surgeons who are uncomfortable with carrying out an intervention that is not clinically indicated will carry out circumcision because they fear the effects of parents taking their male children to unskilled practitioners, with the attendant dangers of significant harm and even death.[23] Nevertheless, judicial attitudes may change if cases arise in the United Kingdom similar to those in the United States where adult males have sought restorative surgery and/or instigated legal actions for battery.[24]

There are other medical procedures that can only be performed lawfully if there has been judicial approval, even where all of those with parental responsibility are in agreement. These include medical treatment or surgery performed on a child primarily for the benefit of another person. *Re Y*[25] concerned an incapacitated adult, but the application of the best-interest principle involves the same considerations whatever the individual's age. Here, the court was willing to authorise a bone marrow donation from the incapax to her sister even though this was not in her *medical* best interests, on the basis that the procedure was in her *social* best interests. If the donation did not take place, the sister was likely to die and the distress of their mother could mean that she would be unable to maintain contact with her other daughter. Connell J cautioned that the case was not to be viewed as a precedent,[26] but similar reasoning could be used in other

[20]   <http://www.who.int/reproductive-health/fgm/index.html>.
[21]   See, eg <http://news.bbc.co.uk/1/hi/health/medical_notes/241221.stm>.
[22]   M Fox and M Thomson, 'Short Changed? The Law and Ethics of Male Circumcision' (2005) 13 *International Journal of Children's Rights* 161, 170.
[23]   Personal communication from J Roberts, above n 19; see also 'Hunt for Nigerian "medic" over circumcision death' *The Sunday Times* (24 August 2003).
[24]   See PW Edge, 'Male circumcision after the Human Rights Act 1998' (2000) 5 *Journal of Civil Liberties* 320 for a useful discussion about male circumcision from a legal and ethical perspective; and G Hinchley and K Patrick, 'Is infant male circumcision an abuse of the rights of the child?' (2007) 335 *BMJ* 1180.
[25]   *Re Y* [1997] Fam 110 at 117.
[26]   *Ibid*, at 116.

cases.[27] While social and other interests may be as important as medical best interests in the impact on emotional wellbeing, it is suggested that only where the indirect benefit to the child from a third party's gain is very clear that the emotional benefit should be seen as justifying the medical procedure on the child. Where non-regenerative human material is concerned, the courts are likely to be more circumspect about any such authorisation.[28]

WHAT DOES THE RESPONSIBLE PARENT DO?

Parents will usually support treatment to keep the child alive on the basis of medical opinion and will generally act in accordance with the best scientific information in the interests of their child's health. An example of this would be participation in immunisation programmes. However, religious and/or cultural views about specific interventions can cause parents to opt out of accepted medical practice. In some cases, this can even threaten the child's life. Parents may disagree with doctors' views of what is in the child's best interests and either demand treatment against the prevailing clinical opinion or, less commonly, refuse to consent to treatment. Such tensions are particularly vivid where life-sustaining treatment is concerned. If such disagreement cannot be resolved locally, a court will be asked to determine the appropriate way forward.[29] How do the courts approach these highly emotive cases, and what does this tell us about what is expected of the responsible parent?

Traditionally, the courts have taken parental views of a child's quality of life into account when determining best interests, but have not allowed these to be the sole determinants of such issues. The case of *Re T (Wardship: Medical Treatment)*[30] has been seen as an aberrant decision[31] or, conversely, as more progressive than most:[32] aberrant if viewed as a reversion to the idea of parents' natural rights; progressive because it took into account the important aspect of the caring relationship. Here, in view of the mother's perception that a liver

[27] D Feenan, 'A good harvest? *Re Y (Mental Incapacity)*: bone marrow transplants' [1997] 9 *CFLQ* 305.

[28] See, eg Art 20 of the influential European Convention on Human Rights and Biomedicine, which prohibits the donation of non-regenerative organs and tissue from an incapacitated person, and Lord Donaldson's ambiguous remarks about organ donation from mature minors in *Re W* [1993] Fam 64 at 78–9 and 83–4, with a recommendation to seek authorisation from the court.

[29] Authorisation will be sought from the High Court under its inherent jurisdiction or for a specific issue order under s 8 of the Children Act 1989, remembering that doctors will not be compelled to act against their clinical judgment: *Re C (a minor) (medical treatment)* [1998] 1 FLR 384.

[30] [1997] 1 WLR 242.

[31] A Bainham, 'Do Babies Have Rights?' (1997) 56 *CLJ* 48; and S Michalowski, 'Is it in the Best Interests of a Child to have a Life-saving Transplantation?: *Re T (Wardship: Medical Treatment)*' [1997] 9 *CFLQ* 179.

[32] J Bridgeman, *Parental Responsibility, Young Children and Healthcare Law* (Cambridge, Cambridge University Press, 2007) 137–42.

transplant was not in the child's best interests, contrary to those of the health team involved, the Court decided not to overrule her wishes. This was understandable given the level of post-operative care that would be required of her:[33] the sacrifices required would have been very significant because the parents lived abroad.[34] If she was less than fully supportive, such care would, undoubtedly, have been compromised. In addition, the mother's view was within the band of reasonable decisions a sensible person could take, that is, she was making an informed, educated decision, rather than a 'merely' religious one.[35] Further, the child had already undergone an unsuccessful operation that had caused pain and distress.

Nevertheless, some commentators have regarded this decision as a regressive step because, inter alia, the interests of the child and the mother were not fully articulated.[36] Great care needs to be taken when considering parents' views.[37] There may be occasions when parents do not have a child's interests truly at heart and it cannot be assumed that the interests of parents and children are exactly aligned.[38] However, this mother was not seen as anything less than a loving parent.[39] The recognition of the caring relationships is to be welcomed, although there is a need to be clear about how they should be valued and acknowledged.[40] Nor should it be forgotten that there is the option of finding a foster carer/adoptive carer if the parent no longer wishes to carry out the parental role.[41]

By contrast, in some cases parents of extremely ill children have insisted on inappropriate (so-called 'futile') medical treatment for children. No doubt, in such cases it is extremely difficult for parents to relinquish the child to its fate. There will always be a need to have sensitive discussions with families. Decisions subsequent to *Re T*[42] have adopted an approach that focuses on the child's best interests, rather than appearing to conflate these with those of the parents. The traditional approach adopted a presumption in favour of prolonging life while weighing up the pain and suffering involved in further treatment against the quality of life that would result from it.[43] Treatment would only be withheld or withdrawn if, from the child's perspective, the child's life would be intolerable.[44]

---

[33]   Above n 30, at 251.

[34]   *Ibid*, at 252.

[35]   *Ibid*, at 250.

[36]   See the discussion in Bainham and Michalowski, above n 31.

[37]   Bainham, above n 31.

[38]   Michalowski, above n 31.

[39]   Above n 30, at 246.

[40]   Fox and McHale, above n 14.

[41]   Bainham, above n 31. This has become necessary in the *Wyatt* case—*Portsmouth NHS Trust v Wyatt and Wyatt, Southampton NHS Trust Intervening* [2004] EWHC 2247 and *Wyatt and another v Portsmouth Hospital NHS Trust and another* [2005] EWCA Civ 1181—discussed below at nn 45 and 46: see SK Templeton, 'Carers sought for baby Charlotte as parents part' *The Times* (15 October 2006).

[42]   *Re T (Wardship: Medical Treatment)* [1997] 1 WLR 242.

[43]   *Re J (Wardship: Medical Treatment)* [1991] 2 WLR 140, drawing on *Re B (a Minor) (Wardship: Medical Treatment)* [1981] 1 WLR 1421.

[44]   *Ibid*, at 147–9 (Taylor LJ).

More recently, the 'intolerability' point was addressed in the *Wyatt* case, where Hedley J was explicit that this was not an additional test to best interests, but part of the process for determining what these might be,[45] with the test sometimes providing a 'valuable guide in the search for best interests in this type of case'.[46]

In *R v Portsmouth Hospitals NHS Trust, ex p Glass*,[47] Lord Woolf MR[48] established important principles of law in such cases, requiring the courts to take into account 'the natural concerns and the responsibilities' of parents.[49] However, the parents' views will be overruled where they are seen to be in conflict with the best interests of the child. In this case, the mother disagreed with the view of the medical team that David, her severely disabled 12-year-old son with a limited life span, should be given no more than palliative care. Following a respiratory tract infection, the doctors prescribed diamorphine to make him comfortable, but this had the effect of further depressing lung function. To make matters worse, they placed a 'Do Not Attempt Resuscitation' order on his medical notes without discussing this with his mother. The family forcibly intervened to resuscitate the child and took him home where he was successfully treated by the family doctor. At this point the trust wrote to the family stating that they could no longer offer life-prolonging treatment to David and that future care should be offered at a nearby hospital.

As her relationship with the team had deteriorated to such an extent, Mrs Glass sought a declaration from the court as to the intervention her son could expect on further admittance to the hospital. The Court of Appeal declined to give such an anticipatory authorisation because it would unduly restrict the doctors involved. The ideal is for doctors and parents to agree in a climate of consultation and full information, but where this is no longer possible the court should only be called upon to adjudicate on actual facts as they occur at the time. At that point, the court would determine the child's best interests.

The *Glass* case was then brought before the European Court of Human Rights,[50] which held that the administration of diamorphine against the mother's wishes had breached the right to respect for private and family life under Article 8 of the European Convention of Human Rights (ECHR) in relation to the child's right to physical integrity.[51] They were particularly critical of the trust's failure to seek an earlier authorisation from the High Court or otherwise defuse the situation.[52] In many ways this case has proved to be a salutary lesson for health

---

[45] *Portsmouth NHS Trust v Wyatt and Wyatt, Southampton NHS Trust Intervening* [2004] EWHC 2247 at [24].
[46] *Wyatt and another v Portsmouth Hospital NHS Trust and another* [2005] EWCA Civ 1181 at [75]–[76], [87] and [91] (Wall LJ).
[47] [1999] 2 FLR 905.
[48] As he then was.
[49] Above n 47, at 911.
[50] *Glass v UK* [2004] 1 FLR 1019.
[51] *Ibid*, at [70].
[52] *Ibid*, at [79].

and legal professions alike, not least because, as one of the judges noted in the European Court, 'maternal instinct has had more weight than medical opinion'.[53] Despite the prognosis, David had survived for more than six years following these events.

Notwithstanding the important recognition of David's individual rights in *Glass v UK*, and also of the requirement that his parents' consent be sought, the decision does little to improve overall decision-making in these cases of very dependent children. The obligation of doctors to consult with David's family was made clear, but the concern remains that if the parents do not agree with the doctors and a court order is sought, undue judicial deference to medical opinion means that the doctors' views will carry much greater weight in the court room. In particular, there is a concern that the medical perception of quality of life will rule the day. The suspicion is that quality of life is seen very much from the able-bodied perspective. In fact, the views of the disabled person themselves should be a major determining factor.[54] Where this is not possible, those caring for them on a day-to-day basis, whether they are relatives, carers or health professionals, should have a central say in determining these matters.[55] Of course doctors understand better than most the most suitable clinical approach to the prevention, cure or relief of disorders. However, it is the patient and/or their carers who understand their temperament, experience of other medical interventions and other important factors.

More recently, *An NHS Trust v MB*[56] provided an unusual example of a case in which the courts have recognised the parents' views as to the quality of their child's life, notwithstanding the profound disability of spinal muscular atrophy. At the time of referral to the court, MB was artificially ventilated and had very limited movement, but was said to be cognitively aware. The mother's view that it was not in the child's interests to have ventilation removed was supported by the court, despite the opposing opinions of no fewer than 14 consultants.

Apart from the decisions in *Re T*[57] (which, arguably, turned on its own particular facts and was subject to widespread criticism) and in *An NHS Trust v MB*,[58] the courts generally support medical opinion[59] and in the eyes of the law the responsible parent is one who accedes to medical opinion. The nature of

---

[53]   (2004) 39 EHRR 15 at 364 (separate Opinion of Judge Casadevall).
[54]   This was the concern of the Disability Rights Commission expressed in *R (on the application of Burke) v GMC* [2005] QB 424.
[55]   A Asch, 'Distracted by Disability' (1998) 7 *Cambridge Quarterly of Healthcare Ethics* 77.
[56]   *An NHS Trust v MB* [2006] 2 FCR 319.
[57]   [1997] 1 WLR 242.
[58]   [2006] 2 FCR 319.
[59]   See *NHS Trust v (1) A (A Child) (Represented by an Officer of CAFCASS as Child's Guardian) (2) Mrs A (3) Mr A* [2007] EWHC 1696 (Fam) for a recent example where the court agreed with the medical team that the 50% prospect of a full, normal life with painful treatment for a seven-month-old child against certain death before 18 months without treatment outweighed all other considerations notwithstanding the parents' faith that God would cure the child and their concern about further suffering.

judicial reasoning often means that, rather than seeing parents as having a fundamental interest in their children's welfare, their interests are seen as in conflict with those of their child. However, not only do parents possess unique, detailed knowledge of their child, they also have high levels of empathy and a stake in the child's wellbeing. More account should be taken of the parental perspective both in practice and in judicial decision-making. Article 8(1) of the ECHR does provide a much stronger means whereby families may challenge any perceived lack of involvement in the health care decision-making process,[60] although to date its impact has been limited.[61]

The Religious and/or Cultural Dimension

Where parental opinions include adherence to religious and/or sub-cultural views, it may be easier to be dismissive of these as being less than rational in the light of clinical judgment. The courts have generally demonstrated an unwillingness to order doctors to carry out medical intervention which parents seek, but which the doctors believe to be medically inappropriate. For example, in *Re C (a minor) (medical treatment)*,[62] Orthodox Jewish parents argued that their 16-month-old daughter, who suffered from muscular atrophy, should continue to be ventilated. This was contrary to medical opinion, which considered such intervention to be futile because ventilation would only prolong the child's life by a few days. The parents' faith dictated that all efforts should be made to preserve life, but the court preferred the doctors' views.

A dramatic example of medical testing against the parents' wishes may be seen in *Re C (HIV Test)*.[63] A local authority applied for a specific issue order[64] permitting a HIV test to be carried out on two children, to ensure the children received the optimal medical care. The parents opposed the application. The local authority relied on medical opinion, which estimated that the children were at a 25 per cent risk of having HIV. The mother, who was HIV positive, breast-fed the baby in question against medical advice and was generally sceptical about the testing for, and treatment of, HIV. She preferred to rely on complementary medicine. She and the father argued that should a test prove positive, subsequent treatment would be more toxic than beneficial and that such sero-positive status would stigmatise the child. The parents challenged the application as an affront to their parental autonomy. Medical opinion considered the children to be at risk without the test because if they developed an illness a doctor treating them would have to cater for the possibility that they did have the virus and overly aggressive

---

[60] *Glass v UK* [2004] 1 FLR 1019.
[61] See, eg *Re L* [2004] EWHC 2713; and *Wyatt v Portsmouth NHS Trust* [2005] EWCA Civ 1181. Cf *An NHS Trust v MB* [2006] 2 FCR 319.
[62] [1998] 1 FLR 384.
[63] [1999] 2 FLR 1004.
[64] Children Act 1989 s 8.

treatment might be adopted if they were, in fact, uninfected. Alternatively, should they be affected by the virus, and were treated in the future by a doctor unaware of this, under-treatment might be advocated in ignorance. The level of intrusion involved in the tests was minimal and the Court was not persuaded by the views of the parents, preferring to concentrate on the welfare and rights of the child.

Further examples have arisen in relation to Jehovah's Witness families. There have been quite a number of cases where doctors have been authorised to give children a blood transfusion, despite the religious objections of their parents and, sometimes, the children themselves.[65] Any challenge under Articles 8(1) and 9(1) of the ECHR—the right to respect for private and family life and to manifest religion respectively—would seem doomed to failure given that neither are absolute rights: Articles 8(2) and 9(2) which, inter alia, provide for the protection of the rights and freedoms of others, could be relied upon to protect the child. Given the courts' commitment to the sanctity of life and best-interest considerations with respect to children, they will not allow parents to make martyrs of their children in the name of religion,[66] and they have had little appetite to permit mature minors to refuse life-saving treatment.[67]

Yet in such cases the parents' genuinely held beliefs that they are acting in the child's best interests are acknowledged.[68] There are also examples of good practice where NHS Trusts engage in constructive dialogue with the Jehovah's Witness community through their hospital liaison committees, which have resulted in useful guidance for health professionals dealing with children from such families.[69] This guidance contains consent forms for parents to sign whereby parents are relieved of their agonising decision-making by an acknowledgement that they would never agree to the use of certain blood products, but equally recognise that the medical team may decide that it is in the child's best interests to do so. This proves acceptable to the Jehovah's Witness community, who then do not ostracise a family whose child has received blood products. The reaction of the religious community has been a key influence on parents in this situation.

Taking Account of the Child's Views

An important aspect of parents' responsibilities is to ensure that their children achieve competent adulthood. Children need to gain experience of decision-making to practice their skills on the road to reaching 'a capacity where they are able to take full responsibility as free, rational agents for their own system of

---

[65] See, eg *Re R (A Minor) (Blood Transfusion)* [1993] 2 FLR 757; *Re S (a minor) (medical treatment)* [1993] 1 FLR 376; and *Re O (a minor) (medical treatment)* [1993] 2 FLR 149.

[66] *Re E* [1993] 1 FLR 386.

[67] *Ibid.*

[68] See the discussion in Bridgeman, above n 32, 143–9.

[69] Personal communication from J Reid, Director of Clinical Operations, Sheffield Children's NHS Foundation Trust.

ends'.[70] All children, whatever their age and circumstance, can provide valuable perceptions that can improve their clinical care.[71] International legal instruments suggest that even very young children should be involved in the decision-making process to an optimal extent.[72] Young children are more competent than is traditionally perceived,[73] particularly where they have experience of a long-term illness.[74] With appropriate techniques, children as young as four can make helpful comments about their experiences of health services[75] and like to be involved in this way.[76] In the light of the empirical evidence, responsible parents should, therefore, give weight to their child's views. The General Medical Council (GMC) has stated that children should be able to influence what happens to them as much as possible,[77] even though the ultimate decision about medical treatment may be taken by those with parental responsibility, or, in the event of a conflict, by the court.[78] However, this only represents good practice and the law does not *require* parents to involve their children in making decisions.

The proposal here is that a rights-based approach where the focus is on the individual child, at least initially, can help to challenge the lack of attention paid to children generally[79] and emphasise their need to be involved in decision-making. The plea for specific legislation, with a code of practice, dealing with all aspects of children's health-care decision-making should be supported, and any departure from such a code of practice should require justification through formal procedures.[80]

---

[70] See M Freeman, *The Rights and Wrongs of Children* (London, Pinter, 1983) 57.

[71] See, eg M Chesney, L Lindeke, L Johnson, A Jukkala and S Lynch, 'Comparison of child and parent satisfaction ratings of ambulatory pediatric subspeciality care' (2005) 19 *Journal of Pediatric Health Care* 221; K Curtis, K Liabo, H Roberts and M Barker, 'Consulted but not heard: a qualitative study of young people's views of their local health service' (2004) 7 *Health Expectations* 149; and R Sinclair, 'Participation in Practice: Making It Meaningful, Effective and Sustainable' (2004) 19 *Children and Society* 106.

[72] See, eg Arts 12 and 13 of the United Nations Convention on the Rights of the Child 1989.

[73] See, eg AL Woodward, JA Sommerville and JJ Guajardo, 'How infants make sense of intentional action' in B Malle, L Moses and D Baldwin (eds), *Intentions and Intentionality: Foundations of Social Cognition* (Cambridge MA, MIT Press, 2001); AN Meltzoff, 'Origins of mind, cognition and communication' (1999) 32 *Journal of Communication Disorders* 251–69; and S Pinker, *The Blank Slate: The Modern Denial of Human Nature* (London, Penguin Books, 2002).

[74] C Eiser, 'Changes in understanding of illness as the child grows' (1985) 60 *Archives of Disease in Childhood* 489; D Fielding and A Duff, 'Compliance with treatment protocol: interventions for children with chronic illness' (1999) 80 *Archives of Disease in Childhood* 196; P Alderson and J Montgomery, 'What about me?' (1996) *Health Service Journal* April 22; and M Bluebond-Langner, *The Private Worlds of Dying Children* (Princeton, Princeton University Press, 1978) passim.

[75] Curtis *et al*, above n 71.

[76] E Elliott and A Watson, 'But the doctors aren't your mum' (1997) 30 *Health Matters* 8.

[77] General Medical Council, *0–18 years: Guidance for Doctors* (2007).

[78] See, eg *R v Portsmouth NHS Trust, ex p Glass* [1999] 2 FLR 905.

[79] A James and AL James, *Constructing Childhood: Theory, Policy and Social Practice* (Basingstoke, Palgrave Macmillan, 2004) passim.

[80] P Alderson and J Montgomery, *Health Care Choices: Making Decisions with Children* (London, IPPR, 1996).

The Mental Capacity Act 2005 provides a possible model. Broadly, section 1(2) of the Act provides that there is a presumption of capacity, while section 4(1) states that assumptions should not be made on the basis of, for example, age or appearance. Section 1(2) requires all practicable steps to be taken to help people make a decision, a non-exhaustive list of which are contained in the Code of Practice,[81] while section 4(4) requires decision-makers to permit and encourage participation in decision-making.

In the absence of these empowering measures, it is even more important that the courts adopt a robust approach to the need to hear young children's views. The use of rights language is having a positive influence on the way in which public bodies deal with more vulnerable members of society,[82] and judicial pronouncements that acknowledge younger children's rights to be heard would help to further foster a culture in which this becomes commonplace.

MATURE MINORS AND PARENTAL RESPONSIBILITY

Yet the natural tendency of parents is to try to maintain a strong influence on the behaviour of their children, not least to protect them from harm. The desire to safeguard children does not diminish as they approach adulthood. This is particularly evident where there is a possibility that the older child may not wish to proceed with life-saving treatment. However, parents do not fulfil their duties if they do not gradually relinquish their proxy decision-making role so that their maturing offspring are given opportunities to make their own decisions, thus developing their skills to become competent adults. As Lord Donaldson stated in *Re W*:[83]

> Adolescence is a period of progressive transition from childhood to adulthood and as experience of life is required and intelligence and understanding grow, so will the scope of the decision-making which should be left to the minor, for it is only by making decisions and experiencing the consequences that decision-making skills will be acquired … [G]ood parenting involves giving minors as much rope as they can handle without an unacceptable risk that they will hang themselves.[84]

In *R (Axon) v Secretary of State for Health (Family Planning Association intervening)*,[85] Silber J emphasised Lord Donaldson's comments in *Re W* when he noted that:

---

81   Ch 3.
82   British Institute for Human Rights, *The Human Rights Act: Changing Lives* (2007).
83   *Re W (A minor) (Medical treatment)* [1993] Fam 64.
84   *Ibid*, at 81 (Lord Donaldson).
85   [2006] EWHC 37.

any right to family life on the part of a parent dwindles as their child gets older and is able to understand the consequence of different choices and then to make decisions relating to them.[86]

Giving them 'as much rope as they can handle' should involve taking 'all practicable steps'[87] to facilitate autonomous decision-making where this is a possibility. With respect to non-life-saving treatment, allowing competent minors to make an independent decision to choose whether to 'consent to treatment, to refuse it or to choose one rather than another of the treatments being offered'[88] would go much further in helping them to develop decision-making skills. Engaging children in all types of decision-making to the extent of their capacity recognises their autonomous interests and the process itself enhances their competence to participate. Meaningful involvement increases 'confidence, self-belief, knowledge, understanding and changed attitudes, skills and education attainment'.[89]

Given the focus of this book, this is not the place to analyse the defects in the *Gillick* test for competence. However, I would argue that if particular minors are assessed to be competent, their autonomous interests should have the potential to restrict the scope of parental responsibility. The extent of this will depend upon the view of children's competence in relation to making decisions about medical treatment. At present, while competent children can consent to treatment without the need for their parents to be informed of the decision,[90] any refusal to accept treatment can be overruled by an order of the court or the consent of a person with parental responsibility.[91] There are arguments that this could be challenged under the Human Rights Act 1998 in the interests of young people's autonomous interests.[92] This has particular force in the case of the experienced child patient who is suffering from a chronic condition where the treatment may offer a limited prospect of success and/or the treatment itself is very distressing.[93]

---

[86]   *Ibid*, at [129].

[87]   As is required by Mental Capacity Act s 1(3).

[88]   The 'absolute right' afforded to competent adults: see *Re T (Adult: refusal of medical treatment)* (1993) Fam 95 at 102 (Lord Donaldson).

[89]   Carnegie United Kingdom Trust, *Measuring the Magic? Evaluating and Researching Young People's Participation in Public Decision-making* (2002) 2; and emphasised by D Koller, '"Making a Difference": Youth Participation in Education and Health Care', presentation at the University of Sheffield (Centre for the Study of Childhood and Youth: Childhood and Youth: Choice and Participation International Conference, 2006).

[90]   See, eg *Gillick v West Norfolk and Wisbech AHA* [1986] AC 112; and *R (Axon) v Secretary of State for Health (Family Planning Association intervening)* [2006] EWHC 37 (Admin).

[91]   *Re R (A Minor) (Wardship: Consent to Medical Treatment)* [1991] 4 All ER 177; and *Re W (A Minor) (Wardship: Consent to Medical Treatment)* [1992] 4 All ER 627.

[92]   Discussed in L Hagger, 'Foundation Trusts and Children's Participation: Some New Opportunities?' (2007) 8 *Medical Law International* 325.

[93]   Interestingly, the US state of Virginia has now passed a law (VA Code No 63.2–100 (2007)) allowing parents of a child aged 14 or over with a life-threatening condition to refuse medically recommended treatment where the parents and child made the decision jointly, the child is sufficiently mature to have an informed opinion on the treatment, other treatments have been considered and they believe in good faith that their choice is in the child's best interests: MR

Certainly, forcible treatment which may involve restraint or even detainment needs strong justification. The reality for practitioners is that without the cooperation of the mature minor, many procedures will be impossible to administer.

A conflicting view is that the current position of concurrent consents[94] is justified because, even if the child can consent, his or her abilities are not such as to extinguish totally the parent's or the courts' role of protection where a child refuses treatment.[95] This position accords with Feinberg's[96] qualms about extending full rights of self-determination to children. His argument is a justification of the right to intervene in the lives of children for the sake of the child's future autonomy, their 'right to an open future'.[97] Where a child's decision or behaviour is such that it threatens his or her own future autonomy, it represents sufficient grounds for intervention. Feinberg emphasises that such measures can be regarded as a means to hold the child's right in trust until such a time as the child reaches maturity and has the competence to exercise such a right. His concerns are with decisions that threaten the child's future autonomy in substantive ways, for example, by threatening future health or mental ability, or affecting reproductive choice and so on. In the light of these concerns, allowing children to refuse life-saving treatment seems proportionate. However, this protective argument is, in principle, problematic for liberals. It inevitably relies upon stipulating an arbitrary demarcation between adult and child, since there is no fixed correlation between age and capacity for autonomy, but rather a loose, contingent relationship, particularly where a child is an experienced patient. There is, therefore, an inevitable Sorites[98] problem that must be addressed. This is not merely a philosophical puzzle, but an issue that strikes at the heart of the consent and children debate.

At the very least, parents, health professionals and the law should ensure that an appropriate decision-making process is in place that best protects children's dignity and autonomy so that decisions are made on the basis of fully informed consent within a human-rights framework that takes a more robust approach to children's interests.[99]

Mercurio, 'An Adolescent's Refusal of Treatment: Implications of the Abraham Cheerix Case' (2007) 120 *Pediatrics* 1357.

[94]   See *Re R* and *Re W*, above n 91.

[95]   See further Gilmore, this volume.

[96]   J Feinberg, *Rights, Justice and the Bounds of Liberty* (Princeton, Princeton University Press, 1980).

[97]   *Ibid*, passim.

[98]   Sorites or the 'heap' problem: the classical philosophical problem of judging when one thing has achieved the transition into another when the transition involves small incremental changes. At what point does the developing child reach the point at which they deserve the respect due to the adult with full capacity?

[99]   Perhaps using the decision-making framework suggested by Alderson and Montgomery, above n 80.

CONCLUSION

While the fact is well established that those with parental responsibility must act in a child's best interests[100] in relation to medical treatment, the parameters of this may yet need extension. We know that 'cosmetic' procedures and even non-therapeutic interventions may be legitimate in certain circumstances. It is also clear that parents are required to support medically necessary treatment where that is underpinned by clinical evidence regardless of their own values. Whether this should be the case is open to question: parents have a unique perspective on the best interests of their children, and the views of children themselves should also be given greater predominance than has hitherto been the case. The law has a crucial role to progress this agenda.

---

[100]   Or at least not against their interests: above nn 13–28.

11

'Don't Spend It All at Once!' Parental Responsibility and Parents' Responsibilities in Respect of Children's Contracts and Property

ELIZABETH COOKE*

INTRODUCTION

O
UR TASK IS to study parental responsibility. Those words live a double life. On the one hand, 'parental responsibility' is a statutory concept, populated with common law content, meted out by the law as something like a status to some but not all parents.[1] On the other, responsible parents and carers, whatever their legal status, take care in countless ways and without reference to legal authority and obligation. They do so in proportion to their abilities and opportunities, over the many complications of their children's lives. One of the more obvious conclusions to draw from this volume is that the two ideas—the statutory concept and the human duty—are different. A study of the extent of parental responsibility for a child's contracts and property is hardly at the cutting edge of child law; but it illustrates that difference very clearly.

The humdrum little details of an everyday shopping trip set the scene. It begins with a visit to the bank:

> Griphook unlocked the door. A lot of green smoke came billowing out, and as it cleared, Harry gasped. Inside were mounds of gold coins. Columns of silver. Heaps of little bronze Knuts.
>
> 'All yours', smiled Hagrid.
>
> All Harry's—it was incredible . . .
>
> Hagrid helped Harry pile some of it into a bag.

---

* I am most grateful to Laura Graham for research assistance.
[1] Children Act 1989 s 3(1), (2) and (3).

'The gold ones are Galleons,' he explained. 'Seventeen silver Sickles to a Galleon and twenty-nine Knuts to a Sickle, it's easy enough. Right, that should be enough fer a couple of terms, we'll keep the rest safe for yeh.'[2]

The money in the bank belongs to Harry. Hagrid does what a good parent would do;[3] he accompanies Harry, provides moral support (a bank, with or without goblins, may be alarming and unfamiliar to an 11-year-old) and helps with the maths. He encourages Harry not to withdraw more cash than he needs. He is not a trustee, but he accepts responsibility for keeping the fortune safe. He keeps track of the shopping list and makes sure that Harry buys the kit he requires for the new term at school.

Hagrid wouldn't let Harry buy a solid gold cauldron, either ('It says pewter on yer list'), but they got a nice set of scales for weighing potion ingredients and a collapsible brass telescope.[4]

There is no difficulty, of course, about Harry's contractual capacity, since the cauldron, etc, textbooks, robes, wand and broomstick are undoubtedly 'necessaries'.[5] So would be Harry's owl,[6] but Hagrid buys Hedwig the owl for him as a birthday present.

There is nothing here that anyone with parental responsibility *has* to do; arguably it all falls within what a responsible parent *would* do. In what follows I explore that contrast, and the purpose of that contrast, in the separate contexts of contract and property.

CONTRACT

The principles behind the rules about a minor's contractual capacity are simple:

The social policy behind special rules for minors and their contracts is to protect the minor against his or her own immaturity and inexperience. It seeks to achieve this purpose, generally, by allowing minors to go back on contracts, or at least enabling them to do so when adults put pressure on them to do so. Minority is viewed as a personal privilege from which none can take advantage but the minor. A second and

---

[2]   JK Rowling, *Harry Potter and the Philosopher's Stone* (London, Bloomsbury, 1997) 58. The Harry Potter books abound in legal puzzles. Might an under-age wizard be regarded as *Gillick*-competent to perform magic outside school? Are the Malfoys vicariously liable for Dobby's misguided attempts to 'protect' Harry? In the final volume it is of course Hermione who proves to be an expert in wizarding succession law. More relevant to our purposes is the fact that one of the themes of the Harry Potter series is: what is a good parent?

[3]   In the unavoidable absence of Harry's parents and guardian. For the present purposes nothing turns on the fact that Hagrid is *not* Harry's parent.

[4]   Rowling, above n 2, 62.

[5]   See below, n 6.

[6]   'Necessaries' extends beyond what is essential for survival to 'goods suitable to the condition in life of the minor' (Sale of Goods Act 1979 s 54), and an animal seems to be a normal expectation of a Hogwarts student; even Ron has a rat.

subsidiary purpose is in conflict with the first. It is to protect honest adults from unscrupulous minors who do not simply take advantage of the privilege, but abuse it.[7]

These conflicting purposes have generated a rather complex set of rules. To summarise: some minors' contracts are valid; some are voidable; the rest are unenforceable against the minor.

In a little more detail:[8] as is well known, a minor's contracts for necessaries, whether goods or services, are valid. 'Necessaries' is a term of art, not limited to subsistence needs;[9] and was stretched as far as the nineteenth-century juries could manage in order to protect their fellow tradesmen.[10] What is the present-day equivalent of the fancy waistcoats,[11] champagne and wild ducks[12] of the frock-coated boyos in the old cases? Is a mobile phone a necessary?[13] Apparently not, or at least the phone companies will not take the risk; a minor is not allowed to enter a phone contract and has to pay-as-you-go.[14] A student loan may well be.[15] The Sale of Goods Act 1979 provides in section 3(1) that '[w]here necessaries are sold and delivered to a minor ... he must pay a reasonable price for them'; so even where the contract is valid, the law adds a further layer of protection.

Moreover, a minor is bound by a contract for services if it is for his or her benefit, and therefore contracts of employment are valid—including apprenticeships, but also the paper round, the Saturday job in Tesco and the full-time job of a minor who has left school. Contracts whose terms exploit the minor will not pass the test.[16] Nor will contracts that involve trading. The rule allows a minor to earn his or her living, but not to risk his or her capital.[17] Nor is there any exemption for contracts for rather special services by exceptional minors; the contract of the 15-year-old footballing prodigy Wayne Rooney with his agent was

---

[7] M Clarke in M Furmston *et al, The Law of Contract* (3rd edn, London, Butterworths, 2007) 775.

[8] Summarised very clearly in Law Commission, 'Law of Contract: Minors' Contracts' (Law Com No 134, 1984) 2. The Law Commission considered, in its Working Paper No 81, substituting for the current law a much simpler system: *all* contracts made by a person aged 16 or over would be fully valid; *no* contract made by a person under 16 should be enforceable against him. The proposal was not supported on consultation, and therefore did not form part of the Law Commission's proposals in 1984; but their recommendations brought about the Minors' Contracts Act 1987, leaving the common law intact, but tidying up some anomalies.

[9] See above n 7.

[10] R Upex and G Benett, *Davies on Contract* (London, Sweet & Maxwell, 2004) 177.

[11] *Nash v Inman* [1908] 2 KB 1.

[12] GH Treitel, *The Law of Contract* (11th edn, London, Sweet & Maxwell, 2003).

[13] Surely: ask any teenager. But the point is undecided (C Sawyer, 'The Child is Not a Person: Family Law and Other Legal Cultures' (2006) 28 *JSWFL* 1, 9) and a phone company would be unlikely to take the risk: see the following note.

[14] See, eg <http://www.adviceguide.org.uk/index/your_world/consumer_affairs/young_people_money_and_consumer_rights.htm> accessed 16 December 2008.

[15] Student loan contracts certainly sound like necessaries, and of course sometimes involve minors; the practice of loan companies seems to be to ask borrowers to ratify when they are 18.

[16] *De Franceso v Barnum* (1889) 45 Ch D 430.

[17] 'The law will not suffer him to trade, which may be his undoing', *Whywall v Campion* (1738) 2 Stra. 1083.

unenforceable against him, which meant that when he was poached by another agent, the latter was not liable in the tort of inducing breach of contract.[18]

Another group of contracts are voidable by the minor to a limited extent: they are valid unless he or she repudiates them, during minority or within a reasonable time of attaining majority. These are contracts that involve an ongoing liability connected with property: contracts concerning land, which impose an ongoing obligation, such as a lease or a contract to purchase land;[19] a subscription for shares;[20] partnership agreements;[21] and marriage settlements. There are complex rules relating to the extent of the right to repudiate.

All other contracts with minors are unenforceable against the minor, unless he or she ratifies them when he or she reaches the age of majority.[22] It is sometimes said that they are voidable, which is a little confusing because of the similarity to the contracts involving land, etc just mentioned; the point is that contracts in this category are fully voidable and remain so unless the minor ratifies them as an adult; the land contracts become valid if not repudiated within a reasonable time after majority is attained. The following story illustrates the consequences of this, from an American point of view:

> A sophisticated adult-looking man enters a car dealer's showroom and purchases a new station wagon for use by him and his family. He shows the salesman a driver's license indicating that he is 25 years old and qualified to operate the vehicle. After signing the contract of sale, the purchaser uses the car for six months and then recklessly collides with another automobile. While he is liable for his criminal behaviour in violating the traffic regulation and for his tortious injury to the other driver's automobile, under the laws of many states if he is actually under the age of 21 years, he can disaffirm (i.e. void) the contract of sale and recover any portion of the purchase price he has paid.[23]

The age of majority in the story, as well as its spelling and vocabulary, reflect its date and origin, but it emphasises the point that this is quite a harsh law for adults. There is no grey area of *Gillick*-competence; these are bright-line rules:

> It was thought necessary to safeguard the weaknesses of infants at large, even though here and there a juvenile knave slipped through.[24]

---

[18]   *Proform Sports Management Ltd v Proactive Sports Management Ltd and another* [2006] EWHC 2903 (Ch).

[19]   *Davies and another v Benyon-Harris* (1931) 47 TLR 424; and *Whittingham v Murdy* (1889) 60 LT 956.

[20]   ie the liability to the company for calls can be avoided. *North Western Railway v M'Michael* (1850) 5 Ex 114.

[21]   *Goode v Harrison* (1821) 5 B & Ald 147.

[22]   This is the effect of the repeal of the Infants Relief Act 1874, by the Minors' Contracts Act 1987.

[23]   RG Edge, 'Voidability of Minors' Contracts: A Feudal Doctrine in a Modern Economy' [1967] 1 *Georgia Law Review* 205.

[24]   *R Leslie Ltd v Sheill* [1914] 3 KB 607. 612 (Sumner LJ), quoted in Clarke, above n 7. There was speculation, after the *Gillick* decision, that its effects might be felt in areas such as the law relating to a minor's contractual capacity: S Cretney, '*Gillick* and the concept of legal capacity' (1989) 105 *LQR* 356. However, that does not seem to have happened; there is much to be said for bright lines.

The law's message is clear: deal with minors at your peril. However, once the age of majority drops to 18, there is far less of a difficulty, since the pool of minors decreases and the ease of identifying those who are underage increases. Of course, there are other ways of protecting minors, and other jurisdictions have taken different approaches. Some began with a rule that the child had no contractual capacity at all, but this proved inconvenient and changed into a qualified rule such as that currently in force in England and Wales.[25] Some have special rules for the validation of contracts in particular contexts: in New York and California a contract for the child's services in sport or entertainment may be rendered fully binding with court approval,[26] a procedure that Mr Rooney's agents might have welcomed. Finally, the invalidity of minors' contracts causes no problems once they are executed, goods or services have been delivered and property has passed. If the young man in the story above had bought the vehicle outright, it would have been his, and there would be no way for him to get his money back, in modern England and Wales as much as in 1960s Georgia.[27] It is deals on credit that are threatened by the invalidity rules, and contracts for services that do not fall within the idea of 'necessaries' or 'beneficial contracts'.

Against this background, what is the content of parental responsibility in respect of minors' contracts? Precisely none. Parents are not liable under their children's contracts unless they expressly undertake such liability, nor can they validate them on the minor's behalf.[28]

So here we seem to hit a brick wall. There is a fair amount of law surrounding the child's contractual capacity, and plenty of room for disagreement about what the rules should be in that context; but no legal content to parental responsibility. Nor is anyone making an argument that there should be. The purpose of the emptiness of parental responsibility in this context is to protect the minor by completing the discouragement effect. If parents *did* have responsibility for their children's deals, there would be no disincentive for anyone to contract with a minor and the law's carefully constructed protection would vanish.

Wayne Rooney's parents signed his agency agreement,[29] and we wonder why. Did the agents think this would validate the deal? Or provide a disincentive to Rooney's disengaging himself, as he was entitled to do and indeed did? Or provide evidence that Rooney was properly advised and had his parents' approval, in case of later accusations of pressure? It may be that popular belief about the function of a parent's approval or even of their signature seems to

[25] MJ Dugas, 'The contractual capacity of minors: a survey of the prior law and the new articles' (1988) 62 *Tulane Law Review* 745.

[26] H Hruby, 'That's show business kid: an overview of contract law in the entertainment industry' (2006) 27 *Journal of Juvenile Law* 47.

[27] Treitel, above n 12, 549.

[28] *Blackburn v Mackey* (1823) 1 C & P 1.

[29] See above n 18.

provide the necessary reassurance to keep the wheels of the sport and entertainment business turning. Certainly there was no suggestion in the litigation that the parents took on any liability under the contract.

What the good parent *actually* does, of course, is extensive. From the days of the first little payments of pocket money to the receipt of the first instalment of a student loan (the latter probably after the end of minority) and beyond, a parent will have things to say, whether welcome or unwelcome. What the responsible parent *does* is quite distinct from the rights and duties that he or she has by law in this area; and it is the *absence* of legal duties to perform their children's contracts that protects the child from third parties.

PROPERTY

The Child's Capacity[30]

The child is not far short of an adult in terms of capacity to hold property; and indeed it is because he or she *can* hold property that his or her contractual capacity is restricted.[31] The only thing he or she cannot do is hold a legal estate. That disability is a recent invention, part of the 1925 drive to make life simple for purchasers; it is set out in section 1(6) of the Law of Property Act 1925, expressed by the draftsman in the same breath as the prohibition on legal tenancy in common:

> A legal estate is not capable of subsisting or of being created in an undivided share in land or of being held by an infant.

The law's nervousness about a child's impact upon purchasers persists: we discovered recently that a child, like a pre-*Boland* woman,[32] could not have an overriding interest by virtue of his or her actual occupation of land.[33] Unlike the pre-*Boland* women, the child undoubtedly holds an interest *in the land*; but that interest cannot find its way into what is now paragraph 2 of Schedule 3 to the

---

[30] For some general comment on capacity, see E Cooke, 'Children and real property—trusts, interests and considerations' [1998] *Fam Law* 349.

[31] See above n 18. The child's earnings, of course, belong to him or her; it is quite startling to discover that in California they belong to his or her parents: J Benbow, 'Rights of Parents: Under My Roof: Parents' Rights to Children's Earnings' (2007) 16 *Journal of Contemporary Legal Issues* 71. See further S Din, 'Instituting proper trust funds and safeguarding the earnings of child performers from dissipation by parents, guardians and trustees' (2004) 35 *McGeorge Law Review* 473.

[32] Recall that until *Williams & Glyn's Bank Ltd v Boland* [1981] AC 487, it was not clear that a married woman who had contributed to the purchase of land registered in her husband's name held an interest in the land, let alone that she could be regarded as having an overriding interest by virtue of actual occupation.

[33] In *Hypo-Mortgage Services Ltd v Robinson* [1997] 2 FCR 422, it was held (actually following *Caunce v Caunce* [1969] 1 WLR 286, and *Bird v Syme-Thomson* [1979] 1 WLR 440!) that a child with an interest in land, in actual occupation, nevertheless did not have an overriding interest by virtue of that occupation. The child's interest, therefore, could not be enforceable against the mortgagee.

Land Registration Act 2002: the child's equitable ownership cannot bind a purchaser because it cannot be an overriding interest.[34] The motivation for this is the protection of purchasers, whether buyers or mortgagees. Moreover, where parents are 'intentionally homeless', the fact that they have a child living with them, who is *not* intentionally homeless, does not put the family back into the 'unintentionally homeless' category; the child cannot represent his or her family in terms of entitlement to local authority housing.[35]

The child's disabilities in respect of property can be seen as a way of managing responsibility, rather than rendering him or her 'absent' from property law,[36] or constituting a failure to protect him or her or to respond to children's needs.[37] Certainly, the protection of third parties is an important element here; why should a mortgagee pick up the mortgagors' responsibility to house their children?[38] Furthermore, it is clear that a child *can* succeed to a statutory tenancy under the Rent Act 1977, although the tenancy will remain equitable while the child remains a minor.[39] As Hale J (as she then was) remarked:

> [T]here is ample reason to conclude that children are not 'non-persons' in the law of landlord and tenant, let alone the law of property generally.[40]

Legal Estates in Land

What happens to the legal estate that the minor cannot hold? Note that it does not automatically vest in a parent or anyone with parental responsibility; any attempt to transfer a legal estate to a minor simply fails, and the legal estate stays where it is unless placed elsewhere. In the delightfully technical days before the Trusts of Land and Appointment of Trustees Act 1996, a conveyance of a legal estate to a minor operated as an enforceable contract to create a strict settlement for him or her.[41] Today things are less picturesque but more convenient: a transfer of a legal estate to a minor *inter vivos* will operate only in equity, leaving the transferor with the legal estate and the status of trustee unless he or she makes

---

[34] [1997] 2 FCR 422 at 426: '... it cannot have been intended that s 70(1)(g) should operate as the second defendant suggests. No inquiry can be made of minor children or consent obtained from them in the manner contemplated by that provision, especially when they are, as here, of tender years at the material date. If the second defendant was right, lenders would never be protected. Their security could always be frustrated by simple devices' (Nourse LJ). The minor's interest cannot be recorded by notice on the register: Land Registration Act 2002 s 32.

[35] *R v Oldham Council, ex p Garlick* [1993] AC 509.

[36] Sawyer, above n 13.

[37] A Barlow, 'Family Law and Housing Law: A Symbiotic Relationship?' in R Probert (ed), *Family Life and the Law* (Aldershot, Ashgate, 2007) 22–6.

[38] Such would be the result of a different decision in *Hypo-Mortgage Services*, above n 33.

[39] *Kingston upon Thames BC v Prince* [1999] 1 FLR 593; and see J Morgan, 'Children are people too' [2000] 12 *CFLQ* 65.

[40] [1999] 1 FLR 593 at 603; quoted by Morgan, above n 39.

[41] Settled Land Act 1925 s 27(1).

other arrangements.[42] Where land is left to a minor by will or as a consequence of intestacy, it will be held on trust; and while inherited money, if any, could be transferred to a child, it will normally be held upon the usual accumulation and maintenance trust, by the trustees who also hold the land.[43] Thus, in many instances responsibility for property belonging to a child falls upon people without parental responsibility, and the content of that responsibility is determined by the law of trusts.

A minor may be appointed as a trustee; but if the trust includes land he or she will not be able to function properly without the legal estate, and so there is a power—but no duty—for the settlor or, if there is none, the other trustees, to replace him or her.[44]

The Content of Parental Responsibility

Before 1925, a minor *could* hold a legal estate; go back a few centuries, however, and he would have had trouble rendering the services due in return for the estate he held. In particular, he might be a bit short in the arm for the more macho varieties such as knight service. Wardship was an incident of knight service and of grand serjeanty, enabling the feudal lord to profit from the ward's property during his minority. When knight service was abolished, the Tenures Abolition Act 1660 put guardianship on a statutory footing, and thus the status of the 'guardian of the estate' was developed; the link to feudal service has disappeared, leaving the idea of someone who looks after the child's property and is trustee of any property or profits he or she holds for the child.[45] Much later, Blackstone discusses the ancient rule that the guardian of an estate inherited by a child must be someone who cannot inherit it if the child dies and would therefore usually *not* be the child's father.[46] And that separate role of the 'guardian of the estate', distinct from that of the father as the guardian 'by nature and by nurture', survived until very recently. According to the Guardianship of Minors Act 1971, testamentary guardians, surviving parent guardians,[47] and guardians appointed by the court in its modern wardship jurisdiction all had the powers of the guardian of a minor's estate under the 1660 statute; and there was authority to the effect that such a guardian had powers that a parent in normal circumstances

---

[42]   Trusts of Land and Appointment of Trustees Act 1996 Sch 1 para 1.

[43]   In *Harry Potter and the Half-Blood Prince* (London, Bloomsbury, 2005), Harry Potter inherits Sirius Black's house; there is no mention of trusteeship, so perhaps under-age wizards can hold a legal estate. The conservatism of the Ministry of Magic is such that it would be unlikely to sanction the enactment of legislation analogous to the 1925 property law reforms.

[44]   Trustee Act 1925 s 36(1). For further comment on this point, see Sawyer, above n 13, 7.

[45]   Tenures Abolition Act 1660 s 12.

[46]   W Blackstone, *Commentaries on the Laws of England: Vol 1* (1765–69) 450. This affords him the opportunity to contrast Roman law, and the pleasure of claiming the authority of Solon (lawgiver in Athens, late sixth century BC) for the English rule.

[47]   That is, where the other parent has died.

had not—in particular, to give a valid receipt on the child's behalf.[48] Therefore, when it came to constructing parental responsibility in the Children Act 1989, it was felt to be worthwhile to make it quite clear that the parent with parental responsibility has two distinct bundles of rights and duties—those of a parent, in section 3(1) of the Children Act 1989, and those of a guardian of a child's estate, in section 3(2) and (3).[49]

So what are the duties of the guardian of the child's estate? The legal sources are ancient and coy.[50] As far back as the seventeenth century there was a reluctance to spell things out: the Tenures Abolition Act 1660 empowered a guardian to 'bring such ... actions ... as by law a guardian in common socage might do'. Blackstone discusses 'Parent and Child' in Chapter XVI of Book I of the *Commentaries*, saying:

> A father has no other power over his son's estate than as his trustee or guardian; for though he may receive the profits during the child's minority, yet he must account for them when he comes of age.[51]

Of guardians, in chapter XVII Blackstone says:

> The power and reciprocal duty of a guardian and ward are the same ... as that of a father and child, and therefore I shall not repeat them: but shall only add, that the guardian, when the ward comes of age, is bound to give him an account of all that he has transacted on his behalf, and must answer for all losses by his wilful default or negligence.[52]

So in considering this aspect of parental responsibility, we run again into the law of trusts. The parent or other person with parental responsibility does not automatically hold legal estates intended for the child; but he or she *may* hold property for the child and in that event he or she is a trustee and is there to take care of the property for the child with all the fiduciary duties that that trusteeship implies.[53]

It is perhaps that diversion of parental responsibility into trusteeship that makes modern writers on family law so reticent about the content of parental

---

[48] The Law Commission in 'Review of Child Law: Guardianship' (Working Paper No 91, 1985) [145] cites *M'Reight v M'Reight* (or *M'Creight*) (1849) 13 I Eq R 314 and S Cretney, *Principles of Family Law* (4th edn, London, Sweet & Maxwell, 1984). In *M'Reight*, the Lord Chancellor stated, *obiter* and referring to some older cases, that 'payment of a legacy bequeathed to an infant is an improper payment. The father is merely the guardian of the person and guardian by nature, but in neither capacity has he any power over the property of the infant.'

[49] The Law Commission, mindful of Blackstone's comment (see text at n 46 above), noted that there was no longer any need to feel that parents could not be trusted in the role of guardian of the estate: Working Paper no 91, above n 48, [3.5].

[50] H Brewer, *By birth or consent* (Chapel Hill, University of North Carolina Press, 2005) ch 7, discusses the pre-1660 position, and explains the magnitude of the change in 1660.

[51] Blackstone, above n 46, 441.

[52] *Ibid*, 450–1.

[53] In contrast to the self-seeking profiteer back in the days of the feudal origins of this role: see Brewer, above n 50.

responsibility vis-a-vis the child's property[54]—that, and the fact that this aspect of parental responsibility tends to be far removed from child protection issues, so that it has not been developed in litigation. It is clear that parental responsibility involves some duties in respect of the child's property; but if we want to know what those duties are, we have to look at the law of trusts. Where the parent is a trustee, he or she has all the powers and duties of a trustee, without any specific extra content arising from his or her parenthood. If the property concerned is land, the Trusts of Land and Appointment of Trustees Act 1996 will answer most questions.[55]

Third parties are free to deal with the child if they choose to do so, and dispositions of property by or to the minor will be valid. However, the 'guardian of the estate' ingredient of parental responsibility makes it safe to pay to a parent anything due to a child in respect of his or her property. Payments do not *have* to be made to the parent—they are the child's property, and the law does not deprive the child of it. However, if a third party prefers to pay rent, or sale proceeds, or presumably even a contractual payment, to someone with parental responsibility, he or she can safely do so and he or she can be given a valid receipt—formally and precisely because of the inclusion of the ancient rights and duties of the guardian of the estate within the content of parental responsibility. Something very similar is seen in section 10 of the Trusts of Land and Appointment of Trustees Act 1996, which states that where a beneficiary whose consent is required to a disposition is a minor, the trustees must obtain the consent of any person who has parental responsibility for him or her, or of a guardian.[56] Parental responsibility gives the trustee(s) a safe person from whom to obtain consent.

However, what about the property held by the child him- or herself, of which the person with parental responsibility is not a trustee? The money in the bank, perhaps, or the share in the French timeshare after a parent's death?[57] The child can do as he or she chooses. There is no content of parental responsibility, no

---

[54] Comments in the 1970s and 1980s, when the scope of parental rights and duties fell under some general scrutiny—presumably in response to the Law Commission's endeavours—are sparse indeed on the subject of responsibilities for property. JC Hall, 'The Waning of Parental Rights' (1972) 31 *CLJ* 248, 249 notes that the parent has the right to 'administer the child's property', but says no more about that; there is no mention of rights or duties in respect of property in J Eekelaar, 'What are parental rights' (1973) 89 *LQR* 210. MDA Freeman, 'What Rights and Duties do Parents Have?' (1980) 44 *JP* 380 says: '[Parents] have a right to receive and recover in their own name for the benefit of the child property of whatever description and wherever stated which the child is entitled to receive or recover.' There is nothing on the point in BM Dickens, 'The Modern Function and Limits of Parental Rights' (1981) 97 *LQR* 462, and only a brief mention in S Maidment, 'The Fragmentation of Parental Rights' (1981) 40 *CLJ* 135.

[55] And in its duties to consult, etc makes it unnecessary to import anything from the idea of *Gillick*-competence into this aspect of trusteeship, at least.

[56] The inclusion of 'guardian' is strange, since guardians of any kind following the Children Act 1989 will have parental responsibility.

[57] As to which see J Denker and C Haworth, 'The property of minors under English law' (2004) *Private Client Business* 376. They argue that a French lawyer dealing with such an inheritance needs to be able to deal with a 'guardian of the estate' with specific statutory powers. It is suggested that the

right or duty in the bundle, to tell us what the responsible parent will do by way of advice or direction—just as the law will not tell us anything about what the good parent does about his or her child's contracts; we have to look at other sources of our culture and values. Hagrid may be as good a mentor as any.[58]

Parental Responsibility and the Parent's Property

The law is equally quiet about a parent's duty towards his child or her vis-à-vis the parent's property. Almost uniquely within Europe we do not have forced heirship. Subject to the requirements of the Inheritance (Provision for Family and Dependants) Act 1975, which relate only to maintenance in the case of responsibility for children,[59] the parent does not have to leave his or her child a bean.

The law's reluctance to recognise any duty to pass on property to children has extended to a reluctance to recognise any moral obligation or even desire to do so. Thus, until very recently it was axiomatic in ancillary relief that a wife claiming financial provision from her ex-husband must not receive anything with a view to passing it on to her children. In the new post-*White* world, that concern no longer arises;[60] but when awards directly for children under Schedule 1 to the Children Act 1989 are under consideration it is still a principle that a capital asset must not normally be transferred outright to the child.[61] Outside a duty to maintain, the parent seems to have no duty to pass on his or her property to a child.

And yet of course most do; or, rather, most do nothing to avoid the consequences of intestacy, which is why Harry has a vault full of gold at Gringott's.

Many parents will open a savings account for their child. The government's recent move to encourage this, through Child Trust Funds,[62] keys into parental responsibility, for the 'responsible person' who can open the account is anyone with parental responsibility (if over 16; and excluding a Local Authority).

---

concern expressed is unnecessary; a parent or other person with parental responsibility can perform the role required and, if property is vested in him or her, will be a trustee so far as English law is concerned.

[58] The Children (Scotland) Act 1995 approaches the Scots equivalent of parental responsibility rather differently, as is well known, and sets out its content. Sections 9 and 10 set out duties in relation to the child's property, and set up a system of direction by the court for the management of the child's property by parents—optional for sums over £5,000 and compulsory for more than £20,000—but *only* where the parent is not a trustee. Therefore, again, trusts law is left to its own devices where possible.

[59] *Re Jennings* [1994] Ch 286.

[60] See *White v White* [2001] 1 AC 596.

[61] *Chamberlain v Chamberlain* [1973] 1 WLR 1557; and *A v A (A Minor: Capital Provision)* [1994] 1 FLR 657. In exceptional circumstances, the Court has taken a different view: see *Tavoulareas v Tavoulareas* [1999] 1 FCR 133.

[62] See N Wikeley, 'Child Trust Funds—asset-based welfare or a recipe for increased inequality?' (2004) 11 *Journal of Social Security Law* 189.

However, the statute adds little to the content of parental responsibility; the management duties of the responsible person authorised to open the account are pretty-much non-existent; and there is opportunity, but no duty, to make private contributions to the account.

The minimalism of parental responsibility in this context is difficult to explain. At its root must be individualism, and a very modern English tendency to dismiss what a French person might describe as a *patrimoine*, or a family asset or heritage. Whether this is quite a virtue is not clear. Certainly it does not seem to deter most people from wanting their children to inherit whatever beans they may have amassed; perhaps love and generosity flourish better without legal constraint—even if that allows a few hard cases of disinheritance.

CONCLUSION

It is perhaps trite law, but worth recalling as we have done here, that it is for the minor's own benefit and protection that his or her parents and anyone else with parental responsibility have no legal responsibility in respect of his or her contracts. In the law of property, the minor's capacity is far less restricted; and parental responsibility is not content-free in the context of property, but can only be defined when we step sideways into the law of trusts.

It is tempting to move into autopoietic theory and to assert that parental responsibility and responsible parenting belong to different discourses and simply cannot talk to each other.[63] In some contexts, an assertion of autopoiesis, while formally useless,[64] can prevent our trying to build impossible bridges. However, parental responsibility and responsible parenting *do* inform each other; the legislation setting out the content of the Scottish version of parental responsibility seems to succeed in constructing a picture of parental responsibility that is informed, at least, by our views of what the responsible parent does. In the context examined in this chapter, namely contract and property, the scantiness in the content of parental responsibility seems purposeful; in contract, to complete the deterrent effect, and in property law the aim seems to be to allow formal responsibility to be defined by the law of trusts, leaving the informal content of responsible parenting to be worked out without legal rules. There seems to be little argument for further regulation. Perhaps this really is an area where responsible parenting works best without too much legal regulation,[65] and where the good things in life, the good ideas that the responsible parent will generate, cannot be made to happen through legal powers and duties. Among such good

[63]   cf M King, 'Children's Rights as Communication: Reflections on Autopoietic Theory and the United Nations Convention' (1994) 57 *MLR* 385.

[64]   M King, 'What's the use of Luhmann's Theory' in M King and C Thornhill (eds), *Luhmann on Law and Politics. Critical Appraisals and Applications* (London, Hart Publishing, 2006).

[65]   Further, as has been noted, it is not an area that receives a lot of legal attention from those interested in child protection when it goes wrong.

ideas might be generosity, and a sense of fun, which the law is not always best placed to generate:

Harry pulled open his trunk, and drew out his Triwizard winnings.

'Take it', he said, and thrust the sack into George's hands …

'You're mental', said George, trying to push it back at Harry …

Listen', said Harry firmly. If you don't take it, I'm throwing it down the drain. I don't want it and I don't need it. But I could do with a few laughs. We could all do with a few laughs.[66]

---

[66] JK Rowling, *Harry Potter and the Goblet of Fire* (London, Bloomsbury, 2000) 635.

12

Children's Representation by Their Parents in Legal Proceedings

CAROLINE SAWYER

INTRODUCTION

B EING A PARTY to court proceedings is the most active and public manifestation of a legal personality. It entails not only holding legal rights, but vindicating them, or being liable to be brought to account. The position of parents and children in legal proceedings is thus significant of their identity within the structures of the law. If children's position were the same as adults', they would be holding rights and responsibilities in the same way as adults; if legal proceedings involving the representation of children were simply impossible, they would have no more legal identity than a household pet. What is more usual is a sort of middle ground, in which children are represented through someone else and thus have a partial identity in the legal process. Given that any manifestation of a child's separate legal personality in the context of the world outside the private family indicates that the child has an autonomous identity, potentially inimical to the integrity of the family structure, it is perhaps unsurprising that the right to represent a child in legal proceedings is a long-standing part of parental responsibility.

One of the striking features of English law is its individualistic, rather than family, structure.[1] This is socially most noticeable in the context of family property, which is widely believed to exist, but is a relatively foreign concept.[2] It can be seen, however, also in the history of child representation. The legal personality of the child survived the Norman conquest,[3] and the idea that the

---

[1] This is not peculiar to the law: see A Macfarlane, *The Origins of English Individualism* (Oxford, Blackwell, 1978).

[2] See, eg A Barlow and G James, 'Why don't they marry?' [2005] 17 *CFLQ* 383.

[3] F Pollock and FW Maitland, *History of English Law: Vol II* (first published 1895, Cambridge, Cambridge University Press, 1968) 437.

Crown was the natural guardian of a child (or anyone) prevailed thereafter.[4] Where there was a dispute in medieval times, it was said that a parent, or father, 'ought not to represent the land' of their children, but should:

> 'pray aid' of his child, or vouch his child to warranty, and the child will come before the court as an independent person.[5]

The occasional flourishing of considering children as parties in their own right has continued, notably in the later stages of the twentieth century, but nevertheless the rule that parents are the representatives of their children in legal proceedings has a long history and is currently well established.

Whilst it may be contentious to suggest that parents have 'rights' rather than 'responsibilities', nevertheless this is the clear message of section 2 of the Children Act 1989. And in reality parents almost always still control how, or whether, any separate right a child may have is vindicated: given this element of parental choice, in reality the rights belong more to the parents. This can militate against the existence of such a right at all if there would be any disadvantage to the parents in pursuing and vindicating the right on behalf of the child. Parents have no *responsibility* to act as their child's representatives; nor indeed is it always clear how the responsible parent exercises the right to do so. Given the dependency of most children on their parents, it is unsurprising either that representation is a long-standing element of parental responsibility or that it presents conceptual and practical problems.

The rationale for the legal disability, whether of children or mental patients, is generally framed in terms of protection of the disabled person from the responsibility of having to take important decisions and from the consequences of unwise decisions. It is entirely usual and practical for parents to deal with children's matters for them, which can also reinforce the separate idea that children's legal disability, like the historical disability of married women, reflects not only social, cultural and economic disempowerment, but also a widespread belief that the fundamental unit of society is the family rather than the individual.[6]

The thrust of the right to represent a child is not to act as that child's legal representative—to stand up in court as their solicitor or barrister—but to stand in for, or with, the child. Although the obvious type of proceedings for children to be involved in may be family proceedings, other forms of the process have a

---

[4] *Ibid*, 446: 'That the king should protect all who have no other protector, that he is the guardian above all guardians, is an idea which has become exceptionally prominent in this much governed country'.

[5] *Ibid*, 440–1: 'An infant can sue; he sues in his own proper person, for he cannot appoint an attorney. He is not in any strict sense of the word "represented" before the court by his guardian, even if he has one ... often enough it happens that an infant brings an action against the person who according to the infant's assertion, ought to be his guardian.'

[6] United Nations Convention on the Rights of the Child 1989: especially the Preamble. See also J Hall, 'The waning of parental rights' (1972) 31 *CLJ* 248.

simpler structure. The civil process, for the enforcement of private obligations, is the simplest and clearest, and will be dealt with first. The criminal process is very different, but is also relatively simple in structure, although it contains considerable ambiguity in practice. Family proceedings necessarily involve relatives and are the most awkward of all, entailing conflicts as well as ambiguities in the position of all of the family members. The right to represent children within the legal process is a part of parental responsibility that is particularly revealing of how parental responsibility and children's separate identity may be variously reconciled—or not—in the context of the different branches of the law.

CIVIL PROCEEDINGS

Children may be involved in proceedings about property or contracts, or about compensation for tortious acts. Practically, the actions in which they are involved are limited, for example, by the rule that children's executory contracts are often unenforceable.[7] But, should they wish to bring or defend a claim, the basic rule—to which there are exceptions—is that children under the age of 18 are not competent to appear as parties or to instruct a legal representative.[8] If they wish to bring a case, the court process generally requires them to do so through an adult, or 'litigation friend'.[9] Recent developments mean that a child may be permitted, at the discretion of the judge and by the court's direction, to proceed without a litigation friend, or for any litigation friend to be removed.[10] A child may also apply for such an order, on notice to any existing litigation friend; such orders may later be rescinded by the court.[11] In practice, however, few judges consider children to be sufficiently competent to proceed without a litigation friend.

The role of a litigation friend is in essence a closely confined legal role without social work aspects. The appointment of a litigation friend is part of the court

---

[7] See Cooke, this volume.

[8] Those incapacitated by age are generally in the same procedural position as the mentally incapacitated. For discussion of that context, see eg J Southcott, 'The psychiatric nurse and the appropriate adult' (1999) 6 *Journal of Psychiatric and Mental Health Nursing* 357. See also 'Report into the death of Maxwell Confait' (London, House of Commons Sessional Papers 1977/78).

[9] Civil Procedure Rules (CPR), r 21.2. These were formerly known as 'next friends' where the child was the plaintiff (claimant) and 'guardians *ad litem*' where the child was the defendant or respondent, whence the terminology in care proceedings came (see below). Note that a married minor woman needs a litigation friend: Law Reform (Married Women and Tortfeasors) Act 1935 s 1(c), amended by Law Reform (Husband and Wife) Act 1962 s 3(2). A litigation friend may be a party (*Sinclair v Sinclair* (1845) 13 M&W 640). See Practice Direction 21, [1.3] and [1.5].

[10] CPR rr 21.2(3) and 21.7. This provision was brought in quietly, following the storm over its counterpart in private law family proceedings under Family Proceedings Rules (FPR) r 9.2A 1991, subsequently almost abandoned. This rule also deals with the substitution of litigation friends. The role of the litigation friend ceases automatically when the child reaches 18 (CPR r 21.9 (1)).

[11] CPR r 21.2(3)–(5).

process:[12] they must conduct the proceedings fairly and competently, but there are no written duties about ensuring the child's welfare or comfort within the process[13] any more than the court rules (as opposed to the professional literature) impose such duties on solicitors for competent parties.[14] There is nothing inherent in this process that requires the litigation friend to be, or not to be, a parent. Nevertheless, it is unlikely that anyone not closely connected with the child would want to become involved in something so potentially awkward and time-consuming, so as a matter of practice most litigation friends for children will be their parents.

A further reason why it might be difficult to find anyone other than a parent prepared to be a litigation friend would be because they may be required to give an undertaking to pay the costs of the legal process, although later reimbursement by the child out of any money recovered is possible.[15] Even if this is successful, a litigation friend will have gained nothing out of the process save personal satisfaction—unless they have some sufficiently close involvement with the child for the child's material reward to be satisfying in itself. Whilst the court may appoint a litigation friend for a child, there is no court service to provide such friends and it would still be difficult to find someone to fulfil the role. It would be unlikely that a child would initiate a claim, thus bringing the matter to the attention of the court, without adult support. The requirements of the legal process therefore make it difficult for children to make claims unless they have parental support: it would surely be difficult or impossible to find someone to be a litigation friend if a child's parents were opposed to the claim's being made. In mitigation of the potential harshness of the situation where a child may have difficulty pursuing a claim, the limitation period, which specifies how long a person has to file a claim, does not run against a minor. A child, therefore, always has at least until the age of 21 to start proceedings.[16]

A situation in which parents most obviously can and do exercise their rights to represent their children is that of making a personal injury claim on the child's behalf. If there is a traffic accident, there is almost always provable fault; the injuries are often serious enough to be worth pursuing; and there will be

---

[12] Although a person may become a litigation friend with or without a court order: CPR rr 21.5 and 21.6.

[13] Nor does the child have any voice in the selection of the litigation friend: *Morgan v Thorne* (1841) M&W 400.

[14] Practice Direction 21 [2.1].

[15] CPR r 21.4(3). The exchange between counsel and Keith J at the end of *Joseph Daniel Hills v Chief Constable of Essex* [2006] EWHC 2633 (Admin) is worth reading on this point. Joseph Hills lost his appeal against his Anti Social Behaviour Order and the Chief Constable sought his costs. It appeared that the possibility of such an order had not been explained to his mother as his litigation friend; it was made nevertheless, with the comment that such orders are rarely enforced. As to recovery, see CPR r 21.12.

[16] This would apply to a claim for damages for personal injury, where the limitation period is as short as three years (Limitation Act 1980 s 11). Note, however, that an earlier claim is more likely to succeed, as a stale claim can be more difficult to win unless much of it is effectively prepared when memories and evidence are still fresh.

someone worth suing.[17] A claim of this kind may be, and often is, made by a child against his or her own parent: the true defendant is not the party sued, but the insurer, and the parent has an interest in the child's getting the damages.[18] There are limits to the proxy role: agreements to settle must be approved by the court—if not, they do not bind.[19]

As well as the awkwardness of using the legal process on behalf of a child, there is also, however, difficulty for a person in using the legal process *against* a child, and here the structural difficulty is built into the process itself. The basic rule is that a child is liable in tort.[20] If a child is sued without a litigation friend, the proceedings cannot easily go beyond the stage of issuing and serving the claim form.[21] Given that children are relatively unlikely to have the personal resources or insurance to be worth suing, notwithstanding any occasional social and moral panic about making parents liable for their torts as for their more criminal sins, there is little pressure to reduce the awkwardness of the process.

In essence, then, in civil proceedings the right of parents to represent their children is not wholly reflected in the rules of court, which allow any adult without a conflict of interest to perform that role. In practice, however, parents will almost always have control of their children's civil proceedings, including the decision as to whether proceedings will be brought at all. The academic literature on children proceedings suggests that judges rarely consider children to be competent, but practical and research concerns about the competence of children in court focus more on child witnesses in criminal cases, or children involved in contested family matters, than on children who wish to sue independently for damages.[22] In any event, the involvement of parents is unlikely to be contentious just for the reason that there will be no dispute as to the desired outcome, and so no conflict among the child's stated or perceived views or interests, the role of parent and the role of litigation friend. It appears, therefore, that in civil proceedings, despite the lack of any specified role for parents as such, and notwithstanding the formal development of the ability for children to act without litigation friends, it is almost inevitable that litigation friends will be required and that the only persons likely to fulfil that role in the civil process are parents.

---

[17] Even in the case of uninsured drivers: the Motor Insurers' Bureau will pay on their behalf.

[18] Note, however, the dangers in agreeing damages privately: see, eg *Drinkall v Whitwood* [2003] EWCA Civ 1547, in which the Court of Appeal held that the defendants were entitled to renege on the damages agreed for a teenage girl injured in a road accident before she reached her majority. Approval by the Court would, however, have rendered the agreement binding: CPR r 21.10(1).

[19] CPR r 21.10(1); and *Dietz v Lessing Chemicals* [1969] 1 AC 170.

[20] The rule is long-standing. 'An infant can be sued', say Pollock and Maitland. 'The action is brought against him in his own name and the writ will say nothing of any guardian' (above n 3, 442).

[21] CPR r 21.3(2) and (4); orders shortening the court process are also generally unavailable, rr 12.10(a)(i) and 14.1(4)(a), Practice Direction 12, [4.2(1)].

[22] See, eg J Masson and M Winn Oakley, *Out of Hearing* (London, Wiley, 1999).

CRIMINAL PROCEEDINGS

The position in criminal proceedings is quite different. The substantive law currently sets the age of criminal responsibility at 10, which means that below that age children do not formally become involved in the criminal process as defendants, although those picked up for crimes under that age may have their names noted informally and thus be more liable to pursuit and prosecution for subsequent offences once they are over age. Where a child defendant appears before a court, the Children and Young Persons Act 1933 couples a presumption of age with a duty of 'due enquiry' if it 'appears to the court that he is a child or young person'.[23] The 'person responsible for his welfare' can be compelled to attend court with the child,[24] but parents are not expected or authorised to represent their children in criminal courts. Nevertheless, the criminal justice system does in practice require them to fulfil an earlier and potentially vital representative role.

A child detained by the police has rights additional to those which require that any detained person be allowed to contact someone to tell them where they are, as well as having a legal representative. The idea that steps must be taken to find out who is responsible for a detained child's welfare and to inform them of the reason for the arrest and the fact and place of the detention is not new, and there has always been a broad construction of the person fulfilling the 'parental' role in the criminal process.[25] The Children and Young Persons Act 1933, now updated and amended, defines who is presumed to have responsibility for a child or young person as anyone who has parental responsibility for the child within the meaning of the Children Act 1989, or is otherwise legally liable to maintain him, and any person who has care of the child; this last would include, for example, any non-custodial granny with whom the child might live.[26] It is specifically stated that persons falling within the definition 'shall not be taken to have ceased to be responsible' for the child by reason only of not, in practice, having care of them.[27] The Act thus also explicitly encompasses non-carer parents.

The details of children's apparent protection are in Code C of the Code of Practice for the Detention, Treatment and Questioning of Persons by Police Officers, which governs day-to-day police procedure. The Code was introduced under the Police and Criminal Evidence Act 1984 (PACE), itself a response to abuses of the investigation process, but largely reflected the previous Judges' Rules. It builds outwards from the original focus on parents. An arrested juvenile[28] has the right to have an 'appropriate adult' informed of the arrest and

---

23 Children and Young Persons Act 1933 s 99.
24 Children and Young Persons Act 1933 s 34.
25 Children and Young Persons Act 1933 s 34(2) and (3).
26 Children and Young Persons Act 1933 s 17 as amended.
27 Children and Young Persons Act 1933 s 17(2) as amended.
28 A person under 17: Code of Practice, C1.5.

present at any interview, unless there are specified risks in delaying questioning.[29] Such an 'appropriate adult' is 'the parent, guardian, or, if the juvenile is in … care, or … looked after … a person representing [the] authority or organisation', or a local authority social worker, or 'failing these, some other responsible adult aged 18 or over who is not a police officer or employed by the police'.[30] In this area, 'the persons who may be responsible for the welfare of a child or young person' are that person's parent or guardian (including the local authority, if a child is in care or looked after) or 'any other person who for the time being assumed responsibility for his welfare'.[31] This resonates with section 3(5) of the Children Act 1989—a phenomenally useful section which is often used in practice, but rarely adverted to by those who draft forms with an insurance company in mind, which effectively allows anyone who has the actual care of the child to perform the fundamental parental role of looking after their welfare. The Notes for Guidance stipulate however that the appropriate adult should not be someone suspected of involvement in the offence, the victim, a witness involved in the investigation, someone who has received a confession before attending as the appropriate adult, or an estranged parent to whose presence the juvenile specifically objects.[32] Whilst it may appear at first entirely reasonable for a child's parent to be with them at such an interview, the more one looks at the contents of the formal role, the more questionable it appears.

The term 'appropriate' may carry connotations of 'responsible', but the nature of the adult's responsibilities is very unclear. According to the Guidance, the appropriate adult's role is:

> first, to advise the person being questioned, then to observe whether or not the interview is being conducted properly and fairly, and thirdly to facilitate communication with the person being interviewed.[33]

It is explained that an appropriate adult is needed because young people are 'prone to provide information which is unreliable, misleading or self-incriminating'; whatever the truth of this, it leaves it ambiguous as to whether the role of the adult is to correct untruths or to protect or comfort the child.

---

[29] Code of Practice, C3.15 and C11.15. The idea of protecting children's position by the attendance of an appropriate adult such as a parent mirrors that in the Council of Europe's Proposal for a Framework Decision on procedural rights in criminal proceedings (Brussels, 28 April 2004, COM(2004) 328 final, 2004/0113 (CNS)). Appropriate adults for children to sit next to in court should also be available, but they would be in addition to legal representatives.

[30] Code of Practice, [1.7]. This was originally in a note of guidance to the first edition of the Code in 1985 and became a full part of the Code in the 1991 revision, which specified that the appropriate adult should be a parent, guardian, social worker or other person not employed by the police, but not a solicitor. Before PACE 1984, the area was governed by the Judges' Rules, specifically para 4 of the annexed Administrative Directions.

[31] Code of Practice, C3.13. Nevertheless, if the child is a ward of court—much less common since the Children Act 1989—permission to interview them must be obtained from the court: *Practice Direction (ward of court: witness in criminal proceedings)* [1988] 2 All ER 1015.

[32] Code of Practice, Note 1C.

[33] Code of Practice, [11.17]. See also *Leach v Gloucestershire Constabulary* [1998] EWCA Civ 1368.

First, the 'advice' to be given is entirely unclear, and may be confused with legal advice. The revised PACE Code of Practice makes it clear that the appropriate adult can ask a solicitor to advise the child (although the child cannot be forced to talk to or see them),[34] but it is clear from the many cases reported on appeal that the situation in which the appropriate adult advises the child what to say is far from uncommon: it is then difficult to see that the appropriate adult is not in effect giving legal advice. Moreover, it appears that a child might well have the adult, or parent, *instead* of the solicitor. For example, in *R v Morse*,[35] it was recorded that both the child and the appropriate adult declined legal advice. The child's confession was subsequently excluded under sections 76(2)(b) and 78 PACE 1984 as the appropriate adult, his father, had well below average intelligence and was virtually illiterate, and the police officers agreed that he gave no 'advice' to the defendant, who was himself of below-average intelligence. It is extremely difficult to imagine that any adult would wish, or be allowed, to be 'advised' by such a person at a police interview. The potential for awkwardness and conflict in the role is far from merely theoretical, albeit there is relatively little research on how appropriate adults are appointed or actually perform their role.

Secondly, the role of the appropriate adult in the interview is also ambiguous. A researcher found that the police:

> often do not explain the role to those involved, or may even actively prevent appropriate adults from carrying out their functions as set out in the Codes ... Where parents colluded with the police in trying to obtain a confession they frequently used abusive or oppressive techniques reminiscent of the worst police practices.[36]

The performance of appropriate adults—parents—as 'advisers' has been productive of appeals; often, although not always, successful ones.[37] In *R v Jefferson*,[38] a boy convicted of public order offences committed in Bedford following a televised football match appealed on the grounds of his father's performance of the role of appropriate adult. In the first of two interviews, lasting almost an hour, the father intervened 11 times, sometimes clarifying the son's answers, sometimes commenting on them and on one occasion contradicting him. The Court found that the father:

---

34   Code of Practice, [6.5(a)].

35   [1991] Crim LR 195. The father of a 16-year-old defendant attended as appropriate adult and both of them declined legal representation. Beezley J said that empathy with the defendant was not sufficient, and if an appropriate adult was incapable of giving advice, he was not an appropriate adult.

36   R Evans, 'Getting Things Taped' (1993) *Community Care* 18 November; see also B Littlechild, 'Reassessing the Role of the "Appropriate Adult"' [1995] *Crim LR* 540.

37   Including the Broadwater Farm appeals: see also D Townsend, 'After Broadwater' *Social Service Insight* 3 April 1987. Contrast *R v Gill and others* [2004] EWCA Crim 3245, a drug-dealing appeal, in which it was held that the lack of an appropriate adult did not give necessarily mean that the confession of a juvenile should be excluded.

38   [1994] 1 All ER 270 at 286B.

intervened robustly from time to time, sometimes joining in the questioning of his son and challenging his exculpatory account of certain incidents.[39]

Counsel submitted that although there was nothing at the outset to exclude the father as appropriate adult, his behaviour during the interview made him an inappropriate person to deal with 'ensuring a fair interview and of assisting if necessary' and the interview—which was a substantial part of the prosecution evidence—should therefore be excluded. Notwithstanding that he regarded the father as a 'critical observer and participant',[40] Auld J found that the functions of advising and observing had been fulfilled, and there was no duty of protecting his son from fair and proper questioning by the officers, for example by advising him to remain silent or by refraining from intervening to encourage him to be truthful.

> Encouragement by an appropriate adult of a juvenile who is being fairly interviewed to tell the truth should not normally be stigmatised as a failure of the adult to fulfil the first of his duties under note 13C, namely 'to advise' him,

he said,

> nor should it have the consequence of turning him from an appropriate adult to an inappropriate adult for the purpose of these provisions.[41]

It is difficult to imagine that an adult so 'advised' would feel that it was appropriate, but then there is no adult analogy for the parental role with a child under police questioning.

The third problem relates to the issue of protection. The appropriate adult is usually reported as advising the child to 'tell the truth', which sounds very well. The provision in the Criminal Justice and Public Order Act 1994 that inferences may be drawn from silence thus adds to the effective and perhaps improper pressure to say something.[42] This has three potentially adverse consequences. First, children may tell what they perceive the adult wants to hear, which may or may not be the truth[43] Secondly, they may tell a version of the truth without, for example, exculpatory elements. Thirdly, they may thus provide the police with their only evidence against them. This last in particular has several ramifications,

---

[39] *Ibid*, at 287E.

[40] *Ibid*, at 287G.

[41] The idea that appropriate adults are helping the police process as much as exercising a parental role to protect the child is perhaps furthered by the comment in *Taylor v Chief Constable of Thames Valley Police* [2004] EWCA Civ 858. A small 10-year-old boy was arrested, some weeks after the event, for public order offences at an animal rights demonstration. His mother, who had been with him throughout his arrest and transportation in a police van over a period of a couple of hours, had also taken part in the demonstration, but 'it was eventually agreed could act as an appropriate adult'. The contravention of the principle in Code C—that she was possibly involved in the alleged crime as well—does not seem to have been addressed, perhaps because it would then have been difficult to find any alternative appropriate adult.

[42] Criminal Justice and Public Order Act 1994 s 34.

[43] 'Juveniles may feel under more pressure from parents to "own up" to get it all over with as soon as possible': Littlechild, above n 36, 542.

even where the confession is accurate. Children may be pushed into plunging themselves into the criminal process when there is little or no evidence against them, thus more easily criminalising them than if they had been adults. Given that once a person has crossed the line into the criminal justice system, they may pursue a criminal identity, this is generally unhelpful. But there is also a point of principle: children should be protected just as much as adults. To give the lay parent, or parent-substitute, an unclear 'advisory' role, and to have the child bear the consequences should that not work fairly, may mean that the process is so unfair on the child that it cannot function, and that bringing the parent in means that in effect the case is taken outside the public, criminal process. The family, not the state, becomes the arena of justice. This may be so unfair to the child that the public legal system has to intervene.

Although the appropriate adult appears to have been intended to be something akin to a criminal equivalent of the civil litigation friend, considerably more problems are apparent if one considers the issue of trying to find a person to perform a role that is, in any event, unclear. In civil proceedings, where children are generally involved as claimants, if no litigation friend can be found, the case does not proceed. In the criminal process, some form of appropriate adult will be found to enable the process to go ahead against the child, regardless of whether the adult really is appropriate. Having 'advisers' who are chosen not by their aptitude and training but by their relationship to the interviewee is perhaps most obviously an odd manifestation of the parental role when the parent is among the last people one would choose. Appeals on this basis sometimes succeed. In *DPP v Blake*,[44] a girl arrested for arson confessed in an interview where her estranged father had been called as appropriate adult, notwithstanding her having made it clear that the person she wanted present was her social worker, not him. However, the local social workers had a policy of refusing to attend as appropriate adult if a parent was available. The estranged father took no active part in the interview and was not within the meaning of an appropriate adult. The Divisional Court therefore excluded the girl's confession. By contrast, in *R v W*, the Court of Appeal declined to exclude a 13-year-old girl's admissions because the 'appropriate adult', the girl's mother, was herself 'mentally subnormal and illiterate' and would herself require an appropriate adult were she questioned.[45] Perhaps part of the reason that the process is capable of encompassing these situations is that the child who is inappropriately 'advised' by a parent is unlikely to be able to object, either at the time or later, since they are unlikely to have the parental support without which it is difficult for children to do anything at all.

More recently, however, there have been signs of a change of approach towards children's formal rights in the criminal process. In *R v Hussain*,[46] a man of 42,

[44]   89 Cr App R 179 DC; [1989] 1 WLR 432.
[45]   [1994] Crim LR 130.
[46]   [2005] EWCA Crim 31.

who had been convicted in 1978 at the age of 16 of the murder of his baby brother, succeeded in his appeal where the only direct evidence against him was a confession made after his arrest and questioning in the absence of an appropriate adult. Two social workers were later found to attend the police station, but his claim that he had made the confession as a result of threats and racial abuse from the police was not believed at trial. However, in 2005 the Court of Appeal, applying modern rules, found that the breaches of the Judges' Rules should have rendered the confession inadmissible. When an adult did attend, it was his father—who was of course also the father of the boy who had just died violently, and the most likely suspect were the appellant to have been innocent. The interventions of the social workers included inappropriate questions to the boy. Longmore LJ said:

> Any useful advice would mainly have been that Abid [Hussain] should consult a solicitor; no social worker would or should take it on himself to give legal advice.[47]

Later, however, he blurred the distinction and spoke of 'how important the presence of a solicitor or an appropriate adult is', explaining how they would have gone on to advise him as to whether to continue to be interviewed,[48] and went on further to speak of 'the absence of a solicitor, the absence of an independent adult and the failure to caution'. Although the appeal was allowed largely on the greater understanding of the vulnerability of young people since the trial, the idea that a young person might be interviewed on a murder charge with the presence only of an appropriate adult is countenanced further later on as well.[49] It might be thought, however, that the minimum appropriate lay advice and participation where a charge of murder is involved would involve giving anyone very strong advice to remain silent whilst awaiting a solicitor, so that parents who allowed children to assume that parental presence and advice was sufficient were only demonstrating their own inappropriateness.

The same idea that a child needs parental help obtained in *R (K) v Parole Board*, where a boy of 14 who had no adult help in applying for parole sought judicial review of the decision not to release him.[50] The Court held that failing even to have 'the opportunity to show his product to some well-meaning adult' rendered his right to make representations 'nugatory', and specifically that it:

> compares unfavourably with the well-known safeguards afforded to children, through the presence of an appropriate adult, in interviews by the police.

McCombe J passed over the issue of whether the advice should be necessarily given by someone likely to understand drafting and paperwork, saying: 'in some cases, I was given to understand, formal legal advice may be available under the

---

[47] *Ibid*, at [40].
[48] *Ibid*, at [45].
[49] *Ibid*, at [48] and [49].
[50] *R (on the application of K) v Parole Board* [2006] EWHC 2413 (Admin).

legal aid scheme'. Even if that were not available, he thought it would be necessary, as well as impliedly sufficient, to offer 'a well-meaning adult in putting the child's "best foot forward"'. The case demonstrates well the particularly awkward situation of a child. K had taken GCSEs and been involved in the Duke of Edinburgh's award scheme whilst in prison. A large part of his problem in being released related to anxieties about his falling back into gangland crimes once he returned home, especially as his father was generally in prison. K was particularly confused by the suggestion that, as on release 'he would be returned to a family in which the male members are pro-criminal role models', in effect his very progress whilst in detention worked against his application.

Human rights legislation has also altered the position. Where the police decide to deal with a child's criminal offence by way of caution,[51] parental consent must be obtained. This is satisfied in the case of a child in care by the consent of the local authority, because they have parental responsibility.[52] However, *R v Durham Constabulary*[53] illustrated the potential for parental 'advice' to leave children vulnerable in the case of a warning, although here the parent also felt inadequately treated. A boy of 14 had been 'pinging' girls' bra-straps at school and harassing them sexually in a way described by the boy as 'horseplay'. He was arrested and his stepfather attended as appropriate adult. They both declined the attendance of a solicitor and the boy admitted the offences so that he could be formally warned, rather than prosecuted. The Court said that the stepfather:

> was recorded as being supportive of police action, which had taught R a lesson and possibly prevented him getting into more serious trouble.[54]

However, in 'an unfortunate departure' from the guidance, neither was warned that the boy would then have to go on the Sex Offenders Register. In discussing whether the boy's appeal under Article 6 of the European Convention on Human Rights (ECHR) should succeed, Baroness Hale of Richmond referred to the process in its wider context and addressed the emotional interactions between parent and child, speaking of 'the pressure, whether implicit or explicit,which is put upon the young person to "admit it and we'll let you off with a caution". Explicit pressure would invalidate the admission and thus the caution; ... but the implicit pressure is always there'.[55] Discussing the need for 'children's admissions to be voluntary and reliable, as adults', she said: 'Corners should not be cut just because the offender is a child.'[56]

---

[51]   This entails an admission of guilt by a defendant, and goes on a criminal record.

[52]   If a child is a ward of court (as children in care before the advent of the Children Act 1989 commonly were), the consent of the wardship court is required: *Re A (a minor) (wardship: criminal proceedings)* [1989] 3 All ER 610.

[53]   *R (on the application of R) v Durham Constabulary and another* [2005] UKHL 21.

[54]   *Ibid*, at [10].

[55]   *Ibid*.

[56]   *Ibid*, at [46]. Revised guidance now requires that children and their parents, carers or other appropriate adult have access to information about the options available, including the final warning

It does appear that the appropriate adult system invites and even implements the cutting of corners. Moreover, as before, a child who suffers a loss of procedural rights as a result will be unlikely to be able to pursue redress without the support of the parent. Only where a parent regrets their actions, or is obviously very incompetent, can the child pursue an appeal, and even then the court may regard the parental role as one closer to the control element of policing than to the protective, forgiving role of the parent, or consider that the child had all the appropriate assistance in any event. Those aspects of the criminal process in which there is a particular role for parents, in theory and in practice, are thus clearly unsatisfactory. That children would be disadvantaged by being subjected to the adult process, and thus that they need extra protection or support, is clearly perceived, even if the Strasbourg Court had not made it necessary.[57]

The appropriate adult role has not been clearly analysed, however, so that the problem for those performing that role is not merely that the role's requirements may not have been sufficiently explained to them, but also that they are unclear and thus somewhat inexplicable. Perhaps the incommensurability of the real role with the lack of will to ensure that it is properly fulfilled lies behind this. Parry has suggested that '[e]quating the appropriate adult with a parental role is at the heart of the problem', because although PACE foresees that they will monitor procedural fairness, 'it is doubtful whether they are equipped to really influence substantive or procedural aspects of the process';[58] White comments that 'the functions of an appropriate adult and a solicitor are similar', but few parents are equipped to function as solicitors.[59] The provision of specially trained social workers in all cases might be helpful, but would clearly present problems of resources.[60] There is no sign of political will to improve this process, although if the courts were readier and more consistent in excluding evidence obtained as a result of poor support for children within the process, as White has suggested, that might have to change. As with civil proceedings, there is no formal requirement that the child be supported by a parent, but there is unlikely to be anyone else to do it. An unwilling or incapable parent will probably mean that civil proceedings do not happen. In criminal proceedings, it may mean anything up to facilitating the oppression of the child, within the meaning of the Act, so that what the child says is excluded from the admissible evidence.[61]

scheme and its consequences before they are asked whether they admit an offence: see 'Final Warning Scheme: Guidance of the Police and Youth Offending Teams' (2002) [4.14].

[57] *T v UK* 30 EHRR 121.

[58] R Gwynnedd Parry, 'Protecting the juvenile suspect: what exactly is the appropriate adult supposed to do?' [2006] 18 *CFLQ* 373, 383.

[59] C White, 'Reassessing the social worker's role as an appropriate adult' (2002) *JSWFL* 55; and *R v Lewis* [1996] Crim LR 260.

[60] Pierpoint in her recent study emphasises the keenness of the Home Office to use volunteers: H Pierpoint, 'Survey of Volunteer Appropriate Adult Services in England and Wales' (2004) *Youth Justice* 32.

[61] Police and Criminal Evidence Act 1984 s 76.

FAMILY LAW

The position of parents in family proceedings is fraught with awkwardness. The Children Act 1989 represents the philosophy of its time: gestated in an age of individualism, it ostensibly put the child at the centre of all proceedings about the family and apparently ended the division that had previously existed:

> the Act created a single code, whether the proceedings directly involve the State ('public law') or are initiated by a private individual.[62]

However, the procedural structures still reflect different branches of the law. Parental representation is reasonable if one assumes that children always wish to defend the integrity of the family, and that that is in their interests, and that parents always wish to, and can, support children. Where, however, parental representation may be inadequate or inappropriate, it appears that the process may in reality be focused on preserving the appearance that families and parents are always good, even where the proceedings will go on to establish that, in the particular case, they are not.

Private Law Proceedings

Parents 'representing' children in proceedings would be vindicating parental rights to the custody and control of children. Children were historically useful as labour, at home or as a source of income by being hired out elsewhere, or as the vehicle for property transactions in marriage in a different social class. The intact family was the model and the legal fact; there was no question of children's being represented by proxies for their individual persons. Ideas about children's welfare, and a growing perception that parents did not always know or do what was good for their children, together with the rise of ideas about individual rights, did lead eventually, however, to the idea of children having their own place in the process, although having an equivalent place to that of parents was, apparently unexpectedly, somewhat shocking.

Things were simpler when the family was represented only through the father. The attribution of legal personality to married women also used to cause scandal. *Agar-Ellis* is generally cited as the high- (or low-) water mark of paternal power,[63] although the nature of parental rights was never clear: 'No part of our old law was more disjointed and incomplete than that which deals with the guardianship of

---

[62]   S Cretney, *Family Law in the Twentieth Century* (Oxford, Oxford University Press, 2003) 724.

[63]   'It is for the general interest of families, and for the general interest of children, and really for the interest of the particular infant, that the Court should not except in very extreme cases interfere with the discretion of the father but leave to him the responsibility of exercising that power which nature has given him' (Cotton LJ); and 'It is not the benefit of the infant as conceived by the court, but it must be for the benefit to the infant having regard to the natural law which points out that the father knows far better as a rule what is good for his children than a court of justice can' (Bowen LJ): *Agar-Ellis v Agar-Ellis* (1883) 24 Ch D 317 at 334 and 337–8.

infants.'[64] The rise of ideas of women's rights and a growing perception that children's welfare was a valid consideration in family proceedings were part of the gradual development of the way in which the legal structure reflected family structure.[65] The quasi-proprietorial rules about parents and children were further overlaid with a welfare-oriented legislative structure.[66] The child's point of view, or at least an independent (ie non-parental) assessment of the child's situation, was provided by apparently neutral Court Welfare Officers, who would interview, assess and present their own social-work-trained views of how the family should be reorganised.

Whilst it is perhaps surprising that the rule of law that the father was the natural guardian of his legitimate children was abolished as late as 1991,[67] this date was also the high (or low) point of the idea that the child had a separate legal personality. The rules of *locus standi* in private law children proceedings contained in the Children Act 1989 replaced the traditional paternal/parental structure by something much looser and more individualistic, giving the greatest rights of standing to legal parents and then step-parents, long-standing carers and, finally, potentially to anyone, including the child concerned.[68] This last, breaking entirely with the traditional family and its structure (which is nowhere mentioned in the Children Act 1989, not even in the 'welfare checklist'[69]), led to the 'children divorcing their parents' scandal of the early mid-1990s, and to a reaction against it, led by the courts, that coincided with a reinstatement of the traditional model of the family, with strong parental status and effective rights, as necessarily good.[70]

Paternal representation thus became parental representation and then passed via increased social work involvement to a solidified view of well-functioning family arrangements, which the legal structure supported. This meant, explicitly, replicating and reinforcing parents' responsibilities (that is, their traditional legal rights), which, according to high authority, would change their hearts and minds

---

[64] Pollock and Maitland, above n 3, 443.

[65] The Custody of Children Act 1891 allowed the courts to refuse *habeas corpus* applications by runaways' parents whom they found to have forfeited their rights to custody, and the Guardianship of Infants Act 1925 put 'the welfare of the child' at its head, obliging courts to treat it as 'the first and paramount consideration'.

[66] See, eg the Guardianship of Minors Act 1971, the Guardianship Act 1973 and the Family Law Reform Act 1987.

[67] Children Act 1989 s 2(4).

[68] Children Act 1989 s 10. A child would need a litigation friend (see civil proceedings, above) unless they were competent (s 10(8) CA 189;, Family Proceedings Rules 1991 r 9.2A and Family Proceedings Magistrates Courts Rules 1991 r 4.12,.

[69] Children Act 1989 s 1(3).

[70] This itself had eventually to swing back: *Re L, V, M, H (contact: domestic violence)* [2000] 2 FCR 404. See also C Sawyer, 'The competence of children to participate in family proceedings' [1995] 7 *CFLQ* 180.

and make them conform to the ideal.[71] This is in keeping with the historical structure of family law, which, as Eekelaar has said, is ambivalent about parental rights;[72] it looks to the child's separate personality or the overall power and responsibility of the Crown as well as the position of parents. Perhaps, rather than the introduction of the adversarial process into the private family that so often attracts criticism, what has really happened is that the Crown as *parens patriae* has been first embodied in the ecclesiastical model of family governance[73] and then usurped or reinforced by the social work profession.

Care Proceedings

The cultural origins of care proceedings are entirely different from those of the private law process. Whereas private law reflects the ecclesiastical construction of the family, overriding individuals in favour of the pursuit of an ideal, care proceedings deal with young people whose lives are going wrong. Whilst there are some clear distinctions between children who are neglected and those who offend,[74] the overall process, and its historical roots, are the same for both.[75] Whether the children are characterised as victims of neglect or as individually evil may depend on the swing of the political pendulum; the result is a decision about the position of children which depends very little on the children's views, and in which the place of parents has always been ambiguous.

The ambiguity about children whose parental care is unsuccessful is not new. Medieval orphans were absorbed into local guilds or taken into religious communities; later, support by parishes was formalised in the Poor Laws.[76] 'Child-saving' movements arose in the late eighteenth and nineteenth centuries,[77] and the criminal law began to incorporate offences that parents could commit against children, demonstrating a growing perception of some form of individual identity in the child which the state would protect *against* parents if need be. However, the orders available for dealing with offending and neglected children

---

[71] 'If a father is granted parental responsibility, then that will no doubt encourage him to behave in a responsible way to those children': *Re P (Parental Responsibility)* [1997] 2 FLR 722 at 729 (Woolf LJ).

[72] J Eekelaar, 'What are parental rights' (1973) 89 *LQR* 210, 215.

[73] See especially Matrimonial Causes Act 1857 s XXII.

[74] Notably in Children Act 1989 s 25: *Re M (Secure Accommodation Order)* [1995] 1 FLR 418; see also Crime and Disorder Act 1998 s 12(6)(a).

[75] Moreover, the results have been liable to be punitive in both cases: see A Levy and B Kahan, *The Pindown Experience and the Protection of Children* (Staffordshire, Staffordshire County Council, 1991); and B Corby *et al*, *Residential child care and the child abuse inquiries: research report I* (Liverpool Business School, Centre for Public Service Management, 1998).

[76] A series of Acts between 1536 and 1601; see generally I Pinchbeck and M Hewitt, *Children in English Society Vol I From Tudor Times to the Eighteenth Century* (London, Routledge and Kegan Paul, 1969).

[77] I Pinchbeck and M Hewitt, *Children in English Society: Vol II From the Eighteenth Century to the Children Act 1948* (London, Routledge and Kegan Paul, 1973) 419.

were largely similar. The Children and Young Persons Act 1933 consolidated in legislation the conflation of the offending and the abused and arguably paved the way for the social abandonment of children in care to whatever 'punishment' the state appeared to find appropriate.[78] Parents' responsibility for their children's condition appeared to be a secondary or incidental issue, thus obscuring any potential for the family as an institution to fail the individual child.

After the Second World War, public concern about children in state care led to the Children Act 1948, but there were few changes to the legislative structure or detail. By the time of the White Papers of 1965 and 1968, however, offending in children was defined as resulting from neglect—that is, not their fault—so that their treatment within the legal process ought to take the form not of criminal prosecution, but of civil care proceedings. Politically, however, change proved unacceptable, and the delinquency framework of the 1933 Act remained in force, even when the perspective had moved away from attribution of blame towards a medicalised model of the process.[79]

The proceedings being technically between the state and the child, the parents did not formally appear within the process, but effectively exercised the parental right of representing the child in the legal proceedings against the child. Solicitors acting for children in care cases where a child had been abused by parents could find themselves, in practice, taking instructions on the child's case from the very parents against whom the state sought to protect the child.[80] Insofar as the case was about curtailing parents' rights, because of their failure to socialise the children, the parents' effective defence of themselves reflected Widgery J's remark in the *Worthing Justices* case that the 'real issue is nearly always between the local authority and the parent'. The illogic and injustice was apparent, and a process had developed whereby magistrates who heard care cases also granted legal aid orders to allow parents separate representation from the child. This inventive solution was brought to an end by the Divisional Court, despite Widgery J's commendation of its 'common sense'.[81]

Public idealisation of parents was changing, however, and this began to affect the legal process. The legislation in force immediately before the 1989 Act was the Children and Young Persons Act 1969 and the Child Care Act 1980. The scope of these, as Dingwall *et al* point out, was 'more or less the same as that of the legislation at the turn of the century'.[82] In the 1960s, however, doctors had

---

[78] It is interesting to note that to this day, and despite suggestion that it be changed, works on child abuse such as *The Pindown Experience and the Protection of Children* (Levy and Kahan, 1991) are filed by the Bodleian law Library under 535 (crime) rather than 520 (persons).

[79] A Allen and A Morton, *This Is Your Child: The Story of the National Society for the Prevention of Cruelty to Children* (London, Routledge and Kegan Paul, 1961) 72.

[80] L Hilgendorf, *Social Workers and Solicitors in Child Care Cases* (London, HMSO, 1981); and R Dingwall, J Eekelaar and T Murray, *The Protection of Children: State Intervention and Family Life* (Oxford, Blackwell, 1983) especially ch 8.

[81] *R v Worthing Justices, ex p Stevenson* [1976] 2 All ER 194.

[82] R Dingwall, J Eekelaar and T Murray, 'Childhood as a Social Problem: A Survey of the History of Legal Regulation' (1984) 11 *Journal of Law and Society* 207, 220.

discovered the phenomenon of 'baby-battering',[83] and by the 1970s it was a cause for widespread public concern. However, what changed care proceedings, and especially the structure of parental representation, was one of those scandals that occasionally rock the nation.[84] The mother and stepfather of seven-year-old Maria Colwell succeeded, in an unreported and unopposed hearing in which only they (speaking for Maria) and the local authority, who did not contest the application, were represented, in having her returned home to them from local authority care. Maria's stepfather killed her.[85] Following that case, section 64 of the Children Act 1975 provided that parents were not to be treated as representing the child in care proceedings, and that instead the relevant adult would be a guardian *ad litem.* After a period during which the appointment of a guardian was discretionary as a matter of law and awkward in practice, panels of professional Guardians ad Litem—trained social workers—were provided at public expense under section 20 of the Children Act 1975. Their role was to assess the child's situation independently for the court, putting in essence the view that Maria might have put had she been in a position to formulate and express it. Thus, in care proceedings, while the basic structure of the criminal process— proceedings between the state and the child, in a magistrates' court—remained, the parental role was taken over by social workers.

The practical position of parents however remained uncertain. The Legal Aid Act 1974 provided for legal aid 'for the purpose of taking such a part in the proceedings as may be allowed by the rules of court'.[86] Courts, however, frequently gave parents rights within the process which the rules did not allow for. Under section 65 of the Children Act 1965, where an order was made under section 64 that the parent was not to be treated as representing the child, because of a conflict of interest, the parent could be given legal aid in order to take part in the proceedings. However, it was not until the Children and Young Persons (Amendment) Act 1986 was implemented in 1988 that parents properly gained a right to be parties and to have legal aid. The right to party status and representation as a matter of course came only with the implementation of the Children Act 1989, which also ended the 'parental rights resolution' procedure that had allowed local authorities to terminate parents' rights without any court process at all.[87]

---

[83]   CH Kempe *et al,* 'The Battered Child Syndrome' (1962) 181 *Journal of the American Medical Association* 17.

[84]   Department of Health and Social Security, 'Child Abuse: a Study of Inquiry Reports' (1982); for examples, see 'A Child in Trust' (Wembley, London Borough of Brent, 1985); and 'A Child in Mind' (London, London Borough of Greenwich, 1987).

[85]   Department of Health and Social Security, 'Report of the Committee of Enquiry into the Care and Supervision provided in relation to Maria Colwell' (1974).

[86]   Legal Aid Act 1974 s 28(6A).

[87]   That procedure had been deprecated by the European Court of Human Rights: *R v UK* (1987) 10 EHRR 74. These changes coincided, however, with the beginning of the end for legal aid.

An alternative process for removing children from their parents' care was in common use before the Children Act 1989. Wardship originated to deal with those medieval children who were important to their families as conduits for the transmission or accumulation of family wealth through the generations. Having begun as a process to protect property, wardship had evolved a jurisdiction which also looked to protection of the child's welfare.[88] The process was easy to use, since proceedings were commenced ex parte by the local authority; the child would immediately become a ward of the court. The courts were accustomed to granting such applications by local authorities.[89] A temporary decision would be taken immediately as to the child's living arrangements pending a more carefully prepared *inter partes* hearing. Thereafter, the child generally remained the court's child until the age of majority unless the wardship was discharged earlier, which it rarely was. Any step in the child's life, such as a change of accommodation or medical treatment, had to be approved by the High Court. The advantages of wardship proceedings to family members were that everyone's view could be put and that legal aid was generally granted to parents.[90] Although the loss of formal custody was often adverted to as the major philosophical problem with wardship, some felt, however, that the burden on the legal aid fund exercised legislators at least as much. The Children Act 1989 abruptly ended wardship on the grand scale.[91]

Following the 1989 Act, which provided that the court should appoint a guardian *ad litem* for the child in all 'specified' (broadly speaking, public law) proceedings unless it was satisfied that the child's welfare would be adequately safeguarded without one,[92] the use of guardians *ad litem* became almost universal in care proceedings. The functioning of care proceedings was the subject of some considerable study, examining, for example, how social workers and solicitors, or guardians and solicitors, actually worked together.[93] The concern was however the position of children rather than that of their parents; if local authority care is appropriate, the parents have failed in their role, and there is often a feeling that the existence of the proceedings itself indicates parental 'guilt', which perhaps

---

[88]   N Lowe and R White, *Wards of Court* (2nd edn, London, Barry Rose, 1986).

[89]   J Masson and M Shaw, 'The use of wardship by local authorities' (1989) 52 *MLR* 762.

[90]   The legal aid rates paid for wardship were the High Court civil rates, higher than the civil rates for Guardianship of Minors work and substantially higher than the matrimonial rates. Notably, notwithstanding the contemporary hyperbole about the importance of children and their proceedings, when children work was transferred wholesale out of wardship and into proceedings under the Children Act 1989, it was also transferred down to the much lower matrimonial rates of pay.

[91]   Children Act 1989 s 100.

[92]   Children Act 1989 s 41.

[93]   I. Hilgendorf, above n 81; M Murch, J Hunt and A Macleod, *The Representation of the Child in Civil Proceedings* (Bristol, Socio-Legal Centre for Family Studies, 1990); M Murch and D Hooper, *The Family Justice System* (Bristol, Family Law, Jordans, 1992); and D Clark, 'The Older Child in Care Proceedings' (1996) 26 *Family Law* 113. The Social Services Inspectorate conducted a study concluding that they were 'generally highly professional': R Ingleby, 'Review of Murch and Hooper (1992)' (1993) 56 *MLR* 766.

explains the sidelining of their role in representing their children or defending their family function.

The publicly-funded Guardian Ad Litem (GAL) system, despite almost universal praise, was integrated in principle with that of the rather different Court Welfare Service following proposals from a range of government departments in the late 1990s. The resulting CAFCASS (Children and Family Courts Advisory and Support Service) continues to be beset by resources issues. The current debate is, again, about how to hear the view of the individual child, rather than that of the parents.[94]

CONCLUSION

The parental right to represent a child in legal proceedings suggests that parental responsibility should be reflected in the legal process. This assumes, however, that parents are necessarily good for children and that they are always willing and capable of fulfilling their parental role properly, which is often not the case. The representative role may also be so unclear or beset by conflict that no one can really say what it is. It may be asking more of parents, on behalf of children, than parents can deliver, and lead to conflicts among the rights of parents, the rights of children and the risk of expense and administrative inconvenience in the legal process.

In civil proceedings, parental responsibility is generally barely touched upon by the legal process: the process requires its fulfilment in most cases until the child reaches majority, and although it may be filled by others than parents, generally that does not happen. In criminal proceedings, the primary offender is the child, and the process is as ambivalent about the parental role within the process as it is about parents' responsibility for the child's offending. Confusion and unfairness surrounds what the legal process allows or requires of parents and what they do as appropriate adults. Family proceedings, however, represent the greatest potential for irreconcilable theoretical and practical conflict. The family should not be before the court, so the parental role has broken down somewhere. Within care proceedings, parental involvement and exclusion reflect the widest range of concerns, to protect family structure in general and maintain practical parental responsibility for looking after children (thus minimising state responsibility and public expense), whilst also protecting children who are victim to parental abuse or incapability. The perceived damaging effect of the legal process in family proceedings, whether it is perceived as responsible for furthering personal conflict in private law or for delay in public law, means that there is a further impetus besides potential expense to reduce the potential for parental involvement in defence of both that individual parent's position and the parental role in general.

---

[94]   L Davis, 'Children in Court' (2007) *Family Law* 37.

The legal process is not a place where parental responsibility can generally shine. Save for the civil process, where the parent may support the child in obtaining compensation for some external problem, the very existence of legal proceedings generally indicates some failure of the parental role. The court process is where the social expectations of parental responsibility confront its failures and expose the potential for failure in the execution of parental responsibility generally, often to the detriment of children. Underlying the debate, and often unexposed, is an ambivalence about the relative importance of individual rights within the family in the context of at least keeping up the appearance of a well-functioning social order.

13

Parental Responsibility and Children's Partnership Choices

REBECCA PROBERT

INTRODUCTION

IN AN AGE when many couples are in their 30s before tying the knot, when fewer than 3 per cent of brides marry as teenagers[1] and when more men marry over the age of 85 than under the age of 18, it is easy to overlook the role accorded to those with parental responsibility in the making of marriage. Yet the issue of parental consent to marriage was for many years an important element of parental responsibility, and it offers an insight into the way in which attitudes to parent–child relations have changed over the centuries. Furthermore, the question of how the responsible parent deals with the issue of consent to marriage is one that has recently been revived in the context of forced marriages, requiring the courts to consider the boundaries of what is reasonable, and when legal intervention is necessary to prevent an abuse of parental power.

The first part of this chapter considers precisely what powers parental responsibility confers in this context: what is the role of parental consent in the making of marriage? Whose consent is required, and to whose marriages?[2] How may the requirement be challenged or evaded? The second part then examines what has been expected of a responsible parent in this context and how this has changed over time. This goes beyond the question of the responsible exercise of the right to consent, and requires consideration of the degree of influence that it is deemed acceptable for a parent to exercise over the choice of a spouse.

---

[1] Office for National Statistics, 'Marriage, Divorce and Adoption Statistics: Review of the Registrar General on Marriages and Divorces in 2005, and Adoptions in 2006, in England and Wales', Series FM2 No 33 (Newport, ONS, 2008) Table 3.19.

[2] Brief mention will be made of the role of consent in the making of civil partnerships, although the shorter history of such relationships provides little scope for analysis in this context.

WHAT POWERS DOES PARENTAL RESPONSIBILITY CONFER?

The Legal Role of Consent

Parents have been accorded an official role in the making of their children's marriages since at least the beginning of the seventeenth century, although the extent of their influence has varied over time. The canon law, as codified in 1604, required that parental consent[3] be given to the marriages of minor children: while a failure to obtain parental consent did not render the marriage void, the rules meant that those seeking to marry without parental consent had to find a clergyman willing to marry them clandestinely.[4] When the law of marriage was put on a statutory basis by the Clandestine Marriages Act 1753, the role of parents was enhanced: a marriage by licence entered into by a minor without parental consent was void.[5] Parents also had the power to prevent a marriage taking place by forbidding the banns;[6] however, once a marriage by banns had taken place, it was valid even if parental consent had not been given.

The case law on the 1753 Act reveals a number of runaway matches, but it was relatively rare for parents to mount a legal challenge to a marriage on the basis that they had not given their consent. Indeed, it was the strategic use of the invalidating provisions of the Act by those who wanted a way out of their marriages that accounted for the bulk of the case law and provided the motivation for reform in the 1820s.[7] The solution eventually adopted in the Marriage Act 1823 was to provide that certain specified defects would only render the marriage void if the parties had 'knowingly and wilfully' failed to comply with certain provisions.[8] This of course meant that marriages by banns might still be found to be void if the parties had, in an attempt to avoid knowledge of the intended marriage reaching their parents, had the banns called in the wrong names.[9] But the lack of parental consent to marriages by licence no longer rendered such marriages void, even if the parties had knowingly and wilfully married without it.[10] By way of deterrence, however, it was provided that

---

[3]   Or, if the parents were deceased, that of the child's guardians: canon 100. See E Gibson, *Codex juris ecclesiastici Anglicani* (London, 1713) 507.

[4]   And would be subject to ecclesiastical censure: see, eg M Kinnear, 'The Correction Court in the Diocese of Carlisle, 1704–1756' (1990) 59 *Church History* 191; and MF Snape, *The Church of England in Industrialising Society: The Lancashire Parish of Whalley in the Eighteenth Century* (Woodbridge, The Boydell Press, 2003) 116.

[5]   Clandestine Marriages Act 1753 s 11. See further R Probert, *Marriage Law and Practice in the Long Eighteenth Century: A Reassessment* (Cambridge, Cambridge University Press, 2009) ch 6.

[6]   *Ibid*, s 3.

[7]   See R Probert, 'The Judicial Interpretation of Lord Hardwicke's Act of 1753' (2002) 23 *Journal of Legal History* 129.

[8]   Clandestine Marriages Act 1753 s 22.

[9]   See, eg *Wiltshire v Prince* (1830) 162 ER 1176; *Tongue v Allen* (1835) 163 ER 13; and *Orme v Holloway* (1847) 5 Notes of Cases 267.

[10]   This was clear from the absence of any annulling provision: see the discussion in *R v The Inhabitants of Birmingham* (1828) 108 ER 954.

minors[11] who obtained a licence by false oaths—for example, by swearing that the parties were of age or had parental consent—might forfeit the property that would otherwise accrue to them by virtue of the marriage.[12] Provision was made for the settlement of the forfeited property, modelled upon the powers of the Court of Chancery in wardship cases.[13] Similar provisions were included in the Marriage Act 1836 when the option of civil marriage, or marriage according to the rites of other denominations, was introduced.[14]

Apart from the provision relating to the forfeiture of property—which was abolished in 1949—this remains the approach of the current law: the Marriage Act 1949, which consolidated the previous law, provides that it will not be necessary to prove that parental consent has been given to the marriage of a minor, and that no evidence may be given to prove the contrary 'in any proceedings touching the validity of the marriage'.[15] Yet this does not mean that the requirement of parental consent has *no* legal role to play: active parental *dissent* may render the marriage void. If the marriage is celebrated according to Anglican rites, the fact that the person whose consent is required has publicly dissented to the calling of the banns means that the banns are void,[16] and so would be the marriage of a couple who knowingly and wilfully intermarried after such dissent has been expressed (in the unlikely event of their finding a minister willing to marry them).[17] Similarly, if any caveat is entered to the granting of a licence, no licence can be granted until the objection has been investigated and dismissed:[18] again, even assuming that a marriage could take place, it would be void if the parties knew that no licence had been granted.[19] In the case of non-Anglican marriages—whether religious or civil—the person whose consent is required may forbid the issue of a superintendent registrar's certificate,

> and where the issue of a certificate has been so forbidden, the notice of marriage and all proceedings thereon shall be void.[20]

Like much of the law of marriage, therefore, the significance of the requirement of parental consent lies in its preventative role, rather than in its effect on

---

[11] Except widows and widowers.

[12] Marriage Act 1823 s 23. The provision also applied to marriages by banns, although in such cases only one party would have flouted the law, otherwise the marriage would not be valid.

[13] See, eg *A-G v Clements* (1871) LR 12 Eq 32; and *AG v Read* (1871) LR 12 Eq 38. See further R Probert, 'Control over Marriage in England and Wales, 1753–1823: The Clandestine Marriages Act of 1753 in Context' (2009) 27 *Law and History Review* 413.

[14] Marriage Act 1836 s 10 (necessary for minors to have the consent of those persons whose consent would have been required for marriage by licence); and s 43 (forfeiture of property).

[15] Marriage Act 1949 s 48(1).

[16] *Ibid*, s 3(3).

[17] Marriage Act 1949 s 25(c).

[18] Marriage Act 1949 s 16(2).

[19] Marriage Act 1949 s 25(b).

[20] Marriage Act 1949 s 30. Similarly, it is provided that a civil partnership will be void if the issue of the civil partnership schedule has been forbidden by a person whose consent is required: Civil Partnership Act 2004 Sch 2, para 6(5).

marriages that have actually taken place.[21] As the Law Commission stressed when it examined the law regarding the solemnisation of marriage, the aim of a sound marriage law should be to prevent, rather than undo, marriages that run counter to the policy of the law.[22] Whether the law has been effective in preventing marriages without parental consent is considered further below.

Whose Consent?

Just as the impact of a failure to obtain consent has varied over time, so too have the persons whose consent is required. The canon law spoke of 'parents', but a guardian appointed by the father's will enjoyed priority over a mother.[23] Under the hierarchy established by the 1753 Act, it was primarily the role of the father to give consent; if he had died then it was the responsibility of any guardian appointed by the father's will; if none had been appointed the mother was entitled to give her consent (assuming she had not remarried, in which case she lost this right); and in the absence of any of the above persons the consent of a guardian appointed by the Court of Chancery was sufficient.[24] The Act also provided that the necessary consent could be deemed, if the Lord Chancellor so decreed, where the person whose consent was required was *non compos mentis*,[25] and also allowed the Lord Chancellor to give his consent to a proposed marriage if a mother or guardian (but not a father) was abroad.[26]

Yet not all parents had the power to give (or refuse) consent. The courts decided that parents who were not married to each other had no power either to give consent to a marriage by licence or to forbid a marriage by banns.[27] As Sir William Scott pronounced in *Horner v Liddiard*,[28] such a privilege should not be given to 'those who bear the title of parents as a title of discredit and disability'. Members of the royal family were (and still are) excluded from the legislation; for them the consent of the sovereign was more important than the consent of a parent, especially after the passage of the Royal Marriages Act 1772, which provided that if any descendant of George II married without the consent of the

---

[21]   See, eg the discussion in *Tejani v The Superintendent Registrar for the District of Peterborough* [1986] IRLR 502.

[22]   Law Commission, 'Family Law: Report on Solemnisation of Marriage in England and Wales' (Law Com No 53, 1973) [49].

[23]   *Mr Justice Eyre v Countess of Shaftsbury* (1722) 24 ER 659.

[24]   Clandestine Marriages Act 1753 s 11.

[25]   Clandestine Marriages Act 1753 s 12.

[26]   There was also scope for a refusal of consent to be challenged: see below, text at nn 55 *ff*.

[27]   Although this was a matter of some debate in the early cases: see *R v The Inhabitants of Edmonton; R v The Inhabitants of Hodnett* (1786) 99 ER 993; and note *Fielder v Smith* (1816) 161 ER 712.

[28]   (1799) 161 ER 573.

Sovereign, the marriage would be void.[29] Jews and Quakers, likewise excluded from the scope of the 1753 Act, similarly lacked any legal power to prevent their minor children from marrying,[30] until the Marriage Act 1836 imposed uniform civil preliminaries on all marrying according to non-Anglican rites.

The hierarchy of consents established in 1753 remained in place until the twentieth century, but the increasing legal power accorded to mothers eventually necessitated changes. The Guardianship of Infants Act 1925[31] included a complex provision identifying whose consent was necessary in different circumstances. If the parents of a legitimate child were living together, both had to consent; if they had divorced or separated, the consent of the person to whom custody had been committed was necessary; and if one had deserted the other, the consent of the deserted parent alone was required. If both parents had been deprived of custody, the law required the consent of the person to whose custody the child had been committed. If the child had been born outside marriage, the consent of the mother alone was required. As under the 1753 Act, the necessary consent could be dispensed with in certain circumstances. These too were simplified and modernised: the necessity of a certain person's consent could be dispensed with if it could not be obtained by reason of their absence, inaccessibility or disability.[32] If this person was the only person whose consent was necessary, the Registrar General might dispense with the requirement of consent; alternatively, the court might grant consent. If there was another person whose consent was required, a superintendent registrar might dispense with the consent of the person who was unavailable to give consent.

These provisions were replicated in the Marriage Act 1949, but later changes have been made in the wake of successive reforms to child law.[33] The shift from parental rights to parental responsibility in the Children Act 1989 resulted in a change in terminology, and the consent of *any* parent with parental responsibility became sufficient,[34] reflecting the legislation's policy that parental responsibility could be exercised unilaterally. If a residence order or care order is in place, the consent of the person in whose favour the residence order has been made, or of the relevant local authority, is required.[35] The Adoption and Children Act 2002

---

[29] Royal Marriages Act 1772 s 1. For a detailed analysis, see SM Cretney, 'Royal Marriages: Some Legal and Constitutional Issues' (2008) 124 *LQR* 218.

[30] Although this did not mean that they lacked other means of control, and in *Goldsmid v Bromer* (1798) 161 ER 568, the Consistory Court upheld the right of a Jewish father to challenge his daughter's marriage: 'every parent is deeply interested in the welfare of his children, as affected by such connexions; and has a right to question a matrimonial contract entered into in the minority of his child.'

[31] See Cretney, above n 29, 569–73.

[32] Guardianship of Infants Act 1925 s 9(1)(a).

[33] For the corresponding requirements relating to civil partners, see Civil Partnership Act Sch 2, para 1.

[34] Marriage Act 1949 s 3(1A)(a)(i).

[35] The consent of the person in whose favour a residence order had been made would be required *instead* of that of a parent; while the consent of the local authority would be required *in addition* to that of each parent in so far as their parental responsibility had not been restricted under Children Act 1989 s 33(3).

added special guardians to the list of those who may consent,[36] and provided that where an adoption agency has been authorised to place a child for adoption, its consent will be required,[37] as will that of the designated local authority if a placement order is in force.[38] If the child has actually been placed for adoption with prospective adopters, their consent will be required in addition to that of the adoption agency or local authority, as appropriate.[39] Such changes reflect the general policy of the law regarding the balance of power where there are potentially competing claims to exercise parental responsibility, but one does wonder whether they are in accord with the underlying purpose of requiring parental consent to marriage. Are prospective adopters, or an adoption agency, or the local authority, best placed to decide whether a proposed marriage is appropriate?

Consent to Whose Marriages?

One category of minors has always been exempted from the necessity of obtaining parental consent to their marriage, namely those who had previously been married and whose spouse had died. This was, of course, a more likely contingency in the eighteenth century than it is today. Perhaps surprisingly, the fact that a minor's marriage has ended in divorce or annulment does not remove the requirement of parental consent to a second marriage. Of course, divorce was still relatively rare when the issue was considered by the Latey Committee in the 1960s,[40] and (more importantly) not available within the first three years of marriage, save in exceptional circumstances. (In addition, it may have been felt that those whose marriages had broken down so quickly might need parental guidance the second time around.) Even today, the bar on divorce within the first year of marriage means that few will have time to marry, divorce and find a new partner before their 18th birthday.[41]

The number of minors affected by the necessity of obtaining parental consent has been affected both by changes to the age at which it is possible to enter into a valid marriage and by the changing age of majority. Under the canon law, as revised in 1604, it was assumed that a girl could give a valid consent to marriage

---

[36]   Marriage Act 1949 s 3(1A)(b). The consent of each special guardian is required, unless: a care order is in place and the parental responsibility of any special guardian has been restricted under s 33(3); a residence order has been made; an adoption agency has been authorised to place the child for adoption under s 19 of the Adoption and Children Act 2002; a placement order is in force; or the child has been placed with prospective adopters.

[37]   Marriage Act 1949 s 3(1A)(e).

[38]   Marriage Act 1949 s 3(1A)(f).

[39]   Unless their parental responsibility has been restricted under s 25(4) of the 2002 Act: Marriage Act 1949 s 3(1A)(g).

[40]   'Report of the Committee on the Age of Majority' (Cmnd 3342, 1967) (hereinafter, 'Latey').

[41]   In 2004 there was one 17-year-old bride who had previously been divorced: 'Marriage, Divorce and Adoption statistics', above n 1, Table 3.19.

at 12, and a boy at 14.[42] It was not until 1929 that the Age of Marriage Act raised the minimum age of marriage to 16 for both sexes.[43] There it has remained, despite some expressions of unease, on account of the principled argument that it would be seen as sanctioning sexual intercourse outside marriage if the minimum age of marriage were higher than the age of consent to sexual intercourse, and the pragmatic recognition that raising the age of consent to sexual intercourse would have little effect.[44]

Forty years after the Age of Marriage Act, the number of those who needed parental consent to marry was more dramatically reduced when the Family Law Reform Act 1969 reduced the legal age of majority from 21 to 18,[45] following the recommendations of the Latey Committee. The Committee had given detailed consideration to the issue of marriage, and concluded that it was 'not wise to demand parental consent to marriage past the age of 18'.[46] This was not, however, a response to the demands of minors who might wish to marry without such consent, even though the number of teenage marriages was far higher then than it is today. Indeed, the Minority Report issued by two members of the Committee noted the survey that had been conducted for the Committee, in which 62 per cent of those aged 16 to 20, and 65 per cent of those aged 21 to 24, felt that 21 was the right age for marrying without parental consent.[47] However, even those who felt that the age should be lowered did not favour dispensing with restrictions altogether. The Committee suggested that the considerations affecting those aged 16 or 17 were 'very different';[48] that young people 'change enormously between 16 and 18'; were 'often still in a state of rebellion'; and were 'more dependent on their parents materially and psychologically'.[49]

Thereafter, it was only those minors aged between 16 and 18 who needed their parents' consent to marry. The Latey Committee took the view that this was likely to be a fairly small constituency: in 1965 there were 56,408 bridegrooms and 151,896 brides under the age of 21,[50] but only a small proportion were under the age of 18.[51] Indeed, the number of those who marry at a young age has fallen precipitously. In 2005, fewer than one in every 1,000 teenage girls was married, and married teenage boys did not even register.[52] The majority of teenagers who

---

[42] See RH Helmholz, *The Oxford History of the Laws of England: Vol 1 The Canon Law and Ecclesiastical Jurisdiction from 597 to the 1640s* (Cambridge, Cambridge University Press, 2004) 267.

[43] On the genesis and passage of the 1929 Act, see S Cretney, *Family Law in the Twentieth Century: A History* (Oxford, Oxford University Press, 2003) 58–61.

[44] Latey, above n 40, [103] and [177].

[45] Family Law Reform Act 1969 s 1.

[46] Latey, above n 40, [165].

[47] Latey, [524].

[48] Latey, [158].

[49] Latey, [160]–[161].

[50] Latey, [139].

[51] In 1964 this was 0.9% of bridegrooms and 6.7% of brides: Latey, [159].

[52] 'Marriage, Divorce and Adoption Statistics', above n 1, Table 1.2.

marry do so only after attaining the age of 18: in 2004, only 11 16-year-old males married, and 67 17-year-olds;[53] while there were 126 16-year-old brides and 308 aged 17.[54]

It should of course be borne in mind that there are many factors—other than obviating the necessity of parental consent—that may lead individuals to marry once they reach the age of 18. The small numbers marrying under that age do not necessarily indicate that the law is deterring others from following suit. As the next section will show, there are ways of challenging, avoiding or simply evading the requirement of parental consent.

Challenging Parental Consent

Ever since parental consent has been a formal element in the making of marriages by minors, some provision has been made for a child to challenge the refusal of consent. As one eighteenth-century commentator noted:

> even the [1753] Marriage Act ... (though most industriously calculated in many respects to defeat the natural right of choice, and free agency) hath yet provided a mode of relief in some oppressive cases.[55]

This was true for some, but not all, cases. Under the 1753 Act, a minor was entitled to apply to the Lord Chancellor to give his consent to the marriage if a mother or guardian was unreasonably withholding consent; however, a father's refusal of consent could not be overridden in this way.[56] The legislators either did not wish to acknowledge that fathers could be unreasonable, or supported their right to be unreasonable in the circumstances.[57]

In 1925, this was replaced by a simpler provision allowing the court to grant consent if *any* person whose consent was required refused to grant it.[58] The figures quoted by the Latey Committee indicated that just over one-half of all applications were granted, suggesting that parents were not always withholding their consent for worthy reasons. Unfortunately, no case law is available to ascertain what kinds of reasons parents gave for refusing consent, or the types of cases in which the courts were willing to override the refusal of consent. Most applications were made to the magistrates' court,[59] and no appeal from their decision was possible.[60] Since the age of majority was reduced in 1969, the numbers seeking the assistance of the court have fallen to such a low level that

---

[53]   *Ibid*, Table 3.18.
[54]   *Ibid*, Table 3.19.
[55]   Anon, *Considerations on the Causes of the Present Stagnation of Matrimony* (London, 1772) 14.
[56]   Clandestine Marriages Act 1753 s 12.
[57]   See *In the Matter of The 4 G. 4, c. 76, ex p I.C., an infant* (1836) 40 ER 1008.
[58]   Guardianship of Infants Act 1925 s 9(1)(b).
[59]   In 1965 only 34 of the 598 applications were brought in the county courts: 'Civil Judicial Statistics for 1965' (Cmnd 3029, 1966–67) 64, Table 23.
[60]   See *Re Queskey* [1946] Ch 250.

official statistics are no longer available,[61] and in *Re K; A Local Authority v N and Others*, Munby J described the jurisdiction—together with the use of wardship to control the marriages of minors—as 'little more than dead letters'.[62]

An alternative for minors faced with parental opposition was to resort to evasive measures. Parental opposition no doubt accounted for a number of clandestine marriages before 1754, and elopements out of the jurisdiction after that date.[63] After 1754, it was possible for minors validly to marry *within* the jurisdiction if the marriage was preceded by banns and their parents did not actively dissent. After the law was changed again in 1823, the possibilities for entering into a valid marriage without parental consent were increased, but all usually involved some dissimilation or outright untruths (which, from the mid-nineteenth century, exposed the parties to prosecution for perjury as well as potential forfeiture of property[64]). That some minors did succeed in marrying without parental consent is clear from the case law[65] and other sources.[66] One might imagine that such evasions were more difficult in a bureaucratic age, but in 1973 the Law Commission opined that the rules were 'notoriously difficult' to enforce and 'easily evaded', a state of affairs that had the effect of bringing the law 'into disrepute'.[67] Having rejected the 'extreme' solution of invalidating marriages celebrated without parental consent,[68] it suggested that uniform civil preliminaries would go some way towards making it more difficult for minors to marry without the necessary consents, and further recommended that parents 'should be required either to attend the register office personally or to have the signature to their consent witnessed by a person of standing'.[69]

As yet, none of the Law Commission's 1973 recommendations has been enacted, and it seems unlikely at this date that any will be. The Immigration and Asylum Act 1999 introduced a single set of civil preliminaries, in place of the previous two-tier system, but did not apply them to all marriages. The identity of those marrying is now subject to more stringent checks, but these do not extend to determining whether parental consent has genuinely been given. Furthermore, there is still no requirement of parental consent for those minors who marry after

---

[61] The last year for which figures are available for applications in the county courts is 1973, when six applications were filed: 'Civil Judicial Statistics for 1973' (Cmnd 5756, 1974–5) 84.

[62] [2005] EWHC 2956 (Fam) at [80].

[63] *Like v Beresford* (1796) 30 ER 1129; and *Bathurst v Murray* (1802) 32 ER 279.

[64] Marriage and Registration Act 1856 s 18, and see now Perjury Act 1911 s 3.

[65] See, eg *Re Sampson and Wall, Infants* [1884] LR 25 Ch D 482; *Re H's Settlement* [1909] 2 Ch 260; *Plummer v Plummer* [1917] P 163; and *Re Crump (An Infant)* [1963] Crim LR 777.

[66] See, eg J McCrindle and S Rowbotham, *Dutiful Daughters: Women Talk about Their Lives* (Harmondsworth, Penguin, 1977) 225, in which one woman recollects how she married at 17—'we just got married in a Registry Office and sent telegrams saying we were married to both the sets of parents, because both of them were opposed to it.'

[67] Law Commission, above n 22, [48].

[68] *Ibid*, [49].

[69] *Ibid*, [50].

the calling of banns in the Church of England,[70] although the figures do not suggest that this is a point exploited by teenage brides and grooms, since the proportion who opt for this procedure is at its lowest within this age group.

The possibility of challenging, avoiding or evading the requirement of parental consent to marriage is far greater than the possibility of challenging other exercises of parental responsibility. The very fact that the legislation makes provision for the refusal of consent to be challenged provides an interesting contrast to other areas in which a child must seek the leave of the court in order to challenge parental authority. Of course, this largely reflects the greater maturity (by definition) of those minors who are seeking permission to marry, who may, if this is refused, vote with their feet by eloping.

Wardship and the Inherent Jurisdiction

If a child is a ward of court,[71] the consent of the court (previously the Court of Chancery and now the Family Division) is required for that child's marriage. A marriage celebrated without such consent remains valid, but the parties commit a contempt by so marrying,[72] and may be punished accordingly.[73] The wardship jurisdiction has operated both as a substitute for parental control (for example, where the parents of the child are dead) and as a supplement to it (where the parents themselves invoke the court's jurisdiction specifically for the purpose of preventing that child's marriage). In either case, the court acted as it thought a prudent parent would do.[74]

The use of the past tense reflects the fact that it appears to be a long time since any such application was made by parents. However, in *Re K; A Local Authority v N and Others*,[75] a rather different situation arose. Here, it was the local authority, rather than the parents, that sought an order under the Court's inherent jurisdiction to prevent a 16-year-old girl from marrying without the consent of the Court. The girl in question had already entered into an arranged marriage when aged only 15: the marriage was not only void, but, in the light of the 'husband's' behaviour, disastrous. Despite this, the girl was keen to marry again, but the guardian took the view that it would be better for the Court, rather than her parents, to determine her best interests in respect of any further proposed marriage, and that the girl herself was incapable 'of making life decisions which

---

[70]   It was recommended in 1967 that 'the consent procedure should be made uniform for all modes of marriage': Latey, above n 40, [185(5)].

[71]   On the development and scope of the wardship jurisdiction, see, eg J Seymour, 'Parens Patriae and Wardship Powers: Their Nature and Origins' (1994) 14 *OJLS* 159; and N Lowe and R White, *Wards of Court* (London, Butterworths, 1979).

[72]   *Mr Herbert's case* (1731) 24 ER 992.

[73]   *Edes v Brereton* (1738) 25 ER 974; and *More v More* (1741) 26 ER 499.

[74]   See, eg *The Lord Raymond's Case* (1734) 25 ER 661; and *Smith v Smith* (1745) 26 ER 977.

[75]   [2005] EWHC 2956 (Fam).

are beneficial to her'.[76] The Court refused to make the order sought. At first sight, the reason for this refusal was respect for the parents' rights:

> The starting point might ... plausibly be said to be that the court should not normally invade the sphere of parental obligation and parental responsibility unless there is real reason to fear that the child will not be adequately protected by the parents or indeed, as in cases of forced marriages, that the child requires to be protected from the parents.[77]

But on closer inspection, pragmatism—a recognition of the limitations of the law in this area—appears to have been more important than the abstract idea of respect for parental rights. As Munby J noted, the 'unintended but nonetheless foreseeable' consequence of restricting the girl's marriage might be to push her into less desirable forms of behaviour—such as absconding or entering into a sexual relationship outside marriage.[78] Moreover, it was evident that he took the view that a court was simply unable to judge whether a proposed marriage was in a child's best interests.[79]

In so holding, Munby J illustrated just how much the role of the court has changed in the past 200 or so years. It is a change entwined with the changing nature of marriage, and with what is expected of a responsible parent, to which we shall now turn.

What Did the Responsible Parent Do?

The power to provide, or withhold, consent to a child's marriage has long been seen as being for the benefit of the child rather than a means of enhancing the power of a parent. Blackstone suggested that it was:

> another means, which the law has put into the parent's hands, in order the better to discharge his duty; first, of protecting his children from the snares of artful and designing persons; and next, of settling them properly in life, by preventing the ill consequences of too early and precipitate marriages.[80]

Two hundred years later, this emphasis on responsibility rather than rights was echoed by the Latey Committee when it refused to retain the requirement of consent as a means of shoring up parental authority and noted that not all parents exercised their power of veto responsibly:

> Mothers forbid marriages which remove their useful daughters from home, fathers have their vision clouded by differences of accent or length of hair; even the wisest and

---

[76]   *Ibid*, at [71].
[77]   *Ibid*, at [90].
[78]   The mother of the girl gave evidence that this would have serious consequences within their own culture, and would have a detrimental impact upon the chance of the girl or her sisters securing an Islamic marriage in the future: *ibid*, at [65].
[79]   *Ibid*, at [81], and see further below.
[80]   W Blackstone, *Commentaries on the Laws of England: Vol 1* (1765–69) 440–1.

kindest of parents may be, by the very nature of their close personal involvement with their children, in a poor position to know what their children's deep psychological needs really are.[81]

But, as these two extracts suggest, expectations of what precisely the responsible parent was meant to do changed in this period. Blackstone's reference to 'settling' one's children hints at an important element in the matchmaking process: namely, money. Eighteenth-century judges agreed: the court acted as it thought a prudent parent would do in deciding whether to consent to the proposed marriage of a ward of court,[82] and money was a most important consideration in determining whether a marriage was suitable. Thus, Lord Hardwicke noted in *Smith v Smith* that while wealth was not the most material consideration:

> parents always take care that such provision shall be made of this kind, as will enable infants to live in the world suitable to that rank to which their birth entitles them.[83]

Yet while parents who were motivated solely by financial considerations were criticised, the alternative was not marriage for love alone.[84] The Enlightenment ideal was money combined with affection, as articulated by Eliza Barter, the heroine of *The Marriage Act*:

> I will never marry for Love, to lie upon straw; or marry for Title, without that Passion to improve it.[85]

This was put into practice by Elizabeth Bennett, whose estimation of Mr Darcy rapidly becomes more favourable once she has seen his house and realised what £10,000 per annum means in practice.[86]

No such mercenary considerations appear in the report of the Latey Committee; instead, it is implied that the choice of a spouse is based on psychological factors unknowable to all but the parties themselves. The emergence of companionate marriage is a trend that has inspired much academic discussion[87] and, as

---

[81]   Latey, above n 40, [152].

[82]   The marriage of a ward of court without the consent of the Court of Chancery did not render the marriage void, but it was a contempt of court: see, eg *Stackpole v Beaumont* (1798) 30 ER 909; and *Millet v Rowse* (1802) 32 ER 169.

[83]   (1745) 26 ER 977.

[84]   See, eg Philagamus, *The Present State of Matrimony: Or, The Real Causes of Conjugal Infidelity and Unhappy Marriages* (London, 1739) 29, who identified one of the principal causes of unhappiness in marriage as being 'that preposterous, unequal, and sometimes unnatural way of matching our young people, very often without taking the least Care in examining and comparing the different Ages, Tempers, and Constitutions, of the Parties'. Yet his was not a plea for marriages based on love alone, his solution being that parents should allow the parties time to get to know one another before the marriage. See also Anon, *Considerations on the Causes of the Present Stagnation of Matrimony* (London, J Ridley, 1772); *Letters on Love, Marriage and Adultery* (1789); and R Lewis, *Reflections on the Causes of Unhappy Marriages* (London, W Clarke & Sons, 1805) 14–5.

[85]   J Shebbeare, *The Marriage Act* (London, 1754) 149. See also T Smollett, *The Expedition of Humphrey Clinker* (1771, Wordsworth Classics, 1995).

[86]   J Austen, *Pride and Prejudice* (London, 1813).

[87]   See, eg E Shorter, *The Making of the Modern Family* (London, Collins, 1976); L Stone, *The Family, Sex and Marriage in England 1500–1800* (London, Weidenfeld & Nicholson, 1977); and R

Collins has noted, has been attributed to every period between the Middle Ages and the 1950s.[88] As with any cultural shift, it is difficult to identify when romantic love ceased to be regarded as a dangerous destabilising factor and began to be regarded as the *sine qua non* for marriage, or when the appropriate role of a parent shifted from actually arranging a match to tactfully providing advice. Examples of marriage for love can be found in every period, as can mercenary marriages; incidents of parental intervention or coercion[89] may be set against those who encouraged their children to make their own choices.[90] Indeed, the very concept of love was one that might mean different things to different commentators at different times. Mrs Sarah Ellis, in a tome with the rather hectoring title *The Daughters of England: Their Position in Society, Character and Responsibilities*, insisted that women should marry for love and made no reference to the desirability of obtaining parental consent or even approval, but at the same time counselled against 'falling in love' and suggested that a young girl should wait:

> until a period of greater maturity of judgment, when ... she will be able to form a correct opinion on that point of paramount importance—suitability of character and habits.[91]

But taken as a whole, it is clear that the 200 years between Blackstone and the Latey Commission did see a profound change both in the factors that were viewed as the basis for a good marriage and in the role of parents in the making of their children's marriages. As the rationale for marriage changed, so did the role that parents *could* play. A parent would be ideally situated to judge the (financial) worth of a potential suitor dispassionately, but the greater the role accorded to individual attraction, the lesser the role that could be accorded to parents. The same was even more true of the role of the judiciary: as Munby J noted in *Re K*, a judge faced with the task of deciding whether to give or refuse consent:

> might find the task ... a matter of no little delicacy and difficulty ... how is a judge in today's society really supposed to decide, and by reference to what criteria, whether or not it is in a 16 or 17-year-old ward's best interests to marry some particular suitor.[92]

Trumbach, *The Rise of the Egalitarian Family: Aristocratic Kinship and Domestic Relations in Eighteenth-Century England* (New York, Academic Press, 1978).

[88] M Collins, *Modern Love: An Intimate History of Men and Women in Twentieth-Century Britain* (London, Atlantic Books, 2003).

[89] The problems of the eponymous heroine in Fanny Burney's *Cecilia* (first published 1782; Oxford, Oxford University Press, 1999) 930, are attributed to the interference of the elder generation; similarly, Susan Ferrier in *Marriage* (first published 1818, Oxford, Oxford University Press, 2001) satirises attempts by parents to control their children.

[90] See generally A Macfarlane, *Marriage and love in England: Modes of Reproduction 1300–1840* (Oxford, Basil Blackwood Ltd, 1986); O Hufton, *The Prospect Before Her: A History of Women in Western Europe, Vol 1 1500–1800* (London, HarperCollins, 1995) ch 3; and A Vickery, *The Gentleman's Daughter: Women's Lives in Georgian England* (New Haven, Yale University Press, 2003).

[91] S Ellis, *The Daughters of England: Their Position in Society, Character and Responsibilities* (London, Fisher, Son & Co, 1842) 400.

[92] [2005] EWHC 2956 (Fam) at [80]–[81].

By the second half of the twentieth century, it could be said that the responsible parent had a right, and even a duty, to advise a minor child thinking of marriage,[93] and in extreme cases to seek the assistance of the court in preventing or at least delaying undesirable associations,[94] but no more. The Latey Committee assumed that parental influence would continue even if parents no longer had the legal power to prevent a marriage;[95] 40 years on, by contrast, the view was expressed that even parents who retained such a power would be unlikely to exercise it:

> I suspect that in modern conditions many wise parents ... would, at the end of the day, claim no more than the three rights that Bagehot famously ascribed to the monarch: the right to be consulted, the right to encourage, the right to warn. Many concerned and loving parents, in the final analysis, might well feel it unwise to stand on their strict legal right to refuse consent.[96]

In the view of Munby J, the wise parent accedes to the child's wishes in such a case not because youthful marriage is desirable, but because refusing consent may simply prevent the formalising of the relationship, not the relationship itself.

At the end of the twentieth century, the focus of debate shifted from parents who unreasonably veto their child's choice of spouse to parents who allow their children no choice at all.[97] Of course, forced marriages are not a new phenomenon, nor is the legal or social[98] condemnation of such marriages. Since the Christian church emphasised that consent was at the heart of marriage, a marriage might be annulled on the basis that one of the parties had not given consent because of duress. The change that has occurred is in the meaning of duress, and thus in the degree of persuasion that a parent can exercise responsibly. From the medieval period to the nineteenth century, a marriage could only be annulled on account of duress if there had been threats that would move a 'constant' man or woman.[99] Poynter, for example, noted that fear must be such as:

---

[93]   EL Johnson, *Family Law* (London, Sweet & Maxwell, 1965) 28.

[94]   See, eg 'Wards of Court' *The Times* (30 June 1965) 13.

[95]   Latey, above n 40, [165]; cf the view of the Minority Report at [149].

[96]   *Re K; A Local Authority v N and Others* [2005] EWHC 2956 (Fam).

[97]   See, eg Home Office, *A choice by right: the report of the working group on forced marriage* (London, HMSO, 2000); and Foreign and Commonwealth Office and Home Office, *Forced Marriage: A Wrong Not a Right* (London, HMSO, 2005).

[98]   See, eg H Fielding, *Tom Jones* (London, 1749; Oxford, Oxford World Classics, 1998) 780: 'Now to force a woman into marriage contrary to her consent or approbation is an act of such injustice and oppression that I wish the laws of our country could restrain it; but a good conscience is never lawless in the worst regulated state, and will provide those laws for itself which the neglect of legislators hath forgotten to supply.'

[99]   RH Helmholz, *Marriage Litigation in Medieval England* (Cambridge, Cambridge University Press, 1975) 94.

may reasonably happen to a man or a woman of good courage, constancy, and resolution, and such as includes some danger of death, or else some bodily torment and distress, otherwise it can have no operation in law to rescind a marriage contract.[100]

By the end of the century, however, the court had accepted a subjective standard that focused on the impact of the threats on the individual in question.[101] And since then there has been a growing appreciation of the subtle pressures that may be brought to bear. As Munby J noted in *NS v MI*:

> where the influence is that of a parent or other close and dominating relative, and where the arguments and persuasion are based upon personal affection or duty, religious beliefs, powerful social or cultural conventions ... the influence may ... be subtle, insidious, pervasive and powerful. In such cases, moreover, very little pressure may suffice to bring about the desired result.[102]

If this is the degree of influence deemed inappropriate—and sufficient to annul the marriage—it would seem that a parent is not entitled to promote particular suitors, even if he or she may warn against those deemed unsuitable.

Although the government resolved against making the forcing of another person into marriage a criminal offence, the powers of the courts to protect individuals—whether adult or minor—from being forced into a marriage have been enhanced by the Forced Marriage (Civil Protection) Act 2007.[103] Once this is brought into force the court[104] will be able to grant a 'forced marriage protection order' to protect those at risk of being forced into marriages against their will.[105] The legislation explicitly provides that force includes coercion 'by threats or other psychological means',[106] thereby echoing the approach taken in the modern case law.

However, there is another type of marriage that poses rather more difficult questions. What does the responsible parent of a disabled child do? As the child reaches adulthood and the parent is faced with the possibility that he or she will not be able to provide care for that child indefinitely, is it more responsible to

---

[100] T Poynter, *A Concise View of the Doctrine and Practice of the Ecclesiastical Courts in Doctors' Commons, relative to the subject of Marriage and Divorce* (2nd edn, London, J & WT Clarke, 1824) 138–9.

[101] *Scott v Sebright* (1886) 12 PD 31. The following century saw a more demanding test being formulated in some cases (see *Szechter v Szechter* [1971] P 286; and *Singh v Singh* [1971] P 226), but the subjective test was applied in *Hirani v Hirani* (1982) 4 FLR 232 and it is widely assumed that this represents the current law.

[102] [2006] EWHC 1646 (Fam) at [34].

[103] The Act inserts new provisions into the Family Law Act 1996 that build on the use of the High Court's inherent jurisdiction in cases such as *Re SK (Proposed Plaintiff) (An Adult by way of her Litigation Friend)* [2004] EWHC 3202 (Fam); *Re SA (Vulnerable Adult with Capacity: Marriage)* [2005] EWHC 2942 (Fam); and *Re K (A Local Authority) v N and Others* [2005] EWHC 2956 (Fam).

[104] Either the High Court or a county court: Forced Marriage (Civil Protection) Act 2007 Sch 1, para 8(1).

[105] Family Law Act 1996 s 63A(1), as inserted by the Forced Marriage (Civil Protection) Act 2007 s 1.

[106] Family Law Act 1996 s 63A(6), as inserted by the Forced Marriage (Civil Protection) Act 2007 s 1.

assume that the child will be cared for by the state, or to arrange a marriage with the aim of securing a carer for the child?[107] And what if the child suffers from learning difficulties and is unable to give a valid consent to marriage within the terms of the law?[108]

In a number of recent cases, the courts have shown themselves willing to put protective measures in place to ensure that a marriage does not take place if either party does not have capacity to consent to it,[109] and indeed to refuse to recognise a marriage celebrated by a person who lacked such capacity.[110] The issue in these cases was not couched in terms of parental responsibility, perhaps because those whose capacity to marry was in question had either attained or were on the threshold of adulthood.[111] But the clear implication was that these parents were not acting responsibly—indeed, in *Westminster CC v IC*, Thorpe LJ described the fact that the parents of the vulnerable adult had engineered a telephone marriage to a woman in Bangladesh as 'potentially, if not actually abusive of IC'[112]—and that the responsible action was to ensure that no marriage took place. It was, however, equally clear that these parents were acting in a way that they perceived to be in their child's best interests.[113] As Sumner J noted in *M v B, A, and S (By her Litigation Friend the Official Solicitor)*, the father:

---

[107]   On the views of the Pakistani community on such matters, see the evidence given by the social work expert in *X CC v MB, NB and MAB (By His Litigation Friend the Official Solicitor)* [2006] EWHC 168 (Fam) at [10]. See also Y Hussain, 'South Asian disabled women: negotiating identities' (2005) *The Sociological Review* 522; and F Hepper '"A woman's heaven is at her husband's feet"? The dilemmas for a community learning disability team posed by the arranged marriage of a Bangladeshi client with intellectual disability' (1999) *Journal of Intellectual Disability Research* 558.

[108]   As set out in *Sheffield CC v E* [2004] EWHC 2808 (Fam).

[109]   See, eg *M v B, A, and S (By her Litigation Friend the Official Solicitor)* [2005] EWHC 1681 (Fam) (23-year-old woman who suffered from a severe learning disability: injunction granted to prevent her parents from taking her to Pakistan to be married); *Re SA (Vulnerable Adult with Capacity: Marriage)* [2005] EWHC 2942 (Fam) (17-year-old girl who was profoundly deaf and unable to speak, but did have capacity: order that she be properly informed about any proposed match); and *X CC v MB, NB and MAB (By His Litigation Friend the Official Solicitor)* [2006] EWHC 168 (Fam) (25-year-old autistic man: undertakings from parents that they would not cause or permit him to undergo any form of marriage ceremony or take him out of the jurisdiction). It has been confirmed that the powers of the court in this respect have not been curtailed by the Mental Capacity Act 2005: *Westminster CC v IC* [2008] EWCA Civ 198.

[110]   *Westminster CC v IC* [2008] EWCA Civ 198. As the Court noted in that case, it is highly unlikely that such a marriage could take place in this jurisdiction: as Wall LJ noted, '[n]o English Registrar of marriages could or would have contemplated celebrating a marriage between IC and NK, for the simple reason (amongst others) that no such Registrar could have issued a certificate of satisfaction that there was no lawful impediment to the marriage': at [45].

[111]   Although note *Re MM (an adult); Local Authority X v MM and another* [2007] EWHC 2003 (Fam) at [108], in which Munby J commented that '[p]arental rights and responsibilities, and the rights and responsibilities of partners or other carers, have in the final analysis to give way to the best interests of a vulnerable adult'.

[112]   *Westminster*, above n 110, at [32]. See also Wall LJ at [45].

[113]   See, eg *X CC v MB, NB and MAB (By His Litigation Friend the Official Solicitor)* [2006] EWHC 168 (Fam) at [8], in which the parents were described as 'devoted and committed in their care … Their only motivation is to do their very best for their sons'. See also *Westminster CC v IC* [2008] EWCA Civ 198 at [44], in which Wall LJ noted that 'the marriage of IC is perceived as a means of protecting him, and of ensuring that he is properly cared for within the family when his parents are

may well be influenced by a genuine belief that if married she might be better off than she is at present. There would be someone to look after her when her parents can no longer do so. The idea that anyone other than the family should provide such care for her would be strongly opposed by him.[114]

However, opposition to state care may be motivated by factors other than cultural commitment to the family: there are sufficient reports of ill-treatment and abuse in the state sector to give any father cause for concern about the future of his daughter.[115] Furthermore, as Munby J pointed out in *Re MM (an adult); Local Authority X v MM and another*:[116]

We have to be conscious of the limited ability of public authorities to improve on nature ... If the State—typically, as here, in the guise of a local authority—is to say that it is the more appropriate person to look after a mentally incapacitated adult than her own partner or family, it assumes ... the practical and evidential burden ... of establishing that this is indeed so.[117]

It is clear that it would be incompatible with the legal and social norms of this jurisdiction to allow a marriage to go ahead if either party was unable to consent.[118] If an individual is incapable of consenting to a marriage, he or she will almost certainly be incapable of consenting to sexual intercourse,[119] and physical intimacy with a person who is unable to consent to it constitutes a criminal offence.[120] It may be that the way forward lies in greater rights for private carers[121] to provide an alternative to marriage consistent with both sides' conception of responsibility.

CONCLUSION

As Munby J noted in *Re K*:

---

no longer in a position to do so'. On the changing attitudes to the marriage of those with intellectual disabilities, see D May and MK Simpson, 'The parent trap: marriage, parenthood and adulthood for people with intellectual disabilities' (2003) *Critical Social Policy* 25.

[114] [2005] EWHC 1681 at [33].

[115] See, eg D Brindle, 'Catalogue of abuse in NHS care homes' *The Guardian* (17 January 2007).

[116] [2007] EWHC 2003 (Fam).

[117] *Ibid*, at [116].

[118] In *Westminster CC v IC* [2008] EWCA Civ 198 at [3], Thorpe LJ described such a marriage as 'inconceivable'.

[119] Although not necessarily vice versa: see *Re MM*, above n 111.

[120] Sexual Offences Act 2003 s 30 (sexual activity with a person with a mental disorder impeding choice). See also *Westminster*, above n 110, at [32] and [45].

[121] On the current legal treatment of carers, see A Stewart, 'Home or Home: Caring about and for Elderly Family Members in a Welfare State' in R Probert, *Family Life and the Law: Under One Roof* (Aldershot, Ashgate, 2007).

Traditionally, the court's powers were invoked in support of parents and parental rights. Now they tend to be invoked in opposition to parents and in order to prevent the abuse of parental power.[122]

The role of parents in the making of marriage has been reduced as the nature of marriage itself has changed. Parental responsibility accords the right to give or withhold consent to a minor's marriage, but the diffusion of parental responsibility among a range of persons and even institutions has undermined the original rationale for the requirement; moreover, the responsible parent is today deemed to be one who leaves the choice to the child and offers no more than advice against an unsuitable choice. Such changes inevitably require us to ask whether the requirement of consent is needed at all. Since the parent who forces his or her child into a marriage has replaced the irresponsible minor as the focus of public concern, it may be time for the law to abolish the requirement altogether, and send a message that parents no longer have any legal role to play in the making of their children's marriages, nor any powers beyond those that their children choose to accord them.[123]

---

[122]   [2005] EWHC 2956 (Fam) at [84].
[123]   eg if the child wishes to have an arranged marriage, in finding suitable candidates.

14

Parental Responsibility, Relational Responsibility: Caring for and Protecting Children after their Death

JO BRIDGEMAN

INTRODUCTION

The death of a child is one of the most disturbing, shocking, unacceptable events that can occur. It is a death out of season. More than the death of an adult, who has at least to some extent 'lived a life', the death of a child is an outrage against the natural order of things, disrupting our sense of purpose, of future promise, of our progeny continuing after our death. For the parents of a child who dies, the loss that is mourned includes not only a shared past, but future hopes.[1]

A T ONE TIME, coping with the death of a child may have been part of life; nowadays, we expect our children to survive us. Thankfully, the death of a child has become a terrible tragedy encountered by most only through media accounts of childhood battles with illness, fatal accidents, horrific accounts of deliberate harm or neglect by adults who were expected to care or the rare and shocking murder at the hands of a stranger.[2]

This chapter explores the legal obligations imposed upon parents, as an incidence of their parental responsibility, following the death of their child. I should make it clear from the outset that this chapter does not consider parents, or other adults with caring responsibilities for children, who through neglect or deliberate harm cause the death of a child in their care. These adults have failed to fulfil their moral and legal obligations, their actions amount to the 'violation of a relationship of trust and duty'[3] with a dependent and vulnerable child and they must be held to account by the law. Rather, by examining the legal

---

[1] D Judd, *Give Sorrow Words: Working with a Dying Child* (London, Free Association Books, 1989) 3.

[2] A pilot study carried out for the Confidential Enquiry into Maternal and Child Health in the South West, North East and West Midlands regions of England, Wales and Northern Ireland in 2006 found that there had been 957 deaths of children aged between 28 days and 18 years: GA Pearson (ed), *Why Children Die: A Pilot Study 2006* (London, CEMACH, 2008).

[3] J Conaghan, 'Tort Litigation in the Context of Intra-familial Abuse' (1998) 61 *MLR* 132, 161.

obligations imposed upon, and responsibilities taken by, parents following the death of a child, I aim to reflect upon the meaning and content of parental responsibility more generally.

As is well known, parental responsibility is given a wide and vague definition in the Children Act 1989.[4] Content has been given to the concept of parental responsibility—what it means for the adult possessed of it and the child in relation to whom it is enjoyed—in the case law, most often in cases involving fragmented families where fathers have applied to court for parental responsibility not conferred automatically or by agreement.[5] And in that context, it is a legal status which entitles the holder to information about, and involvement in major decisions regarding, the child; which appears to be more a matter of conferring rights over the child than recognising responsibility, or encouraging it.[6] Yet both section 3 of the Children Act 1989 and the responsibility exercised and experienced by parents clearly amount to something much more significant for the lives of children than symbolic recognition or distanced decision-making. It is my view that we can, and should, give content to the concept of parental responsibility through consideration of parents' understanding, and experience, of their responsibilities.

Adopting an approach informed by the feminist ethic of care, I argue that we should understand the responsibilities of parents to their children to arise from their relationship; one in which the child is dependent upon their parent for care, protection and nurture. In *The Ethics of Care: Personal, Political, and Global,*[7] Virginia Held identifies four characteristics of the feminist ethic of care developed by a host of theorists from a range of disciplines in response to the seminal study of Carol Gilligan.[8] First, the feminist ethic of care understands the individual to be primarily connected or situated in relationships with others rather than first and foremost separate from others. Secondly, the individual takes responsibility for meeting the needs of others in order to preserve valued relationships. Thirdly, an ethic of care approach looks to the specific context to work out what ought to be done in a particular situation—the needs of the parties, the nature of the relationships, social expectations, institutions including the law—rather than the abstract implementation of universal rules. Finally, it challenges accepted views of the public and private as distinct and separate spheres. Ethics-of-care theorists seek to highlight the interdependency of all and

[4]   See Reece, this volume.

[5]   J Bridgeman, 'Parental Responsibility, Responsible Parenting and Legal Regulation' in J Bridgeman, H Keating and C Lind (eds), *Responsibility, Law and the Family* (Aldershot, Ashgate, 2008).

[6]   S Sheldon, 'Unmarried Fathers and Parental Responsibility: A Case for Reform?' (2001) 9 *Feminist Legal Studies* 93, 95.

[7]   V Held, *The Ethics of Care: Personal, Political, and Global* (New York, Oxford University Press, 2006) 10–15.

[8]   C Gilligan, *In a Different Voice: Psychological Theory and Women's Development* (Cambridge, Mass and London, Harvard University Press, 1982).

the ways in which all individuals continue to be dependent upon others through-out their lives, albeit in different ways and to different extents at different times.

The relationship between parent and child, and thus parental responsibilities, commences before birth, continues throughout their lifetimes and endures beyond death. The exact content of the responsibilities of parents depends upon all the circumstances, including the needs of the child, societal expectations, individual abilities, public support and legal obligations. In this approach, responsibilities are fulfilled in the interests of sustaining the relationship and from a concern for the wellbeing of the child. This conceptualisation of respon-sibility is thus different both from that developed in liberal theory—of responsi-bility as accountability—and the communitarian approach which seeks to balance individual rights with social responsibilities.[9] It is, I suggest, a conceptu-alisation of responsibility which is particularly apposite for intimate relationships such as between parents and children (although, I have argued elsewhere that it can equally provide a framework for responsibilities arising in professional caring relationships).[10] Before exploring the responsibilities of a parent following the death of their child, I first examine the legal obligations imposed after a child's death upon adults with parental responsibility for the child.

LEGAL OBLIGATIONS

The law has relatively little to say about our obligations to the deceased generally: confined to certification, registration and disposal. After death, the primary legal obligation imposed upon others is the duty to dispose of the body. First, the death must be registered by a 'qualified' informant, who may be a relative, someone present at the point of death or the occupier of the premises where the death occurred. The death should normally be registered within five days, but will be delayed if the circumstances of death require investigation by the coroner.

Failure to dispose of a body may amount to a public order offence or infringe public health legislation, but it is not an offence in its own right.[11] As long as they have the means to do so, the legal (as opposed to moral or social) duty to dispose of the child's body falls upon his or her parents[12] in their position as the child's personal representatives,[13] although the majority will consider this to be their

---

[9] J Bridgeman and H Keating, 'Conceptualising Family Responsibility' in Bridgeman *et al*, above n 5.

[10] J Bridgeman, *Parental Responsibility, Young Children and Healthcare Law* (Cambridge, Cam-bridge University Press, 2007).

[11] J Herring, 'Crimes Against the Dead' in B Brooks-Gordon *et al* (eds), *Death Rites and Rights* (Oxford, Hart, 2007).

[12] Although they are not liable in nuisance if they do not dispose of the body because they cannot afford to do so, *R v Vann* (1851) 2 Den 325.

[13] Under the Administration of Estates Act 1923 s 46, imposing a duty to dispose of the body upon the executors appointed under the will or to the personal representatives of the deceased. This does not confer proprietory rights over the body, but possession and custody and the entitlement to

responsibility and an act of care for which they wish to take responsibility. In *Fessi v Whitmore*, the mother and father, both of whom had enjoyed parental responsibility for a child, disagreed over the burial place of their son's ashes.[14] The child, a 12-year-old boy, had lived with his father since the separation of his parents. He died a couple of days after moving away with his father from the area of his family home; buried in the sand whilst playing on the beach near his new home. The court likened its role to one of resolving a dispute between trustees;[15] as his parents had 'like entitlement to the remains', the court employed the principles of justice and fairness to resolve the conflict between them. This led to the conclusion that the child's ashes should be scattered in the cemetery close to where the child's mother and brother lived, where his paternal grandfather's ashes were scattered and in a place 'where all members of the family can come together to see a fitting memorial to [his] life'.

In *R v Gwynedd CC, ex p B*,[16] Balcombe LJ understood a parent to have a 'right or duty to bury', arising from the earlier case of *R v Vann*, although he must have meant 'to dispose of', given that the law does not insist upon burial.[17] The right was enjoyed by the child's birth mother exercisable against the local authority, although in practice against the child's foster carers. The birth mother, who had visited her daughter twice a year, disagreed with her foster parents, who had cared for her for 14 years, as to the child's burial place. Dismissing an application for judicial review of the decision of the local authority, Balcombe LJ approached the conflict as a matter of statutory construction (of the terms of the Child Care Act 1980) and without reference to the 'human and emotional feelings of the parties'. His Lordship concluded that upon death the child could no longer be considered to be in local authority care, so that any right or duty vested in the local authority ceased and reverted to the natural parents. However, if the natural parents cannot be found or do not have the means required to dispose of the body, the local authority has the power of disposal. Although resolved through the niceties of statutory construction, this case supports the view that the duty imposed, or the right enjoyed, is an incidence of the status as parent—in this case her birth mother—becoming an aspect of parental responsibility by virtue of section 3 of the Children Act 1989, which defines parental responsibility as all the '*rights, duties*, powers, responsibilities and authority which by law a *parent* of a child has in relation to the child and his property'.[18]

---

make the necessary arrangements—H Conway, 'Dead, but not buried: Bodies, burial and family conflicts' (2003) 23 *Legal Studies* 423, 426–7.

[14] *Fessi v Whitmore* [1999] 1 FLR 167.

[15] For the suggestion that the parent/child relationship should be reconceived in terms of a trust, of which the child is the beneficiary, see K O'Donovan, *Family Law Matters* (London, Pluto Press, 1993) 104–5.

[16] *R v Gwynedd CC, ex p B* [1992] 3 All ER 317.

[17] Or 'a duty to decently inter', *R v Price* (1884) 12 QBD 247.

[18] Children Act 1989 s 3(1), emphasis added.

That parents have rights, from which duties may arise, with regard to the disposal of the body of their deceased child, is supported by the European Court of Human Rights in *Pannullo and Forte v France*.[19] The Court held that the parents' Article 8 right to respect for private and family life had been violated by the delay of over seven months in returning to them the body of their daughter. The child had undergone treatment in France for a heart condition and whilst there succumbed to a lung infection leading to her death. A postmortem was performed as part of an investigation as to whether there had been medical negligence or error amounting to a criminal offence. As the child's body could have been released within weeks of her death, but was retained until the completion of the forensic report, the interference with her parents' right to respect for private and family life was not necessary in a democratic society. The limits of the Article 8 right in this context can be seen in *Jones v UK*, in which the European Court of Human Rights observed that Article 8 rights 'pertain, predominantly, to relationships between living human beings'. The refusal to grant a father permission to include a photograph on the headstone of his daughter's grave did not impinge 'on the applicant's personal or relational sphere' such as to amount to an interference with his right to respect for private and family life. However, it should be noted that in this case the father had fulfilled his duty to dispose of his daughter's body and thus the final act of care, whereas the rights ascribed to the parents in *Pannullo* supported their endeavour to lay their daughter to rest.

The impact of Article 8 on English law was recently considered by the High Court in a dispute between a biological mother and the 'psychological parents' of a 15-year-old child who hanged himself in his cell at a young offenders institution. Cranston J held that Article 8 required the Court to consider the wishes of the deceased and those of his biological mother with whom he had had little contact for much of his childhood and of his uncle and aunt who had cared for him, had a residence order and whom he described as 'mum and dad'. As there was:

> a conflict in terms of the engagement of family life under Article 8.1, the Court is required to focus intensely on the comparative importance of the different rights being claimed, and to balance those competing rights so as to minimise the interference with each to the least possible extent.[20]

Decisive amongst the factors to be weighed was that his biological mother was 'incapable of assuming the responsibility' for making the funeral arrangements.

The litigation arising from the organ retention scandal revealed to the Bristol Royal Infirmary Inquiry[21] and the subject of a separate inquiry into practices at

---

[19]   *Pannullo and Forte v France*, Application no 37794/97, 30 January 2002.
[20]   *Borrows v HM Coroner for Preston* [2008] EWHC 1387 at [21].
[21]   'The Inquiry into the management of care of children receiving complex heart surgery at The Bristol Royal Infirmary Interim Report, Removal and retention of human material' (May 2000).

Alder Hey Children's Hospital[22] raised the question of parents' rights with regard to their deceased children whilst being fundamentally about parents' responsibilities. One of the lead actions in *AB and Others v Leeds Teaching Hospital NHS Trust*[23] was brought by Susan Carpenter, whose son, Daniel, died at the age of 17 months following surgery to remove a tumour around his brain stem performed at Southampton University Hospital. As with the majority of postmortems performed upon children, the circumstances surrounding his death resulted in the performance of a coroner's postmortem, which required neither consent nor non-objection.[24] Daniel's brain was retained for diagnostic examination and cremated some six months after his death. His mother was only informed of this fact 14 years later. A negligence action was not available and thus the tortious claim, seeking recognition of the wrong done, had to be grounded in the tort of wrongful interference with a body.

Although there was no case establishing the tort in English law, Gage J accepted that the elements of the tort were (i) a duty or right to possess the child's body, (ii) which the defendant, without lawful authority, interfered with by the retention or disposal of organs. The reasoning applied by Gage J to reach the conclusion that no tort of wrongful interference with a body had been committed in the circumstances—which was the retention of organs for the purposes of diagnostic examination and subsequent disposal—was as follows.[25] First was the principle, of dubious origin but now accepted, that there is no property in a dead body, although parts of the body may become subject to possessory rights if, by virtue of the application of skill, it acquires different qualities.[26] As, on the agreed facts, the postmortem was lawfully performed, removal of the organs for the purposes of the postmortem was lawful. Consequently, the pathologist performing the postmortem was in lawful possession of the removed tissue or organs. Gage J concluded that the parent had a duty to dispose of their child's body, but not a right to burial or possession of *organs* lawfully removed at postmortem and retained for the purposes of diagnosis after the burial. The parental duty—to dispose of their child's body—was fulfilled before diagnostic investigations had been completed, so no right to possession of retained organs arose from the parental duty. The application of the principles in this way led to the conclusion that the pathologist had a possessory right to the organs retained, whilst the child's parents had no legal rights. I have argued elsewhere that the conclusion

---

[22] 'The Royal Liverpool Children's Inquiry: Report' (30 January 2001).

[23] *AB and Others v Leeds Teaching Hospital NHS Trust; Cardiff and Vale NHS Trust* [2004] EWHC 644.

[24] The 'Bristol Inquiry Interim Report' found that of the 265 postmortems carried out in Bristol on children who had died following heart surgery or from a heart condition in the period covered by the inquiry's terms of reference, 83% (220) were coroner's postmortems ('Interim Report', above n 21, 6).

[25] *AB and others*, above n 23, at [128]–[161].

[26] *R v Kelly* [1999] QB 621 at 631 (Rose LJ), an application of Locke's theory of property as part of the 'common stock' until value is given to it by mixing labour with it.

that there was no tortious wrong committed against the parents amounted to a symbolic denial of the ongoing relationship with, and hence responsibility towards, their child, compounding the harm caused by the doctors and pathologists.[27]

Thus, the law appears to be fairly straightforward: limited duties are imposed upon parents, and limited rights as against others recognised, with regard to their child following his or her death confined to disposal of the body. It is my contention that parental responsibilities to their children, during their lives and after their death, go beyond legal duties and parental rights and that parents faced with the death of their child understand themselves to have very important responsibilities—arising from their relationship with their child—which they must fulfil. Writing about the organ retention scandal, Mavis Maclean has observed that: 'parental responsibility ... not only transcends the legal relationship of the parents but also continues after death.'[28] It is the transcendental and enduring nature of parental responsibility that I wish to explore. To develop that argument, I wish to examine briefly the other issue raised by *AB and Others*: children and bodies as property or persons.

PROPERTY, PERSONHOOD OR CONNECTION?

There has been much analysis within the academic literature of the body as property and of questions of body ownership, which I do not need to summarise here.[29] Jonathan Herring and PL Chau categorise the approaches adopted in these works into three types: those which demonstrate that in some respects the law does treat separate parts or products of the body as property; those which show that the law protects the body using the tool of consent to recognise rights to autonomy or bodily integrity; and those which argue that the law should adopt a combination of the two. It may be that the parents who brought a group action in *AB and Others* did feel that their child's body had been wrongfully interfered with, although I doubt that they felt that this was interference with their possession or ownership of their child's body, as Gage J himself recognised.[30] It was certainly the case that parents felt that they should have been asked whether organs from their child's body could be removed and retained for the purposes of

---

[27] J Bridgeman, 'When Systems Fail: Parents, Children and the Quality of Healthcare' (2005) 58 *Current Legal Problems* 183.

[28] M Maclean, 'Letting Go ... Parents, Professionals and the Law in the Retention of Human Material after Post Mortem' in A Bainham, S Day Sclater and M Richards (eds), *Body Lore and Laws* (Oxford, Hart, 2002) 81.

[29] J Harris, 'Who Owns my Body?' (1996) 16 *OJLS* 55; P Matthews, 'Whose Body? People and Property' [1983] *Current Legal Problems* 193; P Matthews, 'The Man of Property' [1995] 3 *Medical Law Review* 251; A Grubb, '"I, Me, Mine": Bodies, Parts and Property' (1998) 3 *Medical Law International* 299; L Skene, 'Proprietary Rights in Human Bodies, Body Parts and Tissue' (2002) 22 *Legal Studies* 102; JK Mason and GT Laurie, 'Consent or Property? Dealing with the Body and its Parts in the Shadow of Bristol and Alder Hey' (2001) 64 *MLR* 711; and J Herring and P-L Chau, 'My Body, Your Body, Our Bodies' (2007) 15 *Medical Law Review* 34. See also Reece, this volume.

[30] *AB and others*, above n 23, at [134].

examination, teaching and research, whether or not they were formally required to give consent. To construct the wrong in terms of violation of property interests is to miss the point and, despite the difficulties in its application in this relational context, consent has been the tool selected in the reform of the law in this area.

The broadening of the relationship from one of parental rights over, to parental responsibility for, the child may reflect an understanding that whilst parents have a particular relationship with, and role in relation to, their children, they do not own them and neither do they own their children's bodies after death. David Archard's analysis details how problematic is the attempt to apply classical accounts of property, such as those found in the work of Aristotle and Locke, to children.[31] In his analysis of *Gillick*,[32] Jonathan Montgomery argued that, by approaching the issue as one of parental right to control, the Court of Appeal had treated children as if they were items of property. In contrast, the House of Lords understood parental rights—on the facts of the case to consent to the touching involved in medical examination and treatment— as existing for the benefit of children as separate persons:

> The trend in recent years has been to regard parental rights and duties as existing for the benefit of children ... If parental rights exist for the benefit of children not adults, then the family is to be conceived of as a community of individuals with separable interests and not merely as a unitary state to be controlled by a (benevolent?) despot.[33]

Helen Reece, in this collection, argues that it is a mistake to consider that the law, aided by the tool of parental rights, treats children as the property of their parents, suggesting that the facts that children need to be cared for and that parental rights exist for the benefit of children go without argument.

In their examination of the question, 'Are Persons Property?', Margaret Davies and Ngaire Naffine identify the dominant perception of personhood as self-possessive individualism[34] and the modern meaning of property within law as:

> [D]escrib[ing] a legal relationship *between* persons *in respect* of an object, rather than the relation between a subject and the objects possessed as property of the person. A property right enables the proprietor to exercise control over a thing, the object of property, against the rest of the world. Property thus defines the limits of our sphere of influence over the world; it defines the borders of our control over things and so marks the degree of our social and legal power. The claim of property in oneself is an assertion of self-possession and self-control, of a fundamental right to exclude others from one's very being. It is a means of individuating the person, of establishing a limit between the one and the other: between thine and mine; between you and me.[35]

---

[31]   D Archard, *Children: Rights and childhood* (London, Routledge, 2004) 141–5.
[32]   *Gillick v West Norfolk and Wisbech AHA and another* [1985] 1 All ER 533 (CA); [1985] 3 WLR 830 (HL).
[33]   J Montgomery, 'Children as Property?' (1988) 51 *MLR* 323, 332.
[34]   M Davies and N Naffine, *Are Persons Property? Legal debates about property and personality* (Aldershot, Ashgate, 2001) ch 3.
[35]   *Ibid*, 6.

Furthermore, whilst the relationship of parent and child might be characterised by control and power, the child is not an object, a thing, but rather a person with a claim to self-possession. Yet, whilst each child is an individual, they are also connected to others through emotional ties, practically and financially dependent and cared for by others who have responsibilities to them. Appreciation of this leads us to question whether the borders or limits between individual persons are so clearly defined or, once established, fixed: perhaps we should rather, as Jonathan Herring and PL Chau suggest, understand all persons as connected and their bodies as interacting and changing.[36] They argue that the law should provide a framework which 'reflects, supports, and respects' all aspects of our bodies: individuated and connected; changing, recreating and interacting with our environment; and central to our identities.[37] The examples they offer of the mutual interdependency and relationality of the body are physical—pregnancy, breastfeeding, sex and caring work—of bodies interacting in a physical way with the environment, and changing physically through ageing, or with levels of health and fitness. Whilst offering important insights into the way in which we view, and regulate, the body, the argument which they advance about the interdependency and relationality of persons is neither confined to bodies nor to the physical.

John Harris has expressed the view that people hold ambivalent and inconsistent attitudes towards body parts, disposing of some without a moment's pause and demonstrating sentimental attachment to other parts or to the same parts in different circumstances. The debate about legal regulation of dealing in body parts should not, he argues, be driven by the context of the organ retention scandal:

> The families involved in the misdeeds at Alder Hey deserve our sympathy and respect, not least because they have been deceived and unnecessarily distressed. But they are not the only bereaved families in the world. Almost all families have experienced bereavement, and all will at some point suffer irreparable loss. We should not let the agenda on such an important issue as organ retention and use be set by those forced to view it though the distorting lens of grief, particularly when one result may be that other families may still have to suffer grief prematurely as a result.[38]

I would suggest that the experiences of the families involved in Alder Hey, whilst not *setting* the agenda, should be on it and that the lens of grief is instructive in the development of appropriate legal regulation of such a sensitive issue. In particular, I suggest, the responses of the families involved show that debate about law reform cannot be confined to the dichotomy between consent and property, but rather must engage with questions of relationship and responsibility. As Margot Brazier explains in her response to John Harris, legal regulation of this issue has to accommodate the responsibility of those connected to the

---

[36] Herring and Chau, above n 29.

[37] *Ibid*, 52.

[38] J Harris, 'Law and regulation of retained organs: the ethical issues' (2002) 22 *Legal Studies* 527, 548.

deceased to dispose of a loved one's body according to their religious and family values: to fulfil their final act of caring responsibility.[39] The evidence provided by parents to the Bristol Royal Infirmary Inquiry reveals the extent to which parents continued to perceive their child as an individual for whom they had a continuing responsibility to care and protect even after the child's death. This is captured in the comment of Paul Bradley, father of Bethan, who died following surgery at Bristol Royal Infirmary:

> [T]here was no appreciation of Bethan. It was as if she ceased to have any existence just because she had died. The retention of organs was a violation of her. The manner in which it was done, without reference to us, was an assumption that Bethan's body belonged to the Hospital to do with her as they wished. Yet to us, Bethan was still our daughter even though she had died.[40]

Death does not extinguish the relationship between parent and child: the child remains the child of the parent, and they continue to feel a sense of responsibility towards their child:

> When a child dies that child is still the parents' child—not a specimen, not a case, not an unfortunate casualty of a failed procedure, but someone's baby, someone's child.[41]

As Mavis Maclean observes, parents who gave evidence to the Bristol Royal Infirmary Inquiry spoke not in terms of a parental right to property in their child's body, but of parental responsibility to care and protect enduring after death.[42] The parent/child relationship commences before the child gains legal personhood and endures beyond their death. From this arises the continued responsibility to care for and protect the child as an individual, as explored in the next section.

A CONTINUING PARENTAL RESPONSIBILITY TO CARE AND PROTECT

To be a parent is necessarily a relational status of connection with another, a child. Parenting is an activity, a behaviour and a role to which social, moral and legal responsibilities are ascribed. Whilst there are aspects of parental responsibility which are legally and socially imposed and there are some overarching tenets to parental responsibility, the exact content of parental responsibility arises from the particular parent/child relationship and depends upon the specific circumstances. In other words, parents' responsibilities change as the child matures and will differ according to the child's needs: for example, parents' responsibilities to a child with a chronic condition or severe disabilities are different from those to a

---

[39]   M Brazier, 'Retained organs: ethics and humanity' (2002) 22 *Legal Studies* 550.
[40]   Written statement from Paul Bradley, father of Bethan, <http://www.bristol-inquiry.org.uk> accessed 17 December 2008.
[41]   CMO Summit, 'Proceedings', Bristol Heart Children's Action Group (11 January 2001) 6.
[42]   Maclean, above n 28, 81.

healthy child. The Children Act 1989 requires courts to make decisions regarding the upbringing of children in the child's best interests, and contested decisions made by parents referred to court will be measured by that touchstone. However, on a daily basis compromises have to be made, the interests of other children accommodated and those of parents and other family members included in decisions about daily routines and timetables, menus and activities. Although not a legal obligation, in extreme circumstances such as the serious illness of a child or, in the context of this chapter, the death of a child, other interests become less significant and other demands less pressing as the primary focus of concern is upon the child's interests.

We can start to gain an insight into the meaning and experience of parental, relational, responsibility following a child's death from the evidence offered by parents, whose child died during or after heart surgery, to the Bristol Royal Infirmary Inquiry. A reading of this evidence reveals two very clear aspects to the relational responsibility as felt and understood by these parents following the death of their child. The first was to ensure that their child continued to be treated as an individual and with respect and dignity. The second was that the responsibility they had to care for and protect their child, which existed during their lifetime, continued after the child's death.[43] Furthermore, as with during their child's medical treatment, the parents themselves had to entrust elements of their child's care to other professionals. When these professionals failed to treat their child with respect, parents felt that they had failed in their responsibility to care for and protect their child. Paul Bradley, Bethan's father, commented:

> The worst aspect of Bethan's second operation was the losing of control over her. There was nothing we could do. We had to rely entirely upon the 'experts'. After Bethan's death, the only controls returned to us were the arrangement of her funeral and subsequent burial. We now discover that even this was not so. There was no regard for Bethan's body or our feelings on the matter.[44]

A sense of an ongoing relational responsibility to ensure respect for the child as an individual and to care for and protect their child was also expressed by parents in their evidence to the inquiry into the retention of organs at Alder Hey Children's Hospital in Liverpool.[45] Alexandra's mother expressed her sense of having failed to protect her child by having placed her trust in others who failed to treat her child with respect:

> [A]s a parent ... she would have done anything and everything in her power to protect her child. That was what she was there to do even more so in death because it was the

---

[43] Written statements submitted by parents whose children underwent cardiac surgery in Bristol between 1984 and 1995 to the Bristol Royal Infirmary Inquiry, available from the inquiry website, <http://www.bristol-inquiry.org.uk> accessed 17 December 2008.

[44] Written statement from Paul Bradley, father of Bethan, <http://www.bristol-inquiry.org.uk> accessed 17 December 2008, 18.

[45] 'The Royal Liverpool Children's Inquiry: Report' (30 January 2001), chairman, Mr Michael Redfern QC.

only thing she could do for her child at that stage. She had put her trust in the doctors, the midwives, the pathologists that they would respect her child and that they would deal with her in the way one would wish to deal with a dead person. They did not, they desecrated her. She feels let down. There was only one thing she could do and that was to protect her in death and she did not do it and she has to live with that.[46]

Many parents expressed the sense that they had failed to ensure that their child was treated with respect and dignity and thus had failed to protect them when their child 'needed them most':

She feels her daughter has not been treated with the respect she deserved in death. She feels guilty that having loved her daughter so dearly in life she let her down when she needed her most, namely in allowing her organs to be retained without consent. Overall she feels let down, disgusted, angry, upset and betrayed.[47]

They now feel that they signed the consent because they were under pressure and lied to. Their child lost his dignity and was treated like a piece of meat in a butcher's shop. They feel let down. They feel that their child's dignity was taken away when his organs were retained ... They feel guilty that they did not protect their child in death.[48]

The impression given by Alder Hey was that an individual's identity ends at post mortem examination if not death ... They feel that they protected their child in life but in death when he needed their protection even more than ever, they feel guilty that they let him down in allowing or permitting organ retention.[49]

Whilst there are similarities in the circumstances and hence experiences of the parents who gave evidence to the Bristol Royal Infirmary and Alder Hey Inquiries which might lead one to expect them to have similar perspectives on their relational responsibilities, and whilst I can point to no comparable bodies of evidence or comprehensive research studies on the experience and meaning of parental responsibility to parents whose children died in other circumstances, I suggest that this understanding of parental responsibility is shared whatever the circumstances of the child's death, although exactly how the responsibility to ensure respect for the child as an individual and to care for and protect the child is understood might differ depending upon whether the death resulted from a termination, miscarriage, stillbirth, the limitation or withdrawal of treatment, unexplained causes, congenital disabilities, acute or chronic illness, following surgery, due to an accident or the deliberate actions of another. It is, I suggest, well illustrated by a case which has returned to media attention as I complete the writing of this chapter. In July 2008, the *Times* reported a High Court challenge to the use by Enfield Council of new powers to register the death of Christopher

---

[46] *Ibid*, 408: Alexandra, stillborn.
[47] *Ibid*, 415: Lindsay, died at the age of seven months after cardiac surgery.
[48] *Ibid*, 416: Jordan, stillborn.
[49] *Ibid*, 425: Sam, died following surgery at the age of 18 months.

Blum without giving a cause.[50] Christopher died in June 1987 at the age of four months and had remained in the mortuary for twenty-one years as a result of his parents' refusal to sign the death certificate. His father refused to sign a certificate giving the cause of death as sudden infant cot death. Christopher died hours after administration of the whooping cough, polio and tetanus vaccine. His parents believed that his death may have been the result of a contaminated vaccine and wanted an inquest into the cause of death. His father, Steve Blum, explained:

> We were advised to put Christopher's death behind us and try for another baby. His life had been snuffed out and no-one seemed to give a damn. People seemed to think that because he was only four months old that he didn't really count ... Today we accept that Christopher is dead but we do not accept he died of cot death. It's a matter of respect to have the correct cause of death on the certificate ... The whole thing is horrible and disrespectful. They made a mess of my boy trying to find the cause of death and in the end they copped out and claimed it was cot death. I feel guilty that I haven't been able to do right by him so far. But I will continue to fight until I get the right result. It's the least I can do for the little fellow.[51]

After losing the legal challenge, Christopher was buried in November 2008, by Enfield Council but without his parents or siblings.[52]

There have been studies of parents coping with perinatal death, which is the death of a baby from miscarriage or termination after 12 weeks of pregnancy, stillbirth or in the first 28 days of life. These studies reveal the ways in which parents sought to secure recognition of their child as a unique individual with a clear place in the family,[53] connected through relationships which continued after death.[54] In these cases, where the child had died before or shortly after birth, parents found ways of recognising the presence of the child as an individual and marking their child's place in the family through memories and mementos such as photographs, footprints, a lock of hair or the blanket in which they had been swaddled. In her study, Claudia Malacrida noted the guilt and pain experienced by parents who did not feel that they had been able to give their stillborn child an appropriate funeral because of the failure of others to recognise them as a person. Friends and families of these parents appeared to fail to see the importance of such an occasion, sending the message that there was no real loss:

---

[50] D Brown, 'After 21 years in a freezer, baby boy will be buried against his parents' wishes' *The Times* (28 July 2008) 20.

[51] J Beattie, 'We won't Bury our Baby Until Doctors Say Vaccine is Killer! Baby in Morgue for Nine Years as Parents Dispute Cause of Death' *The People* (22 December 1996) 1 and 11.

[52] R Stansfield, 'Baby Christopher Buried After 22 years' *The Mirror* (8 November 2008) 22.

[53] D Côté-Arsenaulty, 'Weaving Babies Lost in Pregnancy Into the Fabric of the Family' (2003) *Journal of Family Nursing* 23, 36. Although *Znamenskaya v Russia*, Application no 77785/01, 12 October 2005 suggests that recognition of the paternity of a stillborn baby could be an Art 8 right of the parents to respect for their private life.

[54] C Jonas-Simpson and E McMahon, 'The Language of Loss When a Baby Dies Prior to Birth: Cocreating Human Experience' (2005) 18 *Nursing Science Quarterly* 124, 128.

Parents eventually come to understand that they have no right to ask for help, and they come to believe that the responsibility for dealing with this 'problem' rests solely with them.[55]

The last act of caring was very much experienced as their responsibility.

The loss of control noted by the father of Bethan, who had died after heart surgery (above), was also experienced by parents whose children died of a 'cot death' or sudden unexplained infant death (SUID).[56] As the cause of death is unknown, the coroner has to be informed and a postmortem examination must be held in an attempt to establish the cause of death. The formal processes of investigation prevail to exclude the parents in their attempts to care for and protect their child.

For parents whose children have died as a result of the deliberate actions of another, the parents' responsibility to ensure respect of the child as an individual and to care and protect may take the form of the pursuit of justice for their child. As one mother has explained, theirs is the responsibility to represent and 'stand by' their child as the perpetrator is brought to court and punished.[57]

REFLECTIONS UPON PARENTAL RESPONSIBILITY

In his recent book, *Family Law and Personal Life*, John Eekelaar includes responsibility as one of the values which should guide personal law. In his discussion, he contrasts responsibility with two concepts which I have employed in this chapter: rights and obligations. In brief, I understand moral rights to be individual entitlements which, if given legal effect, may become legal rights; and obligations to be those which are, morally or legally, owed to another. The difference between rights and responsibilities is that whilst the former are focused upon individual claims, responsibilities are relational and their content dependent upon the needs of the other in the relationship.[58] The distinction drawn by John Eekelaar between obligations and responsibility is that whilst 'a responsible person follows their legal obligations, responsibility does not stop there'.[59] Relational, contextual and transcending that which is owed to others, Eekelaar suggests that by their nature responsibilities cannot be legally enforced. Law can encourage responsible behaviour, but if it is legally enforceable it is no longer a responsibility, rather it

[55] C Malacrida, 'Complicating Mourning: The Social Economy of Perinatal Death' (1999) 9 *Qualitative Health Research* 504, 515.
[56] In 2004, 357 children under the age of one year, and 20 over the age of one, died from SUID: The Foundation for the Study of Infant Deaths.
[57] JD Schmidt, 'Murder of a child' in TA Rando (ed), *Parental Loss of A Child* (Illinois, Research Press Co, 1986) 218.
[58] J Eekelaar, *Family Law and Personal Life* (Oxford, Oxford University Press, 2006) 128.
[59] *Ibid*, 129.

has been translated into a legal obligation.[60] Perhaps then the legislators were right back in 1989 to define parental responsibility as all the:

> rights, duties, powers, responsibilities and authority which by law a parent of a child has in relation to the child and his property?[61]

By which I mean that whilst parental responsibility includes parental rights, duties and powers, it is more than the sum of these. Going beyond legally enforceable rights, duties or powers, responsibilities are contextual, relational and other-regarding, such that we will not arrive at a single definition of parental responsibility applicable in all circumstances. To give substance to our understanding of parental responsibility, what is required is the development of a conceptual framework of parental responsibility informed by parental experience and understanding of their responsibilities in the variety of circumstances in which it is exercised.

A strict reading of the Children Act 1989 might lead to the conclusion that parental responsibility ends with a child's death. Children are defined in the Children Act 1989 as persons under the age of 18[62] and 'persons' refers to live persons. A reading of the law does not support this view, even if it is only the limited duty and right to dispose of the child's body. However, more importantly, I suggest, parents' relational responsibility transcends legal obligations and endures beyond the child's death. Parents have expressed an understanding of their responsibilities to their deceased child in terms of respecting the child's dignity and individuality and a continuing responsibility to care for and protect them. I have argued that parents' responsibilities vary according to the circumstances, including the child's needs, societal expectations, individual abilities, public support and legal obligations. What I hope to have demonstrated in this chapter is the need for the development of a conceptual framework of parental responsibility informed by parental experience and understanding of their responsibilities to nurture the child as a unique individual, and to care for and protect the child in the variety of circumstances in which it is exercised.

---

[60] *Ibid*, 130–1.
[61] Children Act 1989 s 3(1).
[62] Children Act 1989 s 105(1).

Part III

Responsible Parenting

15

Financial Support for Children after Parental Separation: Parental Responsibility and Responsible Parenting

NICK WIKELEY

INTRODUCTION

THIS CHAPTER EXPLORES the inter-relationship between parental responsibility, responsible parenting and the child support and child maintenance obligations. As the authors of *Bromley's Family Law* explain:

A legal obligation to provide financial support for another member of the family may be seen as the most tangible recognition of the moral ties created by family relationships. Where such an obligation is imposed, it also sheds light on social conceptions of the appropriate scope of those ties. Different societies at different times may impose the obligations upon different degrees of relationship.[1]

Of all such obligations to support family members, the duty to maintain which flows from the parent/child relationship has been one of the most enduring. According to Blackstone, the relationship between parent and child is 'the most universal relation in nature';[2] in his world, the parents of legitimate children owed a threefold duty to their offspring: to maintain, protect and educate them. This triumvirate of parental obligations reflected social norms which were well established by the early modern period.[3] The common law recognised no similar

---

[1] N Lowe and G Douglas, *Bromley's Family Law* (10th edn, Oxford, Oxford University Press, 2007) 914 (footnotes omitted). Unfortunately the example that follows in *Bromley* is only partially correct, as the Poor Law certainly imposed an obligation on grandparents to maintain their grandchildren, but not vice versa: Poor Relief Act 1601 s 6; and *Maund v Mason* (1873–4) LR 9 QB 254.

[2] W Morrison (ed), *Blackstone's Commentaries on the Laws of England: Vol I* (London, Cavendish Publishing, 2001) 343.

[3] See LA Pollock, 'Parent-Child Relations' in DI Kertzer and M Barbagli (eds), *Family Life in Early Modern Times 1500–1789* (New Haven, Yale University Press, 2001) 191, citing William Gouge's treatise *Of Domesticall Duties* (London, 1622), which declared that parents had a threefold task: to nourish, nurture and instruct their children.

obligation of support for illegitimate children, with the result that the liability of reputed fathers evolved through the bastardy jurisdiction as an adjunct to the poor law.[4]

The more comprehensive understanding of 'parental responsibility' as set out in today's family law textbooks includes the obligation 'to protect and maintain the child'.[5] On this basis the child maintenance obligation is merely one example, and a sub-set, of the broader concept of parental responsibility. On another level, however, there is a dissonance between the legal concept of parental responsibility and the child maintenance and child support obligations. Therefore, for example, an unmarried father may lack parental responsibility, yet still owe his child a duty of maintenance and support. Conversely, an adult who is not a genetic parent may enjoy parental responsibility, but will never be liable for child support (at least in the strict sense of that term as maintenance payable under the Child Support Act 1991). However, irrespective of whether that individual has ever acquired formal parental responsibility for the child, he or she may of course be liable to maintain that child (for example, in ancillary relief proceedings) where he or she has treated that child 'as a child of their family'.[6]

It follows that there is at best an uneasy fit between the legal notion of parental responsibility and the specific obligations of child support and child maintenance. This chapter starts by identifying the circumstances in which any such obligations arise as a matter of law. It then considers how the law seeks to quantify the extent of this duty to support and maintain children, and what is known about the incidence of awards in practice. Finally, this chapter considers the moral or philosophical basis for the imposition of such a duty and how far this has been translated into and reflected in the law.

At the outset of this discussion, however, the terminology involved needs to be clarified. For the purposes of this chapter, the term 'child support' refers exclusively to the obligation arising under the Child Support Act 1991, whereas 'child maintenance' refers to the parallel (but not coincident) duties that may be imposed in the context of other legislation (notably, but by no means exclusively, under the Matrimonial Causes Act 1973 and the Children Act 1989). For present purposes, and especially in the latter context, the focus is also on the obligation to provide maintenance by way of regular periodical payments, and so does not include the possibility of capital provision.[7] In the discussion that follows, an

---

[4] N Wikeley, *Child Support Law and Policy* (Oxford, Hart Publishing, 2006) 69 (hereinafter, 'Wikeley').

[5] See, eg Lowe and Douglas, above n 1, 377; and J Herring, *Family Law* (3rd edn, Harlow, Pearson Education Ltd, 2007) 383.

[6] Matrimonial Causes Act 1973 s 52(1); see also to the same effect Domestic Proceedings and Magistrates' Courts Act 1978 s 88(1), Children Act 1989 s 105(1) and Civil Partnership Act 2004 Sch 5, para 80(2) and Sch 6, para 48. See generally Lowe and Douglas, above n 1, 338–40.

[7] Of course, there is no power under the Child Support Act 1991 to make capital orders, unlike under the Matrimonial Causes Act 1973 or the Children Act 1989.

umbrella expression—'the duty to provide for children'—is used to describe the aggregate of these child support and maintenance obligations.

We should note that in future it may prove much more difficult to maintain this conceptual and formal distinction between child *support* and child *maintenance*, not least because since the publication of the Henshaw Report[8] and the subsequent White Paper[9] the Labour Government has insisted on using the language of 'child maintenance' in its programme to reform and re-brand the creaking child support system. Indeed, Parliament has since enacted the Child Maintenance and Other Payments Act 2008, as a result of which the Child Support Agency (CSA) has been abolished and replaced by the new Child Maintenance and Enforcement Commission (CMEC).[10]

WHO IS SUBJECT TO THE LEGAL DUTY TO PROVIDE FOR CHILDREN?

The discussion so far in this chapter assumes that the legal duty to provide for children is a duty that rests with individuals—so parents are, and in certain cases non-parents may be, under an obligation to support their children. In fact, of course, society as a whole accepts some responsibility for providing for children. In terms of cash transfers, the community at large provides support for nearly all children, primarily through the universal child benefit and the means-tested child tax credit, both of which are funded out of general taxation—and so paid for by all taxpayers, irrespective of whether they have children themselves. However, in the United Kingdom, these forms of assistance are typically seen as secondary to individual parental obligations. Repeated social surveys have demonstrated strong support for the proposition that the principal responsibility for maintaining children in the event of divorce or separation lies with their parents.[11] This approach is consistent with international norms. For example, the United Nations Convention on the Rights of the Child (UNCRC) recognises:

> the right of every child to a standard of living adequate for the child's physical, mental, spiritual, moral and social development,[12]

while also acknowledging that:

> [the] parent(s) or others responsible for the child have the *primary responsibility* to secure, within their abilities and financial capacities, the conditions of living necessary for the child's development.[13]

---

[8] DWP, 'Recovering child support—routes to responsibility' (Cm 6894, 2006).

[9] DWP, 'A new system of child maintenance' (Cm 6979, 2006).

[10] See P Parkinson, 'Reengineering the Child Support Scheme: An Australian Perspective on the British Government's Proposals' (2007) 70 *MLR* 812; and N Wikeley, 'Child Support Reform—Throwing the baby out with the bathwater?' [2007] 19 *CFLQ* 434.

[11] The evidence is reviewed in Wikeley, above n 4, 18–19.

[12] UNCRC Art 27(1).

[13] UNCRC Art 27(2), emphasis added.

Formally, as a matter of legal principle, all parents are subject to the duty to provide for their children, including parents in intact families. However, in the absence of family breakdown (and/or serious child neglect), the respect for family autonomy and privacy is such that there is little enthusiasm for questioning the distribution and allocation of resources in intact families, whether or not income and other assets are in fact shared equitably within households. There is, of course, ample evidence that such resources are not shared equally.[14] However, the duty to provide for children and the quantification of that obligation only become a live issue, both in policy and practical terms, on divorce or separation. As Baroness Hale explained in *R (Kehoe) v Secretary of State for Work and Pensions*,[15] the child support and maintenance obligations are essentially parallel means to the same end. As mentioned above, however, one difficulty is that these parallel duties operate in overlapping domains.

The Legal Duty to Provide for Children: Who Is Liable for Child Support?

In particular, we should recognise that the scope of the statutory duty of child support under the Child Support Act 1991 is not perhaps as universal and all-embracing as is commonly thought. For example, it should be noted that under section 1(1) of the 1991 Act, 'each parent of a qualifying child is responsible for maintaining him', but only '[f]or the purposes of this Act'. That limited statement of principle immediately highlights two important qualifications to the scope of the statutory duty of child support.

The first, and for present purposes more important condition, is that only a 'parent' can be liable under the 1991 Act—and a 'parent' means simply 'any person who is in law the mother or father of the child',[16] so leaving the boundaries of the notion of a 'parent' to the combined vagaries of statute and case law. In summary, therefore, parents are 'natural' parents, adoptive parents and parents recognised as such under the Human Fertilisation and Embryology Act (HFEA) 1990.[17] Leaving aside for one moment the latter two rather special and less common types of case, the construction of parenthood in the 1991 Act is often characterised as representing the reaffirmation of the supremacy of biological or genetic parentage over social parenting. The most extreme manifestation of this approach is that a man who acts outside the protection of the HFEA 1990 as a sperm donor for a lesbian couple will be liable for child support when that couple's relationship breaks down, even though he has never acted as a social

---

[14] See, eg J Pahl, *Money and Marriage* (Basingstoke, Macmillan Education, 1989).

[15] [2005] UKHL 48.

[16] Child Support Act 1991 s 54.

[17] But note that there is no scope for the acquisition of the status of 'parent' by estoppel in circumstances which would now be covered by the Human Fertilisation and Embryology Act 1990, but which occurred before the relevant legislation was in force: *Re M (Child Support Act: Parentage)* [1997] 2 FLR 90.

parent for the child in question.[18] In fact, of course, the attribution of child support liabilities to 'parents' is a little more complex than the conventional primacy of the genetic paradigm might suggest.

In the first place, and as a matter of practice, the parties and the law will simply assume paternity in many cases by virtue of the fact that the parties are or were married to each other. Indeed, the Child Support Agency (now CMEC) is entitled to proceed on the basis of this common law presumption as to parentage, which has been translated into statutory form in the 1991 Act.[19] In other cases, albeit without the support of any statutory presumption, the parties will often assume paternity by reason of a long-standing sexual relationship, whether or not that involves cohabitation. Yet we know that the incidence of the misattribution of paternity is probably in the order of about 4 per cent, which adds up overall to many children.[20] It is only if the truth subsequently emerges that an aggrieved assumed 'father' may seek to unravel the child support liability. In this context, the common law in the United Kingdom has responded very differently to its Australian counterpart to claims for reimbursement by 'cuckolded' (or, to put it more neutrally, assumed false positive) fathers. Here, the High Court has held that in certain circumstances a 'duped' father may bring an action in the tort of deceit,[21] an avenue which has been closed off by the highest Australian federal court.[22]

Furthermore, the prioritisation of genetic parentage over social parenthood in the 1991 Act has in any event been tempered over time by changes to the child support formula. Notoriously, the original formula, reflecting Mrs Thatcher's insistence that genetic parenthood (for which read fatherhood) is for life, made very little allowance for 'second family' children, whether they be the father's own children born into a subsequent relationship or his subsequently acquired step-children. This policy was largely abandoned with the March 2003 reforms to the child support system, implemented by the Child Support, Pensions and Social Security Act 2000. The position today is that the new scheme formula seeks to accord broadly equal recognition to all of a non-resident parent's (NRP's) children and step-children.[23] This approach has been maintained under the post-Henshaw reforms in the 2008 Act.

---

[18] Illustrated most graphically in the much-publicised case of Andy Bathie: <http://news.bbc.co.uk/1/hi/england/london/7125895.stm> accessed 17 December 2008. Strictly, as a matter of law, he was of course potentially liable for child support under the 1991 Act even before the couple's relationship broke down.

[19] Child Support Act 1991 s 26 and Case A1.

[20] MA Bellis, K Hughes, S Hughes and JR Ashton, 'Measuring paternal discrepancy and its public health consequences' (2005) 59 *Journal of Epidemiology and Community Health* 749.

[21] *A v B* [2007] EWHC 1246.

[22] *Magill v Magill* (2006) 231 ALR 277 (High Court of Australia); for competing critiques, see KB Handley, 'Paternity Fraud' (2007) 123 *LQR* 337; and N Wikeley and L Young, 'Secrets and Lies: No deceit down under for paternity fraud' [2008] 20 *CFLQ* 81.

[23] So, eg a non-resident parent with one child from a previous relationship and with one new child or step-child will be assumed to devote 15% of his net income to the new child's support and then 15% of his remaining net income to the first child: see further Wikeley, above n 4, 303–4.

The second qualification inherent in section 1(1) is that a child support liability may arise only in relation to a 'qualifying child', that is a child with at least one parent who has the status of being a non-resident parent.[24] Therefore, whereas the concept of a 'child' is at least partially defined by the 1991 Act, in terms of both the age and educational status of the child,[25] the notion of a 'qualifying child' is defined exclusively by reference to the status of that child's parents. Two important consequences flow from this parasitic definition.

First, it inevitably follows from the narrow definition of 'parent' that there can be no liability under the 1991 Act for a step-child, foster-child or other 'child of the family' in the broader family law understanding of that expression.[26] The Child Support Agency's (now CMEC's) statutory writ simply does not run to such cases. Therefore, the only way to enforce any financial provision in such circumstances will be by way of an action for child maintenance in the ordinary courts.

Secondly, and crucially, genetic parentage is a *necessary* but by no means *sufficient* precondition for liability under the 1991 Act. The parent in question must also be a *non-resident* parent—which means that he must not be living in the same household as the child and the child in turn must have 'his home with a person who is, in relation to him, a person with care'.[27] These requirements are in turn further defined and refined in such a way that their application can become highly contentious. Most notably, a father who has shared care for say three nights a week will not for these purposes be living in the same household as his children and they will not have their home with him. He will accordingly be deemed by law to be a non-resident parent,[28] so heightening the sense of injustice perceived by fathers' rights lobby groups. Less controversially, it means that where the adults are estranged but still living in the same household with their child, there can be no child support liability[29]—although in theory a child maintenance claim may be brought in the ordinary courts.

It is, of course, the general rule under the 1991 Act, assuming that there is a non-resident parent, a person with care and a qualifying child (described below as 'the statutory trio') and that each of them is habitually resident in the United Kingdom,[30] that the Secretary of State (in the guise of the Child Support Agency and now CMEC) has exclusive jurisdiction to make a child support maintenance calculation. If any one of the statutory trio is no longer habitually resident within

---

[24]   Child Support Act 1991 s 3(1) and (2).

[25]   Child Support Act 1991 s 55. This definition has been brought into line with the new child benefit definition of 'child' as a result of the amendment in Child Maintenance and Other Payments Act 2008, s 42.

[26]   Unless, of course, the child has been adopted: see Commissioner's decision *R(CS) 6/03*, paras 8–10 and see also *CCS/3128/1995* (grandparent not liable unless adoption has taken place).

[27]   Child Support Act 1991 s 3(2).

[28]   Child Support (Maintenance Calculations and Special Cases) Regulations 2000 (SI 2001/155) reg 8(1); see further Wikeley, above n 4, 245–8.

[29]   See, eg *CCS/14625/1996*, discussed in Wikeley, 242.

[30]   Child Support Act 1991 s 44(1).

the jurisdiction, it follows that the agency cedes its jurisdiction and an application may be made to court for child maintenance.[31] Furthermore, as we have
already seen, the same applies if any one member of the statutory trio loses their
status as, for example, a *non-resident* parent or a *qualifying* child. The courts are
also left with a residual power to make orders in a number of special cases even
where on the face of it all members of the statutory trio fall within the agency's
jurisdiction. These are, for example, where either the parties agree to a consent
order or where the child has extra costs associated with educational or disability
needs, or where a 'top-up order' is appropriate in the case of a high-earning
non-resident parent.[32]

The Legal Duty to Provide for Children: Who Is Liable for Child Maintenance?

If the case is one in which the courts retain jurisdiction in some way, the
boundaries of liability for child maintenance are both narrower and wider,
depending on the ambit of the relevant legislative code which is invoked.
Obviously in ancillary relief proceedings on divorce, only a spouse (or former
spouse) can be made liable to pay child maintenance; but, as we have seen, that
spouse need not be the child's genetic parent, given the court's power to make an
order in favour of a 'child of the family'.[33] Maintenance orders may also be made
under section 15 of, and Schedule 1 to, the Children Act 1989 against any parent,
a term defined so as to include married step-parents.[34] Although the Children Act
1989 may be used to impose a maintenance obligation on unmarried cohabitants
in respect of their own (genetic) children, there is no power to make such an
order in relation to a child treated by the cohabitant as a 'child of the family'.[35]
Furthermore, although a civil partner can never be a liable parent for the
purposes of the Child Support Act 1991,[36] as civil partnership alone cannot
accord the status of being a 'parent',[37] he or she may be subject to a child
maintenance order for any 'child of the family' under either Schedules 5 or 6 to
the Civil Partnership Act 2004 or Schedule 1 to the Children Act 1989, mirroring
the provisions governing matrimonial ancillary relief proceedings.[38]

---

[31] Anecdotally, there is some evidence that some unscrupulous NRPs who are resident overseas
(and so potentially within the UK courts' jurisdiction) will deliberately arrange for themselves to be
paid through a UK company in order to bring them within the deemed habitual residence rules and
so within the jurisdiction of the CSA—thereby ousting the courts' powers, on the not unreasonable
assumption that the CSA will be entirely ineffective in pursuing them.

[32] Child Support Act 1991 s 8.

[33] Matrimonial Causes Act 1973 ss 23(1)(d)–(f), (2) and (4), 24 and 24A; see further s 52.

[34] Children Act 1989 Sch 1, para 16(2)(a).

[35] *J v J (A Minor) (Property Transfer)* [1993] 2 FLR 56. See also *Hill v Morgan* [2007] 1 WLR 855 at
[38] (Thorpe LJ).

[36] Of course, there is nothing to stop a civil partner being a person with care under the 1991 Act,
and so having the requisite standing to apply for child support.

[37] Unless, of course, the civil partner is also an adoptive parent.

[38] See Civil Partnerships Act 2004 Sch 5, para 2(1)(d)–(f) and para 80(2); and Children Act 1989
Sch 1, para 16(2)(b).

In this discussion we must also not lose sight of the historic absence of any coherent fit between (private) family law and (public) social security law.[39] On one level there has traditionally been a close and symbiotic relationship between the two legal domains—so, for example, the liable relative rule in social security law has been used by official agencies over the centuries, to greater or lesser effect, as a means of reinforcing private law norms about the maintenance obligation. (However, note that the Child Maintenance and Other Payments Act 2008 has now abolished the liable relative rule as it relates to children.[40]) On another level, however, the social security system has ignored the formal boundaries of private law obligations. Therefore, for example, the operation of the cohabitation rule means that the social security authorities regard a step-father as being de facto responsible for his step-children, so excluding the child's mother from access to means-tested benefits, notwithstanding the absence of any legal liability on his part to support either her or her children.[41] Indeed, as already noted, on the breakdown of such a relationship, an unmarried step-parent cannot (at present) be required to pay maintenance under the Children Act 1989 for his step-child. This position looks set to continue given the government's less than wholeheartedly positive response to the Law Commission's consultation paper on the financial consequences of ceasing cohabitation.[42]

What Is the Extent of the Legal Duty to Provide for Children?

Assuming that there is a legal duty on a particular adult to provide for the child in question following the breakdown of the relationship with the other parent or partner, either via the child support or child maintenance regimes, what then is the extent of that obligation? This section considers the principles for quantifying that liability, first under the agency-administered child support system and then under the court-based child maintenance jurisdictions.

Quantifying the Duty to Provide for Children under Child Support Law

This chapter is not the place to examine the details of the child support formula, or to be precise, the child support formulae, given that the Child Support Agency (and now CMEC) has the unenviable task of operating an old and a new child support

---

[39] See further N Wikeley, 'Family Law and Social Security' in R Probert (ed), *Family Life and the Law: Under One Roof* (Aldershot, Ashgate, 2007).

[40] See Child Maintenance and Other Payments Act 2008, s 45 ; and N Wikeley, 'The Strange Death of the Liable Relative Rule' [2008] 30 *JSWFL 339–351*.

[41] See Social Security Contributions and Benefits Act 1992 ss 136 and 137(1). Accordingly, if he was in remunerative work, his partner would be denied access to income support. They would also be required to make a joint claim for child tax credit: see Tax Credits Act 2002 s 3(3).

[42] Law Commission, 'Cohabitation: The Financial Consequences of Relationship Breakdown' (Consultation Paper No 179, 2006). See also Ministry of Justice, 'Response to paper on cohabitation and relationship breakdown' (6 March 2008).

scheme in parallel universes.[43] There is certainly not space to examine the minutiae of the difference between the two statutory formulae. However, there are at least five important continuities in terms of principle which are reflected in the quantification of liabilities under both the old and new child support schemes.

First, as we have seen already, both child support schemes operate a bright-line distinction between 'parents' and those who are not (genetic, adoptive or HFEA) parents. There is no space in either the old or new scheme formula for shades of grey when it comes to the status of being a parent and its consequences. In short, formally recognised legal parentage is the hook upon which child support liability is pegged, but the cloth of the coat that hangs on that peg is then cut according to the standard formula. There is, therefore, no possibility of a reduction in liability where the child is the outcome of a casual or even fleeting relationship, nor where the conception was unwanted. In the same way, the departures and variations schemes, allowing modifications to the formula outcomes in exceptional cases, exclude any significance being attached to issues of blame or fault as between the parents.[44] As Hale J (as she then was) observed:

> The policy of the Child Support Act 1991 was that people who had children should support them, whether or not those were wanted children.[45]

There are arguably sound reasons for this approach, whether grounded in terms of individual children's rights or in terms of wider social policy considerations directed towards encouraging responsible sexual behaviour.

Secondly, both the old scheme and the new scheme work on the assumption that the children of non-resident parents are entitled to share in the standard of living of that parent. As we shall see shortly, the common law has traditionally taken a less expansive view of the maintenance obligation. True, the complexity and opaqueness of the original formula are such that the principle that children should share in their parents' standard of living is often difficult to discern in the old scheme. It is also obscured by the old formula's insistence on using basic income support allowances as the starting point for the operation of the formula, so giving the impression that the assessment of child support is a purely needs-based exercise. To that extent the old scheme invites (non-resident) parents to ask the rhetorical question, 'How much does a child cost?', not 'How much is a child entitled to?' However, the calculation of the additional amount which is due under the old scheme formula, once the maintenance requirement is met, is undoubtedly premised on the idea that children should, as a matter of principle, share in both their parents' standard of living. In the new scheme this assumption is articulated more clearly on the face of the formula, given that non-resident parents are liable to pay a set percentage of

---

[43]   In broad terms, the old scheme relates to cases taken on by the Child Support Agency between 5 April 1993 and 2 March 2003, while the new scheme governs applications made on or after 3 March 2003 (when Pt 1 of the Child Support, Pensions and Social Security Act 2000 came into force for most purposes).

[44]   Wikeley, above n 4, 398–401.

[45]   *J v C (child: financial provision)* [1998] 3 FCR 79 at 81.

their net income by way of child support, depending on the number of children involved (and depending on the presence of any second family children).

Thirdly, both the old and new child support schemes operate on the principle that all, or nearly all, non-resident parents are bound to make at least a minimum payment by way of child support in respect of their children. There are, of course, differences of detail as between the two schemes, for example, in terms of the method used to calculate the nominal amount concerned. If anything, however, the principle that all non-resident parents should make at least some contribution to the support of their children is more firmly embedded in the structure of the new scheme. This is because the range of exemptions from the liability for the minimum payment of child maintenance is much narrower under the new scheme than in the old scheme. However, in both schemes the normative message is clear—responsible parents, however low their income, should make and be seen to make a modest contribution towards the support of those of their (genetic) children who do not live with them. Although the contribution is modest (typically in the order of £5 a week), it is more than nominal (in contrast to the 5 pence per year orders commonly made before the 1991 Act).

Fourthly, and at the other end of the income spectrum, both the old and new child support schemes acknowledge the limitations of a formula-based system and allow high-income cases access to the courts for 'top-up' awards. Therefore, for example, there is a limit both to the amount of child support payable under the old scheme formula (as a percentage of the non-resident parent's income) and to the maximum net income which can be factored into the new scheme calculation. If either of those rules applies, an application may be made to court for additional payments of child maintenance over and above the standard formulaic child support liability. So there remains a place in the world of child support for individualised justice, tempered by the exercise of judicial discretion, at least for the super-rich.

Lastly, both the old and new schemes enable non-resident parents who care for their children overnight to obtain a reduction in their child support liability. In the old scheme, the threshold for such a 'discount' is 104 nights a year (on average two nights a week), whilst in the new scheme it is just 52 nights a year (one night a week). The lowering of the threshold was justified in terms of encouraging parents to share care after separation, but it has led to concerns that child support liabilities are fuelling some disputes over contact.[46] Moreover, the existence of the reduction undermines the law's formal claim that contact and child support are separate issues, to be resolved according to different principles, a position which has not commanded widespread acceptance amongst separated parents.[47]

---

[46] Thus, Resolution argues for the threshold to be raised to three nights a week and for consideration to be given to phasing out existing discounts: *Resolution's Policy on CSA Reform* (2007) 2 and 7.

[47] See further Wikeley, above n 4, 312–23; and J Herring, 'Connecting Contact: Contact in a Private Law Context' in A Bainham, B Lindley, M Richards and L Trinder (eds), *Children and Their Families* (Oxford, Hart Publishing, 2003) ch 6.

Quantifying the Duty to Provide for Children under Child Maintenance Law

The rigid and formulaic approach of the child support system to calculating maintenance is often contrasted with the broad discretion afforded to the courts in those cases in which they retain jurisdiction to make orders. Certainly, the statutory checklists of relevant factors for the award of child maintenance are expressed in fairly general terms and the weighting to be attached to individual considerations is a matter of judgement for the court. In addition, it is significant that the various legislative codes for child maintenance[48] all operate a two-tier checklist of factors.

First, there are those matters which must be considered in all cases in which the court is considering whether to make an order for child maintenance, irrespective of the relationship between the adult and child concerned. These are, for example, the child's financial needs, resources, disability and educational requirements, along with the resources, commitments and standard of living of both adults in the relationship in question.[49] These are all, to a greater or lesser extent, matters that can be particularised and quantified in financial terms. The weight to be attached to each of them, of course, is a matter for the judge's discretion.

Secondly, there are those additional considerations, all tinged with a much more normative hue, which must be taken into account, but only in those cases where the person against whom the order is sought is not the genetic parent of the child concerned. In these cases the court:

shall also have regard—

(a) to whether that party assumed any responsibility for the child's maintenance, and, if so, to the extent to which, and the basis upon which, that party assumed such responsibility and to the length of time for which that party discharged such responsibility;

(b) to whether in assuming and discharging such responsibility that party did so knowing that the child was not his or her own;

(c) to the liability of any other person to maintain the child.[50]

The unstructured and open-textured nature of this two-tier checklist is arguably not as problematic as might appear at first sight. In most cases, the court will not need to go further than the factors enumerated in the first tier of the checklist. In

---

[48] Matrimonial Causes Act 1973, Domestic Proceedings and Matrimonial Causes Act 1978, Children Act 1989 and Civil Partnerships Act 2004—there are, of course, some differences of detail and emphasis between the codes: see, eg the discussion of Children Act 1989 Sch 1 and the standard of living point in Lowe and Douglas, above n 1, 972–4.

[49] Matrimonial Causes Act 1973 s 25(3), Domestic Proceedings and Matrimonial Causes Act 1978 s 3(3), Children Act 1989 Sch 1, para 4(1) and Civil Partnerships Act 2004 Sch 5, para 22(2) and Sch 6, para 6(2).

[50] Matrimonial Causes Act 1973 s 25(4); see to the same effect Domestic Proceedings and Matrimonial Causes Act 1978 s 3(4), Children Act 1989 Sch 1, para 4(2) and Civil Partnerships Act 2004 Sch 5, para 22(3) and para 6(3).

practice, moreover, there is a very strong incentive for the parties to bargain in the shadow of the formulaic statutory child support calculation, not least given the fact that in most cases a consent order now only prevents either party applying for an assessment by the agency for a maximum period of 12 months.[51] As Nicholas Mostyn QC, sitting as a Deputy High Court judge, has observed:

> If a child maintenance order, whether made by consent or after a contest, is markedly at variance with the calculation under the new regime then there will be a high temptation for one or other party after the order has been in force for a year, and after giving two-months notice, to approach the CSA for a calculation. Quite apart from the obvious acrimony that this would engender, a calculation in a different amount to the figure originally negotiated or awarded may cast doubt on the fairness of the original ancillary relief settlement between the parties, leading to further litigation. These spectres should be avoided at all costs.[52]

It is, of course, possible that even in the absence of the 12-month rule that court orders and settlements would have shadowed the formula rates. This was the experience in Australia, where the Child Support Agency was not given the authority to make assessments in cases which had already been dealt with under the pre-existing court-based arrangements (so-called 'Stage 1' cases). Instead, the Australian agency only took on responsibility for making assessments in new 'Stage 2' cases (although it did assume the task of collecting and enforcing orders in older cases).[53] Yet in practice the levels of child maintenance ordered in Stage 1 cases tended to rise on variation applications, as the family courts had close regard to the new formula-based assessments as a guideline for old cases.[54]

Certainly, family law practitioners in England and Wales report anecdotally that one (and arguably the sole) resounding success of the March 2003 reforms to the child support formula was the creation of a transparent 'going rate' for children which could be readily explained to clients and put into practice.[55] Therefore, private agreements are often based on the expectation that a non-resident parent will pay, for example, 15 per cent of his net income in child maintenance where there is one child. If this is right, then the meaning attached to the private law parental obligation of support has undoubtedly evolved over time. At common law, of course, a father was under a limited duty (albeit

---

[51]   Under the original scheme a consent order locked out the agency indefinitely (unless the parent with care claimed benefit). The 12-month rule applies only to new scheme cases (ie those arising since 3 March 2003): Child Support Act 1991 s 4(10)(aa).

[52]   *GW v RW* [2003] EWHC 611 (Fam) at [74]. See also, in the context of non-residential parents on low incomes, *E v C (Child Maintenance)* [1996] 1 FLR 472.

[53]   Another important difference is that since the start of their child support system, Australian parents have never had the option of agreeing a court-based consent order for child maintenance—the choice has been between going through the agency (albeit in many cases with private collection arrangements) or making a wholly private arrangement.

[54]   H Rhoades, 'Australia's Child Support Scheme—is it working? (1995) 7 *Journal of Child Law* 26, 29; see further *Beck v Sliwka* (1992) 15 Fam LR 520.

[55]   See, eg House of Commons Work and Pensions Committee, 'Child Support Reform', Fourth report of Session 2006–07, Vol II (HC 219-II), Q86, Ev 19.

unenforceable in practice) to maintain his legitimate children by way of food, clothing, lodging and other necessities.[56] Once the statutory jurisdictions for the award of child maintenance were established, this was translated as meaning that:

a child of a subsisting marriage is simply to be afforded shelter, food and education, according to the means of his parents.[57]

Whilst the reference to the 'means of his parents' introduces a relativistic element to the equation, the overriding conception was that maintenance could be defined solely in terms of meeting needs. There is, furthermore, plenty of evidence that this responsibility was accorded a relatively low priority by courts and practitioners for many years, at least so far as orders for periodical payments were concerned.

This minimalist conception of the child maintenance obligation, based on traditional common law principles, was implicitly questioned by the 1991 Act. That challenge became more explicit with the adoption of the simple percentage rates in the 2000 Act. Following the 1998 Green Paper, Nicholas Mostyn QC argued forcefully in support of the common law position that while children might have an expectation that they could share in their parents' wealth, they had no right to do so—to prescribe otherwise was 'fundamentally unfair'.[58] However, the subsequent White Paper was adamant:

Children have a right to share in the income of their parents—this applies to the children of wealthy parents as much as those whose parents have more modest incomes.[59]

This resounding declaration of principle lost some of its sheen in the course of the 2000 Bill's passage, when a government concession resulted in the imposition of a cap on the maximum amount of a non-resident parent's income taken into account under the formula, meaning that the courts retained their power to make top-up orders.[60]

This detail notwithstanding, there seems to be a developing acceptance in practice that 'according to the means of his parents' presumptively means 'according to the standard formula outcome'. Therefore, if the case may at any point realistically fall within the potential jurisdiction of the Child Support

---

[56] Lowe and Douglas, above n 1, 916.

[57] *Harnett v Harnett* [1973] Fam 156 at 161D, approved by the Court of Appeal in *Lord Lilford v Glynn* [1979] 1 All ER 441 at 447h, and cited by Lowe and Douglas, above n 1, 967. *Lord Lilford v Glynn* was distinguished by the Court of Appeal in *Tavoulareas v Tavoulareas* [1998] 2 FLR 418, but see the criticism of that decision in S Gilmore, 'Case Commentary—*Re P (Child) (Financial Provision)*—Shoeboxes And Comical Shopping Trips—Child Support From The Affluent To Fabulously Rich' [2006] 16 *CFLQ* 103, 113.

[58] N Mostyn, 'The Green Paper on Child Support—Children First: a new approach to child support' [1999] *Fam Law* 95, 98.

[59] DSS, 'A new contract for welfare: Children's Rights and Parents' Responsibilities' (Cm 4349, 1999) ch 2, [36].

[60] Child Support Act 1991 s 8(6); and see Wikeley, above n 4, 332–4.

Agency (now CMEC), then the level of any award or order is likely to track the probable formulaic outcome. Responsible parenting after separation is accordingly seen in terms of a share in parental income and not simply a contribution towards maintenance. Of course, the cultural acceptance of such a 'going rate' may not be uniform across the whole separating population. It also remains to be seen how firmly this norm is embedded in practice. In particular, can it survive in a post-Henshaw world? This new environment will see much greater emphasis on private ordering at the same time as the standard 15/20/25 per cent rule is to be made more complicated as part of the shift towards basing assessments on gross rather than net incomes. In addition, the flight of high street firms from legally aided family work means that many parents will not have ready access to specialist legal advice on the consequences of relationship breakdown.

What Actually Happens to the Duty of Support in Practice?

At this stage it may be helpful to review what we know about the actual volume of child support and maintenance orders in practice. The original policy intention was that assessments made by the Child Support Agency would replace the much-discredited court orders. In fact, the agency's performance has been so dire that, wherever possible, parents have voted with their feet, with the result that private ordering has to a large extent superseded the role of the courts. We have a considerable body of data about child maintenance outcomes generally, although the robustness of these figures may not always engender complete confidence. The statistics suggest that around one-half (51 per cent) of the eligible population have some form of child maintenance provision in place, with 19 per cent of the total eligible population being subject to agency assessments, 23 per cent having private arrangements and about 9 per cent being subject to court orders or some combination of the above.[61] This leaves around one-half of the eligible population (49 per cent) with no child maintenance arrangement in place (or possibly a nominal CSA arrangement, but a nil liability). In any empirical analysis of these data, there are at least three important areas of inquiry—the number of orders and agreements made, the amounts of maintenance involved and the rate of compliance.

First, so far as the actual volume of orders is concerned, in 2006 the agency made some 130,300 new scheme maintenance calculations, but 20,100 of these resulted in nil awards, leaving some 110,200 positive assessments.[62] It should be emphasised that these figures relate solely to maintenance calculations made on new applications in the course of the year. They take no account of requests for reassessments because of changes in the parties' circumstances. In 2006 alone, the

---

[61]   See C Bullen, *Child maintenance: The eligible population in Great Britain* (DWP Working Paper No 41, 2007) 7.

[62]   'Child Support Agency Quarterly Summary Statistics: December 2007', Table 2.3.

agency received over 1.7 million notifications of changes of circumstances concerning its new scheme case load.[63]

By way of comparison, there is much less reliable information about the incidence of court-based child maintenance awards. We do know that in 2006 the county courts disposed of a total of 111,955 ancillary relief orders under the Matrimonial Causes Act 1973, of which 75 per cent were uncontested from the outset, 20 per cent were initially contested but later consented, and 5 per cent were contested at trial.[64] However, this overall total relates to all types of financial provision order for both adults and children. The total of all contested and initially contested orders was 28,492, of which just under one-half (14,184) were made in respect of children.[65] Of this latter figure, there were only 2,844 orders which were orders for periodical payments for children.[66] This figure of 2,844 amounted to 70 per cent of the total of all periodical payment orders across all contested and initially contested cases (for both spousal and child maintenance). If we assume that the same split operates in relation to the total number of never-contested orders for periodical payments (12,681), this implies that there were a further 8,911 consent orders agreed from the outset for child maintenance periodical payments. If so, this means that in 2006 there were somewhere in the order of 11,755 child maintenance orders made in the county courts, whether by consent or otherwise (11,755 is 8,911 (estimated consent orders) plus 2,844 (actual contested court orders)).[67] There will also have been a number of orders made under section 15 of, and Schedule 1 to, the Children Act 1989, but this is unlikely to take the total number of orders much above 12,000 a year.[68] In comparative terms, this would in turn suggest that the aggregate number of all child maintenance orders (for periodical payments) processed by the courts annually represents only about 10 per cent of the total number of new awards made by the Child Support Agency over the same period.

Secondly, as regards the amounts of maintenance ordered, we have fairly comprehensive data on the levels of child support awards made by the Agency under both the old and new schemes.[69] The information on the amounts of maintenance under court orders and voluntary arrangements is much more

---

[63]   *Ibid*, Table 29.

[64]   Ministry of Justice, 'Judicial and Court Statistics 2006' (Cm 7273, 2007) Table 5.6 at 91. The actual number of cases will be less as the figures relate to disposals for each type of order.

[65]   *Ibid*, Table 5.7.

[66]   *Ibid*, Table 5.7: in contrast there were 4,854 property adjustment orders and 3,915 lump-sum orders for children.

[67]   One qualification of this total is that it ignores orders made for maintenance pending suit, but these are only likely to account for another 1,000 orders at most (there were 362 contested or initially contested such orders).

[68]   In 2006, the courts made 592 financial orders under the CA 1989 ('Judicial and Court Statistics 2006', Table 5.4 at 89), but many of these will have been of a lump-sum nature. The discussion in the text ignores the magistrates' jurisdiction, but family proceedings courts received only 290 financial applications in 2006 (*ibid*, Table 5.3 at 87).

[69]   These are discussed in Wikeley, above n 4, ch 15.

patchy.[70] We know that these amounts are typically higher than those in agency assessments, but to a large extent this may simply reflect the different nature of the populations in question. In particular, the deficiencies of the official data mean that we have little information as to the levels of these court-based awards in relation to the parties' incomes. However, for the reasons explained above, it appears that many of the newer consent orders and private agreements will in fact be based on the formula rates. Yet we might anticipate that not all child maintenance awards (and certainly not all private agreements) will necessarily shadow the statutory child support formula.[71] Some of the exceptions will obviously include those cases involving very wealthy non-resident parents, where the child support scheme cedes jurisdiction to the courts in any event. It is also probable that any applications in the courts for child maintenance for a 'child of the family' are resolved according to different benchmarks—not least as the agency can never have jurisdiction in such a case and there are the specific second-tier statutory considerations, as set out above, which must be taken into account. There is a distinct dearth of recent hard evidence as to both the volume and levels of any such awards involving step-children.[72]

Thirdly, the picture with compliance is rather similar. We have a considerable body of statistical data on compliance with child support orders,[73] but the data needs to be interpreted with care. There is much less information on compliance rates with court orders and private agreements, but what there is tends to suggest that these types of arrangement are more likely to result in regular payments of maintenance.[74] On the other hand, this must be in large part a function of the constituencies involved. As the agency's non-resident parents were predominantly conscripts—either because the parent with care had claimed benefit or because the parties had failed to reach a private agreement—one would expect a lower compliance rate amongst the child support population. This will be compounded by the general nature of its constituent population (for example, the agency has handled a much higher proportion of cases than the courts which involve parents on low incomes and those who were not previously married).

---

[70] See generally, however, N Wikeley, E Ireland, C Bryson and R Smith, *Relationship breakdown and child support study* (DWP Research Report No 503, Leeds, Corporate Document Services, 2008).

[71] It must also not be overlooked that the courts' armoury of different types of award (eg lump-sum orders and transfer of property orders) is much more extensive than that available to the agency.

[72] The data which are used for the annual 'Judicial and Court Statistics' do not disclose whether orders are made for (genetic) children or those treated as children of the family: Personal email communication on file with author, Family Justice Statistics, Ministry of Justice, 15 November 2007.

[73] Again, see further Wikeley, above n 4, ch 15.

[74] *Ibid.*

What Is the Principled Basis for the Duty to Support Children?

We have considered the circumstances in which the law currently imposes a duty on particular individuals to provide for children and also how it seeks to quantify that liability. We have also looked in broad outline at some actual outcomes in terms of orders for child maintenance. We now need to go back to first principles. In particular, what is the moral or philosophical basis for the imposition of such a duty of support?[75] We can then determine how far this has been translated into and is reflected in the present law. Drawing on the work of leading scholars, I have argued elsewhere that the starting point is that children have a right to child support:[76]

> Applying the insights of MacCormick and Eekelaar, we may argue that children's basic interests mean that children have a right that their essential needs for food, shelter and clothing are satisfied. This right may be conceptualised in two parallel and complementary ways. First, it might be characterised as a fundamental human right, which is vested in children by virtue of their membership of the wider community and irrespective of their own parents' particular circumstances ... Secondly, the child's right to support might be construed as a correlative claim-right, in the sense that the failure to satisfy those needs would amount to a breach of duty by an individual subject to a corresponding obligation.[77]

As we have already noted, this debate necessarily raises fundamental questions about the respective roles of private and public responsibility in supporting children. Sheldon's suggestion is that meeting children's needs should be seen first and foremost as a collective responsibility.[78] Yet, as we have seen, this view would seem to attract little popular backing, as empirical social survey evidence has consistently demonstrated widespread public approval for the proposition, in keeping with the philosophy of the UNCRC, that parents have the primary responsibility for the support of their children.[79] Certainly, policy-makers have usually acted on that assumption. As Maclean and Eekelaar point out, the Finer Report's ill-fated proposals for a tax-funded guaranteed maintenance allowance for lone parents 'were perhaps a high-water mark in post-war prioritization of communal over family support obligations'.[80] Indeed, a guaranteed maintenance scheme along the lines of other North European states was simply not a realistic political option during the recent round of child support reform which has resulted in the 2008 Act.[81]

---

[75] The discussion that follows is inevitably based on Wikeley, ch 1.
[76] Wikeley, ch 1 and especially 6–11.
[77] *Ibid*, 8.
[78] S Sheldon, 'Unwilling Fathers and Abortion: Terminating Men's Child Support Obligations?' (2003) 66 *MLR* 175.
[79] See Wikeley, above n 4, ch 1.
[80] M Maclean and J Eekelaar, *The Parental Obligation* (Oxford, Hart Publishing, 1997) 43.
[81] Wikeley, 491–3.

The parent's role is thus central in allocating responsibility for the support of children. There is, of course, extensive theoretical literature spanning several disciplines on the nature of parental responsibilities which cannot be detailed here.[82] For some philosophers, the parental obligation of child support 'is a basic moral duty that does not require further justification'.[83] However, as Sheldon pointedly observes:

> to state the existence of a genetic link is to make an empirical rather than a normative claim: it does not in itself provide any moral argument.[84]

In this context, Eekelaar's analysis is arguably the most helpful:

> The duty to care for children is embedded in the *conjunction* of two sources. One is the *a priori* duty to promote human flourishing, which exists independently of the actual organization of any society. That moral duty binds everyone and is not specifically directed towards parents (although it will fall primarily on them for no other reason than their physical proximity to children). The other is derivative from society itself, for social practice determines the application of that duty within its structure ... while social practice does not itself create the duties towards children, it may place a particular responsibility on some people rather than others to discharge them with respect to particular children.[85]

Social practices, as the quotation from *Bromley* at the start of this chapter reminds us, may shift over time. They may also be informed by gender. We know, for example, that mothers tend to view genetic parenthood as the basis for an unconditional support obligation, whereas fathers regard that obligation as mediated by social parenthood.[86] Therefore, as Maclean and Eekelaar explain:

> fathers adjust the extent of the obligation which they feel they owe towards their natural children by reference to subsequent social parenthood whereas mothers do not think that they should do this.[87]

Yet we must also recall that Maclean's and Eekelaar's study was of *separated* parents—such a gendered divergence of views is much less marked in the community at large. In any event, as Maclean herself has waspishly observed, in

---

[82]   See, eg B Hall, 'The Origin of Parental Rights' (1999) 13 *Public Affairs Quarterly* 73, arguing that the genetic tie establishes a moral presumption that the 'natural' parent has parental rights (and so presumably duties). For an alternative view, see P Montague, 'The Myth of Parental Rights' (2000) 26 *Social Theory and Practice* 47.

[83]   S Altman, 'A Theory of Child Support' (2003) 17 *IJLPF* 173, 174, n 4, citing LD Houlgate, 'Ethical Theory and the Family' in DT Meyers, K Kipnis and CF Murphy (eds), *Kindred Matters: Rethinking the Philosophy of the Family* (Ithaca, Cornell University Press, 1993) ch 3 (see especially 63–9).

[84]   S Sheldon, '"Sperm bandits", birth control and the battle of the sexes' (2001) 21 *Legal Studies* 460, 480.

[85]   J Eekelaar, 'Are Parents Morally Obliged to Care for Their Children?' (1991) 11 *OJLS* 340, 351 (original emphasis).

[86]   See also C Burgoyne and J Millar, 'Enforcing Child Support Obligations: the attitudes of separated fathers' (1994) 22 *Policy and Politics* 95.

[87]   Maclean and Eekelaar, above n 80, 142.

practice it is usually only men who have the option of making the distinction between genetic parentage and social parenthood—for women the phenomena are 'almost always coterminous'.[88]

The question then is how far these arguments—whether moral, philosophical or social—are reflected in the current legal arrangements for the provision of child support and maintenance. Arguably there is perhaps a surprising degree of congruence between the (agency-based) child support and (court-centred) child maintenance systems, even if politicians and policy-makers do little to articulate the underlying principles and the complexity of the present arrangements helps to disguise the common themes. The two most important common themes may be identified as follows.

First, the state and parents share responsibility for supporting children in financial terms. The state gives effect to this through universal child benefit, payable for all children, and the means-tested but almost universal child tax credit (CTC). The state's commitment to this task has been reinforced in recent years with the government's pledge to eradicate child poverty and the shifting of extra resources, directed towards all families with children, through the child benefit and tax credit schemes. The parental commitment to supporting children is assumed in the case of intact families and prescribed in the case of separated families by the combination of the various child support and maintenance systems.

Secondly, however, parents are expected to take the primary responsibility for the support of their children—thus, child benefit and CTC are only contributions towards the cost of raising children in intact and separated families alike. In addition, both the child support and maintenance schemes are designed to ensure that this obligation survives divorce or separation. Both systems predicate responsibility on formal parentage, although the court system also enables social parents to be found liable for child maintenance. Given the complexities and nuances involved, there are obvious operational reasons for confining liability for social (and non-genetic) parenthood to the court-based schemes. The UK arrangements are similar to those operating in other common law jurisdictions in this regard.[89]

There are, however, some differences between the agency-based and court-centred systems for supporting children. The most important of these relates to the theoretical basis for quantifying the extent of the duty of support. The statutory child support system is premised on the child's right to share in both parents' standard of living. The court-based child maintenance jurisdictions have traditionally been much less expansive—doubtless reflecting a combination of

---

[88]   M Maclean, 'The Origins of Child Support in Britain and the Case for a Strong Child Support System' in R Ford and J Millar, *Private Lives and Public Responses* (London, Policy Studies Institute, 1998) 230.

[89]   The New Zealand statutory child support scheme is unusual in leaving open the possibility that step-parents may be found liable for support in an agency-based system.

the historic right of the native-born Englishman to leave his heirs without a bean and the common law's preoccupation in other contexts that the contractual liability of minors should extend no further than for 'necessaries'.[90] Recent developments, however, suggest that the effect of the 12-month rule may be to engineer a process of levelling up, so that child maintenance orders and agreements may be beginning to reflect the same 'percentage of income' principles as child support awards.

CONCLUSION

This chapter has explored the focus of the liability to support children and the way in which liability is quantified in both the formulaic child support and the avowedly discretionary child maintenance jurisdictions. It has also considered how far these respective regimes are used in practice and the extent to which they reflect and share certain common values. In many ways, the discourse of the statutory child support scheme dominates the field. However, section 1 of the Child Support Act 1991 is telling in terms of the social message about responsible parenting which is being communicated. In short, non-resident parents are required to maintain their children financially. It is not a question of the rights of either the child or the parent with care.[91] Where a valid maintenance calculation requires payments to be made under the 1991 Act, the sum in question is non-negotiable as a matter of law. Furthermore, the very act of making such payments discharges the parental obligation to maintain, at least 'for the purposes of this Act'. This exclusive emphasis on financial support can also 'be seen as gendered, reinforcing notions that women care and men pay'.[92] As Heather Draper has further argued:

> It is not in the public interest for social fathers to use as a benchmark for fatherhood what is required of absent fathers by the state in child support. Nor is it in the public interest for the view to be perpetuated that merely paying child support is a legitimate means of discharging one's responsibilities to one's children.[93]

The narrow conception of the duty of support and the role of parental responsibility in the 1991 Act is replicated in the Child Maintenance and Other Payments Act 2008. The new Child Maintenance and Enforcement Commission has a main objective:

---

[90]   See Cooke, this volume.

[91]   See *R (Kehoe) v Secretary of State for Work and Pensions* [2005] UKHL 48 and the discussion in chapter one above; see now *Kehoe v United Kingdom* [2008] ECHR 528.

[92]   R Boden and M Childs, 'Paying for Procreation: Child support arrangements in the UK' (1996) 4 *Feminist Legal Studies* 131, 147.

[93]   H Draper, 'Paternity fraud and compensation for misattributed paternity' (2007) 33 *Journal of Medical Ethics* 475, 479.

to maximise the number of those children who live apart from one or both of their parents for whom effective maintenance arrangements are in place,

an objective which is supported by certain subsidiary goals.[94] The new Commission must also:

take such steps as it thinks appropriate for the purpose of raising awareness among parents of the importance of—

(a) taking responsibility for the maintenance of their children, and

(b) making appropriate arrangements for the maintenance of children of theirs who live apart from them.[95]

The language of responsibility is thus central to the new model child support scheme. However, responsibility in terms of the statutory child support jurisdiction remains somewhat detached from broader conceptions of parental responsibility. It is narrower both in terms of its perception of the ambit of maintenance (measured only in financial terms and solely in terms of the non-resident parent's income and not capital) and also in relation to its personal scope (genetic, adoptive and HFEA parents alone). The ultimate test for the current reforms will be whether the new emphasis on private ordering can reinforce rather than undermine the parental responsibilities attached to child support.

---

[94]   Child Maintenance and Other Payments Act 2008 s 2.
[95]   *Ibid*, s 4.

16

Parental Responsibility and the Responsible Parent: Managing the 'Problem' of Contact

JULIE WALLBANK

INTRODUCTION

Making joint birth registration the default position will help to embed a cultural norm that fathers should reach the birth of their child with an expectation that they have clear responsibility for their child ... [B]y publicly encouraging joint registration and by making it understood, the Government can work to change those with more passive attitudes towards joint birth registration.[1]

U NDER THE SUB-heading of 'Clear messages of expectation', the above statement sets out the Department for Work and Pensions' rationale for its Green Paper on joint birth registration.[2] It makes it very apparent that, by adopting an all-in scheme (with exemptions based on enumerated circumstances), the government is striving to establish paternal responsibility for children as a 'cultural norm'.[3] The emphasis is very much upon the idea that mothers and fathers have equal rights and responsibilities in relation to their biological offspring, as illustrated by the following:

There is clearly a significant public policy interest in encouraging parents, fathers as well as mothers, to play a major role in their children's lives throughout childhood. The Government believes that joint registration of births can be a key part of our determination, to develop a culture in which the welfare of children is paramount and people are clear that fatherhood, as well as motherhood, always comes with both rights and responsibilities.[4]

---

[1] Department for Work and Pensions, 'Joint birth registration: promoting parental responsibility', Cm 7160 (London, The Stationery Office, 2007) 6.

[2] *Ibid.*

[3] For a list of circumstances which would exempt biological parents from joint registration, see *ibid*, 15–16.

[4] *Ibid*, 6.

At various points in the Green Paper, the importance of equal parental responsibilities is stressed. For example:

> Our proposal is that legislation around birth registration for unmarried parents should reflect that parenting is a joint undertaking and it should therefore make both parents equally responsible for registering the birth of their child ... The key benefit of an approach that places equal responsibility on both parents to register is that it is in keeping with the Government's desire to promote responsible fatherhood.[5]

What these examples from the Green Paper show is how the current Labour Government's approach to family policy and law is now commonly influenced by norm-oriented approaches to the regulation of family life. Such approaches are also evident in the area forming the subject matter of this chapter, namely the relationship between parental responsibility and contact. The aim of the law governing family relationships is to set down norms which, it is hoped, will become embedded in society and embraced by the population of mothers and fathers. The concept of parental responsibility has increasingly come to be used to create the homogeneous standard of the responsible parent.

As Herring has argued, although parental responsibility is a key concept in family law, its meaning is uncertain.[6] From the statutory formulation in section 3 of the Children Act 1989, it is clear that it incorporates at least two facets: first, that of providing a legal status for parents and others who acquire it; and, secondly, the performance of those duties and responsibilities to the child that arise as a result of his or her conferment.[7] While the statute does not provide a list of the rights, duties, powers, responsibilities and authority that comprise parental responsibility, Lowe and Douglas have named some of the rights and responsibilities which are commonly associated with it.[8] Their list—which includes 'having contact with the child'—is useful for the way in which it supplements the statutory definition, but, as Herring points out, no list of parental responsibilities is ever going to be complete and the government can always add to it.[9] What is perhaps more significant is that Lowe's and Douglas's list is function-based in respect of what might be expected in terms of the norms of family life and the rights, role and responsibilities performed by parents in relation to their children. Indeed, the legal formulation of parental responsibility is very much action-based, with little attention paid to the cognitive aspects of the responsible parent that have been developed more recently. This chapter is an attempt to redress this gap in the legal discussions of parental responsibility and to show how thinking

---

[5]   *Ibid*, 15.

[6]   J Herring, *Family Law* (3rd edn, Harlow, Pearson Education Ltd, 2007), 382.

[7]   See further J Eekelaar, 'Parental responsibility: State of nature or nature of the state?' (1991) 13 *JSWFL* 37.

[8]   N Lowe and G Douglas, *Bromley's Family Law* (10th edn, London, Butterworths, 2007) 377. For the discussion of dutiful behaviour, see 31–3.

[9]   Above n 6, 383.

and acting responsibly now forms a crucial part of parental responsibility in the context of contact.

First, I will examine parental responsibility in the context of social policy on the family generally, paying particular attention to the gendered lives of mothers and fathers. Secondly, I will look at the construction of the responsible parent, as one who facilitates contact between the child and the other parent. Thirdly, I will discuss the cognitive aspects of responsibility, showing how a particular way of thinking about contact is promoted by government publications, and how in fact the responsible course of action may be to deny contact in certain cases. It is my intention to highlight some of the ways in which the attempts to assimilate to a homogeneous norm of the responsible parent impact upon mothers and fathers in the context of contact.

PARENTAL RESPONSIBILITY: EQUAL STATUS OR EQUAL PARTICIPATION?

As noted above, the concept of parental responsibility involves issues of both status and action. Discussion, particularly at the government level, has frequently been concerned with the 'status' aspect of parental responsibility, whilst at the same time conjuring up ideas as to its normative dimensions to be inculcated by all parents in acting as responsible parents. Yet, as this section will show, equal status does not necessarily translate into equal participation in family life.

The extension of parental responsibility to fathers who jointly registered their child's birth was driven in large part by considerations of status. The government was partly responding to research which showed that unmarried fathers lacked knowledge about parental responsibility and its meaning, their lack of legal status in relation to parental responsibility and the consequences arising from this.[10] However, as I have argued elsewhere, these reforms on birth registration can be interpreted as an attempt to assuage fathers' concerns about women's perceived gains.[11]

Issues of status and function have also been debated by judges in contested cases.[12] In a detailed analysis of the case law on parental responsibility orders, Gilmore has identified a number of inconsistencies and anomalies, and has suggested that there is 'no clear and consistent position'.[13] He shows how in some

---

[10]   As per s 111 of the Adoption and Children Act 2002. See further R Pickford, 'Unmarried Fathers and the Law' in A Bainham, S Day Sclater and M Richards (eds), *What is a Parent?* (Oxford, Hart, 1999).

[11]   J Wallbank, 'Clause 106 of the Adoption and Children Bill: Legislation for the "Good Father"?' (2002) 22 *Legal Studies* 276.

[12]   eg in *Re S (Parental Responsibility)* [1995] 2 FLR 648 at 657, Ward LJ distinguished between the rights and powers associated with parental responsibility and the status that parental responsibility confers on the non-residential parent. See also *Re C and V (Parental Responsibility and Contact)* [1998] 1 FLR 392.

[13]   S Gilmore, 'Parental Responsibility and the Unmarried Father—A New Dimension to the Debate' [2003] 15 *CFLQ* 21.

cases the rights and duties within parental responsibility are emphasised, characterising parental responsibility as 'active', whereas in others it is seen as relatively benign, focusing on the importance of parental status.

By narrowly constructing parental responsibility as merely conferring a status on fathers rather than involving any corresponding powers and duties, courts have been enabled to make orders in favour of fathers who have no practical contribution to make to the child's life. Such a status-based approach to parental responsibility does very little to signal the importance of the norm of shared parenting, or the ideal that both parents should play 'a major role in their children's lives throughout childhood'.[14] In this, it is out of step with other developments. Although conferring status upon a wider range of fathers will be an effect of compulsory birth registration, the state is also increasingly concerned with the 'doing' rather than just the 'being' of family life.[15]

The emphasis upon 'doing' as well as 'being' family has been discussed at some length in the work of Collier. His study on the various constructions of masculinity and 'good fatherhood' in relation to parental responsibility and the social policy objectives of the Labour Government reveals how family life is currently premised on the promotion of the norm of full, active and persisting commitment to children on the part of women and men.[16] Moreover, the new and idealised model of fathering is one of 'active parenting', which is quite distinct from the law's earlier construction of a father's primary familial role, which was providing financially for his children. This is illustrative of the shifting nature of the discursive constructions of responsibility and the responsible father, whose role is now more akin to that played by mothers.[17] As Dey and Wasoff have argued, 'regulatory and normative roles can quickly become outmoded as a result of social and cultural change'.[18]

Collier's argument is that the emergence of a confluence of the experiences of women and men in relation to both the workplace and 'attitudes, and expectations surrounding the family' has led to a coming together of women's and men's experiences of the public and domestic spheres, where the norm of the 'good' father is constructed around achieving a successful balance between the two spheres, and to governmental support for and promotion of the new model of fatherhood.[19] However, the promotion of women's participation in the workplace

---

[14]   Above n 1.
[15]   E Silva and C Smart, 'The "New" Practices and Politics of Family Life' in E Silva and C Smart (eds), *The New Family?* (London, Sage, 1999), as cited in H Reece, *Divorcing Responsibly* (Oxford, Hart, 2003) 230.
[16]   R Collier, 'A Hard Time to Be a Father?: Reassessing the Relationship Between Law, Policy, and Family (Practices)' (2001) 28 *Journal of Law and Society* 520, 531.
[17]   R Collier, *Masculinity, Law and the Family* (London, Routledge, 1995) 196–7.
[18]   I Dey and F Wasoff, 'Mixed Messages: Parental Responsibilities, Public Opinion and the Reforms of Family Law' (2006) 20 *IJ LPF* 225, 226.
[19]   Above n 16, 528.

has led to 'a formidable set of expectations of women as parents'.[20] For example, women are more likely to be regarded as responsible for their children's bad behaviour: as Featherstone notes in respect of parenting orders under the Crime and Disorder Act 1998, the national evaluation of the programmes found that 81 per cent of those attending were women.[21] In addition, the provisions of the Children and Adoption Act 2006 (CAA) introduced contact activity directions and conditions under section 11A–P of the Children Act 1989, including parenting programmes, classes and counselling or guidance sessions to facilitate or aid contact. Although the provisions will (when in force) apply to both mothers and fathers, it is not unlikely that it will be resident parents (usually mothers) who will be subject to parenting programmes and classes to help them to understand the benefits of contact. Furthermore, where poverty is a feature of family life, insufficient attention is paid by the government to the:

> (gendered) relationship between financial deprivation and the ability of parents to fulfil the parenting responsibilities expected of them. It is a gendered relationship because … women still carry the main day-to-day responsibility for the care and upbringing of children; this is obscured by the gender-neutral language of parenting.[22]

The above notwithstanding (which shows some unevenness in respect of the gendered nature of parental responsibility or 'doing' family life), a number of government initiatives and policy measures have been implemented in a bid to create a 'democratic family'.[23] These create a sense of (although not necessarily actual) equality.[24] In respect of the social policy objectives of the Labour Government on family life, Collier identifies the prominence of 'social justice, emancipation, equality and social cohesion'.[25] It is certainly the case that a number of developments in family law throughout the 1990s and into the twenty-first century have been founded upon the desire to equalise the position of women and men in relation to their children. Changes in employment law giving fathers paternity leave exemplify both the desire to achieve equality and

---

[20] B Featherstone, 'Why gender matters in child welfare and protection' (2006) 26 *Critical Social Policy* 294, 305.

[21] Citing D Ghate and M Ramalla, *Positive Parenting: the National Evaluation of the Youth Justice Board's Parenting Programme* (London, Policy Research Bureau, 2002). See also J Scourfield and M Drakeford, 'New Labour and the "problem of men"' (2002) 22 *Critical Social Policy* 619, 625.

[22] R Lister, 'Children (but not women) first: New Labour, child welfare and gender' (2006) 26 *Critical Social Policy* 315, 327.

[23] R Collier, 'Fathers4Justice, law and the new politics of fatherhood' [2005] 17 *CFLQ* 511, 528.

[24] *Ibid*, 515. For example, the EU Charter of Fundamental Rights and the National Minimum Wage are aimed at addressing the gender inequality and facilitating male involvement in family life by accommodating a suitable work–life balance.

[25] *Ibid*, 527.

how reality falls short: as Herring points out, only one-fifth of fathers have used it,[26] and fathers in the United Kingdom continue to work the longest hours in Europe.[27]

The extent to which women's enhanced opportunities and increased participation in the labour market has impacted on the state of men and their familial relations and responsibilities has aroused considerable scepticism. Academics like McMahon[28] vehemently refute the existence of the 'new fatherhood' which has emerged as a result of male reaction towards the increasing prevalence of the notion that women are equal to men.[29] McMahon notes a rift between supposed equality and the practical realities of women's lives. Despite acquiring increasing professional prominence, women continue to undertake the majority of menial domestic tasks for the family.[30] Collier terms this the 'gap between rhetoric and reality'.[31] Even though men claim a more significant role compared to that of the past, there may be a tendency to over-estimate the extent to which male behaviour has changed. Scourfield and Drakeford, for example, note that family policies developed to support fathers are founded upon the unproven assumption that men want to spend more time with children and also upon an 'optimistic view of fathering', based on gender equality, which may not represent the reality.[32]

Despite the body of research which shows that in practical terms women may bear the brunt, in responsibility terms, of the confluence of women's and men's lives, the Labour Government continues to pursue equality (particularly through rights attribution) between women and men in respect of their familial roles and responsibilities. As Smart and Neale have argued, family policy on parental responsibility in the 1990s was driven by a 'clear and determined attempt to effect "social engineering" in the area of family life'.[33] On the one hand, the extension of parental responsibility was very clearly designed to make parents, and particularly fathers, conform to the norms of continuing responsibility during and after the parents' relationship has broken down. On the other hand, notions of equality and rights have been central to the Labour Government's policy agenda, combined with an acceptance that there are problems faced by men as fathers. Fathers' lobby groups have successfully channelled the themes of social injustice, rights and inequality in order to address the alleged unfairness which was said to

[26]   J Herring, 'Why Financial Orders on Divorce Should be Unfair' (2005) 19 *IJLPF* 218, citing BBC News Online, 'Dads Shun Nappy Changing for Work' (26 July 2004).
[27]   *Ibid.*
[28]   A McMahon, *Taking Care of Men: Sexual Politics in the Public Mind* (Cambridge, Cambridge University Press, 1999) 2.
[29]   *Ibid.*
[30]   See further F Williams, 'In and beyond New Labour: towards a new political ethics of care' (2001) 21 *Critical Social Policy* 467, 472.
[31]   Above n 16, 539.
[32]   Scourfield and Drakeford, above n 21, 625.
[33]   C Smart and B Neale, 'Wishful thinking and harmful; tinkering? Sociological reflections on family policy' (1997) 26 *Journal of Social Policy* 1, as cited in Collier, above n 16, 530.

exist in child support legislation in the early 1990s.[34] By contrast, the extent to which notions of equality and rights in respect of family life and women's and men's lives achieve what is termed 'social justice', especially with respect to women as mothers, is highly questionable, as has been demonstrated by a substantial body of feminist research.[35] It is clear that equal participation in family life is far from being achieved, and imposing equal status without attention to the gendered realities of family life may be experienced as a further burden on mothers.

PARENTAL RESPONSIBILITY AND CONTACT

Parental responsibility (PR) and contact are linked in a number of ways. The government has clearly conceived the problem as a lack of responsibility, and therefore attempts to inculcate parental responsibility as a norm—whether at the point of birth, registration, participation or post-separation negotiations. At one level, the encouragement of joint registration can be seen as an attempt to reinforce the desirability of paternal involvement. In this way, the government attempts to forestall future problems by embedding the values of responsibility at the earliest possible date. The proposals to make joint registration the default position is an act of iteration in respect of both the ascription of parental status and the norms associated with doing parenthood for life from birth to adulthood. The extension of parental responsibility, influenced by the appeal to equality and the idea that the government is giving something to fathers in the conferment of PR, is a device whereby the government is seeking to manage parents and ensure that men are firmly tied to families.

However, it is in the context of post-separation parenting that concepts of responsibility are most influential. The government has accepted that the law of contact was failing fathers and that the shortcomings might be effectively addressed by improving contact facilitation and enforcement. Thus, obligations on mothers to facilitate contact and on non-resident parents to maintain contact are central to the exercising of the normative requirements demanded of parents and rest upon the central idea that contact benefits children's welfare. However, as

---

[34] On the subject of child support, see J Wallbank, 'The Campaign for Change of the Child Support Act 1991: Reconstituting the "Absent" Father' (1997) 6 *Social and Legal Studies* 191; and R Collier, 'The Campaign Against the Child Support Act, "Errant Fatherhood" and "Family Men"' [1994] *Family Law* 384. See also Wallbank, above n 11, for a discussion of how the themes of social injustice, rights and inequality were used by the Labour Government to justify legislation to extend parental responsibility to unmarried fathers who jointly register their child's birth with the mother.

[35] See, eg J Tronto, *Moral Boundaries: A Political Argument for an Ethic of Care* (London, Routledge, 1993); C Smart and B Neale, *Family Fragments* (Cambridge, Polity Press, 1999); and Wallbank, above n 34, and *Challenging Motherhood(s)* (London, Longman, 2001). See also Collier, above n 34; R Bailey-Harris, 'Contact-challenging conventional wisdom?' [2001] 13 *CFLQ* 361; R Bailey-Harris, 'From Utility to Rights? The Presumption of Contact in Practice' (1999) 13 *IJLPF* 111; S Day Sclater and F Kaganas, 'Contact: Mothers, Welfare and Rights' in A Bainham, B Lindley, R Richards and L Trinder, *Children and Their Families: Contact, Rights and Welfare* (Oxford, Hart, 2003).

will be shown below, contact obligations can be enforced against the residential parent, but have not as yet been enforced against the non-residential parent.

The strength of the assumption that contact is 'almost always in the child's interests' was emphasised in *Re O (Contact: Imposition of Conditions)*.[36] The case concerned an appeal by a mother against the conditions imposed upon her to facilitate indirect contact when she was strongly opposed to it.[37] Bingham MR described the mother's implacable hostility by relying on the first instance judge's view that it was an 'irrational repugnance'.[38] Although there is scant detail on the history of the relationship between the mother and father, there was some evidence of domestic violence. The father had given an undertaking not to pester or molest the mother, which he breached with the result that he received a 21-day suspended prison sentence.[39] Rejecting her appeal, the Court of Appeal noted the caring parent's obligations in respect of facilitating contact, albeit in this instance, indirect contact. As Herring has made clear, the contact order requires the residential parent to facilitate contact or be subject to breach of the order and at risk of imprisonment for contempt.[40] In addition, the Court of Appeal noted the revocability of the residence order, which presumably was designed as a strong warning to the mother.[41]

The 'problem' of contact is correspondingly presented as the difficulty of enforcing contact when the residential parent will not cooperate. The briefest survey of case law illustrates this. One of the most publicised cases was *Re D*, in which Munby J handed down his public judgment on the failings of the court system. His judgement began:

> On 11 November 2003 a wholly deserving father left my court in tears having being driven to abandon his battle for contact with his seven-year old daughter.[42]

In *Re M*, following the example of Munby J in *Re D*, Bracewell J noted the problems with the current law:

> Some parents agree to contact without any intention of making it work ... At present it can take months for a case to be restored to court when contact has been frustrated ... during which time there may be no contact taking place and the residential parent,

---

[36]   [1995] 2 FLR 124 at 124.

[37]   The conditions included that the mother send the father photographs of the child every three months, send reports concerning the child's progress at nursery and medical reports as appropriate and accept cards and presents sent through the post by the father.

[38]   Above n 36, at 126.

[39]   Above n 36, at 125.

[40]   Above n 6, 458.

[41]   Above n 36, at 130. For a discussion of the use of transfer of residence in intractable contact disputes, see J Wallbank, 'Getting tough on mothers: regulating contact and residence' (2007) 15 *Feminist Legal Studies* 189.

[42]   *Re D (a child) (intractable contact dispute)* [2004] All ER (D) 41. See also *Pelling v Bruce-Williams (Secretary of State for Constitutional Affairs intervening)* [2004] Fam 155; *Re O (a child) (Contact: withdrawal of application)* [2003] EWHC 3031 (Fam); *V v V (Contact: Implacable Hostility)* [2004] 2 FLR 851; and *Re M (Intractable Contact Dispute: Interim Care Order)* [2003] EWHC 1024 (Fam).

usually the mother, uses the time to brainwash the child into rejection of the father . . .
At present, enforcement of contact orders creates insuperable problems for the courts.[43]

It is obvious from the statement that although Bracewell J initially chose to use
the gender-neutral term 'some parents', the problem of contact is clearly laid at
the door of the residential parent, 'usually the mother'. As Kaganas and Day
Sclater argue, because contact is so strongly regarded as crucial for children's
welfare, mothers who resist contact and are constructed as 'implacably hostile' to
it are regarded as putting their own desires above their children's needs. They are
therefore positioned as 'bad' mothers because of their perceived irresponsibility
and refusal to see what is good for their children.[44] However, there are now signs
of the judiciary recognising the distinction between cases where the resident
parent has a genuine fear (whether rational or not) and cases where a resident
parent is simply opposed to contact. It is only in the latter cases now that a
mother would likely be characterised as implacably hostile. In one recent case, it
was also noted by Wall LJ that although contact did sometimes break down due
to the implacable hostility, it more often broke down due to the behaviour of the
father.[45]

The courts in fact have a range of possible responses in respect of controlling
the implacably hostile mother. These have been expanded by the new powers of
enforcement of contact,[46] which may be applied for by both resident and
non-resident parents. In practice, the non-resident parent (usually the father)
will not be in breach of the contact order by failing to maintain contact, it being
against the '. . . common law rule that personal services cannot be directly
enforced by court order'.[47] Enforcement orders are, therefore, likely to be most
frequently used against the resident mother.[48] It is not too difficult to conclude
that, despite the existence of formal equality in the legislation, in practice it is
mothers who will be detrimentally affected, and that the enforcement measures
are designed to target individual mothers who are identified as failing to achieve
the norm of the responsible parent in respect of facilitating contact.

Enforcement measures are targeted strategies which seek to address particular
aspects of mothers' behaviour which are seen as falling short of the desired norm.
In respect of contested contact case law, Smart and Neale have identified a

---

[43]   *V v V (Children) (Contact: Implacable Hostility)* [2004] 2 FLR 851 at 853–4 (emphasis added).
[44]   F Kaganas and S Day Sclater, 'Contact Disputes: Narrative Constructions of "Good" Parents'
(2004) 12 *Feminist Legal Studies* 1, 4–5.
[45]   *Bradford, Re; Re O'Connell sub nom B (a Child), Re; O (Children)* [2007] 1 FLR 530.
[46]   Under Children Act 1989 s 11J as inserted by Children and Adoption Act 2006 s 4. The court
may impose an unpaid work requirement on the defaulting parent and in addition make an order for
financial compensation to be paid to any parent financially prejudiced by non-compliance such as the
cost of a holiday which has been missed: Children Act 1989 s 11O-P as inserted by Children and
Adoption Act 2006 s 4.
[47]   J Masson and C Humphreys, 'Facilitating and Enforcing Contact: The Bill and the Ten Per Cent'
[2005] 35 *Family Law* 548, 548.
[48]   *Ibid*, 552.

'double standard at work'.[49] Faced with a mother who is hostile to contact, the courts have constructed her as 'implacably hostile', a phrase which was prominent in case law throughout the 1990s. However, in respect of the father who fails to have contact with his child, no equivalent label for the father, such as 'implacably irresponsible', was employed.[50] There is a sense that despite the construction of the gender-neutral norm of the responsible parent, in practice very little has changed in respect of the gendered impact that enforcement measures will have upon men and women. As Masson and Humphreys have noted, enforcement is biased and one-sided.[51] Moreover, as rightly highlighted by Diduck and Kaganas:

> fathers' rights campaigns[52] appear to have had the effect of galvanising the government and the courts into action against mothers whom they see as obstructive.[53]

It should perhaps be noted that it is only 10 per cent of parents who seek help from the courts to resolve issues regarding post-separation arrangements concerning children.[54] Although the mechanisms to improve enforcement are expanded, these targeted strategies designed to manage recalcitrant parents and to assimilate them to the much desired norm of the responsible parent through punitive devices are only concerned with a small number of parents—namely those who are involved in court-based disputes. Much more interesting for the purposes of this chapter is how the government has elected to manage post-separation parenting by the issuing of general advice to all separating parents on how to become the desired responsible parent in respect of contact.

In order that all parents are able to exercise their parental responsibilities in relation to children, the 'problem' of contact is identified as in need of addressing when the adults' relationship breaks down. It is considered important that mechanisms are in place in order that contact is facilitated. The construction of the lack of contact as a problem by the government rests upon the acceptance that a child's wellbeing is promoted by contact with both parents and damaged by its lack.

Empirical research is viewed as important in 'driving' the impetus to solve the constructed problem of contact.[55] However, the various studies of contact provide inconclusive findings. For example, on the issue of whether it is the

---

[49]   C Smart and B Neale, 'Arguments Against Virtue—Must Contact Be Enforced?' [1997] *Family Law* 332, 336.

[50]   *Ibid.* For a discussion of the construction of the implacably hostile mother, see further J Wallbank, 'Castigating Mothers: the Judicial Response to Wilful Women in Cases Concerning Contact' (1998) 20 *JSWFL* 357.

[51]   Above n 47, 552.

[52]   And, perhaps, to some extent, the European cases on swift enforcement. However, these of course all refer to a balancing exercise, reasonableness and to the undesirability of proceeding against children's wishes. (Footnote reproduced in full from the original.)

[53]   A Diduck and F Kaganas, *Family Law, Gender and the State* (2nd edn, Oxford, Hart, 2006) 561.

[54]   Department for Education and Skills, *Parental Separation: Children's Needs and Parents' Responsibilities* (London, The Stationery Office, 2004) 5.

[55]   L Trinder, 'Introduction' in Bainham *et al*, above n 35, 5.

frequency or quality of contact which is most determinative in respect of outcome, Dunn *et al* claim that it is frequency of contact which has the greater significance.[56] They maintain:

> Earlier studies have reported some inconsistent findings on the significance of contact. Our results were unequivocal: more frequent and regular contact … was associated with closer, more intense relationships with non-resident fathers (relationships that were both more positive and more conflicted), and fewer adjustment problems in children.[57]

In one such earlier study, Rodgers and Pryor on the other hand believe it is both frequency and quality of contact which determine success rather than just the existence of contact.[58]

Other research on the benefits of contact for children displays further contradictions. For example, Kraemer, writing on the benefits of participant fatherhood for all children, suggests that children with input from both mothers and fathers have more effective cognitive skills and suffer less in respect of emotional development.[59] Conversely, studies by Amato and Rezac suggest there is no definite association between contact and a child's wellbeing.[60] Additionally, in a meta-analysis of 63 published studies in the area of contact, Amato and Gilbreth found that frequency of contact was only vaguely linked to a child's greater academic achievement and avoidance of problems like depression and low self-esteem, but that this link was not conclusive.[61]

The different findings in studies may be attributable to different sample types and sizes and other methodological issues, such as the variables identified and analysed.[62] For example, factors such as the quality of pre-existing relationships between parties will unavoidably influence results and may not have been factored into a particular study. If the non-residential parent and child had an emotionally close relationship while the parents were together, the parent–child relationship post-separation is more likely to be successful.[63]

---

[56] J Dunn, H Cheng, TG O'Connor and L Bridges, 'Children's Relationships with their Non-Resident Fathers: Influences, Outcomes, and Implications' (2004) 45 *Journal of Child Psychology and Psychiatry* 553.

[57] *Ibid*, 562.

[58] B Rodgers and J Pryor, *Divorce and separation: the outcomes for children* (York, Joseph Rowntree Foundation, 1998) 40.

[59] S Kraemer, 'What are fathers for?' in C Burck and B Speed (eds), *Gender, Power and Relationships* (London, Routledge, 1995) 209.

[60] P Amato and S Rezac, 'Contact with Non-Residential Parents, Interparental Conflict, and Children's Behaviour' (1994) 15 *Journal of Family Issues* 961.

[61] P Amato and JG Gilbreth, 'Non-Resident Fathers and Children's Well-Being: A Meta-Analysis' (1999) 61 *Journal of Marriage and the Family* 557, 564, as discussed in S Gilmore, 'Contact/Shared Residence and Child Well-Being: Research Evidence and its Implications for Legal Decision-Making' (2006) 20 *IJLPF* 344, 347.

[62] For a brief summary of some of the methodological issues, see Gilmore, above n 61, 346.

[63] J Bradshaw, C Stimson, C Skinner and J Williams, *Absent Fathers?* (London, Routledge, 1999).

Despite the ambiguity in the research findings, it is the empirical research which shows the impact of parental separation as having adverse outcomes for children that is relied upon in the Green Paper.[64] What is interesting about the way in which the government frames the issue is that, on the one hand, it points to factors pertaining to parental separation which have a negative impact upon children, whilst on the other it contrasts this position with the positive aspects of 'effective parenting', where children have fathers who have been actively involved.[65] Yet these are not simple opposites, and the details of what makes the difference to children other than active involvement by fathers are not articulated. Although the Green Paper draws on empirical research to make its point, none of the discrepancies in the research findings mentioned above is referred to. Additionally, framing the issues in this rather simplistic way permits the eclipse of other relevant factors such as social class, poverty, employment patterns and ethnicity. Effectively, the mere participation of the father is made central to the child's future wellbeing. This makes it easier to characterise the responsible resident parent as one who reflects upon and eventually facilitates or assumes contact with children for the child's sake. The resident parent becomes targeted as the origin of the 'problem' of contact and when identified as not promoting the post-separation ideal, in need of normalisation.

THE RESPONSIBLE PARENT

As Reece suggests, responsibility comes to take on another facet which is concerned with the attitude and degree to which a parent reflects upon her choices. For her:

> responsible behaviour has become a way of being, a mode of thought; the focus has shifted from the content of the decision to the process of making the decision . . . Now, he or she shows her responsibility by the attitude with which he or she reflects on the implications of what he or she chooses.[66]

Although her theoretical framework may be different, our points about responsibility are similar, especially as to how it has an expanded meaning in respect of the

---

[64] See further above n 54, 16.

[65] eg adverse outcomes of separation are cited as the following: up to one-half of young offenders come from separated families, girls are at greater risk of teenage pregnancy and children are less likely to obtain formal qualifications. On the other hand, effective parenting produces better outcomes such as higher educational achievements, more satisfactory adult relationships and protection from mental health problems: *ibid*, 16–17.

[66] Reece, above n 15, 210.

normative commitments that it requires.[67] Like Reece, I am concerned with showing the extent to which responsibility becomes displayed by both the decision-making process and the content of the decision on contact. In the context of contact, however, it is the final decision to facilitate contact which makes the resident parent a responsible one. For example, in disputed contact cases, the mother who reflects at some length on the decision about contact, having genuinely held concerns, is likely to be given short shrift. The refusal of contact (the content of the decision) is integral to acting responsibly and is incapable of being excised from the decision-making process. The responsible parent is one who facilitates contact and not one who adopts an, albeit responsible and reflective attitude, to the implications of the refusal.[68] This section will show both how these ideas as to responsible parenting permeate government publications and initiatives, and why a responsible parent might have good cause to refuse contact.

Recent discourses on contact have drawn upon a particular formulation of the responsible parent, who is a person with a set of desirable characteristics—self-regulatory, self-monitoring, facilitative, accommodating, flexible, self-sacrificing, conciliatory and giving—an approach that may be seen as reflecting Foucault's ideas of normalisation and bio-power.[69] The government's second Green Paper, for example, makes clear the characteristics which are attributed to the responsible parent.[70] It is stated that both parents have 'a responsibility to ensure their child has constructive contact with the other parent' and that 'collaborative agreements made between parents should be favoured, as they are likelier to work better'.[71] Whilst it is clear that the former statement constitutes part of the 'doing' role associated with parental responsibility, it also speaks to the thinking part of the responsible parent. Contact is quite simply not enough, it must be 'constructive' and both parents are responsible for ensuring that it is so.

In practice, of course, it is impossible for the law to regulate for constructive contact in respect of monitoring the quality of the actual period of time spent with children unless an order for supervised contact is in place. Furthermore, it is unrealistic to expect one parent to assume any responsibility for the quality of the child's contact with the other; indeed, this would seem to go against the grain of the very concept of parental responsibility, which gives parents the power to act

---

[67]   *Ibid*, citing D Rhode and M Minow, 'Reforming the Questions, Questioning the Reforms: Feminist Perspectives on Divorce Law' in S Sugarman and H Hill Kay (eds), *Divorce Reform at the Crossroads* (Connecticut, Yale University Press, 1990) 210.

[68]   I am very grateful to Helen Reece for her comments on this point.

[69]   See, eg M Foucault, *History of Sexuality* (Vol 1, London, Penguin, 1981, trans R Hurley); M Foucault, 'Power and Strategies' in C Gordon (ed and trans), *Power/Knowledge* (Hemel Hempstead, Harvester Wheatsheaf, 1980); and M Foucault, *Discipline and Punish* (Harmondsworth, Peregrine, 1981, trans A Sheridan).

[70]   Department for Constitutional Affairs, Department for Education and Skills and the Department for Trade and Industry, *Parental Separation: Children's Needs and Parents' Responsibilities: Next Steps, Report of the responses to consultation and agenda for action*, Cm 6452 (London, HMSO, 2005).

[71]   *Ibid*, 7.

independently of each other when there is no court order to the contrary.[72] What the Green Paper is doing is attempting to set down the normative guidelines for post-separation parenting: divorcing parents are offered advice on how best to negotiate their post-separation relationships for both their own sense of wellbeing and for the sake of the children's welfare. Although the advice provided by the government speaks to 'parents' rather than mothers, it could be argued that the message particularly speaks to the residential parent (usually a mother) to, at minimum, facilitate contact.

As outlined above, a main feature of the government's new approach to contact is through the parents' collaborative agreement, which is considered more likely to be successful. In order for parents to become collaborative—ie responsible—parents, the government has elected to focus on supporting parents and children during the separation period to reach agreement without resorting to the courts, and on the facilitation of contact through 'directing people to attend relevant classes or programmes that could help build positive contact arrangements' when recourse to law is relied upon.[73] Educative devices both at the earliest stages of separation and at the level of court intervention are drawn upon in order to establish a template for the responsible parent.[74] Where couples have been unable to reach the ideal and have had to resort to the courts, the emphasis is very much on assisting them to come to amicable arrangements regarding their children through the use of various trained professionals, and the help provided is grounded in highly directional measures through a number of new powers known as 'contact activity directions'.[75] These new powers will be available alongside the existing residence and contact orders provided by the Children Act 1989.[76] As Gillies has argued:

> interventions framed within the discourse of 'parenting support' stress the importance of helping parents to do the best they can for their children.[77]

However, as she also notes, 'tacit moral judgements direct the nature and type of support'.[78] In respect of my argument, this means that the type of support provided through advice-based networks tends towards assimilating parents to the homogeneous norm of the responsible parent, which includes the idea that

---

[72]   For further discussion, see Diduck and Kaganas, above n 53, 280–83.
[73]   *Ibid.*
[74]   The measures provided to support parents on divorce include the wide dissemination of parenting plan templates, access to specialist legal advice, mediation, Family Help Service *via* the existing Family Advice and Information Service and the pilot of a collaborative law model: above n 70, 11.
[75]   The power to direct parties to attend information meetings, meetings with a counsellor, parenting programmes/classes or other activities designed to deal with contact disputes; power to attach conditions to contact orders which may require attendance at a given class/programme: *ibid*, 7.
[76]   Children Act 1989 s 8.
[77]   V Gillies, 'Meeting parents' needs? Discourses of "support" and "inclusion" in family policy' (2005) 25 *Critical Social Policy* 70, 70.
[78]   *Ibid.*

the best way to negotiate contact is through cooperation and collaboration. The effect is to attempt to manage the 'problem' of contact by training parents to manage themselves, thus allowing other modes of response, such as improved social and material resources, to fade into the background.[79]

The government, not surprisingly, uses statements from interested parties and organisations to show the level of support for its new approach to contact.[80] At this point I would like to suggest some problems with the normalising technique of an advice-based system aimed at cooperation and collaboration, particularly in the most difficult cases where there is substantial hostility between parents. As outlined above, only 10 per cent of parents seek help from the courts to resolve issues regarding post-separation arrangements for children.[81] The vast majority of parents, therefore, resolve disputes over contact for themselves, yet the extent to which they assume the norms of 'constructive contact' and collaboration is difficult to assess.[82]

The parenting plan which is adopted by the government begins by outlining 'key facts about children's best interests' and offers advice on what to do if parents are finding it difficult to agree.[83] There is nothing in the document that is not to be expected, and the norms of best interests may be viewed as a culmination of that body of research into post-separation life which shows contact to be in the child's interests.[84] For the purposes of this chapter, what is more interesting is the advice given to parents in respect of what to do if they cannot agree on the arrangements. Aside from the practical advice about how to put together the best parenting plan for children, more targeted advice is provided for those parents who are unable to agree and collaborate. In order to reach the normative ideal of the collaborative parent, it is advised that:

> Most parents find that putting aside their conflicts and disagreements and thinking about their children's needs can provide a way forward to negotiate arrangements.[85]

---

[79] *Ibid*, 87.

[80] See above n 70, 14.

[81] *Ibid*.

[82] Although there is a burgeoning body of empirical work which explores these themes: see, eg G Wilson, 'The Non-Resident Parental Role for Separated Fathers: A Review' (2006) 20 *IJLPF* 286, which reviews the research.

[83] *Putting your children first* (DFES, 2006) 4. Children's best interests may be summarised as: children being raised by both parents, each parent supporting the children to enjoy a positive relationship with the other, children being clear about arrangements, not being exposed to sudden changes, being supported to keep in touch with other important people, new partners to support the arrangements for the child.

[84] See further PD Allison and FF Furstenberg, 'How marital dissolution affects children: Variations by age and sex' (1989) 25 *Developmental Psychology* 540; DA Dawson, 'Family structure and children's health and wellbeing: Data from the 1988 National Health Interview Survey on Child Health' (1991) 53 *Journal of Marriage and the Family* 573; M Maclean, *Foundations: Together and apart, Children and Parents experiencing separation and divorce* (York, Joseph Rowntree Foundation, 2004); Amato and Rezac, above n 60; and Amato and Gilbreth, above n 61.

[85] Above n 83, 21.

Further, 'you will need to decide which things you can compromise on'[86] and 'try to put your own feelings of hurt and pain to one side and focus on your children'.[87]

The advice in relation to both collaboration and cooperation is in the main targeted at getting parents to sideline their own feelings, doubts and disagreements. However, this works on the assumption that the feelings of hostility and doubt can be extricated from the sense of acting in the children's interests. The tone of the advice is glib, over-simplistic, patronising and, in the most difficult cases, unrealistic. Very often, it will be the case that the conflict has arisen as 'an almost inevitable result of trying to do the right thing'.[88] Additionally, mothers who are reluctant to allow contact are often seeking to protect children. In her empirical study of 27 separated unmarried parents, Laing noted that mothers who had primary responsibility for child care during the relationship 'continued and reinforced this role after the separation'.[89] Mothers' concerns over the safety of their children may provide a source of anxiety and indeed hostility in relation to contact. Currently, however, it should be noted that even if violence or sexual abuse is proven in intractable contact disputes, it is only a factor which might dilute the general assumption in favour of contact and will not necessarily act as a bar to it.[90]

As Kaganas and Piper have argued, the *risk* of violence is not sufficient to offset the presumption of contact with the father.[91] There may also be a range of significant forms of behaviour that women identify as placing children at risk, such as substance abuse or mental health problems, yet they are not necessarily taken as sufficient cause to negate the presumption of contact.[92] Anxieties about child welfare may stem from a variety of factors, for example, safety issues raised by the material circumstances of the father's accommodation, problems relating to alcohol, other drugs or the use of pornography, the quality of care offered by the father during the relationship, or hostile conduct in relation to the mother. However, Perry and Rainey's research showed that the legal system tended to:

> downplay genuine concerns ... of a potentially serious nature—there is nothing trivial or unwarranted about concerns that a child may be driven by a drunk parent, or that a parent refuses to use a car-seat . . . [P]arents ... who raised such concerns were made to feel ... that they were making ... contact unnecessarily difficult.[93]

---

[86]   *Ibid*, 22.
[87]   *Ibid*, 23.
[88]   K Laing, 'Doing the Right Thing: Cohabiting Parents, Separation and Child Contact' (2006) 20 *IJLPF* 169, 174.
[89]   *Ibid*, 175.
[90]   See further Kaganas and Day Sclater, above n 44.
[91]   F Kaganas and C Piper, 'Shared Parenting—A 70% Solution?' [2002] 14 *CFLQ* 365.
[92]   *Ibid*.
[93]   A Perry and B Rainey, 'Supervised, Supported and Indirect Contact Orders: Research Findings' (2007) 21 *IJLPF* 21, 39.

They conclude that the "'bias in favour of contact" can clash with the welfare principle in the short-term'.[94]

There is a need to recognise that where the primary care-giver holds a genuine fear of violence or detriment to her and/or the child, it should be the role of family law to send the message that violence or other forms of misconduct against women and children will simply not be tolerated. Genuine anxieties about child welfare may be obscured by the focus on the homogeneous norm of the responsible and collaborative parent. The idea that a mother's hostility to contact can be straightforwardly disentangled from the children's needs—that they are somehow different issues—may simply not be the case. Saunders, on behalf of Women's Aid, has expressed some concerns in respect of the government's increasingly stringent approach to enforcement:

> the Government is pursuing the enforcement agenda whilst failing to address the main reason why so many mothers do not hand over their children.[95]

However, it is not just at the level of enforcement that vigilance is needed in respect of the gendered implications of changes in the regulation of family life. Gilmore's study has shown that the research does not support a presumption in favour of contact, rather that it is 'not contact *per se* but the nature and quality of contact that are important to children's adjustment'.[96] Furthermore, it has shown that a strong presumption in favour of contact can deflect attention from the risks, the effects of domestic violence and rationally based concerns of residential parents.[97]

CONCLUSION

The government is clearly concerned to improve the quality of the separated families' relationships, particularly that between the non-residential parent and child. However, the attempt to assimilate parents to the homogeneous norm through its facilitation and enforcement measures, employing a range of techniques, is not without potential pitfalls, amply illustrated by the research. These may be amplified at both the stage of negotiation and enforcement when the norm of the responsible parent contains such a strong emphasis upon facilitation and collaboration. As Gillies warns:

> Parents who are regarded as lacking in the necessary reflexivity and knowledge are to be supported back to the path of inclusion ... while those who refuse to conform and

---

[94] *Ibid.*
[95] H Saunders, 'Contact must be safe before it is enforced', Policy Article, <http://www.womensaid.org.uk/landing_page.asp?section=0001000100090005000500090007> accessed 17 December 2008.
[96] Above n 61, 358.
[97] *Ibid*, 359.

acknowledge their moral obligations are to be named, shamed, fined and ultimately even imprisoned.[98]

This chapter has considered some of the normative aspects of parental responsibility and the construction of the responsible parent. It has been my intention to provide a framework for thinking about the development of discourses on parental responsibility, its relationship to contact and shifting meanings ascribed to it in the regulation of family life. The concept of parental responsibility has evolved to include the increasing use of norms and normalising techniques in the governance of family life and specifically targeted strategies which seek to address particular aspects of behaviour which are seen as falling short of the desired norm in the context of contact.

This chapter has also illustrated the way in which the Labour Government has put together a programme of social policy and law which draws heavily upon norm-oriented approaches to the regulation of family life. In so doing, the government utilises the idea that mothers and fathers have equal rights and responsibilities in relation to their biological offspring. It has been shown that parental responsibility is concerned not just with 'being' family, but also with 'doing' family, and it has been suggested that discourses on parental responsibility have evolved in response to perceived inequalities between mothers and fathers.

The motivation to extend parental responsibility to the majority of fathers is premised upon the idea that men should participate fully in family life on the same footing as mothers, and the government seems to accept uncritically that the ascription of parental responsibility will be followed by such ongoing commitment to family life. However, research has shown that in practical terms women may bear the brunt, in responsibility terms, of the confluence of women's and men's lives. Despite this, the government continues to pursue equality through the attribution of rights rather than looking at actualities. It has also been argued that in the context of contact the discourse around responsibility has been ascribed a broader significance which draws upon a more common-sense notion of responsibility incorporating 'being', 'doing' and also 'thinking' about what it means to be a responsible parent.

The CAA implements a range of strategies which are concerned with both the facilitation and enforcement of contact by the identification and use of the homogeneous model of the responsible parent. In setting down this model, discourses on contact and the new measures to deal with facilitation and enforcement provide a range of initiatives in order to persuade parents to adhere to an ideal standard for the children's sake. In constructing discourses on children's needs in the post-separation context, the government relies on research studies which show the purported benefits to children of contact with both parents, despite the research evidence being contradictory.

[98]   Above n 77, 83.

When the post-separation parent falls short of the model, the government provides the means through guidance and advice by which the ideal can be attained, which is getting parents to self-govern and conform. The adoption of the homogeneous standard of the responsible parent as understood in its broader sense may be criticised for the way in which it strips away the gendered realities of mothers' and fathers' lives and also erases other important categories of analysis such as social class. Such complications need to be added back into the picture of the responsible parent.

17

Parental Responsibility for Juvenile Offending in English Law

ROGER LENG

INTRODUCTION

THE NOTION THAT parents should share responsibility for the offending of their children has been expressed in criminal law since the passing of the Children and Young Persons Act of 1933 and has become a central plank of the government's criminal justice policies through the 1990s and early part of the twenty-first century. The purposes of this chapter are: first, to trace the development of parental criminal responsibility and to map its current scope in English law; secondly, to consider the nature of parental criminal responsibility; and, thirdly, to explore the rationales for imposing this liability and consider some of the issues which attend its imposition in practice.

PARENTAL RESPONSIBILITY FOR OFFENDING

This chapter is concerned with the circumstances in which a parent is made criminally responsible as a consequence of a court determination that their child is guilty of a criminal offence, but without any need for proof of either parental involvement in the offence or of parental fault. At the outset, it is useful to distinguish this type of responsibility—which may be termed 'pure' parental criminal responsibility—from two other types of responsibility: first, the responsibility that may attach to a parent for complicity in the child's crime under the general law; secondly, the responsibility that may attach to a parent as a consequence of a child's involvement in the criminal process.

A parent may be liable by virtue of complicity in a child's crime in a number of circumstances. Thus, a parent who assists or encourages his or her child to commit a crime may be liable for the offence as an accomplice or, where the child lacks criminal responsibility, under the doctrine of innocent agency.[1] In some circumstances, a parent may be liable for an offence committed by a child by virtue of a legal power to control the child and failure to take an opportunity to do so.[2] Under the recently created offence of familial homicide, a parent may be liable where their child kills another child of the same household where the victim had been at serious physical risk which the parent ought to have been aware of and failed to take reasonable steps to avert.[3] However, in each of these cases, criminal liability attaches by virtue of the general law and subject to proof of the required conduct and fault elements. These are all cases in which a parent is liable, but not by virtue of parental status.

Parental status has a greater role to play in the second type of responsibility, but here the parent is not actually criminally responsible. A child's involvement in the criminal process as either suspect or defendant will generate responsibilities for the parents, typically involving attendance and/or participation in key stages of the process at the police station, court and youth offender panel. These responsibilities are considered in detail by Caroline Sawyer in her chapter. Such responsibilities of attendance and participation are frequently conflated with parental criminal responsibility for two reasons: first, because these responsibilities may be experienced by parents as burdens akin to punishment; secondly, because similar political rhetoric has been employed to justify both types of responsibility (it being argued that both attendance at court and suffering a penalty may serve to 'bring home' to a parent the reality of the child's offending behaviour). However, these commonalities should not obscure an essential difference. Whereas duties of attendance and participation may be explained as applications of the parent's general duty of care and support, that explanation does not extend to the punishment of parents. In practice, of course, there may be a correlation between the parent who accepts the duty to participate in the criminal process and the parent on whom a penalty is imposed at the culmination of the process. The implications of this will be considered below.

Parental Responsibility for Financial Penalties

The earliest measure to impose criminal liability on parents by statute was section 55 of the Children and Young Persons Act 1933, which gave courts a discretion to require a parent to pay any fine levied on a child or young person following conviction.[4] This provision was largely ignored by the courts and was

---

[1]   *Walters v Lunt* [1951] 2 All ER 645.
[2]   *Du Cros v Lambourne* [1907] 1 KB 40.
[3]   Domestic Violence, Crime and Victims Act 2004 s 5.
[4]   It is submitted that the Reformatory Schools Act 1884 and the Industrial Schools Act 1857 requiring parents to maintain their children in these institutions did not impose particular liabilities in relation to juvenile offending as opposed to the duty to maintain; cf R Arthur, 'Punishing Parents for the Crimes of their Children' (2005) 44 *The Howard Journal* 233, 234–5.

accordingly strengthened by section 26 of the Criminal Justice Act 1982. This substituted a new section 55, providing that in all cases in which a child or young person was fined or ordered to pay costs, the duty to pay should fall on a parent unless either the parent could not be found or it would be unreasonable to order the parent to pay with regard to the circumstances of the case.[5] This clear expression of policy had little effect on the practice of the courts and by 1988 the official Criminal Statistics showed that parents were ordered to pay in only 13 per cent of cases in which a juvenile was fined and in 21 per cent of cases in which compensation was ordered. In the White Paper, *Crime, Justice and Protecting the Public*, published in 1990, the government explained this low take-up by suggesting that magistrates would take the view that parents would pay the fine in any event and so a formal order was unnecessary.[6] This explanation was convenient for a government set on making parental responsibility a central element in juvenile crime policy, but it may have been rash to embark upon such a policy without first examining the reasons why magistrates dealing with young offenders and their parents on a daily basis were reluctant to impose parental responsibility.

Following the White Paper, the provisions of the Criminal Justice Act 1991 tightened and extended the rules about parental responsibility for fines, as part of a package of measures which also extended parental responsibilities to include 17-year-olds and strengthened powers to bind over the parents of young offenders. The current law, now absorbed into the Powers of the Criminal Courts (Sentencing) Act 2000, provides that where the court decides to impose a fine, a compensation or costs order, or a surcharge,[7] on an offender under the age of 16, the court must order that the sum be paid by the parent or guardian, unless the court is satisfied either that the parent or guardian cannot be found, or that it would be unreasonable to make an order for payment having regard to the circumstances of the case.[8] Where the young offender is aged between 16 and 18, the court has a discretion whether or not to order the parent to pay any financial penalty.[9]

Although the fines which may be imposed on young people are capped (currently at £1,000 for those under the age of 18 and £250 for those under the age of 14[10]) the amount payable will be fixed by reference to the financial circumstances of the liable parent.[11] The parent may be ordered to provide the

---

[5] For a contemporary criticism of this measure, see H Wilson, 'Parental responsibility and delinquency: reflections on a White Paper proposal' (1982) 21 *The Howard Journal* 23.

[6] Home Office, *Crime, Justice and Protecting the Public* (Cm 965, 1990) [8.8].

[7] Domestic Violence, Crime and Victims Act 2004 s 51, amending Powers of the Criminal Courts (Sentencing) Act 2000 s 137.

[8] Powers of the Criminal Courts (Sentencing) Act 2000 s 137(1) and (2).

[9] *Ibid*, s 137(3).

[10] Powers of the Criminal Courts (Sentencing) Act 2000 s 135.

[11] Powers of the Criminal Courts (Sentencing) Act 2000 s 138.

court with a statement of his or her financial circumstances,[12] and would commit an offence by either failing to furnish the statement or by providing false information.[13]

Parental Bind Overs

The power of a court to bind over any person appearing before it has existed since 1361 as a rough and ready means of influencing the future conduct of those considered likely to cause trouble. The procedure may be used as an alternative to prosecution for minor offending, but may also be applied to other persons before the court, such as witnesses or complainants, as a means of pre-empting anticipated disorder. The person bound over is required, on pain of penalty for refusal, to enter into a promise to the court (known as a recognisance) 'to be of good behaviour and to keep the peace' for a specified period, subject to an obligation to forfeit a specified sum of money in the event of default. Traditionally, the procedure has been understood as a hybrid, employing civil procedure for the imposition of the bind over, but a form of criminal procedure for forfeiture of the recognisance. However, in recent times the procedure has become increasingly formalised and in *Steel and another v UK*, the European Court of Human Rights held that the procedure is properly characterised as criminal.[14] The practical implications of this are that an application to bind a person over is subject to the fair trial rights attaching to criminal proceedings under Article 6(2) and (3) of the European Convention on Human Rights, and in particular, the criminal standard of proof beyond reasonable doubt should be applied.[15]

The bind over power was first adapted for the purpose of requiring a parent to take proper care of, and exercise proper control over, a juvenile, by the Children and Young Persons Act 1969. A feature of the original scheme was that there was no power to bind over a parent where the child was subject to a supervision order. This suggested that parents were, to a degree, relieved of responsibility by the appointment of a supervisor (and was perhaps indicative of a broader principle, now displaced, that the state rather than parents must take responsibility for the most problematic children).[16] More significantly, a bind over could not be imposed without the consent of the parent.[17] Perhaps not surprisingly, the power was used in only a 'handful of cases each year'.[18]

---

[12] Powers of the Criminal Courts (Sentencing) Act 2000 s 136.
[13] *Ibid*, subss (4) and (5).
[14] *Steel and others v UK* (1999) 28 EHRR 603.
[15] *R v Middlesex Crown Court, ex p Khan* (1997) 161 JP 240 (DC).
[16] See J Eekelaar, *Family Law and Personal Life* (Oxford, Oxford University Press, 2006) 104.
[17] Children and Young Persons Act 1969 s 7(7)(c).
[18] Home Office, above n 6, [8.10].

The White Paper of 1990 proposed to remove the consent requirement in order that the power could be used routinely, it being argued that the risk of forfeiting up to £1,000 would provide a strong incentive for parents to improve their supervision of their children. In particular, it was suggested that bind overs might be used to encourage parents to control the movements of young people at night and in tandem with supervision orders, including curfews.[19] The original version of the Bill which gave effect to these proposals would have required parental bind overs in every case in which a juvenile was convicted unless that would be unreasonable in all of the circumstances. This proposal met with a storm of protest and provoked objections from, among others, the Magistrates' Association, the Justices' Clerks' Society and the National Association for the Care and Resettlement of Offenders. Against the proposal it was argued that many young offenders come from families with multiple problems that require support rather than the threat of punishment that is implicit in a bind over. Fears were voiced that binding over parents would damage relationships within families, make parents less willing to cooperate with the criminal justice system, and clog the courts with appeals and hearings to determine whether parents had failed in their duty to exercise control over their children.[20] Out of political necessity, the government ameliorated the proposal by replacing mandatory bind overs with a rule requiring courts to consider a bind over in every case involving a child under 16 and, where a bind over was not ordered, to explain in open court why this was so. The provision is now found in section 150 of the Powers of the Criminal Courts (Sentencing) Act 2000.[21]

Under section 150, in every case in which a young person under 18 is convicted, it is the duty of the court to consider the issue and to bind over a parent or guardian if it is considered that this would be desirable in the interests of preventing further offending by the young person. Whereas a court must give reasons for not imposing a bind over, there is no corresponding duty to give reasons where one is imposed. This reflects a government project to make parental bind over an almost automatic appendix to every juvenile sentence, and may encourage courts to ignore the statutory test.[22] However, if the test is properly applied, there will be many cases in which a bind over would be inappropriate. Thus, where a parent demonstrates no intention to cooperate or has completely lost control of his or her child, it could not be said that to impose a bind over would be in the interests of preventing further offending. Equally, where a parent has been striving to guide and control a difficult teenager, it could not be argued that a bind over would serve the interests of crime prevention.

---

[19] *Ibid*, [8.10] and [8.11].
[20] See, eg Hansard HL vol 529 cols 108–20 (22 April 1991).
[21] The provision was originally Criminal Justice Act 1991 s 58.
[22] See R Noon, 'Binding over parents under s.58 Criminal Justice Act 1991—Some practical problems' (1992) 156 *Justice of the Peace* 803.

The requirement of parental consent is retained, but the element of voluntariness is removed, since a refusal to consent which is considered unreasonable by the court is an offence punishable with a fine of up to £1,000.[23] A parent who agrees to be bound over must enter into a recognisance, for an amount set by the court up to a maximum of £1,000, to take proper care of and exercise proper control over the young person. Following concerns at the vagueness of these duties, the provision has been amended and now specifies that 'care' of a person includes giving him or her protection and guidance and that 'control' includes discipline.[24] These duties are problematic, in that they apparently impose an objective standard of 'proper' care and control, unrelated to the parent's abilities and resources or to the inclinations and temperament of the young person. In particular, the term 'control' suggests a settled relationship of direction and obedience, which may be impossible to achieve in reality. Where the young person has received a community sentence, the recognisance may include a duty to ensure that the young person complies with the sentence. The recognisance can be for any period not exceeding three years and not extending beyond the young person's 18th birthday. There is a right to appeal against the imposition of a bind over as if it were a sentence following conviction.[25]

The potential of the bind over as an instrument of social discipline depends upon the power to punish failure to observe the promises extracted from the subject. The enforcement mechanism for the parental bind over is the same procedure as is used for forfeiting recognisances to keep the peace.[26] In that context, the procedure is quite straightforward and simply involves proof that the person bound over has committed a criminal offence. However, unlike a criminal offence, which is episodic, parental care and control are continuing duties, and proof of a failure of care and control would presumably require evidence of the quality of the parent–child relationship over the period in question. It should certainly not be assumed that failure to care and control can be inferred from the mere fact of a further offence by the child, a breach of curfew, or a failure to fulfil a community sentence.

Parenting Orders and Parenting Contracts

Parenting orders were proposed in the White Paper, 'No More Excuses' in 1997 as part of a programme of measures built around the principle that offenders and their parents should take responsibility for their offending behaviour. Although introduced as part of New Labour's flagship Crime and Disorder Act 1998, the

---

[23]   Powers of the Criminal Courts (Sentencing) Act 2000 s 150(2)(a) and (b).
[24]   Powers of the Criminal Courts (Sentencing) Act 2000 s 150(11).
[25]   Powers of the Criminal Courts (Sentencing) Act 2000 s 150(8) and (9).
[26]   Magistrates' Courts Act 1980 s 120.

orders reflected a political consensus[27] at the time and were designed to answer criticisms of the burdensome impact of earlier parental responsibility provisions by offering a degree of constructive support to affected parents. Notwithstanding that aim, the new orders have themselves been criticised as being unnecessarily coercive,[28] and have now been supplemented by parenting contracts, introduced by the Anti-Social Behaviour Act 2003. The rationale for introducing parenting contracts was that they might produce the same benefits as parenting orders, but without the element of coercion or need for a contested court hearing. As will be discussed below, claims that the contract mechanism is non-coercive and informal may be disputed.

Government guidance on the use of parenting contracts and orders recommends a hierarchy of approaches for Youth Offending Teams (YOTs) in relation to work with parents. Where parents are fully cooperative, work should be conducted on a voluntary basis. For less cooperative parents, a parenting contract may be offered, on the understanding that a refusal to enter into a contract may be used as evidence in support of an application for a parenting order. Thus, in many circumstances, parenting orders will be reserved for those parents who are resistant to engaging in work with a YOT to prevent their child offending.[29]

A parenting contract in respect of criminal conduct or anti-social behaviour[30] under section 25 of the Anti-Social Behaviour Act 2003 may be entered into when a child or young person has been referred to a YOT as a result of receiving a formal warning,[31] or as a result of a referral to a youth offender panel following conviction for a first offence.[32] Before a YOT enters into such a contract, it must have reason to believe that the child or young person has engaged in, or is likely to engage in, criminal conduct or anti-social behaviour, although in most cases this condition will be satisfied either by the fact that the young person has admitted an offence when accepting a warning, or has been convicted in the Youth Court. The parties to the contract will be the parent and the YOT, each of whom give undertakings, although it is specified that the 'contract' will not be legally binding. The parent will normally agree to participate in a programme involving counselling or guidance, coupled with more specific undertakings designed to prevent the child's further offending or anti-social behaviour. The YOT's undertaking will be to support the parent in fulfilling the contract.

---

[27] See proposals of the former Conservative Government: 'Preventing Children Offending: A Consultation Document' (London, Home Office, 1997) ch 5.

[28] D Ghate and M Rumella, *Positive Parenting: The national evaluation of the Youth Justice Board's parenting programme* (London, Youth Justice Board for England and Wales, 2002) 38–9.

[29] Ministry of Justice, Department for Children, Schools and Families and Youth Justice Board, 'Parenting Contracts and Orders Guidance' (2007) [2.22].

[30] Parenting orders may also be obtained in relation to exclusion from school or truancy, under Anti-Social Behaviour Act 2003 s 19.

[31] Under Crime and Disorder Act 1998 s 65.

[32] Under Crime and Disorder Act 1998 s 1.

The range of circumstances in which a parenting order may be made is set out in section 8 of the Crime and Disorder Act 1998 and includes cases in which a child or young person is convicted of an offence, or is subjected to an anti-social behaviour order (ASBO) or a sex offender order (ie following a caution for a sex offence), and where a child under the age of 10 is subject to a child safety order having committed acts which would have amounted to an offence if he or she were over the age of 10.[33] That list has now been extended to include the case where a young person is referred to a YOT having received a formal warning from the police.[34]

Before an order is made, the court must be satisfied that such an order would be desirable in the interests of preventing a repetition of the conduct that gave rise to the order. Where that test is satisfied, an order is mandatory in the case of a child under the age of 16, but discretionary where the offender is aged 16 or 17. The choice of an apparently subjective test indicates a government view that courts should have a discretion to impose orders even in cases where rationally there is little prospect of a useful outcome. Thus, in parliamentary debate, Lord Williams of Mostyn made it clear that the orders might be enforced against unwilling parents without consideration of whether they would be likely to cooperate.[35] A more objective approach to the question of whether an order would be desirable is indicated in *R (on the application of M) v Inner London Crown Court*,[36] in which Henriques J quashed a parenting order on the basis of irrationality following a detailed examination of the facts. A parenting order was considered futile where there was no reason to anticipate further offending by the young person. This case indicates that courts should impose orders only where, on a rational assessment, to do so might serve to prevent further offending.

Parenting orders may last for a period of up to 12 months and will normally involve an obligation to attend counselling and guidance sessions once a week for a period not longer than three months. The order may also specify other requirements (presumably also subject to a rationality hurdle), which might include escorting the child to school or ensuring that the child is supervised by a responsible adult at night.[37]

Parental Compensation Orders

The most recent addition to measures imposing parental responsibility for juvenile offending is the parental compensation order created by section 144 of

---

[33]   Under Crime and Disorder Act 1998 s 11.
[34]   Anti-Social Behaviour Act 2003 s 26. Note also that parenting orders may also be obtained following exclusion from school under the Anti-Social Behaviour Act s 20.
[35]   Hansard HL vol 585 cols 1076–7 (10 February 1998).
[36]   [2003] EWHC 301 (Admin).
[37]   Examples taken from Home Office, 'No more excuses—a new approach to tackling youth crime in England and Wales' (Cm 3809, 1997) 14.

the Serious Organised Crime and Police Act 2005.[38] Whereas a parent may be made liable to pay a compensation order made against a child in criminal proceedings under existing powers,[39] the new procedure extends parental liability to pay compensation for loss or damage caused by the act of a child under the age of 10 that is either judged to be anti-social behaviour or would have constituted a crime if committed by a child older than 10. Quite apart from its impact in imposing liability on parents, the provision continues a trend, started with the Crime and Disorder Act 1998, to re-conceptualise problematic behaviour by young children as criminal. The predominant view for the greater part of the twentieth century was that, however harmful, the conduct of children of 'tender years' should not be characterised as criminal unless the child has matured sufficiently to understand that what was done was wrong. Children under the age of 10 were deemed to lack the capacity to commit crime, whilst children between the ages of 10 and 14 were subject to the presumption of lack of capacity (known as *doli incapax*) unless it was demonstrated that they understood that their actions were wrong. This arrangement reflected two considerations: that society as a whole should share the risks and burdens associated with unpredictable behaviour in childhood, and that criminalisation, with the associated stigma of deviance, is inappropriate until a child has had an opportunity to mature and be socialised to understand society's values.

These protective principles were substantially discarded by the Crime and Disorder Act 1998 in accordance with government policy that wrongdoers must take responsibility for their actions. The Act abolished the presumption of *doli incapax*,[40] replacing the rebuttable presumption of incapacity with an irrebuttable presumption of capacity for 10- to 14-year-olds.[41] The Act also addressed quasi-criminal behaviour of children under the age of 10 with the introduction of the misleadingly named Child Safety Order (CSO).[42] The main grounds for making an order are that the child has committed an act which would have constituted an offence if he or she had been aged over 10, or that the child had acted in a manner likely to cause harassment, alarm or distress to others (ie anti-social behaviour). Under a CSO, requirements may be imposed on the child not only for his or her care, protection and support, but also in the interests of preventing of a repetition of the behaviour which led to the imposition of the order.[43] This explicit deterrent aim suggests that the CSO is simply a means of

---

[38] Serious Organised Crime and Police Act s 144 gives effect to Sch 10 of that Act, which in turn inserts new ss 13A–E in the Crime and Disorder Act 1998.

[39] Powers of the Criminal Courts (Sentencing) Act 2000 s 137 as amended.

[40] Crime and Disorder Act 1998 s 108, see generally R Leng, M Wasik and R Taylor, *Blackstone's Guide to the Crime and Disorder Act 1998* (London, Blackstone Press, 1999) 55–61; and C Walsh 'Irrational Presumptions of Rationality and Comprehension' [1998] 3 *Web Journal of Current Legal Issues*.

[41] *R v T (Child: Doli incapax)* [2008] EWCA Crim 815, disapproving *CPS v P* (2007) 171 JP 349.

[42] Crime and Disorder Act 1998 s 11; see generally Leng *et al*, above n 40, 29–34.

[43] Crime and Disorder Act 1998 s 11(5).

criminalising those under the age of 10. Indeed, the National Association of Probation Officers argued that the order 'reduces the age of criminal responsibility to zero'.[44] Since a child under the age of 10 is not in a position to fulfil the requirements of an order, a responsible officer must be named as supervisor in the order, but it was also envisaged that in many cases the CSO would be complemented by a parenting order, placing the parent under a duty to see that the terms of the CSO were fulfilled.

The parental compensation order confirms the characterisation of young children's wrong-doing as criminal and imposes parental responsibility to compensate for any loss or damage to property caused by behaviour which would have amounted to a criminal offence if the child were aged over 10, or by anti-social behaviour. Rather oddly (for an ostensibly compensatory measure), the court must be satisfied that the award of compensation would be desirable in the interests of preventing a repetition of the (quasi) offending or anti-social behaviour. The significance of this requirement will be considered below.

THE NATURE OF PARENTAL RESPONSIBILITY

In 2006/07, the Youth Justice Board recorded 216,000 final warnings and court disposals for those under the age of 18, each of which might have attracted parental criminal responsibility. Of these, 104,000 involved children under the age of 16 for whom there is, in effect, a presumption that some form of parental responsibility will be applied.[45] Figures are unavailable for the number of cases in which parental responsibility is imposed. However, in view of the huge number of parents potentially implicated, it is remarkable that there has been relatively little consideration of the precise nature of the responsibility imposed.[46]

It appears to have been widely assumed that parental responsibility for a juvenile's offending does not involve the ascription of criminal responsibility to the parent. Thus, discussions of parental responsibility are almost universally absent from textbooks on criminal law and academic treatises on criminal liability and instead are found in works on sentencing. This practice originated with the rules concerning the payment of fines, but has been extended, perhaps without much reflection, to those modern forms of parental responsibility which have developed since 1991. It is undoubtedly convenient to deal with parental responsibility alongside sentencing issues because it arises for consideration at the same stage of the proceedings. However, this classification of convenience should not obscure the fact that the imposition of parental responsibility is a totally different exercise to sentencing. Sentencing is the disposal stage of a

---

[44]   NAPO, 'Briefing on the Crime and Disorder Bill' (February 1998).
[45]   Youth Justice Board, 'Annual Workload Data 2006/07', <http://www.yjb.gov.uk/en-gb/> accessed 17 December 2008.
[46]   But see K Hollingsworth, 'Responsibility and rights: children and their parents in the youth justice system' (2007) 21 *IJLPF* 190.

bifurcated trial procedure in which the first stage involves a determination of liability. Where parental responsibility is imposed following a trial, the parent will not have been a party to the trial, nor will he or she have been the subject of it. Thus, the procedure leading to the imposition of parental responsibility, properly understood, involves not only a disposal (akin to the sentencing of the principal offender), but also the necessary prior determination of liability (akin to the determination of guilt for the principal offender).

The question of whether the imposition of parental responsibility involves a criminal charge was considered briefly in *R (on the application of M) v Inner London Crown Court*.[47] The case concerned an application for judicial review of a decision to make a parenting order in respect of the mother of a 13-year-old girl following the child's conviction for a single incident of malicious wounding. Counsel for the applicant had initially argued that the imposition of the parenting order involved a criminal charge and was therefore subject to the fair trial rights attaching to criminal proceedings under Article 6(2) and (3) of the European Convention on Human Rights. This argument was not pursued at the hearing. However, Henriques J indicated that if he had been required to determine the issue, a consideration of the three criteria set out in *Engel v Netherlands (No 1)*,[48] namely categorisation under domestic law, the nature of the misconduct and the nature and severity of the sanction, would have pointed to the conclusion that no criminal charge was involved.

The view that the imposition of a parenting order does not involve a criminal charge, apparently shared by counsel and the judge in this case, was probably heavily influenced by the House of Lords' decision in *Clingham and McCann*.[49] That case concerned challenges to the propriety of employing civil rules of evidence and burdens of proof in obtaining ASBOs. The Lords' decision that the imposition of an ASBO does not involve a criminal charge may be seen as a ringing endorsement of the modern practice of using civil procedures to achieve criminal justice aims. However, it would be a mistake to assume that the reasoning applied in *Clingham* will necessarily apply to similar challenges. In particular, Lord Steyn emphasised that the imposition of an ASBO involved no immediate penalty and pointed out that in no case had the European Court of Human Rights found that proceedings were criminal in nature where they could not result in a penalty for the defendant. That position may be contrasted with the decision of the European Court of Human Rights in *Steel v UK*, which held that the procedure by which a person is bound over to keep the peace should be considered criminal, because a refusal to be bound over may be punished with immediate imprisonment.[50] Applying this reasoning, it may be argued that a

---

[47] [2003] EWHC 301 (Admin).
[48] [1976] 1 EHRR 647.
[49] *Clingham v Royal Borough of Kensington and Chelsea; R v Crown Court at Manchester, ex p McCann* [2002] UKHL 39.
[50] *Steel v UK* (1998) 28 EHRR 603.

parenting order, like a bind over, but unlike an ASBO, involves the imposition of a penalty. Whereas a person subject to an ASBO must simply desist from specified bad behaviour, a parenting order involves a burdensome obligation to attend counselling for two hours per week for up to three months, and may involve other positive obligations for the full 12 months' duration of the order. In structure the order is similar to community sentences such as community punishment orders, community rehabilitation orders and attendance centre orders, all of which may require attendance at particular places and times and participation in supervised activities. The government has been at pains to emphasise that these sentences are punitive and should not be seen as soft options.[51] In view of this stance, if and when the nature of the parenting order is fully argued before a court, it would be difficult for the Crown to deny the punitive nature of the order and accordingly difficult to resist the claim that the process involves the ascription of criminal responsibility to the parent.

It may also be argued that making a parent liable for a child's financial penalties involves ascribing criminal responsibility to the parent. A fine is a punishment when imposed upon a child as the sentence of the court, and is no less a punishment when shifted to the parent by operation of law. If punishment is the hallmark of criminal responsibility,[52] criminal responsibility is ascribed to the parent by imposition of the fine. A possible objection to classifying parental responsibility as a form of criminal responsibility under the *Engel* criteria would be that those criteria include a consideration of the 'nature of the misconduct'. The problem here is that parental liability for juvenile offending may be imposed without proof of any misconduct by the parent. This objection may be answered by three arguments.

First, if it is accepted that the huge body of strict liability regulatory offences are properly classified as criminal notwithstanding the absence of a fault element, it would appear that an element of misconduct is not a necessary condition for classifying a responsibility as criminal. Secondly, although the parent may not be at fault, the reference to misconduct in *Engel* may be satisfied by reference to the child's criminal act on which the parent's responsibility is founded. Thirdly, although parental misconduct need not be proved, it is arguable that the rationale for imposing parental responsibility is an assumption that offending by the child is indicative of parental dereliction of duties of control, discipline and moral guidance. The force of this assumption is apparent in the decision of the Court of Appeal in *R v Sheffield Crown Court, ex p Clarkson*,[53] in which an order

---

[51] See most recently the Prime Minister's press conference on 14 July 2008, in which he resisted calls for automatic imprisonment for knife possession on the basis that community orders were 'tough sentences': <http://blogs.guardian.co.uk/politics/2008/07/gordon_browns_monthly_press_co. html> accessed 17 December 2008.

[52] 'The criminal quality of an act cannot be discerned by intuition; nor can it be discovered by reference to any standard but one: is the act prohibited with penal consequences': *Proprietary Articles Trade Association v Att-Gen for Canada* [1931] AC 310 at 324 (Lord Atkin).

[53] [1986] Cr App R (S) 454.

imposing a fine on a mother was quashed on the ground that she had rebutted any assumption of misconduct by demonstrating that she had done all that she could to prevent her son offending. This decision suggests that parental responsibility for fines corresponds to a model of criminal liability familiar in regulatory law, ie strict liability subject to a due diligence defence, the burden of proving which lies on the defendant (in this case the parent).

Perhaps the clearest instance of ascription of criminal responsibility to the parent is found in the recently created parental compensation order. This is doubly paradoxical because the order is compensatory (typically a civil matter) and is not based on criminal conduct (for the simple reason that it applies only in relation to the actions of children below the age of criminal responsibility). Although the order is subject to the civil standard of proof and is concerned with compensation payable to those suffering loss, it is apparent that the objectives of the procedure are criminal, rather than civil, in nature. Thus, responsibility for instituting proceedings rests with a local authority rather than the individual victim, indicating that the issue is seen as of public, rather than purely private, concern. The requirement that the award of compensation should be desirable in the interests of preventing a repetition of the offending behaviour indicates that the process is primarily intended as a deterrent (a characteristic of criminal rather than civil liability). Finally, as with criminal proceedings before a magistrates' court, appeal lies to the Crown Court.

The argument advanced here is that current provisions for parental responsibility for juvenile offending involve ascribing criminal responsibility to the parent. This is not simply a sterile argument about legal classification. If accepted it would have a significant impact on the procedures adopted to determine parental responsibility, on the substantive tests applied and on the manner in which parental responsibility is debated at a policy level. In procedural terms, the most obvious implication of classifying the imposition of parental responsibility as a criminal proceeding would be that the criminal rules of evidence and burdens of proof would be engaged. In particular, the procedures would become subject to those fair trial guarantees under Article 6(2) and (3) of the European Convention on Human Rights that apply only to criminal proceedings.

A second consequence of recognising that parental responsibility involves the ascription of criminal liability would be that the substantive rules should be scrutinised according to the normal principles associated with criminalisation. The starting point for such an enquiry is the recognition that punishment and criminal responsibility normally involve the application of damaging stigma, and the infliction of harm to individuals as well as costs to the community as a whole. Accordingly, criminalisation should be used with restraint and as a last resort where the relevant policy objective cannot be achieved by any other means, and only where the benefits from imposing the criminal sanction outweigh the associated costs.

THE RATIONALE FOR CRIMINALISING PARENTS

A consistent theme in political rhetoric concerning parental responsibility has been that offending behaviour by youngsters may be in part attributed to failure to exercise parental duties. Thus, writing about the Bill which would become the Criminal Justice Act 1991, David Waddington, then Conservative Home Secretary, remarked that:

> offenders set off on the road to crime at an early age, because their parents have not bothered to instil in them a sense of right and wrong and respect for other people's property.[54]

More recently, Baroness Scotland, speaking for the government on the Bill which would become the Anti-Social Behaviour Act 2003, argued that parenting orders were necessary for parents who were reluctant to teach their children the difference between right and wrong.[55] Whereas proven failure to fulfil parental duty might justify criminalisation, it should be noted that this is not the model of parental responsibility found in current legislation, under which responsibility may be imposed without any proof of fault on the part of the parent.

The justifications for the current regime of parental responsibility for juvenile crime can be found in the successive White Papers which provided the foundation for the Criminal Justice Act 1991 and the Crime and Disorder Act 1998. Thus, in the 1990 White Paper it was argued that parents have the most powerful influence on their children's development and should help them to develop as responsible, law-abiding citizens.[56] Parents were also considered to be best situated to exercise control over their children:

> parents should know where their children are and what they are doing and be in a position to exercise some supervision over them.[57]

Finally, it was argued that requiring parents to pay financial penalties:

> brings home to the parent the reality of the consequences of their children's behaviour and the implications for their own actions.[58]

These arguments do not provide a satisfactory justification for criminalising parents. Their major flaw is that they conflate quite different concepts of responsibility. It may be accepted that parents shoulder the responsibilities of care and control in relation to the child as described in the White Paper. But responsibility in the sense of a liability to suffer a penalty imposed by a criminal court is a quite different sort of responsibility. The distinction between these two types of responsibility has been examined by Peter Cane, who would describe the

---

[54] *The Evening Standard* (9 November 1990).
[55] Hansard HL vol 651 col 1092 (18 July 2003).
[56] Home Office, above n 6, [8.1].
[57] *Ibid*, [8.7].
[58] *Ibid*, [8.8].

parent's responsibility of future care as a 'prospective responsibility', whereas liability for a criminal penalty relating to past events is described as 'historical responsibility'.[59] Thus, it does not follow that the parent who has responsibilities of superintendence in relation to the child should also bear responsibility for a penalty if the child offends. Where criminal liability arises from a duty imposed by law, the normal requirements are: first, proof that the person in question was subject to the duty; and, secondly, proof that the duty was breached. Although in some instances parental responsibility may be avoided where the parent was not in breach of duty,[60] there is no general rule requiring a court to consider whether or not the parent has fulfilled his or her duties relating to the child as a precondition for imposing parental responsibility.

Equally flawed is the argument that because the parent is best placed to control the child, the parent must bear responsibility if the child offends. Under general principles, where criminal liability arises from the fact that a person has the legal power and practical opportunity to control another's conduct, it must also be shown that the defendant failed to exercise that power.[61] This is not a precondition of parental criminal responsibility.

The government's final argument—that imposing liability 'brings home to the parent' the nature of their responsibilities—is utterly inadequate as a justification for criminalisation. To impose a penalty for the purpose of encouraging future performance of a duty, without any assessment (other than perhaps a generalised assumption) of a past failure, or ignorance of or disinclination to perform the duty, runs contrary to all accepted principles of criminal law.

The government returned to the issue of parental responsibility in its 1997 White Paper, 'No More Excuses', which expressed a determination to reinforce the responsibility of delinquents and their parents, citing the need to end the 'excuse culture' surrounding juvenile crime.[62] By focusing on excuses, the government rather clumsily side-stepped the logically prior question of why the parent should be liable in the first place. The White Paper then cited research indicating a clear link between offending rates and the quality of parenting, and referred to the success of parenting schemes in the United States.[63] This material presented a strong case for state intervention in parenting where children have committed crimes or exhibit other problems. However, this material does not provide any justification for the criminalisation of parents. Indeed, as will be discussed below, studies of parenting schemes operating in England and Wales have noted that where parents take part in parenting programmes under the coercion of a court

---

[59] P Cane, *Responsibility in Law and Morality* (Oxford, Hart Publishing, 2002). The distinction is discussed in the context of parental responsibility by Eekelaar, above n 16, ch 5.

[60] See, eg *R v Sheffield Crown Court, ex p Clarkson (1986) 8 Cr App R (S) 454; TA v DPP [1997] 1 Cr App R (S) 1; R v J-B 2 Cr App R (S) 211; and Bedfordshire CC v DPP [1996] 1 Cr App R (S) 322.*

[61] See, eg *J.F. Alford Transport* [1997] 2 Cr App R 326; and *Rubie v Faulkner* [1940] 1 KB 571.

[62] Home Office, above n 37, [4.2].

[63] *Ibid*, [4.6]–[4.10].

order, this tends to be counter-productive in terms of the parents' willingness to participate in and take full benefit from the programme.

THE IMPACT ON PARENTS

There is a mass of evidence that young offenders are more likely to come from families with grave difficulties, and that the quality of parenting is perhaps the most significant factor in determining whether or not a youngster will offend.[64] This evidence strongly indicates the desirability of state intervention to improve parenting, but does not indicate a need for this to be coercive or punitive. Although the procedure for imposing fines on parents has a long pedigree, there is no evidence of the impact that this practice has on the affected families. Similarly, there is scant evidence on the effects of parental bind overs. In particular, no evidence has been offered to indicate that that the imposition of the fine or bind over encourages better superintendence or parenting of the child. A small-scale study on bind overs concluded that they operated to undermine positive parental support for the child and humiliated and embittered the affected parent.[65] A number of commentators have suggested that parental fines would exacerbate family hardship, and that fines and bind overs would tend to create family tensions which could lead to domestic violence, family break-up or other adverse consequences,[66] although hard evidence is lacking. Recent research evidence on parenting schemes is instructive, but fails to distinguish between parents who attend such schemes voluntarily and those attending under the coercion of a parenting order. The overall picture is encouraging: there is some evidence that parenting schemes have an effect in reducing offending, and parents generally feel that they benefit from the schemes.[67] It is instructive, however, that parents who are forced to attend the schemes suffer anger and humiliation, and that this presents a barrier to be overcome by the professionals offering help. Interestingly, a Mori poll deployed by the government in support of the application of parental responsibility shows that 67 per cent of parents would find professional help useful if faced with a troublesome teenager.[68] If such a high

---

[64]   J Graham and B Bowling, *Young People and Crime* (London, Home Office, 1995), Home Office Research Study No 145.

[65]   M Drakeford, 'Parents of young people in trouble' (1996) 35 *Howard Journal of Criminal Justice* 242.

[66]   H Wilson, 'Parental responsibility and delinquency: reflections on a White Paper proposal' (1982) 21 *The Howard Journal* 23; and Penal Affairs Consortium, *Parental responsibility, youth crime and the criminal law* (London, Penal Affairs Consortium, 1995).

[67]   See generally Ghate and Rumella, above n 28.

[68]   Mori poll on parenting, November 2006, published on the Prime Minister's website at <http://www.number10.gov.uk/output/Page10450.asp> accessed 17 December 2008. See also T Blair, 'Parents need a helping hand' *The Sun* (21 November 2006), <http://www.number10.gov.uk/output/Page10449.asp> accessed 17 December 2008.

percentage might be willing to accept help on a voluntary basis, the need to coerce participation in parenting programmes must be questioned.

Finally, a major objection to the current scheme of parental criminal responsibility is that it is applied discriminatorily against mothers rather than fathers. In relation to all of the parental criminal responsibility provisions, the courts have a choice whether to engage one or other parent or both. Almost invariably, the courts will choose the parent who attends court with the juvenile, which is more likely to be the mother. Recent figures relating to attendance at all parenting programmes (both voluntary and subject to a parenting order) show that the ratio of mothers to fathers is in excess of four to one. Equivalent figures are unavailable for the other forms of parental criminal responsibility, but it seems likely that they would show a similar bias. What is worrying about these figures is that they indicate that the parent (typically the mother) with whom the child lives and who is making some efforts to parent may be subject to a coercive order, whilst the absent parent, as a direct consequence of his or her lack of involvement in the parenting process, will escape liability altogether. Indeed, it has been accepted by the courts that the fact that a child does not live with a particular parent would make it unreasonable for that parent to be subject to a parenting order.[69]

CONCLUSION

The political debate about parental responsibility for juvenile offending is firmly resolved in favour of its imposition. Parental responsibility for juvenile offending is now imposed by a large number of developed countries[70] and continues, as in the United Kingdom, to be a popular area for new policy initiatives. In the United Kingdom, measures against the parents of young offenders appear to enjoy overwhelming public approval, according to a Mori poll published in 2006.[71] However, little attention has been paid to the extent to which these measures criminalise parents and to the theoretical and practical problems associated with criminalisation. At a theoretical level, it is remarkable to legislate for a form of vicarious criminal liability under which one person is made liable for the acts of another (who him- or herself is fully criminally liable) without proof of assistance or encouragement in the offence, or proof of any dereliction of parental duty or indeed proof of any fault whatsoever. At a practical level, it is remarkable to criminalise a very large group of citizens without a detailed assessment of the likely consequences of doing so.

---

[69] *TA v Director of Public Prosecutions* [1997] 1 Cr App R (S) 1.

[70] See, eg EM Brank and V Weisz, 'Paying for the crimes of their children: public support for parental responsibility' (2004) 32 *Journal of Criminal Justice* 465 for a review of parental responsibility law operating in the United States.

[71] See above n 68.

Parental responsibility for juvenile offending is rooted in the empirically supported belief that offending behaviour reflects a person's childhood social experiences, and in particular personal relationships, guidance, example, respect and discipline within the family setting. It is probably correct to recognise a link between levels of offending and changes in social structures and in expectations and experiences within families. However, this general proposition cannot justify the imposition of criminal responsibility on particular parents of offending children where the conditions operating within their family are largely a product of broad social forces beyond the control of the individuals concerned.

The government's attempts to address the roots of juvenile offending by intervention at the family level are showing some early signs of success. However, although the broad idea of parental responsibility for juvenile offending attracts public support, it is doubtful whether the blunt tool of punitive orders furthers the aim of reducing juvenile offending. It is argued that the current provisions contradict accepted theories of criminal liability, operate in an arbitrary manner and are grossly discriminatory in operation.[72] If the government wishes to retain parental responsibility as an aspect of criminal law, the scheme should be remodelled to reflect proper principles of criminal liability. A better option might be to reduce the scope of parental responsibility and divert resources to proven non-punitive measures aimed at reducing juvenile crime.[73]

---

[72] For a comparable critique of parenting orders in Scotland, see R Walters and R Woodward, 'Punishing poor parents: Respect, responsibility and parenting orders in Scotland' (2007) 7 *Youth Justice* 5.

[73] See also R Arthur, 'Punishing parents for the crimes of their children' (2005) 44 *The Howard Journal* 233.

18

Parental Liability for Harm Caused by Children: A Comparative Analysis

PAULA GILIKER*

INTRODUCTION

PARENTHOOD MAY BE one of the most important and joyous events an individual may experience, but from a legal and ethical perspective, it also gives rise to obligations. As Lord Millett stated in *McFarlane v Tayside Health Board*, 'the birth of a normal, healthy baby [is] … a mixed blessing. It brings joy and sorrow, blessing and responsibility.'[1] This chapter will examine the nature of this responsibility in English tort law. Children, by their very nature, are immature and sometimes irresponsible. They are capable of causing serious harm to themselves and others, without fully appreciating the risks of their actions. The parent, as carer and having control over the child, is the obvious person to blame if their child's conduct harms another. In the classic case of *Carmarthenshire CC v Lewis*,[2] for example, a four-year-old boy, left alone for a short period of time, ran into a nearby road in front of a lorry, the driver of which swerved to avoid the child and was tragically killed. In such circumstances, while it is impossible to blame the child, the duties of supervision and control of the responsible adult are called into question. Further, more difficult questions arise when one is dealing with teenagers. Whilst technically minors, they are capable of understanding instructions and appreciating many of the risks associated with their actions. In *Donaldson v McNiven*,[3] for example, the Court of Appeal was asked to consider the conduct of a parent, who had allowed his 13-year-old son (described as 'neither specially obedient nor specially disobedient') to play with an air rifle, having put his son on his honour never to use the rifle except in the cellar of the house. His son had disobeyed these instructions

* The author would like to thank Helen Reece, Ken Oliphant and the editors for their assistance in the writing of this chapter. Any errors remain those of the author.

[1] [2000] 2 AC 59 at 113–14.
[2] [1955] AC 549 at 566 (the carer in question in this case was a schoolteacher, but the same principles apply).
[3] [1952] 2 All ER 691 (parent not found to be negligent).

and accidentally shot a five-year-old child. In such circumstances, to what extent should a parent trust his or her child and rely on the child's relative maturity to prevent any accident occurring?

Parental liability, in such circumstances, raises fundamental questions about how we, as a society, view the parent/child relationship. This chapter will examine the role of tort law in relation to what might be termed the 'parent-child-victim' triangle. By caring for, and taking control of, a child, a parent is deemed to assume responsibility for both the child's welfare and for preventing him or her from harming others. This is a positive duty—in contrast to the normal reluctance of tort law to impose liability for omissions to act[4]—which renders the parent directly liable to the victim injured by the child's action. Yet the extent to which a parent is liable varies considerably between legal systems. As we will see, the courts in France are prepared to use strict liability as a means of ensuring that parents take financial responsibility for the harm caused to third parties by their children. In England and Wales, in contrast, the courts seek evidence of fault in the parents' care and control of the child. A choice therefore lies between using tort law in this context to set standards of parental behaviour or to go further and use it as a mechanism for ensuring that the victim's compensatory needs are met. In examining the balance drawn by the common and civil law courts between the interests of the innocent victim and the hapless parent, we are forced to consider not only our perception of individual responsibility, but the degree to which it is desirable or even necessary to regulate parenting through the mechanism of civil compensation. To what extent should the modern parent worry not only about his or her child's welfare, but the legal implications of the child's actions?

THE 'REASONABLE' PARENT

The common law has long held the view that parents should not be vicariously liable for their children: liability should be based on evidence of actual fault.[5] Liability arises not due to a formal statutory designation of responsibility, but under core tort principle. A parent is deemed to assume responsibility towards his or her child and this responsibility entails potential liability. In negligence, this signifies that the parent must meet the standard of 'the reasonable parent'. Whilst this may appear onerous, in practice the common law courts have shown themselves willing to acknowledge the difficulties of bringing up a child. There

---

[4]   See *Home Office v Dorset Yacht Co Ltd* [1970] AC 1004.

[5]   *Moon v Towers* (1860) 8 CB (NS) 611; 144 ER 1306 at 615: 'I am not aware of any such relation between a father and son, though the son be living with his father as a member of his family, as will make the acts of the son more binding upon the father than the acts of anybody else' (Willes J). See, generally, R Bagshaw, 'Children through tort' in J Fionda (ed), *Legal Concepts of Childhood* (Hart, Oxford, 2001).

are few reported cases, but Lord Reid's comments in *Carmarthenshire CC v Lewis*[6] give a clear indication of the approach taken:

> There is no absolute duty; there is only a duty not to be negligent, and a mother is not negligent unless she fails to do something which a prudent or reasonable mother in her position would have been able to do and would have done. Even a housewife who has young children cannot be in two places at once and no one would suggest that she must neglect her other duties, or that a young child must always be kept cooped up. But I think that all but the most careless mothers do take many precautions for their children's safety and the same precautions serve to protect others ... What precautions would have been practicable and what precautions would have been reasonable in any particular case must depend on a great variety of circumstances.

The general application of the test may be seen in the Australian case of *Smith v Leurs*.[7] Here, Brian, aged 13, had fired a stone from a catapult whilst playing with friends and struck another boy in the eye. His parents had been aware of the catapult and had warned Brian of the dangers of using it. Brian had been instructed not to play with it away from home, but chose to disobey these instructions. It was contended that Brian's parents had been negligent in allowing their 13-year-old son to possess a catapult. The High Court of Australia disagreed. A catapult was a 'common object in boyhood life'.[8] Brian had been warned of its dangers and was old enough to understand this warning. This was sufficient in the circumstances. The courts would not exact an obligation which is 'almost impossible of performance' or which exceeds what is practicable and to be expected according to all the circumstances, including the practices of the community.[9]

The majority of reported cases concern teenagers using firearms who cause severe injury to bystanders. Such cases are interesting in that they demonstrate the changing nature of the parent/child relationship as the child matures and gains greater independence. There is recognition that the parental role will lessen as the child nears the age of majority.[10] It is arguably a necessary part of the child's development towards adulthood that he or she is given more freedom to make his or her own decisions. However, when these decisions lead to injury to others, to what extent is the parent liable? A subjective approach would assess the maturity of the individual child to identify how much parental control his or her parent should reasonably exert, but such a detailed approach is contrary to the

---

[6] [1955] AC 549 at 566. In *Palmer v Lawley* [2003] CLY 2976, for example, the court did not find a mother negligent when her two-year-old child escaped from the back garden by unlatching a side door, walking up an alleyway and then onto the adjoining road. To do so would, according to the judge, place too high a burden on mothers and signify that every child would have to be locked in when playing.

[7] (1945) 70 CLR 256, High Court of Australia.

[8] *Ibid*, at 259 (Latham CJ).

[9] See the judgments of Latham CJ, Starke J and Dixon J.

[10] *North v Wood* [1914] 1 KB 629: father not liable for his 17-year-old daughter's failure to control her dog.

general objective test adopted by common law courts. The decisions therefore attempt to adopt an objective standard, although the courts appear to find it difficult to ignore all subjective factors. Contrast, for example, the treatment of the fathers in *Donaldson v McNiven*[11] and *Newton v Edgerley*.[12] In *Donaldson*, the father had allowed his 13-year-old son to play with an air rifle and was not found to be negligent. His son was mature enough to understand his father's warning and this would suffice.[13] In *Newton*, however, the father was liable for giving his 'young, immature' 12-year-old boy a 'lethal' shotgun without proper instructions on how to use it if others were present.[14] There is clearly some scope for interpretation.

Liability will thus depend on whether the parent has taken reasonable and practicable steps to prevent their child harming another individual. In light of the courts' willingness to appreciate the stresses of bringing up children, there have been few successful claims. The courts take into account the fact that:

> [t]he studied calm of the Royal Courts of Justice, concentrating on one point at a time, is light years away from the circumstances prevailing in the average home.[15]

Parental liability for the acts of their children is, as a result, a neglected area of tort law.

A number of reasons may be identified for this, apart from the difficulty of identifying fault on the part of the parent. First, parents and children are generally not seen as worth pursuing. Injuries caused by children may often be minor and therefore dismissed as an unfortunate consequence of youth.[16] Whilst there is clearly a greater willingness to pursue claims for serious injury, litigants appear to be discouraged by the fear that the parent or child will be unable to meet any large financial award of damages. Oliphant has argued that this argument is misconceived. Household insurance policies tend to include provision for personal liability and a large proportion of parents and children are covered by liability insurance policies taken out by the parents.[17] Nevertheless, a

---

[11] [1952] 2 All ER 691.

[12] [1959] 1 WLR 1031, distinguishing *Donaldson v McNiven* [1952] 2 All ER 691.

[13] See also *Gorely v Codd* [1967] 1 WLR 19 (father gave son sufficient instructions on the use of air rifles); and *Rogers v Wilkinson, The Times* (19 January 1963) (father adequately instructed 12-year-old son in use of gun).

[14] See also *Bebee v Sales* (1916) 32 TLR 413 (father liable for airgun fired by 15-year-old son when he failed to confiscate it after a previous incident).

[15] *Surtees v Kingston upon Thames RBC* [1992] PIQR P101 at 124 (Lord Browne-Wilkinson VC).

[16] Note also that where a child has injured another child, if there is no permanent injury, the claim is unlikely to be high due to the absence of a claim for loss of earnings and the provision of free health care on the NHS.

[17] K Oliphant, 'England and Wales case note to *Cass Ass Plén* 13 December 2002' (2004) 12 ERPL 718, 724. Insurance cover may be obtained as part of the buildings insurance policy (liability as owner of building) or through the household contents policy, either as occupier or for personal liability, and it may extend to losses caused by immediate family. All are subject to caps: see <http://www.abi.org.uk> accessed 17 December 2008. However, the take up of household contents insurance is variable in the United Kingdom. An ABI ORC survey reported that under one-half of households in the lowest income group held home contents insurance (44%), compared to over 80% of those with average

perception still exists that compensation might not be covered by insurance. Research additionally indicates that even when the accident has serious consequences, litigants will be reluctant to face the trouble and bother of a legal claim.[18]

Secondly, there is no actual obstacle to pursuing the actual culprit. Children may be sued in tort and there is no minimum age for liability.[19] In practice, however, this right is often illusory as children will be incapable of meeting the requirements of intention or foresight necessary to fulfil the conditions for liability. Nevertheless, the potential for such an action may have discouraged the development of a direct action against the parent.

Finally, the misconduct of children tends still to be seen as a matter of criminal or family law. The courts are reluctant to intervene and impose liability in familial situations and prefer to respect the autonomy of the family. The so-called 'blame' culture has yet to target children or parents as obvious defendants.[20] It is not insignificant that it was only in 1997 that the Court of Appeal formally set the standard of care expected of a minor.[21] Children are by their very nature accident-prone and the common law courts have displayed no great willingness to impose tortious liability on either the child or the parent in such circumstances.

A CHANGE OF APPROACH?

The common law courts demonstrate a distinct reluctance to impose liability on parents for the acts of their children in the absence of clear evidence of negligence. Whilst a duty of care will be imposed, in determining breach, the judiciary take into account the pressures of family life and the unpredictability of

incomes: see *Access for all: Extending the reach of insurance protection* (ABI, October 2007). Such insurance, in contrast to France, will also exclude deliberate or criminal acts, which diminishes the impact of such cover.

[18] See H Genn, 'Who claims compensation: Factors associated with claiming and obtaining damages' in D Harris *et al*, *Compensation and support for illness and injury* (Oxford, Clarendon Press, 1984) 61, who reports that less than 10% of victims of domestic and leisure accidents even consider the question of compensation.

[19] Contrast the position in Germany where a child cannot be found liable in tort below the age of seven, rising to 10 in traffic accidents (see para 828 BGB) and in the Netherlands, where a child cannot be found liable in tort until the age of 14 (Art 6:164 BW).

[20] Although note the media coverage concerning a first instance finding that a parent hiring a bouncy castle would be liable for failing to supervise adequately children at play: *Harris v Perry & Ors* [2008] EWHC 990 (QB); 'Boy severely hurt on bouncy castle likely to get £1m payout' *Guardian* (9 May 2008). The decision was, however, overturned on appeal ([2008] EWCA Civ 907); the Court of Appeal ruling that it would be quite impractical for parents to keep children under constant supervision and it would not be in the public interest for the law to impose a duty upon them to do so.

[21] *Mullin v Richards* [1998] 1 WLR 1304, relying on the Australian case of *McHale v Watson* (1966) 115 CLR 199 and case law on contributory negligence and children (see *Gough v Thorne* [1966] 1 WLR 1387). The decision itself appears lenient—15-year-old girl not able to foresee injury due to plastic ruler breaking during a play fight. See also *Etheridge v K (a minor)* [1999] Ed CR 550.

children. Two factors may, however, require the courts to reconsider their approach. As seen below, the trend in both English criminal law and most other European states is to increase parental responsibility and offer greater protection to victims injured by minors. The potential impact of these two influences will be examined below.

Parenting in Criminal Law

In recent years, the UK Government has placed more emphasis on encouraging parents to take responsibility for the criminal acts of their children. The latest initiatives to tackle anti-social behaviour and create a modern culture of respect focus, inter alia, on poor parenting skills, a weak parent/child relationship and a family history of problem behaviour.[22] The statutory provisions described by Leng in his chapter in this volume seek to increase parental involvement in the punishment of minors and to force parents to recognise their duty to care for, and control, their own offspring.[23]

Such measures are by their very nature controversial. They interfere with family autonomy and signify state regulation of the task of raising a child. Some commentators have suggested that parenting orders may be seen 'as fundamentally authoritarian, an attack on civil liberties and an extraordinary invasion by the State into family autonomy.'[24] Such measures do suggest a policy divide between criminal and civil law. Whilst civil law accepts that parents should allow their children to grow up and take greater responsibility for their own actions as they mature, criminal law increasingly looks to parents to exercise more control over potential young offenders and thereby reduce youth crime. If criminal law represents a gradual societal acceptance of the need to increase regulation of the parent/child relationship to prevent harm to others, would a similar evolution be desirable in civil law? If we accept that family autonomy must, at times, give way to the protection of innocent victims, there is a clear argument that tort law should also adopt a greater regulatory role and that the civil courts should at least reconsider their current leniency towards parental responsibility.

---

[22]   The Respect Action Plan, for example, published in January 2006 set out a framework of powers and approaches to: promote respect positively; bear down uncompromisingly on anti-social behaviour; and provide support to local people and local services. It recognised (at 3) that '[p]arents have a critical role in helping their children develop good values and behaviour': see <http://www.respect. gov.uk> accessed 17 December 2008. See also the government White Papers of 1990 and 1997: 'Crime, Justice and Protecting the Public: The Government's Proposals for Legislation' (Cm 965, 1990) and 'No more excuses—a new approach to tackling youth crime in England and Wales' (Cm 3809, 1997).

[23]   For a critical study of the statutory provisions, see K Hollingsworth, 'Responsibility and rights: Children and their parents in the youth justice system' (2007) 21 *IJLPF* 190. See generally A Bainham, *Children: The Modern Law* (3rd edn, Bristol, Jordan, 2005) ch 14.

[24]   Bainham, above n 23, 640.

A Strict Liability Approach?

Further, English law is far more generous towards parents than the law in other European states. Continental legal systems, in general, impose greater levels of responsibility on parents for the harmful actions of their child, either by virtue of a reversed burden of proof or by the imposition of strict liability on the parent. A number of recent studies have emphasised the distinction between the special forms of liability imposed in civil law systems and the ad hoc approach of the common law:

> In almost all the European countries, it is possible to find some form of special liability imposed on parents for the harm caused by their minors. This is true for France, Germany, Greece, Italy, Poland, Portugal, Spain, Switzerland, Belgium, the Netherlands and the Czech Republic. In contrast, Austria and England do not have any particular rule ... [Parental liability] is sufficiently well established in a majority of European countries for it to appear as a 'common European rule'.[25]

The position in France is of particular note. French law in recent years has completely remodelled its treatment of parental responsibility for children and moved from a fault-based to a strict liability system. This has been achieved by a complete rereading of its civil code (with only limited legislative modifications) and an open discussion of the use of the insurance market to create a no-fault compensation mechanism. France thus provides an excellent example of what can be achieved if one is prepared to impose strict duties on parents to protect others from the harm their children may cause. Express provision was made for parental liability in the 1804 Civil Code. Article 1384 of the Code (as amended) provides:

> (4) The father and mother, in so far as they exercise 'parental authority', are jointly and severally liable for the damage caused by their minor children who live with them.[26]

> (7) The above liability exists, unless the father and mother ... prove that they could not prevent the act which gives rise to that liability.[27]

Until the 1960s, these provisions were deemed to rest on a presumption of fault by the parents (originally the father), to be rebutted on proof that the harm suffered was not due to a failure to take reasonable steps to look after or educate the child (*une faute de surveillance ou d'éducation*).[28] However, since that time, the courts have

---

[25] S Galand-Carval, 'Comparative report on liability for damage caused by others Part I' in J Spier (ed), *Unification of Tort Law: Liability for Damage Caused by Others* (The Hague, Kluwer Law International, 2003) [17]–[18].

[26] '*Le père et la mère, en tant qu'ils exercent l'autorité parentale, sont solidairement responsables du dommage causé par leurs enfants mineurs habitant avec eux*.' As amended by *loi* No 70–459 of 4 June 1970 and *loi* No 2002–305 of 4 March 2002. All translations of the *Code civil* are taken from <http://www.legifrance.gouv.fr> accessed 17 December 2008 and are by G Rouhette with the assistance of A Rouhette-Berton.

[27] '*La responsabilité ci-dessus a lieu, à moins que les père et mère ... ne prouvent qu'ils n'ont pu empêcher le fait qui donne lieu à cette responsabilité*.' As amended by *loi* of 5 April 1937.

[28] Cass (2) civ 12 October 1955 JCP 1955 II 9003 note P Esmein; D 1956.301 note R Rodière.

interpreted the law in favour of victims. The most significant steps were taken in the 1980s and 1990s. In 1984, the *Cour de cassation* moved first to remove the condition that the child had to commit a tortious act.[29] It is sufficient that the child's act was the direct cause of the damage. This was followed in 1997 by *l'arrêt Bertrand*.[30] Here, Sébastien, aged 12, had collided with a moped while riding his bicycle onto a main road. It was argued that the Bordeaux Court of Appeal had been wrong in failing to consider whether his father could show that the accident was not due to any fault on his behalf. The *Cour de cassation* disagreed: the question of fault would now be deemed irrelevant. In the absence of *force majeure* or contributory negligence, the parent would be strictly liable. No other excuse would suffice. The *Assemblée Plénière* in 2002 confirmed this change of approach.[31] To establish liability on the part of the parents:

> it is enough that the damage pleaded by the victim has been directly caused by the act, even if it is without fault, of the minor ... only *force majeure* or contributory negligence can exonerate the father and mother of this liability.[32]

In so doing, the French courts (notably without any intervention from the legislature) imposed strict liability on parents for children over whom they exercise parental authority until the age of majority (18).[33] As long as this authority continues, they will be liable regardless of the absence of fault on the part of themselves or their children. A number of examples demonstrate the scope of this doctrine. In the 2002 case mentioned above, a schoolboy had injured another pupil, having lost his balance during a physical education lesson. It was not clear why he had fallen over. The court nevertheless found the parent (not the teacher) liable for the injury.[34] Parental authority does not end at the classroom, but will continue until legally removed. Although liability is confined to children 'living with their parents', courts have interpreted this condition loosely. Provided that the child can be deemed 'usually' to live at home, strict liability will ensue. In an extremely generous interpretation of this condition,[35] a mother, who had sent her son to a holiday centre which was 1,000 kilometres

---

[29] See *l'arrêt Fullenwarth* Ass plén 9 May 1984 D 1984.525 concl J Cabannes, note F Chabas, JCP 1984 II 20255 note N Dejean de La Bâtie and *l'arrêt Levert* Cass (2) civ 10 May 2001 Bull civ II No 96; D 2001 Jur 2851 rapp P Guerder, note O Tournafond; JCP 2001 II 10613 note J Mouly; D 2002 somm 1315 obs D Mazeaud; JCP 2002 I 124 No 20 obs G Viney; RTDC 2001.601 note P Jourdain.

[30] Cass (2) civ 19 February 1997 Bull civ II No 56 p32; JCP 1997 II 22848 concl R Kessous, note G Viney, D 1997.265 note P Jourdain, chron 297 par Ch Radé (giving a strong defence of the judgment) and Somm 290 obs D Mazeaud; [1997] Resp civ et assur, chron 9 par F Leduc; [1997] Gaz Pal 2 572 note F Chabas; RTDC 1997.648 obs J Hauser and 668 obs P Jourdain.

[31] Cass Ass Plén 13 December 2002 Bull Ass plén No 4, p7; JCP 2003 II 10010 note A Hervio-Lelong; D 2003 Jur 231 note P Jourdain; Droit et Patrimoine February 2003 obs F Chabas.

[32] My translation.

[33] Parental authority will also be terminated by emancipation of the child: Art 371–1, C civ.

[34] See also Civ (2) 3 July 2003 Bull civ 2003 II No 230 p 191; JCP 2003 II 10009 note R Desgorces (schoolboy injuring friend in play-fight organised and supervised by PE teacher). An alternative action can be brought against the schoolteacher, but will require proof of fault.

[35] And one which arguably negates its entire utility!

from the family home, was found strictly liable for the thefts and violent acts committed by her son in the nearby camping site.[36] It is not surprising that a number of academics have questioned the continued utility of this condition.[37]

The defences have also been interpreted narrowly, in particular that of *force majeure* by which the defendant must show that the injury occurred due to the occurrence of an external, unforeseeable and unavoidable event. In the classic case of *Sté Aube-Cristal*,[38] a 14-year-old girl, Delphine, had accompanied her mother to the claimant's shop and, for some unknown reason, slipped and knocked over a cabinet, breaking its contents. Although no fault could be attributed to Delphine's mother and there was no reason to foresee the accident, the *Cour de cassation* found that, as there was no proof of *force majeure* or contributory negligence,[39] the mother would be strictly liable.

As a number of French commentators have indicated, these decisions render the parent the 'guarantor' of his or her offspring: liable to compensate for any damage he or she directly causes.[40] In the note to the *Bertrand* decision,[41] Professor Jourdain explained the rationale. Children, by their very nature, create the risk of injury to others due to their immaturity and inexperience. It will not always be possible to find fault by the parent, which may leave innocent victims uncompensated. In choosing between the innocent victim and the parents who, by virtue of their parental authority, have the ability to intervene, the latter appear to be the most logical persons to respond, particularly when the burden of strict liability can be met by insurance. Liability thus rests on the imposition of social risk on the parents as a counterpart to their parental authority over the child.[42] Such cost will be distributed within society via the mechanism of insurance.

---

[36] Cass crim 29 October 2002 D 2003 Jur 2112 note L Mauger-Vielpeau; RTDC 2003.101 obs P Jourdain; JCP 2002 IV 3080. See also Cass (2) civ 28 June 2000 Bull crim No 256; D 2001 somm 2792 obs L Dumaine; JCP 2000 I 280n obs G Viney (divorced father liable for armed robberies of daughter after she had left home to live with her boyfriend with whom she had a child!).

[37] See M Fabre-Magnan, *Les Obligations* (Paris, Presses Universitaires de France, 2004) 324. Viney argues at No 876 that the condition should be removed, but this would require legislative intervention due to the wording of Art 1384(4): see G Viney and P Jourdain, *Les conditions de la responsabilité* (3rd edn, Paris, LGDJ, 2006).

[38] See Cass (2) civ 2 December 1998 Bull civ II No 292, p 176; D 1999 IR 29; JCP 1999 II 10165 note M Josselin-Gall; RTDC 1999.410 obs P Jourdain.

[39] See Civ (2) 29 April 2004 Bull civ 2004 II No 202 p 170; D 2004 IR 1429. Note that this does not include third-party contributory negligence, which is usually a defence to strict liability in French law.

[40] See D Mazeaud, *Famille et responsabilité (Réflexions sur quelques aspects de l'idéologie de réparation), Etudes P Catala* (Paris, Litec, 2001) 569 ; and D Pohé, *Jurisclasseur Responsabilité civile:* fasc 141 [1]. See also F Boulanger, 'Autorité parentale et responsabilité des père et mere des faits dommageables de l'enfant mineur après la réforme du 4 mars 2002. Réflexions critiques' D 2005.2245.

[41] See P Jourdain D 1997.265. See also P Jourdain D 2003 Jur 231 at [7]: '*c'est parce que l'activité des mineurs, en raison de leur fragilité et de leur inexpérience, expose les tiers à des risques objectifs de dommage que l'on estime juste d'employer la responsabilité des parents.*'

[42] Alternatively by virtue of the voluntary decision to have a child: see J Julien, *La responsabilité civile du fait d'autrui: Ruptures et continuités* (Presses Universitaires d'Aix-Marseille, 2001) No 121–35. In his view, parenthood brings with it powers ('*les prérogatives parentales*'), but also duties.

The advocates of such an approach do concede that the current approach does not seem to go far enough. Compulsory insurance, and some mechanism for those unable to afford such insurance, would appear to be the natural corollary of such a development. This has not occurred, despite long-standing calls from academics.[43] About 97 per cent of French citizens take out '*multirisques habitation*' (home and contents) insurance,[44] which, in 90 per cent of cases, includes '*responsabilité civile familiale*', that is, liability for all damage caused by minors in their care wherever it takes place.[45] This still leaves a deficit of about 10 per cent which will generally consist of less well-off families.[46] Such insurance, in contrast to that available in England, will cover intentional misdeeds by the children. Article L121–2 of the Insurance Code provides that:

> The insurer guarantees the losses and damages caused by persons for whom the insured is civilly liable by virtue of article 1384 of the civil code, whatever the nature and severity of the fault committed by these persons.[47]

Commentators have noted that the 1997 *Bertrand* decision has led to a significant decrease of litigation in this area and that the extreme narrowness of the *force majeure* defence is a powerful incentive for insurance companies to settle claims.[48]

The concept of parent as guarantor of the risk caused by his or her child's conduct does require an acceptance of a particular view of tort law in which compensation for risks arising in society is its primary goal. Notions of individual responsibility are rejected in favour of the greater social goal of dealing

---

[43]   See, notably, G Durry RTDC 1978.655; F Terré, P Simler and Y Lequette, *Droit civil, Les Obligations* (9th edn, Paris, Dalloz, 2005) No 823; Viney and Jourdain, above n 36, No 892; and the classic article of André Tunc (A Tunc, 'L'enfant et la balle' JCP 1966 I 1983). Note the comments of the *Cour de cassation* in its 2002 Report, at 23 (<http://www.courdecassation.fr/> accessed 17 December 2008).

[44]   Which is compulsory for tenants, but not for freeholders: see *loi* no 89–462 of 6 July 1989 and arts 1732 *ff*, C civ. Indeed, a landlord may insert a clause in the tenancy agreement allowing him or her to terminate the tenancy if the lessee does not possess adequate insurance.

[45]   This data was used by the *avocat général* Gouttes in his report prior to the December 2002 decision (Ass plén Cass Ass Plén 13 December 2002 Bull Ass plén No 4, p 7; JCP 2003 II 10010 note A Hervio-Lelong; D 2003 Jur 231 note P Jourdain), and was supplied by the *Centre de documentation et d'information de l'assurance* (<http://www.ffsa.fr/>). In addition, schools will often insist on the provision of school insurance. On registration of the child, the parent will be asked to supply an *attestation d'assurance scolaire*, which confirms that the child has insurance cover for damage to school property and for personal injury to others. Whilst this should be included in the civil liability insurance part of the householder policy, additional insurance will be required for school trips and extracurricular sporting activities.

[46]   Although the *Commissions d'indemnisation des victimes d'infractions* (CIVI) and *Fonds de garantie des victimes des actes de terrorisme et autres infractions* both offer some supplementary support for victims.

[47]   By this means, a parent (liable for children under art 1384) will be a preferable litigant to the child him- or herself (personal liability being dealt with under art 1382, which is not covered by this provision).

[48]   S Galand-Carvel, 'Comparative report on liability for damage caused by others' in J Spier (ed), n 25 above, [29].

with injury to individuals in what is deemed to be the most efficient means possible. A reduction in process costs (ie litigation) is considered to be preferential to the costly and unpredictable trial of individual responsibility on the facts of each case. France thus follows a particular model of responsibility, which is reflected in its treatment of road accidents,[49] and its readiness to impose strict liability on employers and other organisations which control and direct the activities of others.[50] Innocent third parties are no longer forced to bear the cost of the misdeeds of children and a clear compensatory structure exists to deal with the consequences of their actions.

TAKING PARENTING MORE SERIOUSLY

The position taken in France and the policy choices of English criminal law do appear to be inconsistent with the current common law system of tort which, in practice, all but discourages litigation in this context. Vague standards of care are set with a limited expectation of claims. However, many would hesitate before advocating a move to the French approach outlined above. It represents a particular view of how to treat parental liability, premised on the assumption that the benefits of no-fault liability outweigh any normative role of the law of tort. Not all French commentators have taken the view of Professors Viney and Jourdain. Desgorces, for example, has asked how children are to mature and gain a sense of responsibility for their actions if any resultant injuries are merely absorbed by a system of insurance.[51] No provision is made for the increased maturity of the child between the ages of 0 and 18, thereby failing to recognise the important developmental stages from childhood to adulthood.

Other authors have complained of the 'objectification' of children.[52] The French system treats them as 'devices' capable of creating damage to others, thereby depicting parenthood as the acquisition of a risk which a parent chooses to undertake. Many would baulk at such a picture of the parent/child relationship, which may be termed at the very least 'unduly legalistic'. It is significant that a number of authors draw parallels between liability for children and for motor vehicles; both of which are now based on strict liability. Whilst legal parallels may

---

[49] See *loi Badinter* (*loi* no 85–677, 5 July 1985), which imposes strict liability on drivers in traffic accidents. As a result, from 1985, a major source of tortious injuries has been dealt with outside the French Civil Code.

[50] Notably the Blieck case of 1991 (Ass plén 29 March 1991 D 1991.324 note C Larroumet, chr G Viney p 157, JCP 1991 II 21673, concl H Dontenwille, note J Ghestin) and the Costedoat case of 2000 (Ass plén 25 February 2000 JCP 2000 II 10295 rapp Kessous, note M Billiau, JCP 2000 I 241 obs G Viney, D 2000.673 note Ph Brun).

[51] See Desgorces, note under Civ (2) 3 July 2003 JCP 2003 II 10009.

[52] Note, eg the views of Tournafond (D 2001.2851): treating children like inanimate objects or even animals clearly ignores the intelligence and initiative displayed by children. See also H Groutel Resp civ et assur 2001.chron No 18 and J Mouly JCP 2001 II 10613. Such an analogy has been firmly rejected by the English House of Lords in *Carmarthenshire CC v Lewis* [1955] AC 549.

be drawn, there are clearly ethical and moral differences between a parent's relationship with his or her car and child. Treating the child as just another source of liability which one incurs by virtue of one's choices in life ignores society's interest in the development of new citizens and in promoting familial stability. Added to this, parenthood is not always a choice. Legal responsibility should, surely, not depend on whether or not the pregnancy was intended.

Criticism has also been made of the centrality of insurance, which has led to what has been termed the '*privatisation du droit*' (privatisation of law) in which compensation is placed in reality in the hands of insurance companies, not the courts.[53] One might also question whether the result is even an equitable form of loss distribution when it places a burden on parents disproportionate to the parental authority they assume. The Irish Law Reform Commission in 1985 found it 'too drastic a solution' to impose strict liability on parents which would cause 'injustice' to parents who had done their best.[54] Further concerns may be raised. Certain authors have suggested that the current system is in fact 'anti-natal', in that the only real means to avoid liability is not to have children![55] In addition, potentially arbitrary results may occur when the injury has been caused by a teenager on the cusp of adulthood. At the age of 18, the child gains majority and therefore is subject to the ordinary principles of fault-based liability, as set out in article 1382 of the Civil Code.[56] The result is that entirely different systems of liability will arise depending on which side of his or her 18th birthday the culprit commits the act in question.

This would suggest that French law takes the principle of parental responsibility too far. Insufficient attention is paid to the negative consequences of the imposition of strict liability, and the ability of tort law to set normative standards of behaviour for parent or child is lost. However exemplary the parental behaviour, if the child is the direct cause of damage, the parent will pay. Unrealistically onerous duties are imposed on parents without a clearly proportionate gain to society.[57] Yet the gulf between the English system of fault-based liability and the French strict liability system suggests that there is middle ground to be found, capable of taking parenting more seriously without placing unjust burdens on parents.

---

[53]   See Desgorces, note under Civ (2) 3 July 2003 JCP 2003 II 10009.

[54]   'Report on the liability in Tort of Minors and the Liability of Parents for Damage Caused by Minors', <http://www.lawreform.ie/publications/publications.htm> accessed 17 December 2008 (LRC 17–1985) 70.

[55]   See H Lécuyer, Droit de la famille 1997.3; H Capitant, F Terré and Y Lequette, *Les grands arrêts de la jurisprudence civil* t2 (11th edn, Paris, Dalloz, 2000) 314.

[56]   See art 1382: 'Any act which causes harm to another obliges the person whose fault caused the harm to make reparation.'

[57]   And with a risk of bankruptcy for those unfortunate enough not to insure against such risks!

A PROPORTIONATE RESPONSE TO PARENTAL LIABILITY FOR THE TORTS OF
THEIR CHILDREN

In reality, the majority of civil law systems rely on fault-based systems, where a reversed burden of proof is placed on parents to demonstrate that the injury was not due to their fault.[58] Section 832 of the German Civil Code (BGB) provides a good example of this approach:

(Liability of a person with a duty of supervision or *Haftung des Aufsichtspflichtigen*)[59]

(1) A person who is obliged by operation of law to supervise a person who requires supervision because he is a minor or because of his mental or physical condition is liable to make compensation for the damage that this person unlawfully[60] causes to a third party. Liability in damages does not apply if he fulfils the requirements of his duty to supervise or if the damage would likewise have been caused in the case of proper conduct of supervision.

(2) The same responsibility applies to any person who assumes the task of supervision by contract.[61]

As can be seen, German law provides a useful contrast to English law.[62] The reversed burden of proof has allowed the courts to be more demanding, particularly where the child is in possession of an object with an obvious associated risk of danger, for example a shotgun or a match. As a parent, one is

---

[58] See J-P Le Gall, Internat Ency Comp Law—Vol XI Torts Ch 3: *Liability for the Acts of Minors*.

[59] Translations of the German Civil Code are taken from the German Ministry of Justice website: <http://bundesrecht.juris.de/englisch_bgb/index.html> accessed 17 December 2008.

[60] Liability is thus conditional on an objectively 'unlawful' act by the minor infringing one of the interests protected by § 823, but the child need not be personally charged with fault. Liability will be excluded where the injury was caused by the child's behaviour which would not be qualified as wrongful if performed by an adult: G Wagner, 'Children as tortfeasors under German law' in M Martin-Casals (ed), *Children in Tort Law Part I: Children as Tortfeasors* (New York, SpringerWien, 2006) [68].

[61] Those paid to care for children are thus expressly dealt with under the Code, although the courts have been anxious to exclude neighbours helping with child care temporarily from such provisions: see Landsgericht Karlsruhe in [1981] VersR, 142 (143). Liability, it will be noted, is not confined to parents. Note also the relevant provisions in Spanish law: Art 1903 II *Código Civil español*—'*Los padres son responsables de los daños causados por los hijos que se encuentren bajo su guarda*' (Parents are responsible for the damage caused by their children who are under their guard); and Art 1903 VI, *Código Civil español*—'*La responsabilidad de que trata este artículo cesará cuando las personas en él mencionadas prueben que emplearon toda la diligencia de un buen padre de familia para prevenir el daño*' (The liability referred to in this article shall cease when the persons mentioned in it prove that they employed all care of a reasonable person to prevent the damage). M Martin-Casals, J Ribot and JS Feliu, 'Children as tortfeasors in Spanish law' in M Martin-Casals (ed), *Children in Tort Law*, above n 60, [68], comment, however, that in Spanish law the 'reversal of the burden of proof is watered down to a great extent, since the courts render it impossible to escape liability by proving the diligence of the parents who are held liable for the acts of their children'. As such, it may be subjected to many of the same criticisms as the French system.

[62] See, generally, H Brox and W-D Walker, *Besonderes Schuldrecht* (33rd edn, Munich, CH Beck, 2008) 554–5; MJ Schmid, 'Die Aufsichtspflicht nach § 832, BGB' VersR 1982, 822; and D Haberstroh, 'Haftungsrisiko Kind—Eigenhaftung des Kindes und elterliche Aufsichtspflicht' VersR 2000, 806.

required by law to supervise the minor,[63] and demonstrate that this duty has been correctly exercised when injury to a third party occurs. The standard of care is objective, namely that of the reasonably prudent parent in the particular situation of the case.[64] The German courts, however, go further than the English courts in examining 'the age, disposition, characteristics, development, education and all other individual features of the minor'.[65] One commentator has warned that the vague phraseology used 'should not conceal a discernible trend in recent cases to raise the standard of care expected of modern parents'.[66] Whilst explicit orders to a child who is generally obedient and law-abiding may serve to rebut the presumption of fault,[67] parents will be found liable if they fail, for example, to inform children of the dangers associated with playing with fire and ensure that matches are stored out of the child's reach.[68] One case even suggests that a search of the child's body may be necessary if it is believed that the child has taken the matches and has a tendency to play with them.[69] This would indicate that, in addition to a reversed burden of proof, the courts set a higher standard for parents in Germany.

This assumption is supported by the 2003 study of the European Centre of Tort and Insurance Law on liability for the acts of others in different European states.[70] Faced with the question of how the courts would deal with a parent who gives his 13-year-old child an air rifle with proper instructions on safety, the English reporter predicted that such conduct would not be found negligent if damage was caused by the child: the parent would only be liable 'in the case of want of instruction or, where necessary, supervision'.[71] In contrast, his German counterparts believed that the parent probably would be held liable under § 832 BGB.[72] High standards of care are required for dangerous objects, such as bows and arrows, catapults and air rifles, and for dangerous activities, for example playing football on a road. They acknowledged that 'some academics go as far as to claim that dangerous objects of this kind simply do not belong in the hands of minors'.[73]

---

[63] See §§ 1626(1) and 1631(1) of the BGB, which establish the parental right to custody. In particular, § 1631(1) specifies that parental care (*elterliche Sorge*) includes the duty to supervise the child.

[64] BGH (29 May 1990) BGHZ 11, 282; BGH (26 January 1960) [1960] VersR, 355, 356; and BGH (27 October 1965) [1965] VersR 48.

[65] See RGZ 52, 73; and BGH MDR 1997, 643.

[66] See BS Markesinis, *The German law of obligations Vol 2, The law of torts* (3rd edn, Oxford, Clarendon Press, 1997) 899.

[67] See OLG Frankfurt (28 March 2001) [2001] MDR, 752.

[68] BGH Vers R 1983, 734 (parents of seven-year-old liable for fire child caused using easily accessible matches), BGH (28 February 1969) [1969] MDR 564; BGH (17 May 1983) [1983] NJW 2821; BGH (1 July 1986) [1987] NJW-RR 13, 14.

[69] BGH (1 July 1986) [1987] NJW-RR 13, 14.

[70] J Spier (ed), above n 25.

[71] WV Horton Rogers, 'Liability for damage caused by others under English law' in Spier (ed), *ibid*, [37].

[72] J Fedke and U Magnus, 'Liability for Damage caused by others under German law' in Spier (ed), above n 25, [32].

[73] *Ibid.*

The German system demonstrates two key means by which the English system may be rendered more responsive to victims' needs: by reversing the burden of proof and increasing the standard of care expected of parents.

Reversing the Burden of Proof

Such a reform was suggested by Waller in 1963,[74] and was considered by the Irish Law Commission in their 1985 'Report on the Liability in Tort of Minors and the Liability of Parents for Damage Caused by Minors'.[75] For Waller, such a reform would be 'much more moderate', but would acknowledge the limited truth that in a large number of cases, young children injure others due to the parent's failure to control the child. Further, the parent is best placed to meet questions of proof. The Irish Law Commission accepted that generally it would be the parent, not the victim, who possessed knowledge of how the incident occurred and what parental steps were taken to prevent this. Nevertheless, such arguments did not convince the Commission to recommend a reversal of the burden of proof. There would be occasions where neither parent nor victim could explain exactly what had happened and why, and, in such circumstances, it would be unjust to find a parent, who was not guilty of any lack of care, liable.[76] In the Commission's view, simply being a parent did not by itself justify the creation of a presumption of negligence.

There is much to be said for this view. A presumption represents a view taken in terms of the distribution of risk between the relevant parties—here, that where the evidence is indecisive, the risk will lie with the parent, not the victim. To dress this up in terms of who is best placed to bear the burden of proof cannot disguise this policy decision. Bearing in mind the ingenuity of children, one might legitimately question whether it is a 'limited truth' that behind every mischievous child stands a negligent parent. It will also only be determinative in a small number of cases. Gerhard Wagner, a leading German writer on European private law, comments that:

> the reversal of the burden of proof provided by §832 subs.1 BGB does not really change much. Its main effect is that once the court has fixed the scope of the duty to supervise it is for the parents to prove that they did in fact take all the safety measures required. In this respect, the allocation of the burden of proof to the parents comes naturally as the victim has no access to the sphere of family life and thus lacks the relevant information. In practice, cases rarely turn on the burden of proof.[77]

---

[74] PL Waller, 'Visiting the sins of the children' (1963–4) 4 *Melbourne University Law Review* 17, 39–40.
[75] (LRC 17–1985).
[76] *Ibid*, at 71. It was also argued that there was no similar provision for employers or producers of goods which equally create risks of injury to others and that the provision would be difficult to draft.
[77] See Wagner, above n 60, [51].

The most important question, therefore, is the standard of care expected of the 'reasonable' parent. Whilst a reversal of the burden of proof may in a limited number of cases leave the risk of uncertainty with the parent (if this is considered desirable), in the majority of cases it is in setting the standard of care expected of the parent that the normative power of the courts lies.

Increasing the Standard of Care Expected of Parents

If tort law is to become active in this area of law, there is therefore a need both to clarify the law and to set more stringent standards of care and thereby facilitate the role of tort law in setting behavioural standards. Both trans-European comparisons and criminal policy suggest that tort law should take parenting more seriously and establish a stricter standard of care.

Yet this is something the common law courts have expressed no willingness to do. As seen above, common law judges are slow to condemn those struggling with the trials and tribulations of bringing up a child. As Bagshaw acknowledges:

> The effect of this approach is that, to an extent at least, everyone in society must take the risk of being injured by children behaving like children.[78]

One reason for this is the distinction drawn by the courts between the roles of criminal and tort law. As Lord Scott stated recently in *Ashley v Chief Constable of Sussex Police*,[79] whilst criminal law provides punitive sanctions for behaviour which is categorised as criminal because it damages the good order of society, the function of tort law is different:

> Its main function is to identify and protect the rights that every person is entitled to assert against, and require to be respected by, others.[80]

Tort law, therefore, traditionally places greater importance on individual choice and self-determination. Whilst this value retains its force in the common law, it will be difficult to encourage change. Further, one must consider the traditional respect for the autonomy of the family. Even if the policy goals of criminal law justify intervention—and this is disputed by Leng[81]—civil law has been more reticent. A practice of confining civil liability to clear examples of neglect by the parent is entirely consistent with this division of roles.

One may add to this a more pragmatic obstacle. Claimants, in practice, are very unlikely to pursue uninsured defendants and, even if Oliphant is correct, there will still be a proportion of parents with no insurance cover at all. As we have seen, the French expansion of liability was funded by the fact that the vast majority of households possess liability insurance. In the absence of a culture of

---

[78]   Bagshaw, above n 5, 149.
[79]   [2008] UKHL 25.
[80]   *Ibid*, at [18].
[81]   See Leng, this volume.

parental liability insurance, a more demanding standard of care will make very little difference. There is therefore a further hurdle to be surmounted: the absence (or at least perceived absence) of insurance cover. It may be argued that if a stricter form of liability was imposed by statute, as seen in the United States,[82] or by clear judicial statement, then insurance cover would have to follow, but the continued reluctance of English civil law judges to address the question of parental liability for the acts of children and the focus of the present government on criminal law suggest that this is unlikely to occur.

Thus, whilst clarity of reasoning and more demanding standards will encourage greater liability, the hurdle of changing attitudes towards litigation is still to be overcome. Perhaps the real question we must address is what we perceive to be the role of tort law in relation to family matters. The majority of state-based parental compensation legislation in America was introduced in the 1950s and 1960s[83] to combat the problem of juvenile delinquency—in essence supporting criminal policy goals via a compensatory mechanism.[84] Alternatively, the French system utilises insurance-funded tort compensation to provide a no-fault system of liability for those injured by the acts of minors. The common law has yet to embrace fully either of these goals.[85] It is important, therefore, to recognise the limited role of tort law. Tort law is not a compulsory state-based compensation scheme, capable of responding to teenage delinquency and social unrest; it is part of private law. Its role is therefore to establish appropriate standards of care exercised by parents to third parties for those persons for whom they assume responsibility. By retaining its focus on individual responsibility for one's actions, evidence of fault remains an essential component of liability. Part of taking parenting seriously, therefore, is not only to appreciate the weaknesses of the present common law system of civil liability, but to recognise the limitations of private law in responding to social ills. To do so is to gain a better understanding of the positive role that tort law can play in modern society.

---

[82] All 49 states (excluding New Hampshire) have statutes imposing some form of vicarious liability on parents for damage arising from the acts of their children: see PK Graham, 'Parental responsibility laws: Let the punishment fit the crime' (1999) 33 *Loyola of Los Angeles Law Review* 1719, 1725–9; and L Gentile, 'Parental civil liability for the torts of minors' (2007) 16 *Journal of Contemporary Legal Issues* 125, who lists, in the appendix, the parental liability provisions of every American state.

[83] Although the first piece of legislation on parental civil liability was found in the Hawaii Territory in 1846.

[84] Although damages are generally limited by statute and the aim of the legislation is clearly juvenile crime control, not restitution. See, eg California Civil Code art 1714.1.

[85] Note, however, the Animals Act 1971 s 6(3), which imposes strict liability on the parent as 'head of the household' for injuries caused by animals owned or possessed by a child of that household under the age of 16.

CONCLUSION

This chapter has identified the limited role played by the common law of tort in the regulation of parental liability for harm caused by their children. The courts continue to be unwilling to permit tort law to play a significant role in regulating child care and favour a traditional picture of a family, struggling to bring up children, but working as a supportive family unit. In contrast, policy-makers in criminal law have determined that such a model represents an unrealistic picture of modern society and that more needs to be done to encourage parents to take greater responsibility for their children's actions. While other civil law systems have sought to meet changing societal structures by adapting their interpretation of 'fault', French law has gone further, providing a model based on risk allocation via the mechanism of insurance. It is argued that this is a step too far. By removing any notion of fault by either the parent or child, and yet not rendering insurance compulsory, it provides a model incapable of setting behavioural standards and imposing an unduly onerous burden on the parent. As one commentator has suggested:

> it shows that in France today the child is seen not as a sign of luck and the promise of a future but as a source of trouble and risk.[86]

Such divergence demonstrates that very different views exist of the parent-child-victim triangle. Whilst the common law courts have refused to set 'impossible' standards for parents,[87] it is submitted that modern parenting requires a more thorough consideration of parenting duties and a move away from the indulgence of the past. The approach of the German courts, for example, in setting more realistic standards than the English courts, in particular for children given access to potentially dangerous objects, such as matches or guns, is to be praised. Nevertheless, the role of tort law in this area will always be limited. The weaknesses of the French system—unaccountability of children, an uneasy relationship with ordinary fault principles, an onerous burden placed on parents to be met by insurance premiums or bankruptcy—render a system of strict liability questionable at best. In essence, one has a clash of legal philosophies: should tort law develop on the basis of ideas of social risk met by the community via household insurance, or should tort law retain its focus on ideas of individual responsibility?

It is submitted that tort law should aim to provide a compensatory structure which weighs the pressures of parenthood against the risk of injury to others. A legal system should establish realistic standards of care, whilst acknowledging the limits of a fault-based system in correcting anti-social behaviour. It goes without

---

[86]   H Capitant, F Terré and Y Lequette, *Les grands arrêts de la jurisprudence civil* t2 (11th edn, Paris, Dalloz, 2000) 316 (my translation).

[87]   See the majority in *Surtees v Kingston upon Thames RBC* [1992] PIQR P101, Beldam LJ dissenting.

saying that such standards should not condemn parents to untold levels of liability until the child's 18th birthday. In this way, a sensible balance may be found between the rights of victims, parents and children, acceptable to society as a whole.

Index

abortion, 66
Adam, 105
adoption, 5–8, 11, 39, 131ff, 242, 278
Alder Hay, 260
American Law Institute, 43
appropriate adult, 220–7
arrest, 220
ASBO, 325
autonomy, 4, 63ff, 70, 72, 197–8, 215, 337–8

baby manuals, 1
banns, 238–9
bind over, 318–20, 330
biopower, 307
Blackstone, 120fn, 208–9, 247–8, 273
blood, 112, 194
Bristol Royal Infirmary, 259, 264ff
broomstick, 202
Bundesverfassungsgericht, 44
burial, 258

care, child in, 110, 131ff, 241
care order, 7, 13
care proceedings, 230–4
catapult, 335
child, definition of, 9, 242
childminder, 11
Children's Commissioners, 173
child safety order, 323
child support 9, 19, 273ff
circumcision, 93, 127, 130ff, 139, 187
citizenship, 153, 164
civil partnership, 91, 237, 279
cohabitation, 34, 279
confession, 221ff
confidentiality, 67, 79–80
contact, 28–30, 125, 282
contact activity directions, 299, 308
contracts, children's, 202ff, 217
contraception, 65
corporal punishment, 9, 18, 133–6, 166ff
criminal law, 13, 18, 156, 299, 315ff, 338
cuckold, 277

Darcy, Mr, 248
death of child, 188, 255ff,
see also registration

disability, 251
disposal of the body, 257
doli incapax, 323
domestic violence, 302, 310–1, 330

education, 10–11, 125–6, 128–9, 143ff

Elvis, 109fn
ethic of care, 256, 300fn
European Convention on Human Rights
    Art 3, 166ff, 174ff
    Art 6, 318
    Art 8, 24, 67–8, 80, 177ff, 191, 194, 259
    Art 9, 129, 133ff, 166ff, 194
    Art 2, Protocol 1, 129
Every Parent Matters, 15

father, definition, 5
fathers' rights groups, 29, 300, 304
female genital mutilation, 187–8
filiation, 44–5
fines, 316–8, 330
forced marriage, 18, 250ff
French law, 211, 334, 339ff

given names, 106
genetic link, 34, 274
German law, 44, 48ff, 56ff, 345ff
Gillick, 3, 4, 17, 63ff, 186
Gillick-competence, 118, 127, 129, 197
guardian, 6, 8, 40, 209, Ba22, S17

heirs, 211
Henry VIII, 107
HIV, 81–2
Hohfeldian privilege, 3

ideal parent, 12
immunisation, 82
innocent agent, 316
insurance, 336, 344

Jordan, 106

kinship, 107, 113

Labour Government W2, W 29. Wi2, M 21
land, 206ff
Lesbian, H14, R 9, Ba16
liberation, child, 70
limb-lengthening, 187
litigation Friend, 217–9

marriage, 18, 237ff
masculinity, 298
matronymics, 107
medical treatment, 64ff, 185ff,
mother, definition of, 5

nudity, 14

organ donation, 189
organ retention, 260–1

parentage, 5, 276
parental custody, 48
parental compensation order, 322–4
parental discretion, 2, 15, 26ff, 79ff, 121, 126ff,
    186ff
parental liability, 333ff
parental responsibility
    allocation, 6, 7–8, 46, 88ff
    ending, 54ff
    exercise of, 59ff
    establishing, 51ff
    meaning , 2
    order, 7, 9, 52
    shared, 8, 17
    terminology, 4, 87
parenthood, 5–6, 33ff
parenting contract, 156, 320
parenting order, 156, 320, 338
paternity leave, 299
patronymy, 112–3
Poor laws, 230, 273–4
Potter, Harry, 201
Pregnancy, 33, 263, 267
*Principles of European Family Law Regarding
    Parental Responsibilities,* 43
property, children as, 23, 86, 261–3
property, of children, 206ff
public law, 13, 30, 37, 280
public/private divide, 17

religion, 8, 16, 18, 27, 93, 113, 123ff, 145ff, 166,
    189, 193ff
recognizance, 318
registration of birth, 107–9, 295ff

registration of death, 257
representative, parent as, 215ff
residence order, 6, 7, 52, 54, 91, 93, 109, 241,
    302
rights,
    children's 9, 19, 67ff, 118, 124, 136ff, 192,
        195, 273ff
    parents', 3, 23–4, 66, 85ff, 124, 146, 189
Rooney, Wayne, 203

sex education, 129, 147
Shelley, 125
silence, inferences from, 223
social engineering, 300
special educational needs, 157
special guardians, 7, 242
step-parents, 7, 91, 97, 119
surnames, 18, 93, 106ff
surrogacy, 37
status quo, 115
stillbirth, 266–7

tort, 18, 19, 260, 333ff

unmarried fathers, 44, 50ff, 90, 107, 274ff, 297ff
UN Convention on the Rights of the Child,
    Ch5, Wi3

Vegetables, 13

Wardship, 208, 246
Welfare principle, 24, 53, 64, 111, 115, 118, 126,
    186

Youth Offender Panel, 316
Youth Offender Teams, 321

Zowie Bowie, 118